SECOND EDITION

Competent Communication at Work

strategies & standards for success

Kendall Hunt
publishing company

Jacqueline A. Irwin
Sacramento State University

Holly J. Payne
Western Kentucky University

Pamela Davis Hopkins
East Carolina University

Patric Spence
University of Kentucky

Book Team

Chairman and Chief Executive Officer   Mark C. Falb
President and Chief Operating Officer   Chad M. Chandlee
Vice President, Higher Education   David L. Tart
Director of Publishing Partnerships   Paul B. Carty
Senior Developmental Coordinator   Angela Willenbring
Vice President, Operations   Timothy J. Beitzel
Senior Production Editor   Sheri Hosek
Senior Permissions Editor   Caroline Kieler
Cover Designer   Mallory Blondin

Cover images © Shutterstock.com

www.kendallhunt.com
Send all inquiries to:
4050 Westmark Drive
Dubuque, IA 52004-1840

Copyright © 2010, 2015 by Kendall Hunt Publishing Company

ISBN 978-1-4652-7059-7

Printed in the United States of America

brief contents

contents

SECTION II
General Communication Competencies   65

SECTION III
Social, Group, and Professional Competencies   143

SECTION V
Presentation Competencies 379

preface

In order to perform work-related tasks successfully and regardless of the type of work in which you are involved, you need to be able to competently communicate with others. It's that simple. Whether your goal is to quickly ask a coworker where a client file is located or to develop a long-term mentor relationship with a colleague, your communication skills are a critical component of your performance. The fact is that your communication skills could mean the difference between triumph and failure in countless situations in your professional life.

Competent Communication at Work is designed to help you become an effective and successful communicator. Section V contains two chapters designed for use at any time during your Business and Professional Communication course.

The text comprises five sections:
Section I: The Business and Professional Environment
Section II: General Communication Competencies
Section III: Social, Group, and Professional Competencies
Section IV: Presentation Preparation Issues
Section V: Presentation Competencies

SECTION I: THE BUSINESS AND PROFESSIONAL ENVIRONMENT

Chapter 1: An Introduction to Business and Professional Communication Processes

An understanding of the definition and centrality of communication competence in the workplace is key to professional success. This chapter describes the communication model and its components, the basic principles of communication, and identifies specific communication patterns in organizations.

Chapter 2: The Coming of Globalization: Communication and Culture in a Diverse New World

The forces of globalization and its impact on business communication are explained. Specific intercultural differences in communication styles along with the forms and impact of diversity in the workplace are identified, as well as specific communication behaviors that enable more successful interaction with diverse groups.

SECTION II: GENERAL COMMUNICATION COMPETENCIES

Chapter 3: Verbal and Nonverbal Communication

This chapter explores the difference between verbal and nonverbal communication and describes how verbal and nonverbal communication function in the communication process. Techniques for successful verbal communication and characteristics of nonverbal communication are explained, as well as the definition of sexual harassment.

Chapter 4: Listening: The Key to Credible Communication

Listening as a central component of communication is a focus of this chapter. The process of hearing, listening, and the creation of meaning is explained. It offers ways to improve your listening skills and also describes the distinction between active and passive listening.

Chapter 5: Working with Text: Writing for Business and Professional Communication

The importance of the writing process in business and professional communication and the proper use of style, voice, grammar, usage, and citations are outlined.

SECTION III: SOCIAL, GROUP, AND PROFESSIONAL COMPETENCIES

Chapter 6: Interpersonal Communication Skills at Work

There are different types and functions of relationships at work, and this chapter describes them, along with the role of interpersonal communication in the workplace. Different approaches to conflict and how certain conflict styles work are determined, along with exploring negotiation strategies, providing constructive feedback, and creating positive work climates.

Chapter 7: Working in Small Groups, Team Building, and Running a Successful Meeting

This chapter defines small group communication and identifies the advantages and disadvantages of working in a group. It explains the life cycle of groups and how individual roles function within groups, as well as steps involved in conducting a successful business meeting.

Chapter 8: Résumé Building and Social Media Strategies

Social media has become an important tool in the employment process. This chapter helps you develop a professional networking profile as well as choose the right type of résumé for yourself, and construct it to ensure that you land the job you want.

Chapter 9: Interviewing: Processes and Best Practices

To better prepare yourself for an interview, this chapter explores the types of interviewing questions that are often asked, as well as questions you may want to ask a potential employer. It also discusses appropriate follow-up messages after an interview.

SECTION IV: PRESENTATION PREPARATION ISSUES

Chapter 10: Audience Analysis and Delivery Dynamics

This chapter describes how to analyze your audience and explains the importance of audience adaptation. It delineates the four delivery methods and offers techniques for a successful presentation.

Chapter 11: Information-Seeking and Traditional Library Skills

The research process and how it can apply to your coursework is defined as well as how to find information that you need for assignments by understanding the concepts behind information organization. Proper source documentation is outlined.

Chapter 12: Presentation Development

The focus on choosing a topic and having a clear general purpose, specific purpose, and central idea is discussed in this chapter. Organizing your speech into a clear introduction, body, and conclusion and recognizing the patterns of organization used in informative and persuasive speaking, as well as creating a speech outline, are explained. A demonstration of the correct usage of connectives, main points, supporting material and citing sources is included.

Chapter 13: Visual Aids and Electronic-Enhanced Presentations

The role of visuals in public presentations and selecting the most appropriate visual aid as well as listing the types of visual aids and how to create the most effective visual for your presentation are explained.

SECTION V: PRESENTATION COMPETENCIES

Chapter 14: Informative and Special Occasion Business Presentations

This chapter helps you form an organizational pattern for a business presentation, understand the difference between business speaking and public speaking, and select a topic for your speech. It also discusses different types of informative speeches and special occasion speeches within the workplace.

Chapter 15: Persuasive Business Presentations

The concept of persuasion and the historical and modern approaches to persuasion are discussed. Choosing a direct goal for your persuasive presentation and understanding the role of the audience in persuasion are also explored.

STUDENT ORIENTED PEDAGOGY

Because we recognize the importance of assessing student learning, we have included features that facilitate student learning and help instructors measure learning outcomes.

- **Chapter Objectives** preview the chapter content, focusing on the main points

- **Chapter Outlines** serve as a map to guide students through the content of the chapter and focus on key points

- **Key Terms Lists/Running Glossary** highlight the important terms in the chapter and provide clear definitions

- **Real-world Examples and Strategies** illustrate chapter concepts, as well as help students apply those concepts in their own work

- **Activities** provide additional opportunities to apply students' knowledge of chapter material

- **Glossary of Terms** serves as a helpful reference tool at the end of the text

- **Web Material** is integrated with the text to enrich student learning. The web access code is included on the inside front cover of the textbook. Look for the web icon in the text margins to direct you to various interactive tools.

acknowledgments

We gratefully acknowledge the constructive comments of the colleagues who provided reviews for individual chapters of this text. They include:

Alice Griswold	Clarke College
Amy Childers	North Georgia College & State University
Amy Drees	Defiance College
Autumn Edwards	Western Michigan University
Barbara A. Grayson	University of Arkansas at Pine Bluff
Beth Hallquist	Palm Beach Atlantic University
Beth Hoger	Western Michigan University
Beverly Payne	Missouri Western State University
Catherine Green	University of Memphis
Carla Bevins	University of Kentucky
Chad Edwards	Western Michigan University
Chris Ward	The University of Findlay
Chrisann Merriman	University of Mary Hardin-Baylor
Christine R. Day	Eastern Michigan University
Claire Jerry	MacMurray College
Clive Muir	Winston-Salem State University
Dave Ramsey	Southeastern Louisiana University
David Westerman	North Dakota State University
Deb Halsey-Hunter	Bluefield State College
Brian Wilson	College of Marin
Debrah Richardson	Louisiana College
Elizabeth A. Cameron	Alma College
John J. Cronin	Western Connecticut State University
Joyce Monroe Simmons	Florida State University
Keith West	Sul Ross State University
Kim Rocha	Barton College
Warren Mason	Plymouth State University
Eric Nasalroad	Reedley College
Jan Gabel-Goes	Western Michigan University
Jean Bush-Bacelis	Eastern Michigan University
Jeff Lewis	Metro State College of Denver

Jeffrey Penly	Catawba Valley Community College
Jie Wang	University of Illinois at Chicago
Joanne Cattafesta	University of Kentucky
Joel Kline	Lebanon Valley College
Joyce Lopez	Missouri State University
Karelia Stetz-Waters	Linn Benton Community College
Katherine Hansen	Stetson University
Kathy L. Hill	Sam Houston State University
Keli Wilkes	Valdosta Technical College
Kenneth Lachlan	University of Connecticut
Kim Holloway	King College
Leah Omilion-Hodges	Western Michigan University
Marcia Metcalf	Northern Arizona University
Marilyn Shaw	University of Northern Iowa
McClain Watson	University of Texas at Dallas
Megan Endres	Eastern Michigan University
Merry E. George	Pikeville College
Michael Penneli	University of Rhode Island
Mike West	Missouri Western State University
Nancy Goehring	Monterey Peninsula College
Niecy LeBright	Wilmington University
Pamela A. Braden	West Virginia University at Parkersburg
Pat Cunningham	Dawson Community College
Patricia McArver	The Citadel
Peter Cardon	University of South Carolina
Philip H. Kelly	Gannon University
Phyllis Bunn	Delta State University
Rachel Price	University of Kentucky
Rathin Basu	Ferrum College
Richard B. Teter	Friends University
Richard Lacy	California State University, Fresno
Roberta Pittore	MIT
Ronald J. Thomas	Oakton Community College
Susan Meyeraan	Wartburg College
Teresa Chance	Harding University
Thomas Clark	Xavier University
Tiffany Daniel	Sandersville Technical College
Tim Hartge	The University of Michigan-Dearborn
Toni S. Whitfield	James Madison University
Valerie Evans	Lincoln Memorial University

Virginia Dumont-Poston	Lander University
Janis Moore Campbell	Temple University
Valerie Giroux	University of Miami
Kimberley Holloway	King College
Larry Honl	University of Wisconsin-Eau Claire
Susan Johnson	University of Massachusetts-Amherst
David Lydick	Paul D. Camp Community College
Gerald Plumlee	Southern Arkansas University
Xialing Lin	University of Kentucky
Christina J. Gentile	University of Kentucky
Timothy Sellnow	University of Kentucky
Deanna Sellnow	University of Kentucky
Diane Krider	Central Michigan University
Matthew Seeger	Wayne State University

about the authors

JACQUELINE A. IRWIN (Ph.D., University of Kansas) is an Associate Professor of Communication Studies at Sacramento State University and teaches courses in rhetorical criticism, business communication, sport and media, political rhetoric, and gender. Her research interests include crisis in sport communication, visual rhetoric, narrative, and social movements. She finds joy in advising, seeing students break down social barriers, and working for the greater good in the community.

PAMELA D. HOPKINS (Ph.D., East Carolina University; M.A., Penn State) is a Teaching Assistant Professor and Director of the Speech Communication Center at East Carolina University. She teaches both face to face and on-line sections of Public Speaking, Fundamentals of Speech Communication, Communication Theory, and Business and Professional Communication. As Director of the Speech Communication Center, Dr. Hopkins meets with students, faculty and staff members who need help with verbal communication skills, including organization and delivery, managing anxiety, and professional communication skills. She also presents workshops on communication related topics to various classes and groups across campus. She is a member of the National Communication Association.

HOLLY J. PAYNE (Ph.D., Communication, University of Kentucky) is an Associate Professor in the Department of Communication at Western Kentucky University. Her research focuses on dissent expression and communication competence in the organizational context. Her work in this area is published in *Communication Research Reports*, the *International Journal of Business Communication*, the *Journal of Leadership and Organizational Studies*, and *Employee Relations*. More recently her research has focused on the impact of identification within the non-profit sector as it relates to potential donors and volunteers and school crisis communication. She is the former director of basic speech courses and graduate program director at WKU, and is now current editor of the *Kentucky Journal of Communication*. Dr. Payne is an active member of the National Communication Association and is an engaged member of her campus community. She may be contacted at holly.payne@wku.edu.

PATRIC R. SPENCE (Ph.D., Wayne State University) is an Associate Professor and director of Business Communication in the School of Information Science and College of Communication and Information at the University of Kentucky. He is also affiliated with the Communication and Social Robotics Labs and the Center for Rebuilding Sustainable Communities after Disasters. His research focuses on communication during crises and other extreme events, communication of risk, social media and social robots. His research has appeared in outlets such as Computers in Human Behavior, Journal of Applied Communication Research, Communication Theory and Risk Analysis.

section
one

The Business and Professional Environment

chapter
one

An Introduction to Business and Professional Communication Processes

After reading this chapter you will be able to:

- Understand the definition and centrality of communication competence in the workplace
- Describe the communication model and its components
- Understand the basic principles of communication
- Identify specific communication patterns in organizations
- Describe major changes in today's business communication settings

CHAPTER OUTLINE

key words

Organizational communication competence
Communication context
Encoding
Paradigm
Channel
Decode
Noise

External noise
Internal noise
Formal network
Downward communication
Upward communication
Horizontal communication
Informal network

INTRODUCTION

Recent college graduate George Stevens is finishing his third month on the job at Health Matrix, Inc., which manages digitized health-care information for hospitals and insurance companies. His new position as an accounts coordinator involves marketing products to new and existing customers and managing existing accounts. A large part of his job involves customer service, where he works to ensure that health-care information can be seamlessly entered online and transferred between health providers. Although he feels that everything has been going well so far, he is still learning the ropes of this organization and the preferences of his clients. He spent the first month in training, where he met several other recent graduates working in various departments. They had been going out after work to debrief the day and provide support. He was still getting to know the people in his direct work area and had mainly had the chance to meet with them at weekly staff meetings. He was learning that his new role was more autonomous than he thought his first job would be, but decided that this motivated him to do his best work. He was quickly getting the feeling that his ideas would be listened to, as long as he put together well-thought-out plans and ideas. This also carried over with his customers. As long as his proposals were developed to meet their specific needs, they paid attention and worked to negotiate features as well as fees. He remembered learning about the importance of communication to workplace success, but this was the first time he was really seeing the concepts in action. He was quickly finding out how to communicate in this environment and to whom to communicate. So far, the only major bump in the road had been e-mailing a proposal to a client before sharing it with his director. Even though he hadn't covered this in training and the other new account coordinators weren't following this protocol, George's director wanted to see his proposals first. Instead of e-mailing them to clients, he was supposed to present them face-to-face. After meeting with his director, George learned that this was standard protocol with new account coordinators in his department and was aimed at teaching new employees the ins and outs of putting together proposals and giving more "face time" with clients to allow new hires to form stronger relationships.

George Stevens's experience is similar to that of many new employees. Starting a new position is a time filled with uncertainty, which is why many organizations spend time and resources training workers and socializing them to their institution. Through training and on-the-job experience, employees negotiate their new roles and form relationships with coworkers, managers, and clients. Many new employees will learn by making mistakes here and there, which frequently involve communication. Employees find that a new job involves more than knowing how to do the actual job, but also knowing how to navigate their way through the new organization, including the people, communication rules or norms, and organizational values. Understanding the basic elements of the communication process can go a long way toward helping you be successful in any organization.

How do organizations train workers to become better communicators?

This chapter emphasizes the importance of communication to your personal success at work. Specifically, you will learn about the components of the communication process along with the basic principles of communication and how communication functions in organizations. Becoming a competent communicator at work will assist you in maximizing understanding, avoiding communication breakdowns, adapting your messages to enhance your credibility, and meeting your goals. Effective and appropriate communication is the key to improving your work life and the work lives of those around you.

IMPORTANCE OF COMMUNICATION IN THE WORKPLACE

The importance of communication in all human relationships cannot be overstated. Communication is the process of exchanging ideas with others to form relationships at a variety of levels within a variety of contexts, including the workplace. Some communication scholars consider communication to be not just a quality of relationships, but to be the relationship itself. This connects to the view of communication as constitutive, which means it is the very ingredient necessary for relationships to exist. In the workplace, relationships come in a variety of forms, including supervisor-employee, coworker, and customer. Within each exists the dynamics of power, position, credibility, and competence. In addition to the successful development and maintenance of workplace relationships, many other communication skills are in high demand in today's workplace. Surveys of new graduates, employers, and university professors show that communication skills are one of the most important and underdeveloped employee skills.[1,2] Human resource managers with *Fortune* 500 corporations frequently identify listening, speaking, communication of information, and small-group or team communication skills as most important for graduates in the 21st century.[3] In 2005, a survey of employers recruiting in the Silicon Valley area reported a need for college graduates to improve their oral and written communication skills, including vocabulary and self-expression.[4] Good communication skills directly connect with increased pay, promotion opportunities,[5] performance evaluation,[6] and job mobility.[7] Throughout this book, we'll explore the process of communication in various forms in an effort to help you become a competent business communicator.

figure1.1

Communication Competence Model

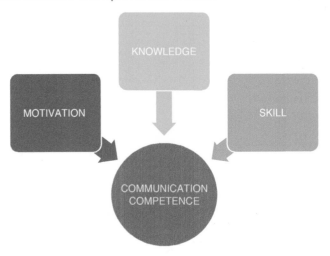

COMMUNICATION COMPETENCE

On the surface, the term *communication competence* sounds pretty straightforward, but competence is more complex than communication that is simply considered good, excellent, or successful. According to O'Hair, Friedrich, Wiemann, and Wiemann, "Communication competence is the ability of two or more persons to jointly create and maintain a mutually satisfying relationship by constructing appropriate and effective messages."[8] As you can see, this definition focuses on relationships and the satisfaction of both people involved. It also places emphasis on communication that is appropriate and effective within a specific relationship. For example, competent communication between you and a friend might not be competent for you and your boss, so adapting your messages to fit different people and situations is critical.

Another definition to consider is that of **organizational communication competence**, which is the impression of successful communication where the goals of the people in the interaction are met based on messages that are appropriate and effective within the organizational context.[9] This definition emphasizes that communication competence is an impression or a judgment made by others and involves both parties in a relationship achieving goals. Like the general definition of communication competence, this definition demonstrates the complexity of not only getting the things that you want

Organizational communication competence: The impression of successful communication where the goals of the people in the interaction are met based on messages that are appropriate and effective within the organizational context.

out of communication but also making sure that others' needs are met. This involves what communication scholars Brian Spitzberg and Bill Cupach identify as motivation, knowledge, and skill.[10] First, we have to be motivated not only to have successful and constructive communication with others, but also to learn how to communicate and approach a variety of communication situations. Next, we need to have knowledge of how to construct and deliver messages in a way that is appropriate to different situations. Finally, we must have the skill or the ability to adapt our messages and to perform the communication act. All the components of communication competence are important, but translating our motivation and knowledge of communication into skillful action can be a challenge and takes practice.[11] As a competent communicator in the workplace, you have to know what is considered appropriate in your organization or with your customers/clients and use the most effective strategies for delivering your messages in terms of the words you use or the way you choose to send your messages. Becoming a competent communicator involves having a thorough working knowledge of the communication model and its essential components.

How do you define communication competence?

© Dragon Images/Shutterstock.com

How skillful of a communicator are you? Complete the assessment in Table 1.1 to find areas of strength and weakness.

TABLE 1.1: Communication Skill Assessment

Read each of the following items carefully and select the response that most describes your communication patterns using the following scale:

5 = Strongly Agree   4 = Agree   3 = Sometimes Agree   2 = Disagree   1 = Strongly Disagree

1. I involve others in conversations in an effort to make them feel valued. _____
2. I always seem to say the right thing, at the right time. _____
3. I often initiate new topics in conversation. _____
4. I effectively make others feel important by listening to and confirming their feelings. _____
5. I disclose information at the same level that others disclose. _____
6. I offer follow-up comments or feedback in conversations. _____
7. I consider others' feeling when talking. _____
8. I communicate in a way that helps others fit into the organization. _____
9. I offer my opinions freely. _____
10. I am appropriately empathetic toward issues affecting different employees. _____
11. I know how to effectively communicate with people in various levels of authority. _____
12. My conversations with others have a natural flow. _____
13. I smile when conversing, encouraging others to participate. _____
14. I appropriately adapt my communication to my conversational partners. _____
15. I balance the amount of time I speak in conversations. _____

This self-assessment measures your communication skill in three areas: empathy, adaptability, and interaction management. In short, *empathy* is your ability to identify with others on an emotional level, *adaptability* is your ability to change your communication based on the person you're conversing with, and *interaction management* is your ability to manage the interaction or conversation with others. To determine your score, add the items as follows:

Empathy	Adaptability	Interaction Management
1. _____	2. _____	3. _____
4. _____	5. _____	6. _____
7. _____	8. _____	9. _____
10. _____	11. _____	12. _____
13. _____	14. _____	15. _____
Total: _____	Total: _____	Total: _____

If you scored between 25 and 19, you exhibit a **High** level of skill in this skill area.
If you scored between 18 and 12, you have a **Medium** or moderate level of skill in this area depending on the context.
If you scored between 11 and 5, you have a **Low** level of skill in this area.

*Adapted from the Workplace Communication Skill Survey (Payne, 2003).[12]

A MODEL OF THE COMMUNICATION PROCESS IN ORGANIZATIONS

At the beginning of this chapter we stated that communication is a process that includes an exchange of messages; however, communication itself is actually much more complex than this definition suggests. Consider the last time you posted a message on a friend's Facebook wall or your last job interview. Even though these are extremely different situations, you still engaged in an exchange that involved your thinking of the best way to construct a message for that specific person to achieve a specific outcome. Perhaps you were posting a joke on your friend's Facebook page in an effort to make people laugh and to stay connected to that person. This involves creating a funny message that is non-offensive to your friend or any others who might read their wall. In the case of a job interview, you were probably working to send a message to a potential employer that you are responsible and would make a good worker. You adapted your message to try to persuade them to hire you. Goal achievement is a major reason people communicate the way that they do. In other words, communication is largely strategic, but that's not to say that it is not sincere. We constantly work to create desired images and desired outcomes in our lives, and communication is the primary way we do this. To be successful, we have to adapt our messages to the person and situation to which or within which we are speaking. This exchange involving constructing, sending, and receiving messages is captured in the basic communication model (**Figure 1.2**).

First, all interactions take place within a specific **communication context** or situation. Contexts vary from micro to macro levels such as friendships, classrooms, organizations, or cultures. Every context has specific norms of behavior and specific spoken and often unspoken rules that people must follow to be considered competent communicators. Although this textbook focuses on the business context, which has generally agreed-on rules for communication, it is important to recognize that each organization has its own way of doing things, often referred to as organizational culture. Rules for appropriate and effective communication differ from place to place based on organizational culture or context.

Within a context, people exchange many different messages, typically in accordance with the rules of that context. This includes relationship rules. Using an organizational context as an example, you can see how the types of relationships affect the messages you send and the way you send them, whether it's communicating with a coworker, a supervisor, or a customer. Following the norms of these relationships, we begin the

Communication context: The situation or setting in which communication takes place.

Consider different places you have worked. Can you identify specific rules for ways employees should communicate? How did the rules of this organization differ from other organizations you have been a member of?

figure 1.2

The Communication Model

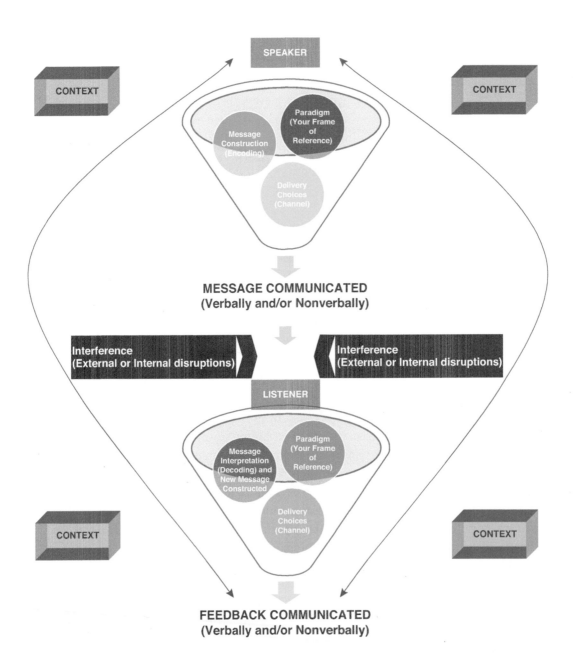

process by constructing or encoding a message. Encoding is the process of putting your thoughts and feelings into language. When constructing messages, it is not only important to consider the rules of the context, but also to consider the other person's paradigm. Think of your paradigm as your window through which you see the world. In other words, it is your frame of reference. Your window frame is made up of your thoughts, ideas, beliefs, upbringing, culture, values, and so on. All your life experiences go into constructing this lens through which you view others and events. Your paradigm affects everything about how you construct, send, and interpret messages. One great complexity of communicating with others is that we all have a different paradigm, a different life experience. This is why it's so important to construct messages in a way that is open and sympathetic to the interpretations of others. It also explains why communication is a process because it takes more than one message sent to achieve understanding. Hence, communication is a transactional process, a give-and-take of messages that if effectively crafted are aimed at ensuring that the message sent equals the message received. Having this success involves adapting your communication and messages to your audience.

Once you construct a message, you communicate it verbally and/or nonverbally using spoken or written words, facial expressions, and vocal variations that substitute, contradict, or emphasize your spoken words. Messages are communicated in various ways, whether it is face-to-face, text messaging, e-mail, or by phone. These are considered communication channels. Communication channels are the means or mechanisms we use to send messages. Selecting the right way and the right channel to communicate our ideas and feelings is much trickier than it sounds. Sometimes the decision is easy; for example, if you need to terminate an employee, you wouldn't send them an e-mail. Channel selection can take thought and planning, especially in the workplace. If you were implementing a new company policy, how should you best communicate that message? Often, communicating important policies requires utilization of more than one channel such as face-to-face and written channels. In today's high-tech workplaces, it's easy to rely too heavily on e-mail, so make sure to distinguish what is appropriate for e-mail versus a paper memo or face-to-face interaction. Typically, more sensitive messages require face-to-face channels or written forms such as formal letters or policies.

Once a message is communicated to others, it follows a similar process of message interpretation and construction. When people hear or read your message, they decode, or translate it and assign meaning. Again, this

Encoding: The process of putting your thoughts and feelings into language.

Paradigm: Your frame of reference or worldview, which includes your thoughts, feelings, beliefs, experiences, values, and assumptions.

Channels: The means or mechanisms we use to send messages.

Decode: Translating messages and assigning meaning to messages.

is where a person's paradigm comes into play as well as their knowledge of you and the specific context you're communicating in.

In addition to the listeners' paradigms, you also have to be aware of things that might interrupt the reception and understanding of your message; this is called noise. Noise is anything that interferes with or interrupts the communication process. Noise can be either external or internal. External noise is anything in the environment that disrupts or distorts a message. If you're sending an e-mail, and the server goes down, this can delay the transmission of your message, or if you're making a sales presentation at a product expo and there are so many people around other booths talking that it's difficult to hear, then someone or something external to you and your audience is interfering with the communication process. Internal noise is the interference experienced within or internally to the communication event. For example, if you are listening to your supervisor instruct you on a new work process and you don't understand one of the steps, then this could become a form of internal noise because you may not hear or keep up with the information that came after the point you misunderstood. Internal noise is often psychological in that we become distracted from the communication process due to boredom, confusion, or a general lack of focus caused by emotional states. Nevertheless, internal noise can be overcome, as the listener or receiver of the message focuses his/her attention and communicates his/her feedback to the speaker. This is the transactional element of the model. The receiver communicates a follow-up message either verbally or nonverbally that lets the sender know their message was received and understood. Although this sounds like a time-consuming model, these things happen instantaneously as we send and receive messages simultaneously. Sometimes it's so fast that the speaker may not process the fact that the receiver didn't fully comprehend the message, but because the back-and-forth continues, common understanding is often found, especially if both parties are sincerely interested in common understanding.

Noise: Anything that interferes with or interrupts the communication process.

External noise: Anything in the environment that disrupts or distorts a message.

Internal noise: The interference experienced within or internally to the communication event.

Table 1.2: Sample Elements of the Communication Model	
Contexts	Relationships with coworkers, managers, clients An organization An industry A situation such as an employment interview, performance appraisal, or sales call
Messages	New company policy Major company announcement Sales proposal or cost estimate Mission or vision statements Meeting announcement Training or business presentation
Channels	Phone or voicemail e-mail, instant messaging Letters or memos Videoconferencing Face-to-face meetings or presentations Brochures, newsletters Web sites and intranets
Noise	Technology problems Message overload Time differences Cultural differences Low employee morale Stress and fatigue Disagreement over policies

Dealing with Communication Overload

With the influx of technology into our everyday work lives comes a massive amount of information, e-mails, Web links, cell phone calls, chat features, and so on. Some researchers speculate that managers and knowledge workers receive anywhere from 100 to 200 new messages each day and that millions of dollars are wasted as employees try to sort through the messages to prioritize.[1] Needless to say, today's employees often struggle with how to manage their communication load. The Harvard Management Update[1] provided a 12-step program for managing information overload. Here is a summary of their tips:

1. **Set aside a specific time** for checking e-mail throughout the day and consider checking only three times a day.

2. **Don't open every e-mail**; instead scan subject lines and delete as necessary. When working on projects with colleagues, agree on a subject line that indicates the code name for the project.

3. If working on a team, **set up an e-mail system of communication** and consider using intranet bulletin boards.

4. **Polish your technology skills** by taking the time to learn new methods of using programs. Many times there are useful tools we never learned or overlook that can help us manage information.

5. **Set up an organized filing system** that makes it easy for you to sort and save the files and e-mails that are most important.

6. **Archive messages**. If your inbox is full with too many messages to organize, then create an archive folder on your local workstation and save everything. If you really need any of the information, you at least know where to start looking, plus it will give you a fresh start for implementing your new filing system.

7. **Never wait to organize your files** and messages. Always put files in the appropriate folders so that you'll always know where to find them and you won't end up with duplicate copies.

8. Just as you set aside time to respond to e-mail, also **set aside time to return phone calls**. Instead of moving between communication activities, let phone calls go to voicemail and then return calls in batches.

9. If you're good at **multitasking**, then work to organize your files while doing other things like printing documents or talking on the cell phone.

10. **Print documents** and e-mails that you can read at later times. Many times we receive attachments of information items that don't need immediate attention, so to keep the clutter out of your inbox, print it to read and respond to later.

11. **Set time limits** for your Internet activity. Whether it's conducting online research or reading the newspaper online, you should set a specific cutoff time for your usage. It's easy to get sucked into the Internet only to waste more of your precious time. Focus on the best search engines and sources of information so you don't waste time fruitlessly looking for information.

12. **Unsubscribe** to as many e-mail lists as possible. Many organizations send out advertisements, newsletters, and announcements that plug up your inbox. Delete and unsubscribe as new organizations add you to their list.

PRINCIPLES OF COMMUNICATION

In addition to the communication model, specific communication principles further clarify and highlight the complexity and nature of the communication process. The following sections provide important considerations for communication in the business and professional environment.

Communication Is a Basic Human Need, but Effective Communication Is Not a Basic Human Ability

We are born communicating. Even though an infant's level of communication may not be very sophisticated, the tone and pitch of a baby's cry communicates to caregivers. Perhaps it's a cry of hunger or sleepiness or even the desire to be held and nurtured; it is nevertheless a powerful form of communication that sets people into action. An extensive amount of research has confirmed the basic physical and mental need for communication; in fact, our brains are formed through interaction and experience with different stimuli. In addition to brain formation, the positive and negative health effects of communication are undeniable. For example, a recent study shows that affectionate communication has a direct impact on lowering stress levels,[13] whereas another study found interpersonal conflict can increase the risk for heart disease.[14] In organizations, positive communication climates translate into more productive and more satisfied employees. Many needs are met through communication, including social, identity, and practical needs. Being a member of an organization includes more than just sitting at a cubicle with no human interaction; it involves working with groups of people and developing relationships with customers, clients, and numerous others. Being a member of different social groups becomes a part of our identities. In other words, we learn more about who we are as people from our interaction with others. We also communicate to meet very practical needs, such as earning a paycheck or learning how to complete a new work process. We learn how to perform our jobs via communication. Even

Being a member of an organization involves working with people and developing relationships.

though communication is a basic human ability and basic human need, *effective* communication is a different story. Enrolling in communication courses and practicing your communication skills can give you a leg up in the business world and set you on a course for developing satisfying workplace relationships.

Communication Is Intentional and Unintentional

This basic principle of communication is typically discussed in the form of a question, Can one not not communicate? The beauty of communication is that we have the power to control our messages, and so we have great opportunities to formulate, practice, and deliver the most effective messages possible. In the business world, this means that we can intentionally construct e-mails, phone calls, newsletters, and brochures to create a desired impression. A job interview is a perfect example of how we work to put our best foot forward to intentionally communicate our enthusiasm for a particular position or company and portray a certain level of professionalism. On the other hand, what if we are sending messages that are less strategic? For example, what if during your job interview you nervously bounce your leg under the table, or what if you shake hands with an administrative assistant when you leave the interview, but not the manager? Messages are communicated unintentionally when you either do not realize that you're communicating something such as nervousness or boredom or when the actions you take, such as shaking hands with someone of a lesser status and skipping the manager, results in others making an interpretation of your behavior that is unintentional. There is nothing wrong with unintentional messages; they are simply an element of existence and human cognitive processing; however, being able to manage and construct your messages and adapt to a variety of contexts can help you to become a more competent communicator.

Communication Is Irreversible

Another common principle of communication is that it is irreversible. This essentially means that once a message is communicated, you cannot adapt, correct, change, or retract it. You can only continue to communicate follow-up messages that assist you in achieving common understanding. This principle of communication is a bit disconcerting because it truly speaks to the power of our words. Communication is a powerful tool that we use in all relationships with others. With that power comes the opportunity to communicate messages for better or worse, to build or to destroy, which is why it is important to take our time in constructing the best messages possible. An example of the irreversible nature of communication is social networking sites such as Facebook. Many employers are not only using these sites as a way to connect with potential customers, but also as a research tool for potential employees. Specifically, they are looking to see if pictures or postings on personal pages are a match with the image the organization is trying to project. This not only exemplifies the intentional and unintentional nature of our communication, but also the fact that once a message is posted, it cannot be taken back. The beauty of communication is that we rarely have just one interaction with another person, so if we communicate something we'd like to retract, we have other opportunities to adapt our messages.

Communication Is Contextual and Rule Based

As indicated in the communication model, communication takes place in specific contexts or situations that have spoken and unspoken or written and unwritten rules for communication. A context can be a specific type of relationship such as between coworkers or between employees and supervisors or it can even be specific organizations or industries. Competent communicators learn the rules of a specific context or situation and then communicate accordingly. For example, some organizations have different procedures for communicating important work policies. Some may communicate all important messages via e-mail, whereas others may use more formal written memos on official company letterhead. As members of many types of organizations, it's important for us to learn the ins and outs of how certain messages are communicated in order to avoid violating norms. This can be a confusing process, but asking questions and observing others at work can go a long way toward helping us tailor what we say and how we say it.

Communication Has Ethical Dimensions

Another important part of communicating competently involves ethics. As mentioned earlier, Spitzberg and Cupach described competent communication as being appropriate and effective.[15] This definition is in essence value-neutral. In other words, if communication is strategic, then you could very skillfully communicate in a way that is appropriate and effective within a specific context and at the same time use unethical means for achieving your goals. We are especially susceptible to unethical means of persuasion in the workplace, where our livelihood relies on our ability to gain compliance from others, including coworkers, clients, and managers. Ethics in communication seems like a no-brainer. Doing the right thing, being honest, and communicating openly seem like fairly easy things to do; however, organizations are complex communication networks where competing goals exist. Consequently, we may find ourselves thrust into frequent ethical dilemmas related to coworkers, clients, or shareholders and we might feel at odds with the ways our organizations want us to communicate. Mumby (2013) states "Communication is ethical when (a) it promotes genuine dialogue and understanding amongst different organizational stakeholders, (b) contributes to individual and relational growth amongst organization members, (c) recognizes the possibility of different organizational realities operating simultaneously, (d) acknowledges the multiple and often conflicting interests of different organizational stakeholders, and (e) facilitates democratic and participatory decision-making processes across all levels of the organization."[16] Many professional communication organizations such as the National Communication Association (NCA) and the International Association of Business Communicators (IABC) provide guidelines for ethical communication. Both organizations stress the importance of communicating honestly and accurately, encouraging free speech, providing access to information, seeking understanding by valuing diverse perspectives including being sensitive to cultural values, giving credit for information borrowed from others, and protecting private and confidential information.[17]

> Ethical dilemmas can make us feel at odds with the way our organization communicates.

© Rawpixel/Shutterstock.com

Table 1.3 highlights IABC's Code of Ethics for Professional Communicators. As you can see, communicating ethically is central to developing organizational relationships in its many forms.

COMMUNICATION IN THE WORKPLACE

Communication in organizations can take many different forms. As outlined in the communication model, many different messages are sent using various channels and to a number of stakeholders , including customers, clients, employees, government agencies, and investors. Communication within organizations takes place in both formal and informal communication networks. **Formal networks** are patterns of communication designed by management and inherent to a person's specific role within an organization. In other words, you use formal networks when you communicate with people based on your specific position in the organization. Formal communication in the workplace can travel in many directions, including upward, downward, and horizontally. All organizations have a certain structure or formal network that influences not only the content of messages, but also the methods for transmitting messages. A review of a company's organizational chart can tell you a lot about how messages travel. Organizational charts are typically characterized by their breadth and depth or their flatness or tallness. Companies with many different levels of authority are considered "tall" structures, and organizations with power that is spread among employees and divisions are considered "flat." **Figure 1.3** demonstrates what a tall or flat organizational chart looks like.

Downward communication describes messages that travel "down" the organizational chart from members with power to those with lower levels of power. These messages typically include policies, procedures, manuals, vision statements, or annual reports. **Upward communication** includes messages that travel "up" the organizational chart from employees upward to managers. Messages that travel upward include status reports, suggestions for improvement, and satisfaction surveys. **Horizontal communication** involves messages that flow between employees of similar status within or across the same departments, including status reports or updates, reminders of policies, and suggestions. Organizations with flatter structures have more upward and horizontal forms of communication. These organizations may or may not use a team-based structure that encourages creative ideas and plans that flow from the bottom up or from employees to managers. An organization's structure varies; however,

Formal network: Patterns of communication designed by management and inherent to a person's specific role within an organization.

Downward communication: Messages that travel "down" the organizational chart from members with power to those with lower levels.

Upward communication: Messages that travel "up" the organizational chart from employees upward to managers.

Horizontal communication: Messages that flow between employees of similar status within or across the same departments.

TABLE 1.3: International Association of Business Communicators Code of Ethics for Professional Communicators

1. Professional communicators uphold the credibility and dignity of their profession by practicing honest, candid and timely communication and by fostering the free flow of essential information in accord with the public interest.
2. Professional communicators disseminate accurate information and promptly correct any erroneous communication for which they may be responsible.
3. Professional communicators understand and support the principles of free speech, freedom of assembly, and access to an open marketplace of ideas and act accordingly.
4. Professional communicators are sensitive to cultural values and beliefs and engage in fair and balanced communication activities that foster and encourage mutual understanding.
5. Professional communicators refrain from taking part in any undertaking which the communicator considers to be unethical.
6. Professional communicators obey laws and public policies governing their professional activities and are sensitive to the spirit of all laws and regulations and, should any law or public policy be violated, for whatever reason, act promptly to correct the situation.
7. Professional communicators give credit for unique expressions borrowed from others and identify the sources and purposes of all information disseminated to the public.
8. Professional communicators protect confidential information and, at the same time, comply with all legal requirements for the disclosure of information affecting the welfare of others.
9. Professional communicators do not use confidential information gained as a result of professional activities for personal benefit and do not represent conflicting or competing interests without written consent of those involved.
10. Professional communicators do not accept undisclosed gifts or payments for professional services from anyone other than a client or employer.
11. Professional communicators do not guarantee results that are beyond the power of the practitioner to deliver.
12. Professional communicators are honest not only with others but also, and most importantly, with themselves as individuals; for a professional communicator seeks the truth and speaks that truth first to the self.

Reprinted by permission of the International Communication Association.

many organizations in today's business environment recognize that the hierarchical structures of the past did not value or maximize employee input. Today's employees must have greater communication skills to be successful in an interactive workplace.

In addition to formal communication networks, **informal networks** are based on friendships or relationships formed based on similarity in professional goals or personal interests. Informal networks may be influenced by social characteristics such as age, shared activities, or co-cultural group membership. Messages within informal networks travel in many different ways, but the company grapevine is commonly referenced as a channel for informal communication. The company grapevine is often considered a powerful form of communication and is surprisingly accurate. Even though it may be a vehicle for rumors and distortion, the company grapevine is known to be a good indicator of employee opinions and morale.[18]

Informal network: Communication patterns based on friendships or relationships that are formed based on similarity in professional goals or personal interests.

figure 1.3

Organizational Chart

Flat vs. Tall Organizational Hierarchy

Tall Organizational Structure

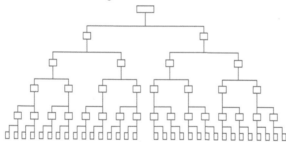

Flat Organizational Structure

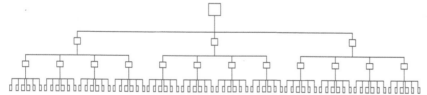

What is horizontal communication within an organization?

In addition to knowing about the communication model and the basic principles of communication, employees must learn the basic flow of communication within their specific organization. Learning the processes and procedures for exchanging information is critical to reaching your communication goals and maximizing your success and productivity.

THE CHANGING NATURE OF TODAY'S ORGANIZATIONS

As discussed throughout this chapter, communication in organizations is a complex process involving people, messages, channels, meaning, and structure. In addition to these concepts, there are also important contextual elements to consider. Organizations do not exist in a vacuum; they are a part of an intricate conglomeration of environmental factors. Organizations are embedded in environments made up of people, governments, cultures, technologies, beliefs, traditions, etc. To understand an organization and how to communicate within it you must be aware of and understand the environment in which it thrives. Three important environmental factors that have greatly changed organizations include globalization, technology, and participative organizational structures.

First, if you've heard the phrase, "The world is flat," it is in reference to the changing nature of our economy from one that focuses on national and regional competition to one that is global in size. Consider for example what might happen if the Chinese real estate bubble bursts. The Chinese government may decide not to bail out construction companies which means they may need to sell off their ownership in U.S. debt, which means that the Federal Reserve might decide to raise interest rates so as to increase the attractiveness of U.S. debt for investors. Even if this scenario does not play out, if the Chinese real estate bubble bursts, it can have serious effects on their economy which will negatively affect American investors in China. As you can see, we live in a complicated global network. Governments and natural forces affect our economy even on something as simple as rattan, a reed used to make baskets and furniture. The Indonesian government recently prohibited the export of products in an effort to build their economy at the same time that they were experiencing a shortage of rattan due to forest depletion. The result? U.S. companies have either been unable to obtain rattan or they have had to pay double the price for it. Fueled by technological advances and improved logistics, we are now more globally connected than ever before. These changes have led to increased multicultural diversity in our organizations and widespread dissemination of technology tools.

As a business communicator you will need an understanding of our global connectedness and must be able to adapt your communication to other cultures. As organizations become more globally dispersed, you will more than likely work with counterparts in other parts of the world, so you can anticipate not only coordinating work across time zones, but you will also need a more in-depth understanding of how to interpret communication patterns of your colleagues and an understanding of consumer behaviors in the international marketplace. Consider the introduction of U.S. fast food to Asia. In 2011 YUM! Brands, owner of KFC, Taco Bell, and Pizza Hut, opened a store in Asia every 18 minutes. Part of the popularity of KFC in the region can be attributed to their inclusion of local foods on their menus. They have been able to adapt to different markets to ensure their success. Another element of doing business in different cultures is understanding cultural practices. For example, when the first drive-through fast food restaurants opened in China, customers didn't quite understand the concept. First, many bikers went through the drive-through as opposed to vehicles, because that's how many people traveled. Next, customers would order the food at the window, park, and take the food inside. Why would anyone want to eat food in their car? This development was unanticipated as Western values of efficiency and time-saving surrounding mealtimes were not cultural values in Asian societies where sitting down to savor a meal is respected and expected. Understanding culture is an important aspect of being a competent business communicator. Chapter 2 provides an even more in-depth discussion of what to expect when interacting with diverse cultures.

It's difficult to discuss globalization without focusing on the important role of technology. Can you imagine life without a reliable e-mail system, or a cell phone, or social media? Indeed, we have become so reliant on technology that many of us have trouble taking a break from it even when it serves as a distraction to our productivity and creativity. The impact of technology on organizations cannot be overstated. Technology is central to how work gets accomplished and how much work can be accomplished by one person. Additionally, technology has provided organizations with a vast array of processing and storage capabilities and improved inventory control and logistics. Marketing, branding, and new product development have also changed with the technological boom. Consider how organizations use a whole range of social media to connect with customers and constituents from Facebook to Twitter to Tumblr. For the purpose of this textbook, we'll focus on how to use technology in competent ways from job search processes to networking to telemeeting. Appropriate and effective use of new communication technologies is critical to your success in business.

Finally, the last major organizational change we'll discuss relates to the way organizations are structuring themselves. As discussed earlier in the chapter, an organizational chart is a visual representation of how a company is organized in terms of how decisions are made and who holds power at various levels. Organizational structures can be tall with many layers of decision-making and power concentrated in the hands of those higher up or flat with fewer layers and more communication horizontally among members at the same level of the organization. Even an organizational chart can be a bit misleading when it comes to describing exactly how decisions are made. One thing is certain; many organizations are using team-based decision-making regardless of the structure they have on paper. Some organizations use a pure form of team management or project management where there are very few levels of hierarchy while others use teams even though they have many layers. Today's students need to know how to work in groups. Working in groups not only involves developing and accomplishing tasks as a group, but also the ability to navigate relational issues that arise. What does it mean to be a team player? Do leaders emerge in a team or are leaders assigned? What happens when power and decision-making are dispersed among employees? The answers to this and other questions are addressed in Chapters 6 and 7 on interpersonal communication and team building. Understanding the role of participation in different organizations is essential to business success. As organizations strive to remain innovative and responsive to market demands, they seek flexible structures that eschew formal hierarchies and slow-moving bureaucracies.

CONCLUSION

This chapter provides the basic concepts for understanding the complex process of communication within the workplace, including the components of the communication model, the principles of communication, and the patterns and flow of communication in organizations. As described in the opening paragraph, George Stevens has experienced some of the complexity of being a new member of an organization. For example, he is learning the most appropriate and effective ways to communicate messages, specifically to his supervisor and to his clients. He is also forming a support system by developing relationships with people outside his department with whom he spent time training. These relationships connect him to the informal communication network at Health Matrix, Inc. In addition, he is learning the best ways to communicate formally with his coworkers and clients by investing time in adapting his messages for staff meetings and sales calls. These are just a few examples of the ways George is learning the ropes and developing his communication competence.

Throughout this course and textbook, you will study many facets of workplace communication, including foundational elements such as listening and verbal, nonverbal, and written communication, as well as processes of interpersonal communication, small-group decision-making, and effective business presentations. As you make your way through each chapter, stay focused on the tools you need for communicating competently in any organization. You might be surprised at how much you'll learn about the complex process of communication and how you can improve the quality of your personal and professional relationships.

ACTIVITIES

1. Working with a partner, develop a list of common communication breakdowns you have experienced in organizations. At what point in the communication process did the problem(s) occur? How did you deal with the situation, and what was the outcome? In retrospect, what elements of the communication model or the principles of communication were most relevant?

2. Considering the communication model, what sources of internal and external noise are most prevalent in organizations? Would you consider information overload as a form of noise? What suggestions might you give for managing large amounts of information?

3. After completing the self-assessment on your communication skills (**Table 1.1**), write down three areas of communication in which you would like to improve. Think about someone you perceive to be a competent communicator or a communication role model. What characteristics do they exhibit? How might you work to achieve some of these same skills?

4. Draw an organizational chart that represents the structure of a company you have worked for or been a part of as a volunteer or as a student. What types of messages travel upward, downward, and horizontally? Would you consider the company's hierarchy as tall or flat? What recommendations would you make for the flow of communication based on the structure?

5. What types of information are shared in the company grapevine? Can you think of an example when information you received from the grapevine was accurate or inaccurate? How can employees and managers use and evaluate information gleaned from the grapevine?

6. Using the IABC Code of Ethics for Professional Communicators (**Table 1.3**) brainstorm examples of ways employees might be ethically challenged. You might consider guidelines for how meetings are run to how messages are marketed to customers. How can organizations assist employees in communicating ethically?

REFERENCES

[1] Maes, J. D., Weldy, T. G., & Icenogle, M. L. (1997). A managerial perspective: Oral communication competency is most important for business students in the workplace. *Journal of Business Communication, 34*, 67–80.

[2] Morreale, S. P., Osborn, M. M., & Pearson, J. C. (2000). Why communication is important: A rationale for the centrality of the study of communication. *Journal of the Association for Communication Administration, 29*, 1–25.

[3] Porterfield, S. C., & Forde, C. M. (2001). Competencies required in the 21st century of entry-level *Fortune* 500 employees with four-year business degrees. *NABTE Review, 28*, 25–32.

[4] Stevens, B. (2005). What communication skill do employers want? Silicon Valley recruiters respond. *Journal of Employment Counseling, 42*, 2–9.

[5] Haas, J. W., & Sypher, B. D. (1991). *The impact of communication abilities on individual success in organizational settings.* Paper presented at the annual meeting of the Speech Communication Association, Atlanta, GA.

[6] Ferris, G. R., Witt, L. A., & Hochwarter, W. A. (2001). The interaction of social skill and general mental ability on work outcomes. *Journal of Applied Psychology, 86*, 1075–1082.

[7] Kilduff, M., & Day, D. V. (1994). Do chameleons get ahead? The effects of self-monitoring on managerial careers. *Academy of Management Journal, 37*, 1047–1060.

[8] O'Hair, D., Friedrich, G. W., Wiemann, J. M., & Wiemann, M. O. (1994). *Competent communication.* New York: St. Martin's Press.

[9] Payne, H. J. (2003). Revisiting a nebulous construct: Exploring the impact of relational communication competence on job performance. *Dissertation Abstracts International, 64*(01), (UMI No. AAT 3078403).

[10] Spitzberg, B. H., & Cupach, W. R. (1984). *Interpersonal communication competence.* Beverly Hills, CA: Sage.

[11] Payne, H. J. (2005). Reconceptualizing social skills in organizations: Exploring the relationship between communication competence, job performance, and supervisory roles. *Journal of Leadership and Organizational Studies, 11*, 63–77.

[12] Payne, H. J. (2003). Revisiting a nebulous construct: Exploring the impact of relational communication competence on job performance. *Dissertation Abstracts International, 64*(01), (UMI No. AAT 3078403).

[13] Floyd, K., Mikkelson, A. C., Tafoya, M. A., Farinelli, L., La Valley, A. G., Haynes, M. T., et al. (2007). Affectionate communication accelerates neuroendocrine stress recovery. Human affection exchange. *Health Communication, 22*, 123–132.

[14] Smith, T. W., & Ruiz, J. M. (2002). Psychosocial influence on the development and course of coronary heart disease: Current status and implications for research and practice. *Journal of Consulting and Clinical Psychology, 70*(3), 548–568.

[15] Spitzberg, B. H., & Cupach, W. R. (1984). *Interpersonal communication competence.* Beverly Hills, CA: Sage.

[16] Mumby, D.K. (2013). *Organizational communication: A critical approach.* Los Angeles, CA: Sage.

[17] National Communication Association (NCA) and the International Association of Business Communicators (IABC). https://www.natcom.org/ and http://www.iabc.com

[18] Goldhaber, G. (1990). *Organizational communication.* Dubuque, IA: Wm. C. Brown.

chapter two

The Coming of Globalization: Communication and Culture in a Diverse New World

After reading this chapter you will be able to:

- Explain the forces behind globalization
- Describe the impact of globalization on business communication
- Identify specific intercultural differences in communication styles
- Describe the forms and impact of diversity in the workplace
- Understand specific communication behaviors that enable more successful interaction with diverse groups

CHAPTER OUTLINE

key words

Globalization

Culture

Power distance

Uncertainty avoidance

Individualism

Collectivism

Masculine culture

Feminine culture

Long-term orientation

Short-term orientation

High-context

Low-context

Monochronic time
   orientation

Polychronic time orientation

Co-cultures

Glass ceiling

Sexual harassment

Hostile work environment

Quid pro quo

Stereotype

Intercultural communication
   competence

Diversity maturity

INTRODUCTION

PHM Inc., a large appliance manufacturer located in the United States, is expanding their manufacturing base internationally with their newest location in Bangalore, India. The North American division of PHM will still provide accounting oversight for the locations abroad, which will require sending a team of auditors to the plant in India twice a year. As a senior accountant with seven years of experience at PHM, Haley Esparza Carter has been asked to serve on the team of auditors. She accepts the assignment and looks forward to the challenge. She is no stranger to diversity, as she feels like she has lived a double cultural life as a Cuban American. Her parents are native Cubans who immigrated to the United States, and she is fluent in Spanish. Growing up in Southern Florida, she was accustomed to going to school with a diverse student body, and she had not given her cultural background a lot of thought until she went away to college in the Midwest, where she was clearly in the minority. After graduation, Haley stayed in the Midwest, where she met her husband and took her first accounting job. At her former company, she was the only Hispanic accountant, and she found that people made interesting comments to her, such as, "We didn't know you were Cuban" and "What does your husband's family think about that?" Her former manager also made comments in front of others about not making Haley mad because of her "Latin temper." When she felt her career was stalling, she took the senior accountant position at PHM. She feels comfortable working for an organization that actively recruits a diverse workforce nationally and internationally. Taking this overseas assignment seems perfect for her because she is aware of some of the challenges she might face when traveling abroad. Beyond this, she needs to educate herself on how culture influences communication patterns. The following sections offer Haley more to contemplate in the way of international cultural differences, but also provide some reflection on the challenges faced by co-cultures or diverse groups within the United States. Read on to see how these topics might help Haley as she prepares for her trip to India.

GLOBALIZATION AND THE NEW ECONOMY

If you have traveled abroad recently, you have more than likely observed some of the dramatic effects of globalization. For example, imagine eating at Kentucky Fried Chicken (KFC) in Barcelona, Spain, or going to Wal-Mart in China, or maybe you noticed homegrown American brands such as the Ford Ranger truck in Brazil or Coca-Cola Light in Europe. The catch phrase and book title *The World Is Flat,* made popular by Thomas Friedman, author of the *New York Times* bestseller, addresses the radical changes in business since the year 2000.[1] He explores how technological, economic, and political developments are allowing organizations worldwide to compete globally. The result of this shift is a wider availability of products and services, more advanced supply networks for major manufacturers, and the outsourcing or offshoring of businesses and/or specific business functions.

Globalization:
The term used to describe how the global economy is becoming interconnected through technology, more open trade agreements, and transportation.

According to Cynthia Stohl, an organizational communication scholar, globalization is "the process through which the global economy becomes increasingly interconnected, through which global and domestic organizations merge, and through which communication technologies blur traditional spatial and temporal boundaries."[2] Consider that large American organizations such as General Electric, ExxonMobil, Ford, and General Motors are among the world's top 10 nonfinancial transnational corporations worldwide.[3] In fact, U.S. multinational corporations employ 10.3 million people abroad.[4] In addition to the large number of U.S. brands and products abroad, many organizations are outsourcing services. If you called for assistance with your cable bill, new computer, or even an order for clothing placed online, you may have noticed the customer service

© michaeljung/Shutterstock.com

coworkers. Understanding the impact of culture on our communication patterns is important to accomplish the work of our organizations. The following sections explore the major differences that have the most impact on communication between members of varying cultures.

Chances are that in your professional life you will work with various multicultural audiences.

CULTURAL DIMENSIONS OF COMMUNICATION

Culture Defined

Culture is defined as a common set of beliefs, attitudes, customs, and ways of knowing agreed on and used by a group of people. Although we are familiar with some American cultural values such as freedom of speech and individual rights, many of our behaviors reflect our cultural norms, which we enact subconsciously. The subconscious nature of cultural behavior makes it difficult to recognize how we communicate differently from those outside our culture and promotes a tendency to view others who act outside our norms as strange. Although it is human nature to prefer things (including

Culture: A common set of beliefs, attitudes, customs, and ways of knowing agreed on and used by a group of people.

people) that are familiar to us, we have to be careful when applying our cultural standards to others. This means you must avoid the expectation that others should conform to your culture because you think it is superior, which is ethnocentric. Ethnocentrism is the belief that one's culture is superior to others. Any time we interact with someone new, we face a great deal of uncertainty, but when interacting with someone from a different culture, that uncertainty is amplified as both parties struggle to make sense of the other due to differences in language, appearance, or nonverbal communication. By expressing openness and tolerance for differences, you can reduce the uncertainty and anxiety for you and your communication partner.

Geert Hofstede described five dimensions of communication that vary by culture: power distance, uncertainty avoidance, individualism/ collectivism, masculinity/femininity, and long-term/short-term orientation.[8] Hofstede and his colleagues categorized many different cultures along these dimensions and identified their levels of each along a continuum. The following sections review these primary differences within the context of business and professional communication.

Power Distance

Power distance: A cultural dimension describing the degree to which a society respects people, symbols, or structures of power.

A culture's approach to power distance describes how a society views people, symbols, or structures of power. In thinking about this concept, consider how much power you afford different groups such as government officials, teachers, police officers, the rich and famous, or CEOs. Cultures have different systems of power and different attitudes or levels of respect toward people with power. Cultures with a high power distance exhibit respect and gratitude toward groups such as elders, teachers, bosses, and politicians. In high power distance cultures the gap between those with and without power is great, signifying inequality between groups. In the workplace, this might translate into authoritarian forms of management or the reluctance of employees to communicate disagreement with supervisors. Hofstede categorized the Philippines, Mexico, Venezuela, India, and Singapore as the top five high power distance cultures. Low power distance cultures have a greater focus on balancing inequities between groups such as between managers and workers and generally do not view those with power as being better than others or commanding or deserving of more respect. These cultures believe that power should be used appropriately and by those who have legitimate or traditional power roles. In the workplace, employees in low power distance cultures expect to be consulted and are unhappy if perks are given to others without license. Austria, Israel, Denmark, New Zealand, and Ireland are the top five low power distances cultures with the United States coming in at fourteenth on the low power distance list.

Uncertainty Avoidance

Uncertainty avoidance, the next of Hofstede's cultural communication dimensions, describes a culture's tendency to avoid things that are unknown or uncertain. High uncertainty avoidant cultures operate from a need to reduce the level of ambiguity, particularly in future events. One way these cultures control uncertainty is by creating complex rule structures. For example, organizations help to reduce uncertainty and promote predictability by creating processes and rules for operation. Cultures with high levels of uncertainty avoidance want clarity and predictability; therefore, they are not as open to differing ideas and prefer complex rule structures for guiding behavior and decision-making. This also translates into a focus on relationships in terms of building long-term agreements with people who are familiar. Greece, Portugal, Belgium, Japan, Peru, and France are considered high in uncertainty avoidance. Cultures low in uncertainty avoidance are more tolerant of differences and view uncertainty as a normal part of life. Singapore, Denmark, Sweden, Hong Kong, Ireland, Great Britain, and the United States are low in uncertainty avoidance. Ultimately, members of these cultures are comfortable with risk and feel lower levels of stress. Change is expected in the business world, and organizations in low uncertainty avoidant cultures look for opportunities to grow and explore.

Uncertainty avoidance: A cultural dimension describing the degree to which a culture avoids things that are unknown or uncertain.

Cultures low in uncertainty avoidance expect and look for growth opportunities.

© foto infor/Shutterstock.com

Individualism and Collectivism

Individualism: A cultural dimension describing the degree to which a culture places emphasis on the achievements of individuals.

A third quality of differing cultures is their individualistic or collectivistic orientation. Individualistic cultures place emphasis on the achievements of individuals. For example, people in the United States gauge their success based on their individual accomplishments such as raises, promotions, or education. Individualistic cultures believe in each person's individual rights and freedoms as well as an individual's ability to complete tasks and make decisions on their own. The United States, Australia, Great Britain, Canada, and the Netherlands rank among the most highly individualistic cultures. Other cultures do not place the individual as the most important component of the social structure; instead, their main concern is for that of the collective or the group. Members of collectivist cultures focus on the success of their groups, including organizations and families. These cultures have a greater tendency toward teamwork and group decision-making and view success as a way to raise the status and well-being of their families or organizations. These cultures seek harmony among groups and focus on relationships as opposed to tasks. Venezuela, Colombia, Pakistan, Peru, Taiwan, and Thailand rank among the highest in collectivistic orientation.

Collectivism: A cultural dimension describing the degree to which a culture focuses on the success of the group of which they are a member, including organizations and families.

Masculine and Feminine

Masculine culture: Culture that values assertiveness, competition, strength, and achievements; this culture also has more rigid sex roles for men and women, with women holding fewer power positions within the organization.

A fourth way to classify different cultures is as masculine and feminine. These labels have drawn some criticism because of stereotypical references to sex; however, Hofstede was looking at the significance of sex roles within cultures and specifically how these roles affect family, organizations, and social norms.[9] Masculine cultures value assertiveness, competition, strength, and achievements. Masculine cultures also have more rigid sex roles for men and women, with women holding fewer power positions within the organization. Japan, Austria, Venezuela, and Italy are among the most highly masculine cultures, whereas the United States is moderate in its masculine orientation. Contrary to the label, feminine or nurturing cultures are more androgynous, with less-rigid sex roles and more openness to equality. Feminine cultures focus on relational qualities of work environments and seek to resolve conflict using compromise and collaboration. Women are more likely to hold managerial positions, and men are expected to be caring, supportive, and people oriented. Sweden, Norway, the Netherlands, and Denmark are feminine cultures.

Feminine culture: A feminine or nurturing culture is more androgynous with less rigid sex roles and more openness to equality; this culture focuses on relational qualities of work environments and seeks to resolve conflict using compromise and collaboration.

As mentioned earlier, the masculine/feminine dimension reflects how a culture views sex roles, so knowledge of this dimension is important especially for women working and traveling abroad. Highly masculine cultures have more rigid sex roles, where there is an expectation that men will hold more positions of power and that women will primarily be responsible for home matters and caretaking, even if they are also expected to work outside the home. Though many cultures honor women in their nurturing roles, religious and cultural beliefs may manifest in very unequal and discriminatory treatment of women in the workplace. This may present certain challenges for businesswomen working internationally, especially in places where women and girls are denied educational opportunities, are not allowed to make direct eye contact with men, and are not expected to hold positions of power. Smooth intercultural interactions can occur with the appropriate approach. Tracey Wilen, a researcher on women in international business, provides the following pointers for women working abroad:[10]

© dboystudio/Shutterstock.com

Women may face cultural challenges when working internationally on business.

- **Be visible** by hosting and attending meetings because it shows that you are a key decision maker.
- **Get introduced**, especially by the right people (those with power who have a relationship with the other party) and in the right way. If you can't be introduced in person, make sure your information, title, and position description are shared with the other party ahead of time.
- **Include a distinct title on your business cards.** Make your position and title clear, and offer your cards freely to reinforce your status.
- **Lead business discussions.** If a woman is leading a business team abroad, she should take an active role in the discussion, and the team should defer to her. This helps shore up credibility, and it makes a clear point when male employees defer answers and questions to women.
- **Be professional in appearance and communication.** Be careful of coming on too strong when trying to establish credibility; just be yourself.
- **Be aware of women's roles in other countries.** Cultural knowledge is important for being aware of your host county's perception of women. Keep these things in mind as you tailor your messages.

Long-Term and Short-Term Orientation

■■■■■■■■■

Long-term orientation: A cultural dimension emphasizing the importance of methodically making decisions based on tradition.

■■■■■■■■■

Short-term orientation: A cultural dimension describing a culture's tendency to make quick decisions and expect quick results.

The fifth dimension posed by Hofstede is long-term and short-term orientation. A culture with a long-term orientation emphasizes the importance of methodically making decisions based on tradition. In the business world, long-term orientation requires perseverance, patience, and a focus on decisions that are best for the group. China, Taiwan, Japan, and South Korea have long-term orientations. This orientation is evident in Japanese work environments where employees rarely make impulsive decisions and thoroughly contemplate and test anything affecting the organization's success through methodical business models. Cultures with a short-term orientation make quick decisions and expect quick results. These societies are focused more on the present and the bottom line. Pakistan, Nigeria, Philippines, Canada, Great Britain, and the United States share a short-term orientation.

OTHER CULTURAL CONSIDERATIONS

In addition to Hofstede's dimensions, other intercultural researchers have documented differences in language use, formality, nonverbal communication, and time orientation. The following section reviews these common differences and addresses ways to break down barriers.

If you would like to compare your culture's communication dimensions with another or research Hofstede's findings check out his Web site.

■■■■■■■■■

High-context: How a culture relies on different elements of a situation in communicating a message, which means noticing subtle cues in interaction and preserving harmony.

High- and Low-Context Language

In addition to Hofstede's work, Edward T. Hall, an anthropologist, studied other communicative variations across cultural contexts and found differences in the use of language.[11] Language use varies along a high-context and low-context continuum. High-context cultures rely on different elements of a situation in communicating a message, which means noticing subtle cues in interaction, and preserving harmony. Many Asian cultures use high-context communication, which can be viewed by those in low-context cultures as indirect. For example, in a meeting with Japanese employees where a major decision is under discussion, you may not realize that others are disagreeing with your ideas. Instead of directly expressing disagreement, the Japanese employees may ask more questions about your idea and then postpone further discussion. In these situations, it is important to understand the subtle cues of the situation, including a focus on group harmony, to make sense of how your counterparts view your ideas. Low-context cultures focus on the specific meaning of spoken words or messages and expect clarity, especially when giving an opinion. Communication in low-context cultures is considered much more direct. The United States and Canada are examples of cultures that prefer low-context communication.

Formality

Just as there are differences in the directness of our language, there are also cultural variations in the formality of our behavior and language. Knowing the level of formality of one's culture can give you insight on how to address people (such as calling them Ms., Mr., Sir, by their title, or first name). There are differences in the formality and directness of our language. People in the United States often communicate messages simply to be polite, such as suggesting that you "get together sometime," which means you want to keep in contact.[12] Members of other cultures might take this phrase literally and expect an invitation. Formality in writing is also important, especially when writing reports and memos.

Low-context: How a culture focuses on the specific meaning of spoken words or messages and expects clarity, especially when giving an opinion.

Knowing the level of formality of one's culture can give you insight on how to address people.

Some cultures have specific ways to address members of the organization. For example, in the United States recipients' names are often listed in alphabetical order; however, in Japan, names are listed by order of rank. Although these are subtle differences, they make a big impact and can help you save face.

Nonverbal Communication

Another critical area of communication awareness is the variety in nonverbal communication forms across cultures. Although we know that the nonverbal expression of certain emotions are universal, such as smiling when happy or frowning when sad, certain facial expressions and body movements differ among cultures. Take the possible confusion you might feel when a Japanese employee nods her head in response to something you have proposed. Although you might think she is agreeing with your statement, in actuality she is communicating that she has heard what you are saying; in other words, she is listening and processing your message. There are also other distinct differences in eye contact, proxemics (the use of personal space), greetings such as handshakes or bows, and tonal vocal qualities such as volume. **Table 2.1** reviews how cultures may contrast in the ways they introduce each other.[13] These and other topics are reviewed in depth in Chapter 3 on nonverbal communication.

Time Orientation

Monochronic time orientation: The view of time as something to be compartmentalized, segmented, or scheduled.

Polychronic time orientation: The view of time as something that is free flowing and naturally occurring.

Time orientation is the final dimension of cultural communication. In the United States, we frequently hear the phrase, "time is money." We relish and protect our time, and we segment and schedule ourselves to optimize activities. This view of time as something to be compartmentalized is a **monochronic time orientation**. We schedule one thing at a time and limit the amount of time we devote to certain activities. Other cultures function very differently with regard to time, viewing it as free flowing and naturally occurring. This **polychronic time orientation** is seen in Latin cultures, where meeting times and dinner parties rarely begin and end as scheduled. Understanding this difference means that you must make a cultural shift in your expectations for when and how events may take place.

Table 2.1: Cultural Contrasts during Business Introductions

	North Americans	Japanese	Arabs
Cultural Objective	Find out who you are; add to network of contacts; gain control	Discover your position in the company and your mission; maintain harmony	Establish personal rapport
Business Cards	A formality; a record of contact	Important to show company affiliation and level	Formality; no intrinsic value
Opening	What do you do? Job identity crucial	Put yourself in group context: 1. Company 2. Department 3. Individual	Establish personal status/family context; general conversation
Self-Image	Independence	Member of group	Part of rich culture
Use of Language	First name; informal; friendly	Little talking	Expression of admiration; flattery; formal greeting
Nonverbal Messages	Direct eye contact; firm handshake	Bowing level; minimal facial expression	Facial expression; body language
Spatial Orientation	Individual space; maintain distance	Groups maintain distance; structured	Close distance, informal
Time Orientation	Short period of introduction	Give lead to others	Long range; take initiative
Information Exchange	Business-related; level of responsibility	Company related	Personal
Closing	Get down to business; take the initiative	Period of harmony; response to initiative	Expression of hospitality/personal relationship
Applied Cultural Values	Informality; openness; directness; action oriented	Harmony; respect; listening; nonemotional	Religious harmony; hospitality; emotional support; status/ritual

This article was published in *Multicultural Management 2000*, table 5.1, page 113. Copyright Elsevier, 1998, used with permission.

Tips for Dealing with Language Barriers

In addition to navigating your way through numerous cultural differences, another significant issue you may face is a language barrier. Language difficulties can increase the anxiety level of all parties; however, there are effective and appropriate ways to navigate these difficult interactions. Mary Ellen Guffey, a business communication expert, offers the following tips for improving your verbal intercultural communication, particularly when there are language barriers:[14]

- Familiarize yourself with basic phrases and greetings used by members of the other culture.
- Speak slowly (not loudly) and choose basic English when communicating messages. Be sure to avoid jargon, clichés, or colloquialisms, as this can be confusing.
- Ask questions frequently to ensure comprehension and encourage the other person to ask questions at any time.
- Listen to the other person and be patient in allowing them to finish their statements, even when their English is slowly articulated.
- Follow up your verbal messages with a written message to ensure clarity. Like most languages, most people learn to read before perfecting conversational speaking, so following up in writing gives the other person time to reflect and interpret.

DOMESTIC DIVERSITY IN THE WORKPLACE

In addition to working with multicultural audiences abroad, there are other forms of diversity to consider within the United States. Even though it is likely that most employees share the same culture, such as being American, many also hold memberships in other groups based on race, ethnicity, religion, gender, age, sexual orientation, or disability. These are considered co-cultures. Co-cultures are subgroups of a larger culture who share a common set of values, beliefs, or attributes. According to Fred Jandt, an intercultural communication scholar, subgroups or co-cultures share language patterns, values, and media outlets and are targeted by organizations as markets for specific products.[15]

The United States is becoming increasingly diverse. According to the Census Bureau, Hispanics and Asians had the largest population increase between 2000 and 2010, with Hispanics growing by 43 percent. Even though those identifying as non-Hispanic, white make up the largest

■■■■■■■■■

Co-cultures:
Subgroups of a larger culture who share a common set of values, beliefs, or attributes.

© EDHAR/Shutterstock.com

proportion of the population at around 64 percent, this group is also the slowest growing.[16] A more diversified work environment results from an increasing number of Hispanics, Asians, and African Americans in the United States. In addition to employees of diverse ethnicities and races, more women are in the workforce than at any time in history, making up approximately 46.8 percent of the total U.S. labor force.[17] Despite the growing diversity of organizations, many groups still face challenges. For women and minorities, the glass ceiling is still a very real experience. The **glass ceiling** describes an invisible barrier preventing women and minorities from advancing in organizations, specifically into upper management positions. Along with the struggle to advance, pay inequities also exist. According to the Bureau of Labor Statistics, in 2010 women earned 81 percent of men's earnings.[18] The following sections introduce you to some of the challenges faced by different co-cultures.

Along with the struggle to advance, pay inequities also exist for women and minorities.

Glass ceiling: An invisible barrier preventing women and minorities from advancing in organizations, specifically into upper-management positions.

Gender

Even though the number of females entering the workforce continues to rise, women still face inequalities with regard to pay, promotion, and employment into historically male occupations. As mentioned earlier, women of equal education and experience make less money than their white male counterparts and hold fewer upper-management positions. One interesting indicator of the glass ceiling is the number of female CEOs of large organizations. In 2014, only 24 women were CEOs of the *Fortune* 500 companies.[19] Recently, large organizations such as Boeing and Morgan Stanley have paid out close to $130 million in class-action lawsuits related to gender discrimination in unfair hiring, pay, and promotion practices.[20] Clearly, even as the number of women in the workforce increases, structural, cultural, and institutional policies and practices still have a negative impact on their advancement and working conditions.

Other research shows that even as the number of dual-income families increases, the division of labor between spouses remains uneven. Women are still the primary caretakers of home and children, making their work lives even more stressful. Many organizations recognize these challenges for women and develop innovative approaches to helping families manage through programs like on-site day care, job-sharing (where full-time jobs are split between two part-time employees), and flexible working schedules such as four-day workweeks or options for telecommuting. Based on some of these programs, *Working Mother* magazine cites Ernst and Young, General Mills, IBM, and Prudential Financial as among the 2014 top places to work for moms.[21] The National Association for Female Executives also listed IBM and General Mills in their list of top employers.[22]

Another significant issue women face in the workplace is sexual harassment. Although most companies have basic written policies regarding harassment, lawsuits abound. **Sexual harassment** is defined as any unwanted physical or verbal action of a sexual nature, which creates a hostile work environment.[23] This definition is somewhat vague in that many different messages can be considered harassing, depending on contextual or situational factors. For example, jokes, e-mails, and pictures of a sexual nature may create a **hostile work environment**—an uncomfortable workplace stemming from sexually charged messages. A second type of sexual harassment is *quid pro quo*, Latin for "this for that." This type of harassment is where a person with power in the organization withholds resources until the employee complies with sexual requests. Survey data suggest that sexual harassment is still a significant issue for women and men in the workplace, and it is the responsibility of management to promote positive, respectful communication among employees using zero-tolerance policies for harassing behavior. Keep in

Sexual harassment: Any unwanted physical or verbal action of a sexual nature, which creates a hostile work environment.

Hostile work environment: An uncomfortable workplace stemming from sexually charged messages.

Quid pro quo: A type of sexual harassment in which a person with power in the organization withholds resources from another employee unless offered sexual favors.

mind that although sexual harassment is most often directed at women it does occur with men and can be directed to members of the same sex.

Race and Ethnicity

Even though many organizations understand the value of diversity, especially among racial and ethnic groups, many employees experience discrimination and prejudice on the basis of their membership in these groups. The Equal Employment Opportunity Commission (EEOC) reported 33,068 charges of race discrimination in 2013, resulting in $112.7 million in settlements.[24] Title VII of the Civil Rights Act of 1964 protects employees against discrimination on the basis of race, sex, religion, and national origin. Discrimination takes the form of inappropriate hiring, recruiting, and advancement practices, harassment or the creation of a hostile work environment, and unfair compensation or other terms of employment, segregation, and retaliation. These forms of discrimination are the result of prejudices individuals hold toward certain groups based on stereotypes.

Our attraction to people who are similar to us and our brain's need to categorize people based on their differences has the ability to increase our reliance on stereotypes. A **stereotype** is a judgment made about individuals based on any observable or believed group membership.[25] We use stereotypes to make judgments about how others will communicate. Often, we are so distracted by the cultural differences that we overlook the similarities and miss the potential for innovation brought about by a diverse workplace. Learning about other cultural values related to race and ethnicity is important for breaking through inappropriate generalizations.

In an effort to raise awareness about racial discrimination in the workplace, in 2008 the EEOC partnered with jazz musician Wynton Marsalis to create two public service announcements. Check out the video.

The terms *race* and *ethnicity* are often confused, but the U.S. Census Bureau considers them separate concepts.[26] Ethnicity describes a person's origin, meaning their family's country of birth, nationality group, heritage, or religious heritage. The complexity of our labels is seen in the use of the term *Hispanic*. Instead of broadly using the term *Hispanic*, some members of this group identify themselves as being Spanish, Hispanic, or Latino. Although they are all Spanish-speaking countries, people with a Mexican, South American, or Cuban heritage may use different labels to identify their ethnicity. In addition to selecting ethnicity, the Census Bureau sets five basic categories for race, including African American or Black, White, American Indian or Alaska Native,

Stereotype: A judgment made about individuals based on any observable or believed group membership.

Asian, and Native Hawaiian or other Pacific Islander. For the 2000 and 2010 Census, participants were allowed to assign themselves as more than one race. This supports Jandt's point that race can be defined sociohistorically because of its changing nature in different societies and cultures. Race is traditionally defined biologically as groups of people who share biological similarities with regard to skin, hair textures, and other physical features.[27] As the diversity of our population grows, so too does the way we define ourselves.

Obviously, our ethnic and racial backgrounds are integral parts of our identities, which influence our communication styles, even in the workplace. Understanding and respecting the cultural values of others can take us a long way toward communicating more competently. **Table 2.2**, developed by interracial communication scholars Orbe and Harris, demonstrates common perceptions of communication style differences based on racial and ethnic group membership.[28]

Age

The United States has experienced a shift in the age of its workforce because of the large population of baby boomers (people born between the years 1946 and 1964). Two major changes related to this include a loss of employees to retirement and simultaneously an increase in the number of workers remaining in the organization beyond age 65 either in the same career or in a second career. According the U.S. Bureau of Labor Statistics, in 2013 the number of older workers in the labor force aged 55 to 64 employed or seeking work increased to 64.4percent.[29] **Figure 2.1** shows the shifting trends of older workers (those 65 and over) between 1980 and 2013; the numbers have more than doubled.[30]

The Age Discrimination in Employment Act of 1967 (ADEA) protects employees 40 years and older from discrimination with respect to terms and conditions of employment in hiring, firing, promotion, layoff, compensation, benefits, job assignments, and training and protects employees from retaliation related to the opposition of discriminatory practices.[31] However, many older employees experience discrimination. The AARP (American Association of Retired Persons) reports that older job seekers often experience age discrimination as indicated in the greater amount of time needed to find positions, lower salaries on rehire, and the amount of court settlements resulting from discrimination claims.[32] In 2013, the EEOC received 21,396 charges of age discrimination and recovered $97.9 million in monetary benefits.[33]

Table 2.2 Guide to Perception of Interracial Verbal and Nonverbal Behaviors

The information included in this table highlights some specific examples of how verbal and nonverbal cues can generate various meanings depending on in-group and out-group perceptions. They are offered here not as generalizations applicable to all ethnic group members in any one group, but as information to assist in recognizing potential sources of miscommunication.

Specific Behavior	Possible In-Group Perception	Possible Out-Group Perception
Avoidance of direct eye contact by Latino/as	Used to communicate attentiveness or respect	A sign of inattentiveness; direct eye contact is preferred
An African American who aggressively challenges a point to which she or he disagrees	Acceptable means of dialogue; not regarded as verbal abuse, nor a precursor to violence	Arguments are viewed as inappropriate and a sign of potential immediate violence
Asian American use of finger gestures to beckon others	Appropriate if used by adults for children, but highly offensive if used to call adults	Appropriate gesture to use with both children and adults
Interruptions used by African Americans	Tolerated in individual/group discussions: attention is given to most assertive voice	Perceived as rude or aggressive; clear rules for turn taking must be maintained
Silence used by Native Americans	A sign of respect, thoughtfulness, and/or uncertainty/ambiguity	Silence indicates boredom, disagreement, or a refusal to participate/respond
The use of touch by Latino/as	Perceived as normal and appropriate for interpersonal interactions	Deemed as appropriate for some intimate or friendly interactions; otherwise perceived as a violation of personal space
Public displays of intense emotions by African Americans	Personal expressiveness is valued and regarded as appropriate in most settings	Violates U.S. societal expectations for self-controlled public behaviors; inappropriate for most public settings
Asian Americans touching or holding hands of same-sex friends	Seen as acceptable behavior that signifies closeness of platonic relationships	Perceived as inappropriate, especially for male friends
Latino/as use of lengthy greetings or the exchange of pleasantries prior to business meetings	Regarded as an important element of establishing rapport with colleagues	Seen as a waste of time; getting to the business at hand is valued

Interracial Communication: Theory into Practice by Orbe, Mark P. Reproduced with permission of Sage in the format Republish in a book via Copyright Clearance Center.

figure 2.1

Workers 65 and Over 1980–2013

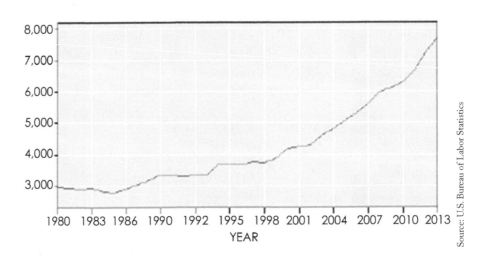

Source: U.S. Bureau of Labor Statistics

In the Older Workers Survey conducted by the Society for Human Resource Management, HR professionals cited willingness to work different schedules, ability to serve as mentors, and invaluable experience as the top three reasons for hiring older workers.[34] The top three disadvantages reported were not keeping up with technology, rise in health expenses, and less flexibility. According to researchers at the Urban Institute, there is no connection between age and job performance, so many of the concerns of employers and coworkers are unfounded.[35] Organizations should work to develop a tolerant workplace respectful of potential generational differences, and they should focus on targeting training to the specific needs of different employees.

Ability

According to the U.S. Census Bureau's American Community Survey, in 2013 6.73 percent of the U.S. population (noninstitutionalized) over the age of 16 reported a disability.[36] Disabilities range in type and severity from physical to mental and can make it difficult for an individual to complete daily activities. The Americans with Disabilities Act of 1990 (ADA) was designed to protect disabled persons from discrimination

Older, experienced workers can serve as valuable mentors for other employees.

and increase their opportunities for employment.[37] The ADA prohibits private employers, state and local governments, employment agencies, and labor unions from discriminating against qualified individuals with disabilities. This bill also requires employers of 15 or more employees to make reasonable accommodations for disabled employees, including facility modifications for access, modified job assignments, and modified or adjusted equipment or materials, or providing readers or interpreters. Despite this legislation, disabled Americans still experience discrimination in the workplace. According to the EEOC, 25,957 charges of disability discrimination were filed in 2013, and $109.2 million in benefits were awarded.[38] Data from the Current Population Survey identifies 22.5 percent of the disabled population were employed in 2013, which means only one in five disabled persons age 16 and above are employed.[39] Surprisingly, the employment trend for people with disabilities has been steadily declining. These numbers not only represent diversity of people with abilities in the workplace, but also a wealth of potential employees who for various reasons are not in the workforce.

Organizations looking to tap this employee pool are taking innovative approaches to accommodate employees. For example, Walgreens has opened a second distribution center in Windsor, Connecticut, designed to employ people with disabilities.[40] The company's goal is to fill at least one third of their open positions with disabled persons. Organizations such as Walgreens are expanding their thinking beyond the limitations of individuals to the potential of human capital, an important business move given the aging workforce and increasing disability rates. Organizations using flexible work schedules, telecommuting, and other technologically enhanced operations are experiencing the benefits of employing workers with special needs. By developing open and flexible work climates and enhancing training for disabled and able-bodied workers, organizations can create comfortable places for people to work.

To see how organizations are building their workforces with an eye to diversity, go to Walgreens corporate Web site and read their diversity statement and brochure.

Regional Differences

Another element of a co-culture relates to regional differences, including differences in communication and psychological patterns grouped along geographic areas. Members of these groups may follow the same customs and have similar forms of speech, which run along geographic clusters. For example, regional groups might include geographic locations along latitudes and longitudes such as North, South, East, or West or with regard to population size (whether you are from an urban or rural region). Although some researchers report that regional cultural differences are lessening because of ease of travel, the media, and technological advancements, others claim that regional differences are as strong as ever.[41] According to communication researchers Andersen, Lustig, and Andersen, "a regional communication pattern is a repository of cultural or institutional plans, patterns, scripts, goals, values, attitudes, beliefs, views, and behaviors that are shared within a social region."[42] Scholars have created different maps to display the regional cultures of the United States similar to the one in **Figure 2.2**.[43]

Other than the study of dialects between regions, the study of differences in how people communicate with others interpersonally based on regions has not advanced. Several researchers note differences in nonverbal communication as well as other patterns. For example, according to nonverbal communication researcher Birdwhistell, in

figure 2.2

Map of Cultural Regions of America

From *Journal of Geography*, Volume 79. No. 6. November 1980. Reprinted by permission of Taylor and Francis. Permission conveyed by Copyright Clearance Center, Rightslink.

addition to the contradictory use of a smile (people smile when happy or when under pressure), people from different parts of the country smile more frequently than others.[44] He observed that people in Georgia, Kentucky, and Tennessee smile more than any other regions; however, even within these states variations exist. Specifically, those living in the Appalachian regions smiled less. Andersen and his colleagues cited studies which found differences in level of talk, importance of friends, and level of activity.[45] New Englanders and those from the Mid-Atlantic region are more introverted and less talkative, whereas New Yorkers are more verbally powerful, using faster rates of speech.[46] Southerners focus more on relationships, affiliations, and friendships and make more eye contact.[47]

These style differences are easy to adjust to once you recognize them. The issue of tolerance remains important particularly because many regional stereotypes exist. As a member of an organization, you should also consider the impact of these regional differences on messages, particularly when constructing sales messages marketing products to these groups.

Sexual Orientation

A final co-culture for consideration is based on sexual orientation. A long-discussed and often controversial topic, the United States currently has no federal laws protecting employees from discrimination based on sexual orientation. Eighteen states have laws prohibiting job discrimination, many organizations set their own policies, and many communities are passing fairness ordinances banning such practices. In those states or organizations without such laws or policies, lesbian, gay, bisexual, and transgendered (LGBT) individuals may be discriminated against in hiring, firing, promotion, and pay and have little legal recourse.

According to Hofstede, a culture's acceptance of homosexuality is connected to their masculine and feminine orientation; masculine cultures are less accepting.[48] In cultures where homosexuality is stigmatized, LGBT individuals are cast as separate from the norm. This minority status has solidified the LGBT community as a co-culture. Many members of the LGBT community strongly identify with their co-culture to the extent that some share specific communication styles, live in specific areas, and patronize businesses that are open and accepting of their needs and interests. Stereotypes abound for members of the LGBT community, which often translate into active forms of discrimination. However, many LGBT individuals have taken pride in their out-group status as they actively fight for rights. Jandt also points out how describing homosexuality as an identity or as a co-culture is problematic for many LGBT individuals who don't "fit the mold" or what leaders of the gay pride movements have portrayed.[49] Categorizing people into a group based on sexual orientation is problematic just as any label has the potential to create inaccurate stereotypes; therefore, keeping an open mind and valuing the contribution of your fellow coworkers is essential to working skillfully with diverse groups.

TIPS FOR COMMUNICATING WITH DIFFERENT CULTURES AND CO-CULTURES

The previous sections explored many facets of international and domestic diversity in the workplace. Organizations that capitalize on these forms of diversity are better able to navigate change. However, organizations must constantly review their policies and practices and look for ways to train employees on issues of diversity. Communicating with members of groups different from your own requires understanding, patience, and time. Many communication skills are important for developing your intercultural communication competence.

Intercultural communication competence is your ability to communicate appropriately and effectively across various situations or settings.[50] Interacting with businesspeople from different cultures requires motivation, knowledge, and skill. Your communication competence in the workplace involves your ability to (a) adapt your communication to different audiences, (b) manage interactions or conversations, and (c) communicate empathy, which means identifying with and managing the emotions of others.[51] The key to communicating competently is that you must be appropriate and effective across situations. In other words, every situation or context has certain rules, norms, or expectations for communication. The business context is a broad area where there are typical norms for behavior and interaction, but even across organizations, norms can vary significantly. This difference between organizations is drastically influenced by culture. Developing your intercultural communication competence can be even more complex when dealing with groups or individuals with diverse cultural backgrounds. Studying the ways culture affects our communication (as described earlier) is the first element of developing your competence. R. Roosevelt Thomas, founder of the American Institute for Managing Diversity, uses the term **diversity maturity** to describe individuals, managers, and organizations with a clear understanding of diversity principles and the ability to practice this knowledge.[52] According to Thomas, diversity-mature individuals:

- Accept personal responsibility for enhancing their own and their organization's effectiveness.
- Demonstrate contextual knowledge. That is, they know themselves and their organizations, and they understand key diversity concepts and definitions.
- Are clear about requirements and include/exclude decisions about differences based on how they affect the ability to meet these requirements.
- Understand that diversity is accompanied by complexity and tension and are prepared to cope with these in pursuit of greater diversity effectiveness.
- Are willing to change conventional wisdom.
- Engage in continuous learning.

Intercultural communication competence: The ability to communicate appropriately and effectively across various situations or settings.

Diversity maturity: Having a clear understanding of diversity principles and the ability to practice this knowledge.

Thomas also suggests that individuals explore their personal feelings toward diversity by contemplating the following questions:

- Am I comfortable working with people from all demographic groups?
- Is there a group or groups that I struggle to accept?
- If so, how have I attempted to overcome my biases?
- How will my comfort or lack of comfort with people different from me affect my ability to advance within this workplace?
- Do I enjoy diversity?
- If so, what kind?
- If so, how much?

If you would like to see how diversity mature you are, take a few minutes to complete Thomas's Diversity Maturity Index. By understanding yourself, learning about the cultural backgrounds of others, and being willing to navigate the tension that diversity can sometimes bring, employees can develop their intercultural communication competence for success in today's business world.

How do you communicate effectively and appropriately in various situations?

© Stephen Coburn/Shutterstock.com

Read each of the 10 individual scenarios in its entirety and review the possible responses to each given situation. Write the letter of the response that most closely reflects how you would respond to that scenario on the score sheet.

1. You manage a fast-food restaurant that had typically been staffed by younger people. Recently, you've added two older workers to the crew taking orders from customers. You're beginning to hear some mutterings from the younger staff about the older workers taking longer to prepare orders, chatting with customers, and being tentative about your computerized ordering system. What do you do?
   a. Call a team meeting so that everyone can discuss what's going on at work and talk through their concerns.
   b. Ignore the problem. Your younger staff tend not to stay at the job for very long, so they'll soon be gone. The older staff will already be in place when newer young ones are hired, and these new staff will simply take the older workers' way of doing business in stride.
   c. Assess the situation. Are the older workers doing a good job? Are their different work styles producing customer satisfaction or customer annoyance?
   d. Create teams of older and younger workers so that they can learn from each other. If that doesn't work out, reassign the older workers to jobs that aren't as time sensitive.

2. You are active in a suburban, mostly white church that recently "adopted" an inner-city school that is 95 percent African American. You are responsible for working with 20 church members who will act as mentors to children at the school. All who have volunteered to mentor are white. How would you address the situation?
   a. Let matters rest. What's important is the commitment and personality of the individuals who will be mentors, not their skin color.
   b. Discuss the matter with African-American members of your congregation to see what their thoughts are.
   c. Try to recruit more people of color to participate as mentors.
   d. Leave the need to better "match" mentors and students to other churches and community organizations.

3. What is the most important reason to respond to diversity effectively?
   a. It's the moral, right thing to do.
   b. It will make my company more competitive.
   c. The law requires it.
   d. It will help me get promoted.

4. You are the local manager of a large chain hardware store, and you know that a competitor will soon open a new store nearby. The two stores are located in a middle-class, predominantly black neighborhood. You have 3 days to prepare a proposal for a special event designed to draw positive attention to your store. Which of the following best describes what you would do?
   a. You call your staff together to attend a meeting where you present the overall charge and hand out assignments. The staff forms into small groups and sends you daily reports. On day 3, you pull the individual reports together into a package.
   b. Given the short time frame, you decide that this is a responsibility you will handle yourself. You consult with your staff, but you handle all the details.
   c. You recently worked with two people who really do razzle-dazzle stuff. There was a lot of creativity, which led to some tension and disagreement, but the results were terrific. You call those two people and give them the assignment.
   d. You choose four employees who live in your store's community. You ask the four to help plan an event that will be responsive to the community's particular interests and priorities.

5. You are the office manager of a large accounting firm that has a central pool of word processors and data entry personnel. One of your staff has very strong religious beliefs. A Bible is on his desk, and biblical pictures adorn his cubicle walls. During breaks, he often speaks to other staff about his church and encourages them to attend a service. Several of the staff have complained that they are having increasing difficulty remaining focused on their work. What would you do in this situation?
    a. Provide suggestions to the staff about how they might open a dialogue with this individual to explain their feelings.
    b. Not do anything and hope things will settle down. You're concerned about infringing on his freedom of religion.
    c. Talk with the employee. Explain that although he is free to practice any religion of his choosing, his attempts to proselytize are interfering with the ability of others to do their job. Tell him he is free to keep the Bible and pictures where they are but that you expect him to refrain from discussing religion with others while in the work area.
    d. Send out a memo to all staff stating that although your company welcomes differences in politics and religion, neither has any place in the office and should be confined to other activities they engage in.

6. You belong to a 10-member technical group that meets weekly to go over progress and business developments. One member is an Asian-American woman whose technical skills are superb and are valued by the group. However, the group has a strong preference for active verbal participation, and she tends to sit quietly during these meetings. How would you handle this situation?
    a. You recognize that there are probably some cultural factors at work here. But you also know that she's doing an excellent job. So you don't call the matter to your coworker's or anyone else's attention.
    b. You speak to your supervisor about your observations and ask her to encourage your coworker to participate more in the meetings.
    c. You seek out your coworker and discuss your observations. You ask her if there's anything you can do to help her become more involved in these meetings.
    d. During the meetings, you actively solicit input from your coworker.

7. You work in the research and development department of a manufacturing industry. Sales staff are always on your case, wanting to know when a "new, improved" product will be ready for market. They accuse the R&D folks of playing scientist and not realizing the importance of the company's bottom line. What do you do?
    a. Don't say anything. Salespeople will never understand R&D people, so there's no point in trying to get them to comprehend what you're trying to do.
    b. Acknowledge that the salespeople have some legitimate concerns, but let them know they don't fully understand the scientific development process.
    c. Establish a cross-functional group with representatives from R&D and sales. Set up lunch meetings for the purpose of problem solving around the issues and develop action plans that are compatible with the company's objectives.
    d. Look at your company's bottom line. Is sales making unreasonable demands that will adversely affect your company's ability to develop high-quality new products and stay competitive? Is R&D more interested in the beauty of scientific discovery than in your company's profitability? Base your decisions on your answers.

8. Your firm, which had previously done business only in the United States, has recently expanded overseas. You've assigned a woman to head the team moving into a South American country. But word has come back that your major customer there is having a hard time accepting a woman heading up the effort. How do you respond?
    a. Look into the situation further and determine whether it is her gender or some other factors (such as personality or skills) that are affecting the customer's views.

b. Leave her in that position, but assign a man to be her special assistant and work with that customer.

c. Replace her with a man because it is very important that your company demonstrate its commitment to customer needs.

d. Contact the customer and ask what the company expects in the way of results from a team leader. Determine whether the current team leader can meet these expectations. If she can, tell the customer this and explain that you plan to keep her in the position. If she cannot meet expectations, assign the job to someone who can.

9. Which of the following is likely to demonstrate the most diversity?
   a. A conference attended by scientists of both genders and multiple ethnicities.
   b. A communitywide meeting for the purpose of determining how best to use a tax windfall.
   c. One white male, one African-American male, one Hispanic male at a local sports event.
   d. I wouldn't know without observing and talking to the individuals present.

10. You are a regional manager of a drugstore chain. You are getting ready to go into one of your stores when you hear two elderly women talking about a particular cashier. You introduce yourself to them and explain that, as a manager, you would like to know how their shopping experience was. One of the women explains that she felt very uncomfortable with the cashier who rang up her order. As the cashier was bagging the order, his shirtsleeve slid up and the woman noticed a tattoo on his forearm. She said, "I've been shopping here for years, and I always thought that you hired clean, presentable young people!" How should you respond to this customer?
   a. Explain that your store prides itself on hiring quality employees who provide good service to customers, but also prides itself on letting employees express their individuality as long as it does not affect the service customers receive.
   b. Tell the customer you will talk to the cashier and ask him to cover the tattoo so that customers will not see it.
   c. Sympathize with the customer about "kids these days," but explain that the company's hands are tied—you can't interfere with an individual's right to express himself or you may get sued.
   d. Apologize for her experience and offer her a five-dollar coupon toward her next purchase at the store.

KEY:
1. a = 5, b = 5, c = 10, d = 7   2. a = 5, b = 10, c = 7, d = 5   3. a = 7, b = 10, c = 5, d = 5
4. a = 5, b = 5, c = 10, d = 7   5. a = 7, b = 5, c = 10, d = 5   6. a = 10, b = 5, c = 5, d = 7
7. a = 5, b = 5, c = 7, d = 10   8. a = 7, b = 5, c = 5, d = 10   9. a = 5, b = 7, c = 5, d = 10
10. a = 10, b = 7, c = 5, d = 5

High Diversity Maturity (85–100)	Moderate Diversity Maturity (70–85)	Low Diversity Maturity (50–70)
You demonstrate substantial diversity maturity when dealing with the differences and similarities that people bring to the workplace.	You have thought about diversity and are open to learning new ideas and behaviors for addressing it. You have demonstrated a desire to address diversity more effectively but are unclear as to how to go about it.	You have not thought much about differences and similarities in the workplace or about how these can be addressed in the most productive way. You still have a long way to go toward becoming as effective as you can in addressing diversity.

Reprinted by permission of the publisher, from *Building a House for Diversity* by R. Roosevelt Thomas, Jr. © 1999 R. Thomas & Associates, Inc., AMACOM books, division of American Management Association International, New York, NY. All rights reserved. www.amacombooks.org

CONCLUSION

This chapter provides a wealth of information for communicating with diverse groups in the workplace. Whether working on an international, globally dispersed team or working in the United States with members of various races, ages, genders, abilities, regions, or sexual orientations, competent intercultural communication is essential. The impact of globalization on our economy demands that workers develop their skills, especially in the area of communication. Working with diverse others provides opportunities for continued economic success.

Signing up to travel internationally with a team of auditors, Haley Esparza Carter, the senior accountant for PHM mentioned at the beginning of this chapter, will experience the challenges and the rewards of working with diverse groups. She seems to have three things going for her as she prepares for her frequent trips to India: (1) She understands her own culture and the complexity of culture in general; (2) she is motivated to communicate effectively with her international counterparts; and (3) she understands the feeling of being an outsider in another culture. These elements of intercultural communication competence will ensure her travels are pleasant and productive. By studying intercultural communication, business women and men ensure their success in the global economy.

ACTIVITIES

1. Look through local newspapers, national newspapers, or weekly news or business magazines and find stories directly related to globalization. See if you can identify the specific reasons organizations are doing business abroad and describe the ways in which they operate. Bring this information to class to share with your classmates.

2. Select a country in which you would like to travel or work internationally (such as Germany, India, China, Taiwan, Japan, United Kingdom, Mexico, or France). Research the culture and identify their values according to Hofstede's categories. What communication challenges might you face in traveling to this new location? Identify the business practices, rituals, or customs of this culture and be prepared to share your findings with your classmates.

3. Consider the following proverbs from different countries. How do these correspond with Hofstede's and Hall's cultural values?
   - Fish or cut bait. (U.S.)
   - Good fences make good neighbors. (U.S.)
   - Don't put all your eggs in one basket. (U.S.)
   - The early bird gets the worm. (U.S.)
   - A bird in the hand is worth two in the bush. (U.S.)
   - Early to bed, early to rise makes a man healthy, wealthy, and wise. (U.S.)
   - After lunch; rest; after dinner walk a mile. (Arab)
   - The first day you meet, you are friends. The next day you meet, you are brothers. (Afghan)
   - After victory, tighten your helmet cord. (Japanese)
   - Deceive the rich and powerful if you will, but don't insult them. (Japanese)
   - Fast ripe, fast rotten. (Japanese)
   - Behind an able man there are always other able men. (Chinese)
   - Be not afraid of growing slowly, be afraid only of standing still. (Chinese)
   - He who doesn't risk never gets to drink champagne. (Russian)
   - Experience is the comb that nature gives us when we are bald. (Belgian)
   - Don't think there are no crocodiles because the water is calm. (Malayan)
   - Punctuality is the politeness of kings. (French)
   - Better to bend than to break. (French)
   - One can't be at the oven and the mill at the same time. (French)

   Source: http://www.quotesandsayings.com/proverbial.htm;
   http://www.readwritethink.org/lessons/lesson_view.asp?id=186;
   http://french.about.com/library/express/blex_proverb.htm.

4. Imagine you are planning a first business meeting abroad with someone from one of the following countries (or one of your choosing): Germany, India, Saudi Arabia, Japan, China, France, Spain, Malaysia, Mexico, or Honduras. Collect information on the country of your choice and develop an outline of exactly how the meeting might be run. Be sure to include greetings, arrangements, meeting etiquette, and even nonverbal forms of communication. Be prepared to present your research to the class.

5. In groups or pairs, describe your cultural memberships. Explain how you identify with your specific nationality, but also consider your co-cultures. Share with your group or partner your experience in or with another co-culture. Describe the challenges you faced from an intercultural communication perspective. What are some recommendations you might make for improving workplace communication among diverse groups?

REFERENCES

[1] Friedman, T. L. (2005). *The world is flat: A brief history of the twenty-first century.* New York: Farrar, Strauss, and Giroux.

[2] Stohl, C. (2001). Globalizing organizational communication: Convergences and divergences. In F. M. Jablin & L. L. Putnam (Eds.), *The new handbook of organizational communication* (pp. 323–375). Thousand Oaks, CA: Sage.

[3] Mataloni, R. J. (2005). U.S. multinational companies: Operations in 2003. *Survey of Current Business, 85,* 7, 9–20. Retrieved July 29, 2008, from http://www.bea.gov/scb/pdf/2005/07July/0705_MNCs.pdf

[4] Wessel, D. (2011, April 19). Big U.S. firms shift hiring abroad. *Wall Street Journal.* Retrieved October 13, 2014, from http://online.wsj.com/news/articles/SB10001424052748704821704576270783611823972

[5] CBS News. 2004, August, 1). Out of India: More American companies are sending jobs overseas. *60 Minutes.* Retrieved July 29, 2008, from http://www.cbsnews.com/stories/2003/12/23/60minutes/main590004.shtml

[6] Wessel, D. (2011, April 19). Big U.S. firms shift hiring abroad. *Wall Street Journal.* Retrieved October 13, 2014, from http://online.wsj.com/news/articles/SB10001424052748704821704576270783611823972

[7] U.S. Bureau of Labor Statistics. (2007, August). *Charting the U.S. labor market in 2006.* Retrieved July 29, 2008, from http://www.bls.gov/cps/labor2006/home.htm

[8] Hofstede, G. (2001). *Culture's consequences: Comparing values, behaviors, institutions and organizations across nations* (2nd ed.). Thousand Oaks, CA: Sage.

[9] Hofstede, G. (1998). Comparative studies of sexual behavior: Sex as achievement or as relationship? In G. Hofstede (Ed.), *Masculinity and femininity: The taboo dimension of national cultures* (pp. 153–178). Thousand Oaks, CA: Sage.

[10] Wilen, T. (2001, May). Women working overseas. *TD,* 120–122.

[11] Hall, E. T. (1977). *Beyond culture.* New York: Anchor.

[12] Elashmawi, F., & Harris, P. R. (1998). *Multicultural management 2000: Essential cultural insights for global business success.* Houston, TX: Gulf Publishing.

[13] Elashmawi, F., & Harris, P. R. (1998). *Multicultural management 2000: Essential cultural insights for global business success.* Houston, TX: Gulf Publishing.

[14] Guffey, M. E. (2003). *Business communication: Process and product* (4th ed.). Mason, OH: South-Western.

[15] Jandt, F. E. (2004). *An introduction to intercultural communication: Identities in a global community* (4th ed.). Thousand Oaks, CA: Sage.

[16] U.S. Census Bureau. (2011, March 24). *2010 Census Shows America's Diversity.* Retrieved October 13, 2014, from http://www.census.gov/2010census/news/releases/operations/cb11-cn125.html

[17] U.S. Department of Labor, Women's Bureau. (2011). *Quick stats 2010.* Retrieved October 13, 2014, from http://www.dol.gov/wb/factsheets/QS-womenwork2010.htm

[18] U.S. Department of Labor, Women's Bureau. (2011). *Quick stats 2010.* Retrieved October 13, 2014, from http://www.dol.gov/wb/factsheets/QS-womenwork2010.htm

[19] Fairchild, C. (2014, June 3). Number of Fortune 500 women CEOs reaches historic high. *Fortune*. Retrieved October 13, from http://fortune.com/2014/06/03/number-of-fortune-500-women-ceos-reaches-historic-high/

[20] Gill, J. (2005, April). Gender issues: Sex-discrimination lawsuits are on the rise: Is your company at risk? *Inc. Magazine*. Retrieved July 15, 2008, from http://www.inc.com/magazine/20050401/law.html

[21] Focus on the 100 best-top ten 2007. (2007). *Working Mother*. Retrieved July 30, 2008 from http://www.workingmother.com/web?service=vpage/859

[22] National Association for Female Executives. (2013). The NAFE top 50 companies for executive women 2013: Executive summary. Retrieved October 13, 2014 from http://www.wmmsurveys.com/NAFE_Executive_Summary_2013.pdf

[23] Equal Employment Opportunity Commission. (2008, March 4). *Sexual harassment*. Retrieved July 16, 2008, from http://www.eeoc.gov/types/sexual_harassment.html

[24] Equal Employment Opportunity Commission. (2013). Race-based charges FY 1997-FY 2013. Retrieved October 14, 2014, from http://www.eeoc.gov/eeoc/statistics/enforcement/race.cfm

[25] Jandt, F. E. (2004). *An introduction to intercultural communication: Identities in a global community* (4th ed.). Thousand Oaks, CA: Sage.

[26] U.S. Census Bureau. (2008, April 10). *Racial and ethnic classification used in census 2000 and beyond*. Retrieved July 30, 2008, from http://www.census.gov/population/www/socdemo/race/racefactcb.html

[27] Jandt, F. E. (2004). *An introduction to intercultural communication: Identities in a global community* (4th ed.). Thousand Oaks, CA: Sage.

[28] Orbe, M. P., & Harris, T. M. (2001). *Interracial communication: Theory into practice*. Belmont, CA: Wadsworth.

[29] U.S. Bureau of Labor Statistics. (2013). Labor force statistics from the current population. Retrieved October 13, 2014, from http://www.bls.gov/cps/cpsaat03.htm

[30] U.S. Bureau of Labor Statistics. (2014. Workers 65 and over 1980-2013 in data tools. Retrieved October 13, 2014, from http://www.bls.gov/cps/tables.htm

[31] Equal Employment Opportunity Commission. (2008, March 4). *Age discrimination*. Retrieved July 3, 2008, from http://www.eeoc.gov/types/age.html

[32] Rix, S. E. (2006). Update on the aged 55+ worker: 2005. *Data digest, 136*, 1–4. Retrieved July 3, 2008, from http://www.aarp.org/research/work/employment/aresearch-import-347.html

[33] Equal Employment Opportunity Commission (2014). Age Discrimination in Employment Act (includes concurrent charges with Title VII, ADA and EPA). Retrieved October 13, 2014, from http://www.eeoc.gov/eeoc/statistics/enforcement/adea.cfm

[34] Collison, J. (2003, June). *SHRM/NOWCC/CED 2003 older worker survey report*. Alexandria, VA: Society for Human Resource Management.

[35] Eyster, L., Johnson, R. W., & Toder, E. (2008, January). Current strategies to employ and retain older workers. *Urban Institute*. Retrieved July 30, 2008, from http://www.urban.org.url/cfm?ID=411626

[36] U.S. Census Bureau (2014). *Selected economic characteristics for the civilian noninstitutionalized population by disability status:* 2013 American Community Survey 1-Year Estimates. Retrieved October 13, 2014, from http://factfinder2.census.gov/faces/tableservices/jsf/pages/productview.xhtml?pid=ACS_13_1YR_S1811&prodType=table

[37] Equal Employment Opportunity Commission. (2008, February 29). *Disability discrimination.* Retrieved July 7, 2008, from http://www.eeoc.gov/types/ada.html

[38] Equal Employment Opportunity Commission. (2014). Americans with Disabilities Act of 1990 (ADA) Charges (includes concurrent charges with Title VII, ADEA, and EPA) FY 1997- FY 2013. Retrieved October 13, 2014, from http://factfinder2.census.gov/faces/tableservices/jsf/pages/productview.xhtml?pid=ACS_13_1YR_S1811&prodType=table

[39] U.S. Census Bureau (2014). *Selected economic characteristics for the civilian noninstitutionalized population by disability status:* 2013 American Community Survey 1-Year Estimates. Retrieved October 13, 2014, from http://factfinder2.census.gov/faces/tableservices/jsf/pages/productview.xhtml?pid=ACS_13_1YR_S1811&prodType=table

[40] Wells, S. J. (2008, April). Counting on workers with disabilities: The nation's largest minority remains an underused resource. *HR Magazine, 53*(4), 44–49.

[41] Jandt, F. E. (2004). *An introduction to intercultural communication: Identities in a global community* (4th ed.). Thousand Oaks, CA: Sage.

[42] Andersen, P. A., Lustig, M. W., & Andersen, J. F. (1987). Regional patterns of communication in the United States: A theoretical perspective. *Communication Monographs, 54*, 128–144.

[43] Bigelow, B. (1980). Roots and regions: A summary definition of the cultural geography of America. *Journal of Geography, 79*, 218–229.

[44] Birdwhistell, R. L. (1970). *Kinesics and context: Essays on body motion communication.* Philadelphia: University of Pennsylvania Press.

[45] Andersen, P. A., Lustig, M. W., & Andersen, J. F. (1987). Regional patterns of communication in the United States: A theoretical perspective. *Communication Monographs, 54*, 128–144.

[46] Gastil, R. D. (1975). *Cultural regions of the United States.* Seattle: University of Washington Press.

[47] Rubenstein, C. (1982). Regional states of mind: Patterns of emotional life in nine parts of America. *Psychology Today, 16*, 22–30.

[48] Hofstede, G. (1998). Comparative studies of sexual behavior: Sex as achievement or as relationship? In G. Hofstede (Ed.), *Masculinity and femininity: The taboo dimension of national cultures* (pp. 153–178). Thousand Oaks, CA: Sage.

[49] Jandt, F. E. (2004). *An introduction to intercultural communication: Identities in a global community* (4th ed.). Thousand Oaks, CA: Sage.

[50] Spitzberg, B. H., & Cupach, W. R. (1984). *Interpersonal communication competence.* Beverly Hills, CA: Sage.

[51] Payne, H. J. (2005). Reconceptualizing social skills in organizations: Exploring the relationship between communication competence, job performance, and supervisory roles. *Journal of Leadership and Organizational Studies, 11*, 63–77.

[52] Thomas, R.R. (1999). *Building a house for diversity: How a fable about a giraffe and an elephant offer new strategies for today's workforce*. New York: AMACOM.

OTHER READINGS

Gudykunst, W. B. (2003). *Bridging differences: Effective intergroup communication* (4th ed.). Thousand Oaks, CA: Sage.

Gudykunst, W. B., & Kim, Y. Y. (2003). *Communicating with strangers: An approach to intercultural communication* (4th ed.). New York: McGraw-Hill.

section two

General Communication Competencies

chapter
three

Verbal and Nonverbal Communication

After reading this chapter you will be able to:

- Understand the difference between verbal and nonverbal communication
- Describe how verbal and nonverbal communication function in the communication process
- Explain techniques for successful verbal communication
- Describe characteristics of nonverbal communication
- Define sexual harassment

CHAPTER OUTLINE

key words

Verbal communication	Nonverbal communication
Ambiguous word	Vocalics
Concrete meaning	Paralanguage
Slang	Kinesics
Jargon	Gesture
Tag question	Adaptor
Hedges and qualifiers	Emblem
Vocal filler	Regulator
Polite language	Illustrator
Articulation	Proxemics
Pronunciation	Chronemics

INTRODUCTION

Elizabeth Martin, a senior at a large university on the East Coast, is enrolled in her required communication class. She has put the class off as long as possible, not because class times don't fit into her schedule, but because she is afraid of standing up and speaking in front of her peers. She feels fine about her conversational skills with her friends, but whenever she has spoken to a group, her grade has been low. Comments from teachers include, "We have trouble hearing and understanding what you say," and "Be specific in your remarks. Talk to your audience," and, "Slow down. You talk too fast." Elizabeth can't understand why she seems successful in communication with her family and friends and unsuccessful when communicating with peers, supervisors, professors, and strangers. Now, her confidence about her communication skills is low, and she dreads the semester to come. But her business degree requires the class, and she has too much time and money invested to change majors now.

Elizabeth doesn't comprehend the importance of verbal and nonverbal communication skills. She is comfortable talking with friends and colleagues because she sees that as an informal activity—something that is a part of everyday life. But, when she has to speak solo in front of a group, or even when she speaks as part of a group in front of others, she lets her fear take over. She forgets that her mission is to communicate her message to her specific audience, whether that is six people or 600.

Elizabeth fears public communication. She is not alone. Many people—just like you, perhaps—dread taking any class that involves public speaking in college. Many professionals won't take a job if public speaking is a requirement of that job. Some professionals do accept jobs where public speaking is required, but they don't do that part of the job well. The book *I'd Rather Die Than Give a Speech*[1] states that many executives called on to make presentations before such groups as boards of directors, analysts, stockholders, regulators, employees, or franchisees experience some form of apprehension, or some form of concern.

Most people fear speaking in public or speaking to or in front of their supervisors, colleagues, and peers because they don't want to look foolish or to fail. What they might not realize is that excellent verbal and nonverbal communication skills are essential to success as a communicator in various settings—interviews, group presentations, sales proposals, meetings, and speeches. Once you realize the importance of both your verbal and nonverbal communication, you can then work to improve these areas.

Excellent verbal and nonverbal communication skills are essential to success.

Consider this scenario for a moment: you are sitting in your required Business and Professional Communication or Public Speaking class on the first day of the semester. The professor hands out the syllabus, which contains the assignments for the semester. You scan it quickly, noting a

SECTION 2: General Communication Competencies

group project, an interview project, a sales speech assignment, and an informative speech assignment. Your first thought is, "Help. I can't do this. I'll just drop this class and take it another time." But, what if you see those assignments and feel fully confident that you can successfully complete them all? What if you are confident in your verbal and nonverbal communication skills? These hypothetical questions become real very quickly. Both verbal and nonverbal communication skills are crucial to your success as a communicator in today's workplace.

By understanding what makes communication successful, you can change your outlook and change your effectiveness as a communicator.

VERBAL COMMUNICATION

Verbal communication refers to *what* you say, or the message that you send. Do you speak clearly? Is your *intended* message always the message that is received?

Della Manchella, a speaker and trainer for companies who want to ensure the successful performance of their employees, says that when we speak, only approximately 10 percent of the words we use get through to others. If we want our message to be understood, we must be careful of the words we use. Boaz Keysar and Anne S. Henly[2] researched whether speakers overestimate their own effectiveness. They concluded that speakers expect their audiences to understand their intentions more than is warranted. Speakers perceive their own utterances as more transparent than they really are. The concern here is that if speakers believe their listeners understand them, they might be less likely to verify that the listener did indeed arrive at the intended meaning.

When you are writing down your thoughts and remarks for a verbal presentation, make sure you remember to write for the ear, and not for the eye. You are writing words that a person or a group of people are going to hear. They will not have your remarks in front of them. They will only have their ears, and they will only get one chance to hear and understand you.

If you are reading a book, an article, or an e-mail and are interrupted, you can reread the material or even flip back to another page to remind yourself what you were reading before the interruption. You can also read one passage several times for clarification. If you read a word, and you don't know its definition, you can leave the passage, look up the definition, come back, and continue to read. When you are listening to someone speak, you only have one shot to understand what they say. You can't

Verbal communication: What you say or the message that you send.

rewind a DVD or ask them to do it over. If you don't understand what someone is saying, then you might stop listening.

When you speak to people whom you know well on an informal basis, you might take it for granted that you communicate clearly. Your conversation might contain run-on sentences, incomplete thoughts, jargon, slang, ambiguous words, and vocal fillers. Still, your message has a good chance of being communicated successfully for several reasons: (a) Your listeners know you well; (b) your listeners are familiar with your speaking style; (c) your listeners have similar interests and hobbies; and (d) your listeners can ask questions to clarify what they hear.

If you take that same style of speaking and use it when asking the boss for a raise or a promotion, or with a new client with whom you are trying to make a sale, or even as you address your coworkers in a meeting, your communication might be unsuccessful. If people have to work hard at trying to understand what you are saying, they probably will not put forth the effort.[3] You need to write or compose your thoughts differently for an audience of listeners than you do for an audience of readers. You need to write down your thoughts and then read them out loud, editing as you read to ensure that your meaning is clear.

Tips for Successful Communication

Do your words match your meaning?

The tips in the following sections will help you produce successful verbal communication.

CLARITY

Be clear. Misunderstandings and miscommunications cost a business time and money. If your boss needs a committee report to be completed *before* the staff meeting at the end of the month, and you understand that it isn't due until *after* the staff meeting, then no one involved with your project can move forward on time. When *you* are the recipient of verbal communication, clarify, paraphrase, or ask questions about the message. Make certain you understand exactly what is expected of you. If your boss gives you verbal directions, take notes as she speaks. Paraphrase what your boss tells you, repeat it back to her, and ask if you understand the directions clearly. If you initiate the communication, check your message for any ambiguities. An **ambiguous word** leaves receivers uncertain of its meaning; **concrete meaning**, on the other hand, is specific.

Ambiguous word: Leaves receivers uncertain as to its meaning.

Concrete meaning: Specific; leaves no uncertainty in its meaning.

SLANG, JARGON, AND BUZZ WORDS

Examples of ambiguous statements:
1. I need that committee report soon. (When exactly do you need that?)
2. I'll be there in a little while. (When will you actually arrive?)
3. You did pretty well. (How exactly did I do?)

Example of concrete meaning or specific statements:
1. That report needs to be 2 pages long, double-spaced, using 12-point font.
2. I'll be there in 25 minutes.
3. Your report was well organized with a clear beginning, middle, and end, but I would like to see more specific examples of your sales figures.

Be careful with slang and jargon. **Slang** and jargon are both "shortcut" talk, and their use is fine when you're talking to family, friends, and colleagues. But in a more formal group or speaking situation, this "shortcut" talk becomes a distraction. You might be asked to present research to supervisors, colleagues, and laypersons in hopes of gaining necessary funding to continue to research and publish your results. If you supplement your speech with **jargon**—or words only known by those people in your area of specialty—then you will confuse and lose the attention of the laypeople unfamiliar with the language you use. They will not write a check if they don't understand what you need it for. Always remember who is in your audience, whether it's two people or 200 people, and tailor your message to each specific audience. Jargon and slang are only clear to those people who know what they mean. People who don't know the meaning will feel left out, and so they will tune you out.

Slang: Informal language typically used or shared by groups.

Jargon: Words known only by those people in your area of specialty.

Have you ever been confused by a doctor using medical jargon?

Most career fields have their own jargon or buzz words. Some jargon has become well known. For example, you are probably familiar with military terms like AWOL, MIA, Jeep, and SNAFU. If you've seen the movie *Saving Private Ryan* or the Ken Burns PBS documentary *The War*, you are also familiar with the term FUBAR. From the medical field, you probably recognize STAT, upper GI, and preemie.

In the financial world, investment brokers might refer to the "dead cat bounce" when talking about a stock that's been sold off a lot, makes a short, sharp rebound, but then continues its decline. Brokers also use the term *bull market* to refer to a good market, *bear market* to refer to a market that is down, and *short sale* to refer to selling a stock you don't own. They might use the term *naked call* when they are talking about selling a call on a stock you don't own. If the stock is called away, you have to then buy it and sell it, leaving you exposed or naked.

Familiar slang also includes words like *awesome*, *dude*, *cool*, *hot*, *like*, and the phrases, "What's up?" and "What's good?" Slang can also reflect words found on popular television shows. The word *cliffhanger* was made a household word after the now infamous "Who shot J.R.?" season finale of the long-running television show *Dallas*. Rachael Ray, from the

Food Network, has introduced "Rachaelisms" such as *yummo*, *sammie* for sandwich, and *stoup*, which she says is a cross between a soup and a stew.

CNET.com lists jargon that was popular in the 1990s for dot-commers. These terms include the following:
1. **Mind share**: A company's ability to retain a piece of the public's consciousness
2. **Eyeballs**: The amount of traffic on a Web site
3. **Off-line**: Describes a private setting outside a meeting
4. **Sync-up**: The sharing of information between two or more people

Some business buzzwords or jargon include the following:
1. **Drive**: A multipurpose word. You can drive out cost, drive the project, or drive the organization.
2. **Incent**: This is a nonword used as a verb in business. Management may try to incent their team to sell more. Other commonly "verbed" words include: She likes to office from home, and text me the address.
3. **Narcisssurfing**: Googling yourself to see how often you show up on the Internet
4. **Al desko**: I often dine al desko to save time. (I eat at my desk.)[4,5]

Texting slang includes the following:[6]

LOL: laughing out loud
OMG: Oh, my God
IDK: I don't know
UOK?: You Okay?
BBIAS: Be back in a second

POWERFUL AND POWERLESS LANGUAGE USE

It's not only important to use language that is clear and free of slang and jargon, but also to examine our speech in terms of powerful and powerless language. Of course, the language you use should reflect the context or situation you are in, so being a competent communicator relies on how flexible you are in adapting your language to fit different situations. Powerful language is thought to be more direct and task-related while powerless language is thought to be indirect or hesitant.

Powerless speech includes the use of tag questions, hedges, qualifiers, verbal fillers, and polite forms. **Tag questions** are statements that end with

Tag question: A statement that ends with a question which serves to seek agreement or confirmation from others.

a question. The question seems to seek confirmation or verification from others, therefore lessening the strength of the primary statement. **Hedges and qualifiers** are words and phrases which make statements sound more tentative. These tentative statements serve to weaken the primary statement by making a person sound unsure. The end effect is that the statement is self-defeating; in other words, the speaker discredits the thought they are about to share. Intensifiers are another form of powerless language demonstrating an effort to make the subject of a sentence seem more important. We often use words such as "very" or "so" to emphasize the importance of something. These types of words are not very creative and add little color to our speech. **Vocal fillers** are words or utterances used to fill the gaps in our language when we should allow a pause in order to articulate a specific word. Examples of vocal fillers include the words "like," "uhm," and "okay." Finally, while being polite and courteous is important in the business world, being excessively so serves to weaken your language. Overly **polite language** includes unneeded apologies or excessive expressions of thanks.

Tag questions:	"We need to double our quota for next quarter… *don't you think*?"
Hedges/Qualifiers:	"*This might not be a good time to ask this question*, but…"
	"*You might have already thought about this*, but…."
Intensifiers:	"We are *very* glad to have you as a new customer."
	"This account is so complex and so time-consuming.
Vocal Fillers:	using like, uhm, okay
	"Uhm, the layout of this ad is like, so busy."
	"I, uhm, wonder if I could, like, take a vacation day next week?"
Polite Language:	"I'm sorry the copy machine broke on you."
	"Thanks for allowing me to take a vacation day next week. I'm sorry I gave such short notice."

These powerless forms of speech are conversational and mostly intended to provide support and express understanding to other parties;

however, excessive use of them or using them in the wrong context can lessen your credibility. According to Deborah Tannen,[7] a leading researcher in the area of gender and discourse, women are more likely to use these powerless forms of speech in business settings in an effort to establish and maintain relationships, while men are more likely to engage in report-talk or task-oriented, direct communication. Many professionals have figured out the key to success is to be flexible, and adjust their communication according to the organizational culture and the situation. A mix of both "powerful" and "powerless" language or "task" and "relational" communication can go a long way toward establishing your credibility.

ARTICULATION AND PRONUNCIATION

Be clear in your articulation and pronunciation. Do you speak clearly? Do other people frequently ask you to repeat yourself? **Articulation** refers to pronouncing the individual speech sounds. For example, the word *asks* has the consonant blend *sks*. When some people say this word, it sounds like *aks*. This is an articulation error. Another example is the word *going*. The *ing* on the end needs to be clearly pronounced. Instead, many people will

Articulation: Pronouncing the individual speech sounds.

Many professionals have concluded that the key to success is to be flexible in your communication style.

© Andresr/Shutterstock.com

say *goin*. The words *want to* can often sound like *wanna* instead. Some people run these words together. Your verbal communication needs to be clear and clean. Make sure you say each sound correctly.

Pronunciation refers to the way you put the sounds together to form a word. It also includes knowing which syllable of the word is emphasized. Here are some examples of words that are commonly mispronounced:

Athlete is not *ath uh lete*. You don't want to add a syllable.
Library does have an *r*. It is not *li bar y*.
Probably is *pro ba bly*. Some people say *prob ly*.
Subtle is *sut-ul*. The *b* is silent.
Candidate is *can-di-date*. The error here is usually *can uh date*.
Barbed wire is not *bob wire*.
Et cetera leaves out the *x* sound.
Regardless is a word. *Irregardless* is not.

We can use tongue twisters to help with our articulation and our pronunciation. Tongue twisters are words, phrases, or sentences that are put together in a way that makes your mouth work hard to say all the sounds correctly. You are probably familiar with the tongue-twister "Peter Piper picked a peck of pickled peppers." For more practice, try saying these sentences out loud, clearly:

She sends sappy soliloquies southward.
Mary mopes much in March.
Seth searches silently, sending signals surreptitiously.
Westward wanders William, while Waylon weighs wood.

Practice your articulation and pronunciation with these tough tongue twisters:
1. If I assist a sister-assistant, will the sister's sister-assistant assist me?
2. Alice asks for axes (say this one three times).
3. A big bug bit a bold bald bear and the bold bald bear bled blood badly.
4. Blake the baker bakes black bread.
5. The brave bloke blocked the broken back bank door.

SECTION 2: General Communication Competencies

6.	Clean clams crammed in clean cans.
7.	A canner exceedingly canny, one morning remarked to his granny, "A canner can can anything that he can, but a canner can't can a can, can he?"
8.	A chapped chap chopped chips.
9.	Cuthbert's cufflinks (say this one three times).
10.	The fish-and-chip shop's chips are soft chips.
11.	Does this shop stock cheap checkers?
12.	Crisp crust crackles (say this one three times).
13.	Few free fruit flies fly from flames.
14.	She sells Swiss sweets.
15.	Strange strategic statistics.[8]

USING WORDS CORRECTLY

In addition to articulating and pronouncing words correctly, it is also important to use them accurately. Sometimes people get words mixed up and use the wrong word when they speak. *The English Composition and Grammar* textbook lists words that are often confused:[9,10]

Advice is a noun that means to give counsel. (He gave me some excellent advice.)
Advise is a verb that means to give advice. (She advised me to finish high school.)

Affect is a verb that means to influence. (What he said did not affect my final decision.)
Effect is a verb that means to accomplish or a noun that means a consequence will result. (The mayor has effected many changes during her administration. The effect of these changes has been most beneficial.)

All ready is a pronoun plus an adjective that means everyone is ready. (When he arrived, we were all ready to go.)
Already is an adverb that means previously. (Sharon has already gone.)

Capital is a noun that means a city or money used by a business. It can also be an adjective meaning punishable by death or of major importance or excellent. (Raleigh is the capital of North Carolina.

Mrs. Dawson will need more capital to modernize her equipment. Killing a police officer is a capital crime.)

Capitol is a noun meaning building or statehouse. (In Raleigh, the capitol is located on Fayetteville Street.)

Choose means to select and is used for present and future tense. (You may choose your own partner.)

Chose is used with past tense and rhymes with hose. (They chose pizza for lunch.)

Formally means properly, according to strict rules. (Should he be formally introduced?)

Formerly means previously, in the past. (The new counsel was formerly a senator.)

Its is the possessive of it. (The bird stopped its singing.)

It's means it is. (It's an easy problem.)

Passed is a verb, and it is the past tense of pass. (He passed us on the highway.)

Past is a noun, and it means the history of a person. It can also be an adjective meaning former, or a preposition meaning farther on than. (I didn't inquire about his past. Her past experience got her the job. I went past the house.)

Than is a conjunction used for comparisons. (Jimmy enjoys swimming more than golfing.)

Then is an adverb or conjunction indicating at that time or next. (Did you know Barbara then? I ate my lunch, and then I went for a walk.)

NONVERBAL COMMUNICATION

Our verbal communication, specifically our language use, is incredibly important for establishing credibility, but our nonverbal communication is equally important. Many people think of nonverbal communication as body language. And it is. But that's only part of what makes up this aspect of communication. **Nonverbal communication** refers to the unspoken messages that we send.

Read the following paragraphs and see if you can determine the role and nature of nonverbal communication:

Nonverbal communication: The unspoken messages that we send.

1. You have scheduled a lunch meeting with your boss to run through some ideas for a new product line. In the restaurant, there are several large-screen television sets scattered about, all tuned to news channels. One is in back of you, but clearly visible to your boss. As you carry on the conversation, you find that your boss continually looks at the screen instead of you. You wonder if she's even listening to you. Eventually, you stop talking.

2. Your colleague catches you in the hall as you leave for a meeting upstairs. He begins a conversation about a ball game on television the evening before. You want to be cordial to your colleague, but you also want to be on time for the meeting because you have a short presentation to deliver. You glance at your watch several times and turn away slightly from your colleague. Your colleague wraps up the conversation and you make it to the meeting on time.

3. You have been asked to deliver a brief presentation at the weekly staff meeting. Your team is leading the sales department, and the boss has asked you to share your successful techniques. You are nervous about speaking, but carefully write out a brief outline to help you stay on track. As you begin to speak, you notice that many people are nodding their heads and giving you great eye contact. You begin to feel good about what you are saying. Then you notice one or two people who have their arms folded and their eyes closed. They don't seem to be paying attention, and you begin to panic. You must be boring them! You lose your confidence and begin to stumble over your words as you rush to finish. After

Some nonverbal symbols speak louder than words.

your presentation, one of the people who had her eyes closed congratulates you on your great sales figures, paraphrasing your presentation in a brief statement.

These are three examples of nonverbal communication in action. Lack of eye contact, use of subtle regulators to control the flow of conversation, and even misperceptions play a part in our nonverbal communication.

Some Things to Know About Nonverbal Communication

CONTRADICT, COMPLEMENT, OR REGULATE

What is the role of context in determining the appropriateness and effectiveness of appearance?

Nonverbal communication can contradict or reinforce or regulate verbal messages. If you are having a good day, you usually will have a smile on your face, your posture will be upright, and you will walk and move in a confident manner. If you have received bad news or if you are having a frustrating day at work, you may move more slowly, your shoulders may stay hunched, and you may have a frown on your face instead of a smile. These nonverbals match or complement the mood of the communicator, but sometimes nonverbals contradict our verbal messages. If someone approaches you and

© Dragon Images/Shutterstock.com.

asks if you're having a bad day (due to the frown on your face and your hunched shoulders) and you say, "No, I'm good," this serves to contradict the nonverbal message. In business and professional settings, we may use contradictory messages in an attempt to hide how we truly feel, but sometimes our nonverbals communicate more than we intend.

Involuntary or Unintentional

Nonverbal communication can be involuntary or unintentional. Nonverbal communication includes those behaviors that are mutually recognized and socially shared codes and patterns with a focus on message meaning (Show me what you mean). For example, an unintended frown when reading a memo may function as a message because most people regard it as a sign of displeasure. You may not be aware that you are frowning, but it will be interpreted negatively by someone else.

We also use nonverbal communication to regulate other people's communication with us. If a coworker stops in your office or cubicle to gab and you have a deadline, after a courtesy chat you might glance at your watch, read something on your computer screen, or shift in your seat. These nonverbal behaviors are your way of regulating the conversation or of trying to signal that you need to get back to work.

Powerful

Nonverbal communication is powerful. People pay a lot of attention to nonverbal behaviors and are more likely to trust nonverbals over verbal messages. Sometimes we dislike a neighbor or a coworker, and we're not sure why because their verbal communication has always been quite pleasant. Something about them, though, just bothers us. Usually, you are picking up on some nonverbal behavior that they exhibit. You may not be aware of what it is, but you know that something is not right. Because competency judgments are strongly impacted by nonverbals, business communicators must be aware of their appearance, body language, and eye contact. You might not hire someone because of a nonverbal behavior, and you might not get a particular job because of your own nonverbal behavior.

Tied to Culture

Nonverbal communication is tied to culture. Did you know that the popular American "thumbs-up" sign is considered to be an obscene gesture in Australia? It's important to be familiar with other cultures' views on nonverbal communication. If you plan to travel or do business in other countries, remember that culture plays a huge role in nonverbal communication. Before you can even say a word, your posture, gestures, and eye contact convey a message to your audience. Crossing your legs in the United States is completely natural: sitting in the same position in Kuwait may be impolite.[11]

Here are some tips on nonverbal communication in other countries:

- **Germany:** It is considered rude to leave your hands in your pockets while doing business. People in Germany may not smile to indicate that they are pleased about something.

- **Hong Kong:** A bow is an appropriate greeting when meeting a business contact. Punctuality is important. You should maintain a two-arm's-length distance from your contact. Touching and patting are considered taboo. Men should not cross their legs when sitting. You should present your business card and gifts with both hands.

- **Indonesia:** You should eat with your right hand, not your left. It is considered good manners to take a second helping of food. Hugging and kissing in public is considered inappropriate. In a private home, remove your shoes and point them toward the door you entered.

- **Japan:** Be prompt. This culture is time sensitive. The American "okay" sign means "money" in Japan. Be aware that, similar to other Asian cultures, extended direct eye contact is considered disrespectful.

- **Singapore:** Gesture with your entire hand. Pointing with one or two fingers is considered rude.

- **Korea:** Cover your mouth when laughing in public. Loud laughter is considered rude. Nose blowing should be done in private. Lower your eyes to show respect for elders.

- **United Kingdom:** The victory sign with the palm facing inward is considered to be an obscene gesture. Make sure your palms face outward. Point with your head rather than with your fingers.[12]

How would you interpret this gesture?

Nonverbal communication can be ambiguous. Much of our understanding of nonverbal communication is not learned in school. We learn from past experience, and we learn as we face new situations. Body language conveys important but unreliable clues about the intent of the communicator.[13] The more information you can get about the clues you are trying to decode, the more likely you will be to decode them correctly.[13] If you are presenting a plan to your team to increase sales in your division, and some team members look away, yawn, and glance at their watches, you might interpret these nonverbal cues to mean that your audience is bored. You might hurry to finish your presentation and leave out important facts. The reality might be that they are listening to you, but several of them had late nights, two are hungry and check the time to see how close lunch is, and one is shy and has a hard time meeting your eyes. Although many nonverbals are universal, they can be difficult to interpret.

Examples of our inability to interpret ambiguous nonverbals is seen in the research on deceptive communication. University of San Francisco psychology professor Maureen O'Sullivan studies how well people detect deception by relying on nonverbal cues from others. Given a video of subjects to review in controlled studies, most laypeople detect lying about 60 percent of the time—barely above a flip of the coin. "Most people are pretty terrible at discerning whether other people are lying," O'Sullivan says. "But if you ask them, 'Is the person you're watching uncomfortable?' most will be able to determine that the liar is less comfortable than the nonliar, but they won't go to the next step of calling them a liar."[14]

Types of Nonverbal Communication

We use nonverbal communication to help represent who we are through our appearance, our posture, our facial expressions, gestures, use of time and space, use of our voices, use of touch, and even the arrangement of furniture in our home and our office.

Keep in mind nonverbal messages are shaped by three primary factors: the culture, the relationship, and the situation.[15]

VOCALICS: THE VOICE

The term **paralanguage** refers to vocal characteristics, which include the following:
- **Volume**: loudness or softness
- **Rate**: the speed at which you speak

Vocalics: The voice.

Paralanguage: Vocal characteristics, including volume, rate, pitch, inflection, vocal fillers, resonance, and pauses.

- **Pitch**: high or low
- **Inflection**: change in pitch or loudness (usually done for emphasis)
- **Vocal fillers**: um, ah, er, like, you know
- **Resonance**: richness or thinness of the voice
- **Pauses**: silences; used for emphasis.

Good communicators are aware of vocal characteristics and use them appropriately when speaking to add variety to their words and delivery. Breathing from the abdomen instead of shallow breathing (where your shoulders go up and down) will help steady your pitch. When you are nervous, your pitch will be higher, making you sound less confident. Practice breathing from your diaphragm. You'll know when you are doing this correctly because your abdomen will move in and out instead of your shoulders moving up and down. Another problem with shallow breathing is that you will run out of air before the end of a sentence, making your communication choppy and breathless sounding. Stand up whenever you are asked to speak. It will allow you to straighten up, and that will make breathing from your diaphragm much easier. You will have more volume, and you will sound more confident. You will also be more comfortable physically because you won't feel as breathless.

Stand up whenever you are asked to speak to better project your voice.

© Blend Images/Shutterstock.com

Don't be afraid to pause for emphasis. The pause is one of the most underutilized vocal techniques that you have at your disposal. A pause of a few seconds at a strategic place in your communication will allow your listeners to catch their breath and wonder, "What's next?" Many speakers avoid the pause because they are afraid of the silence, or they think that the audience will wonder if they've lost their place. Use the pause. It will demonstrate confidence to your listener.

Before you speak, look over your notes. Say the words out loud to practice. Which words need to be emphasized? Which words need to be spoken a little slower? Where do you need to get louder or softer?

For example, look at this sentence: *This is what I believe.* Say it out loud, placing the emphasis on the word *this*. It changes the meaning of the sentence. Now try it with the emphasis on the word *I*. The meaning changes again.

Be especially aware of eliminating vocal fillers from your communication. Nothing is worse than hearing someone fill their sentences with the words *like* or *you know*, or *um*. These are distracting, and they interrupt the communication process. If you aren't sure if you overuse these fillers, tape yourself having a normal conversation for about 5 minutes. Play it back and see if these words crop up. These fillers become a distraction and even an annoyance to your listener, so you want to work hard to eliminate them from your communication.

Appearance

Appearance is another important nonverbal because it's often the first thing your audience will notice. This includes your clothes, hairstyle, makeup, cologne, perfume, fragrance from other products, use of jewelry, tattoos, piercings, and posture. People will judge you by your appearance. In a perfect world, you should be able to dress as you please, have multiple piercings, dye your hair any color you wish, and have many visible tattoos. But people will make judgments about you as soon as they see you, so be aware of what is appropriate for different contexts or situations.

Remember that you *can* smell too good. The only thing worse than being near someone who smells bad because of lack of personal hygiene is being near someone who smells too good from using too many fragrances. Be careful when you splash or spritz on perfume, cologne, or aftershave. Also be aware of hair styling products, shower gels, and moisturizers with a strong smell.

How do you know what is appropriate dress for work? The easiest thing to do is to ask someone during the interview or observe those who interview you. As you walk through the building, look at other people who will be working alongside you. Some organizations have a written dress code. For women, that may include wearing pantyhose, wearing closed-toe shoes instead of sandals, and a restriction on ear piercings and other jewelry. For men, it can require wearing a jacket and tie every day. It may dictate the color of your belt or your shoes or the length of your hair. Many organizations don't have a dress code, but they expect you to dress professionally. If you meet clients every day, you will be expected to dress more conservatively than if you don't. Get familiar with terms like "business casual" and "professional business attire." If you don't know, ask someone who works in a position similar to yours. If you do business across the country, you'll need to do some research. "Business casual" in Boston might be different than "business casual" in the Midwest or even on the West Coast.

The book *Business Etiquette*[12] states that you will be judged by your personal appearance, and this is never more apparent than on "dress-down" days when what you wear can say more about you than any business suit ever could. When dressing in "business casual" clothes, recognize that the real definition of business casual is to dress just one notch down from what you would normally wear on "business professional" attire days. Avoid jeans; worn, wrinkled polo shirts; sneakers; scuffed shoes; halter tops; and revealing blouses. For men, try wearing any pair of pants and a button shirt with long or short sleeves that has more color or texture in the fabric. For women, wear skirts or tailored pants with blouses, blazers, and accessories that mean business yet convey a more casual look than your standard business attire. Avoid wearing clothes that reveal too much or leave little to the imagination. Remember, there are boundaries between your career and your social life. You should dress one way for play and another way when you mean business. Always ask yourself where you're going and how other people will be dressed when you get there. When in doubt, always err on the side of dressing slightly more conservatively than the situation demands. Remember, you can always remove a jacket, but you can't put one on if you didn't think to take it with you![12]

You also need to learn to be flexible. Bill Jones is an investment broker who wears a suit or jacket and tie to work at a bank every day. He has several clients who farm for a living, and during the planting season, those farmers can't always take time to come to the bank to do their business. So, Bill Jones changes into khakis, a collared shirt, and work boots and meets his clients in their fields. Business is done over the back of the client's truck in casual attire to be more equal to the client. It also just makes sense.

Body language, or **kinesics**, is the study of human body motions and movements. This includes facial expressions, gestures, eye contact, and posture. How comfortable are you with eye contact? Most people are uncomfortable with prolonged eye contact—lasting more than a few seconds. But, we are also uncomfortable if someone never looks us in the eye. When you are communicating, eye contact will help you establish a relationship with your listener. Looking at the ceiling, at your listener's ear or nose, or past his or her head will be quite apparent. It is perfectly acceptable to look at your listener for several seconds and then glance away. You can also regulate other people's conversation with your eye contact. If you are having a conversation with two people, and a third person approaches your group, you all may not give them immediate eye contact, preferring to finish your thoughts before visually "inviting" them into the group.

Smiles are nice. A smile usually lets your listener know that you are confident and comfortable. It also can indicate friendliness or approachability. People do smile for all sorts of reasons (Morgan). Whatever their origin or motivation, smiles have a powerful effect on us humans. As Daniel McNeill points out, "Though courtroom judges are equally likely to find smilers and nonsmilers guilty, they give smilers

Kinesics: The study of the human body's motions and movements.

Do your gestures become distracting when you're nervous?

© tmc photos/Shutterstock.com

lighter penalties, a phenomenon called the 'smile-leniency effect.'"[13] Keep in mind that a smile can also have multiple meanings, so be careful about assigning meaning to this nonverbal message.

Posture is also important. Standing up straight will allow you to breathe from your diaphragm, which will help your voice sound stronger. It also indicates confidence.

Gestures are also part of nonverbal communication. We all talk with our hands to some extent. If you get nervous, you may use more gestures and not realize it. These can become distracting. If you do have to speak in front of other people or deliver a speech, you might try recording yourself to check your gestures. You can hold note cards or papers in your hand, not just as your notes, but also to keep yourself from fidgeting. Don't hold a pen, ruler, or anything else that you can tap or click or make noise with. When you get nervous, you're not always aware of your own fidgeting. Gestures should be used for emphasis. This is another reason to practice a presentation before you deliver it in front of other people.

People can also use gestures to supplement or to take the place of verbal communication. Several examples include the following:

1. **Adaptors:** Touching your hair, your face, or your body or adjusting your glasses or your clothes. These are comforting gestures that help us calm down or reassure ourselves. They can become distracting, however.

2. **Emblem:** Takes the place of a word or phrase. The classic example is when a hitchhiker sticks his thumb out, indicating that a ride is needed. Another example is the extension of the middle finger, the V for victory sign, the peace sign, or the thumbs-up sign.

3. **Regulators:** These help control the flow of conversation. Students might start packing up their books before class is actually over. They want to make sure the professor is aware that class time is ending. If we are trapped by a chatty coworker, we might glance at our cell phone for the time, or turn slightly away as if we need to leave. If a colleague we don't know that well gets a little too close, we might cross our arms or move back.

4. **Illustrators:** Hand gestures that help explain or illustrate what we are talking about. When giving directions, we might point down the street. When describing someone, we might indicate with our hands how tall they are.

PROXEMICS

Proxemics is the use of personal space. We all have our own personal space.

Anthropologist Edward Hall categorizes four distance zones: *intimate space*, which ranges from physical contact to about 18 inches (arm's length); *casual-personal*, which ranges from 18 inches to about 4 feet; *social distance*, which is from 4 feet up to 12 feet; and *public*, which is 12 feet and beyond.[16] We usually allow family, very good friends, a partner, spouse, or significant other into our personal space. We get uncomfortable when other people get too close. If you're standing in the checkout line at the grocery store, you might feel crowded when the person next in line gets too close behind you, especially if you are using a credit or debit card. It's an unwritten rule at the ATM machine that the next person in line stands a certain distance away from you. In business situations, you usually move into the intimate space zone for a handshake and then move back to the casual distance that is acceptable. In a meeting, you might sit closer than the 18 inches to 4 feet dictated by social distance, but you are usually side by side or sitting in front or behind someone, and not face-to-face. In a college classroom, you might be crowded together, but you are usually in rows, so that you are facing the back of someone. In this situation, your personal space does not seem violated. This shows that proxemics differ based on different contextual rules.

Proxemics: Use of personal space.

How do you feel about your personal space? Who do you let in your personal space?

CHRONEMICS

Chronemics refers to the use of time: Are you always late wherever you go? Do you always arrive at your destination early? Do you love to be on time? Your use of time is part of your nonverbal communication. If you are late to class, the professor may not let you in, or you may be docked points for tardiness. If you are late for a job interview, you can knock that job off your list of possible job opportunities. If you are consistently late to work, you will probably be reprimanded, and if it continues, you might be fired. Lateness to important events is usually a sign that you had other, more important things to do. That might not be true, but it is the perception that other people will have. People who hold more power in organizations have greater control over their use of time; however, how they use their time is often scrutinized by other employees, especially subordinates.

Chronemics: Use of time.

Sexual Harassment

As discussed in Chapter 2, sexual harassment is real, and you might encounter it in the workplace. It may be expressed through verbal or nonverbal communication. It might be blatant—your supervisor tells you

Two Web sites that will tell you more about sexual harassment are the following: www.de2.psu.edu/harassment/legal/EEOC.html and www.eeoc.gov/facts/fs-sex.html

that you will get a job promotion or an increase in salary if you grant him or her certain sexual favors (*quid pro quo*). It might also be less obvious because a supervisor or coworker can create an atmosphere that makes you feel uncomfortable (hostile work environment). This could include allowing questionable pictures to be displayed, allowing offensive jokes and remarks to be part of the workday, and tolerating personal space violations. Clearly, sexual harassment involves inappropriate verbal and nonverbal elements.

Sexual harassment is a form of sex discrimination that violates Title VII of the Civil Rights Act of 1964. Title VII covers all private employers, state and local governments, and education institutions that employ 15 or more individuals. These laws also cover private and public employment agencies, labor organizations, and joint labor management committees controlling apprenticeship in training. Unwelcome sexual advances, requests for sexual favors, and other verbal or physical conduct of a sexual nature constitutes sexual harassment when submission to or a rejection of this conduct explicitly or implicitly affects an individual's employment, unreasonably interferes with an individual's work performance, or creates an intimidating, hostile, or offensive work environment.

- The victim or the harasser may be a woman or a man.
- The victim does not have to be of the opposite sex.
- The victim does not have to be the person harassed but could be anyone affected by the offensive conduct.
- The harasser can be the victim of supervisor, an agent of the employer, a supervisor in another area, a coworker, or a nonemployee.
- The harasser's conduct must be unwelcome.[17]

Sexual harassment can be obvious or obscure depending on the work environment.

© Photographee.eu/Shutterstock.com

You do want to do a reality check to make sure that you didn't misinterpret the intended communication. Words and behavior can be misinterpreted. If you feel that you are the victim of sexual abuse, document the incident or incidents. You can then approach the harasser personally, take your complaint to your supervisor or the personnel office, or even pursue legal action.

CONCLUSION

Elizabeth Martin, the college senior from the beginning of this chapter, enrolled in her Business and Professional Communication class with fear and anxiety. She didn't understand the importance of verbal and nonverbal communication, and she dreaded the group and individual speaking assignments. But, she knew her senior year at college meant lots of interviews for career opportunities, and she wanted to do well. She also wanted to feel confident when asked to present information to her professors, colleagues, and peers. So, she stayed in the class. By the end of the semester, she successfully completed one group presentation, one professional interview at the Career Center, and two individual presentations. She didn't perform perfectly, but she felt confident in her newfound knowledge and eager to sharpen her skills. Elizabeth strengthened her verbal communication by working to create clear, formal, and powerful messages free of slang and jargon. She also paid closer attention to her use of nonverbals and was able to overcome her nervousness, project her voice, and express enthusiasm and confidence.

After reading this chapter, you should now understand the difference between verbal and nonverbal communication. You should also understand how verbal and nonverbal communication function in the communication process. You've learned some tips for successful verbal communication, the difference between powerful and powerless styles of language, and the importance of clear articulation and pronunciation. This chapter explained the characteristics of nonverbal communication and stressed the importance of the cultural aspects of nonverbal communication. It also looked at the types of nonverbal communication and the concept of sexual harassment.

ACTIVITIES

1. Test your knowledge of commonly misused words. Use the following words in a sentence to make sure you understand the correct usage of these words.

   a. accept: a verb meaning to receive
   b. except: a verb meaning to exclude
   c. allusion: an indirect reference
   d. illusion: a misconception or false impression
   e. your: a possessive pronoun
   f. you're: a contraction of you are
   g. there: an adverb specifying place
   h. their: a possessive pronoun
   i. they're: a contraction for they are

2. List the jargon that you are familiar with—words that are associated with your major, field of study, or hobby. How might these words confuse someone from outside your chosen field of study?

3. Get a book of tongue twisters or access a Web site devoted to tongue twisters and practice saying these words out loud to perfect your articulation and your pronunciation. For more practice, challenge yourself to say each tongue twister with different inflection. For example, make one sentence into a question and say the next sentence as though you are angry. For a final challenge, record yourself and listen to how clearly you speak and which areas need improvement.

4. Visit www.abcnews.go.com/print?id=4889014 and read the article titled "For Some Clinton Supporters, Sexism Is the Only Explanation" for insight into gender and communication.

5. Visit the Web site newsvote.bbc.co.uk/mpapps/pagetools/print/news.bbc.co.uk/1/hi/world/middle_east/… and read the two articles about the U.S. sniper who shot at the Koran in Iraq and President Bush's response to understand the importance of nonverbal communication.

6. As you eat a meal in the dining hall or walk across campus, observe the nonverbal communication of fellow students or even faculty members. What do you observe? Think in terms of appearance, posture, eye contact, facial expressions, personal space, treatment of time, and gestures. Does any behavior surprise you? What did the nonverbal communication tell you?

REFERENCES

[1] Klepper, M. M. (with Gunther, R.). (1994). *I'd rather die than give a speech*. Burr Ridge, IL: Irwin.

[2] Keysan, B., & Henly, A. S. (2002). Speakers' overestimation of their effectiveness. *Psychological Science, 13*(3), 207–213.

[3] Menechella, D. (2001). *How to master the art of verbal communication*. Edison, NJ: Personal Peak Performance Unlimited.

[4] Aemmer, M. (2008). *Top ten business buzzwords*. Retrieved from http://encarta. msn.com/encnet/departments/elearning?article=business_buzzwords

[5] German, K. (2008). *Power of ten: Top ten buzzwords*. Retrieved from http:// www.cnet.com/1990-11135_1-6275610-1.html

[6] NoSlang.com. (2005–2008). *25 Internet slang terms all parents should know*. Retrieved from noslang.com/top20.php

[7] Tannen, D. (1994). *Talking from 9 to 5: Women and men in the workplace: Language, sex, and power*. New York: William Morrow.

[8] Rosenbloom, J. (1986). *World's toughest tongue twisters*. New York: Sterling.

[9] Warriner, J. E. (1988). *English composition and grammar*. Orlando, FL: Harcourt Brace Jovanovich.

[10] Hacker, D. (2009). Commonly misused words and phrases. In *A writer's reference* (6th ed.). New York: Bedford/St. Martin's.

[11] Naguib, R. (2005, October). International audiences. *Toastmaster*.

[12] Sabath, A. M. (1998). *Business etiquette: 101 ways to conduct business with charm and savvy*. Franklin Lakes, NJ: Career Press.

[13] Morgan, N. (2002). The truth behind the smile and other myths. *Harvard Management Communication Letter, 5*(8), 3–4.

[14] Zielinski, D. (2007, September). Body language myths. *Toastmaster*, p. 27.

[15] Ciccia, A. H., Step, M., & Turkstra, L. (2003). Show me what you mean: Nonverbal communication theory and clinical application. *The ASHA Leader, 8*(22), 4–34.

[16] Adler, R. B., & Elmhorst, J. M. (2008). *Communicating at work*. Boston: McGraw-Hill.

[17] U.S. Equal Opportunity Commission. (2002). Facts about sexual harassment. Retrieved from http://www.eeoc.gov/facts/fs-sex.html

chapter four

Listening: The Key to Credible Communication

After reading this chapter you will be able to:

- Describe the process of hearing, listening, and the creation of meaning
- Understand what you can do to improve your listening skills
- Describe the distinction between active and passive listening

CHAPTER OUTLINE

key words

Hearing
Listening
Deafness
Partially deaf
Awareness

Psychological noise
Meaning
Dialogue
Passive listening
Active listening

INTRODUCTION

Cecilia Ramirez was a third-year attorney at a highly respected corporate law firm in downtown Atlanta, Georgia. She frequently worked with different types of clients, but mostly focused on torts (civil issues) as a specialty area. She liked working with "torts" because of their abstract theory-based orientation. However, she worked some 60 hours per week on average and found that she consistently lacked the necessary mental focus for her work. Even though she got a good night's sleep regularly and took care of herself by exercising and eating a well-balanced diet, her focus always seemed to be a bit "off." This concerned her a great deal because in her line of work, being alert and vigilant was not simply a professional virtue—it was absolutely mission critical. If she missed the interpretation of a clause in a contract according to the federal or state legal code, both she and her client could be in serious trouble. The stakes were high.

What Ramirez did not fully realize was that she had a significant listening problem that was rooted in her psychological history; in fact, this problem extended back to her early years of elementary and middle school. Sure, she was a successful undergraduate student in communication studies, held a prestigious law degree, and was a standing member of the Georgia Bar Association. Her life, to date, had been very successful, fulfilling, and rewarding. But, her overarching problem was that she had difficulty paying consistent attention to client contract details and had not yet learned some of the fundamental skills that, once acquired and properly applied, help many professionals succeed in tedious workplaces. She often allowed her mind to wander and lacked cognitive focus, and she knew it. Ramirez is not alone in this regard, either. Many businesspeople and professionals throughout the world have this very same issue. Cecilia's problem is not just tied to her workplace performance. It is a pervasive issue that has affected her entire communication-based life from education, to work, to personal relationships. She simply finds it hard to focus and actively "listen."

The International Listening Association (ILA) tells us *why* listening is such a decisive personal and professional skill (see http://www.listen.org/). Consider these all-too-telling statistics. Multiple studies have confirmed that we listen at only about a 25 percent overall comprehension rate. Think about that for a second, if you will. This means that we only understand about 25 percent of the total verbal and nonverbal meaning sent our way! What could happen to our overall communication aptitudes if we increased that margin? What could happen to our grade point averages, our careers, and even our personal and professional human relationships? Listening, we argue, is central to all our communication practices—across the board. Accordingly, this chapter reviews (a) how hearing, listening, and creating meaning are processes in and of themselves, (b) what you can do to develop your listening skills generally, and (c) how to apply these enhanced skills in the business and professional communication context through *conscious active listening*. Why will we do this? Because effective listening builds the very foundation from which all credible communication flows.

Do you ever find your mind wandering off the topic when you should be focused?

© Blend Images/Shutterstock.com

figure 4.1

The International Listening Association's Web site, which can be found at www.listen.org

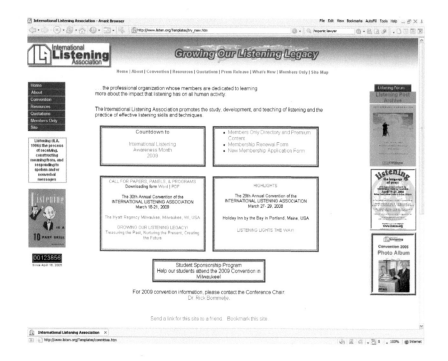

HEARING, LISTENING, AND CREATING MEANING

One of the common mistakes that some tend to make when trying to understand *listening* is to assume that hearing and listening are, in fact, the same thing. Nothing could be further from the truth, however. You see, hearing is entirely a physiological act. **Hearing** is *the ear's physical response to the auditory reception of sound waves*. It is what happens with our ears when we encounter sound. Listening, on the other hand, is entirely a psychological act. And moreover, it is a uniquely distinct psychological act for each and every human being. **Listening** *occurs when we are receiving and appraising the stimuli that surround us*. Listening is where *meaning is made* in the individual.

Hearing: The ear's physical response to the auditory reception of sound waves.

Listening: Occurs when we are receiving and appraising the stimuli that surround us.

You should note that listening does not just involve verbal or auditory stimuli. Listening is also open to the visual realm, dealing with the sights and symbols we take in with our eyes. Listening is olfactic and has to do with the tastes and smells we encounter. Finally, listening is also haptic, and is related to *touch* and *feeling*. So, in a vast, open sense, listening is commingled with the five natural human senses: (a) sight, (b) hearing, (c) taste, (d) touch, and (e) smell (**Figure 4.2**). Through these five human senses, we attempt to make order and sense of the universe. Sometimes we are accurate in doing so, and sometimes we are not.

figure4.2

How meaning is made through listening

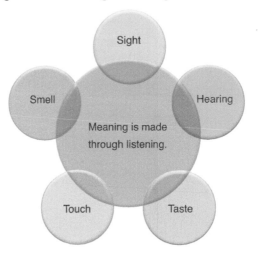

Hearing as a Process: The Basic Auditory System

At a fundamental level, we must be able to hear in order to listen fully and interpret verbal messages. Clearly, hearing is the body's capacity to receive sound through physical vibrations. The main conduit by which this is done is through the human ear. When one cannot physically perceive these vibrations as sounds, we call this deafness. Those who can only moderately hear sounds are referred to as partially deaf. The human auditory system consists of the (a) outer ear, (b) middle ear, and (c) inner ear (**Figure 4.3**). This entire apparatus is connected to the central auditory system.

Deafness: When one cannot physically perceive vibrations as sounds.

Partially deaf: Refers to one who can only moderately hear sounds.

figure4.3

The outer, middle, and inner human ear

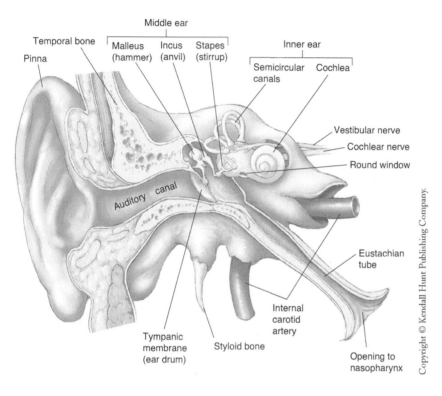

Listening as a Process: The Basic Psychological System

There are many steps in the psychological listening process that we must cover in this chapter. Even though listening is more a function of **awareness**, or a state of consciousness when one is prepared to encounter, interpret, mentally record, and psychologically manage incoming stimuli of all types, we will focus on the traditional "hearing–listening" model to illustrate the point (**Figure 4.4**).

Awareness: A state of consciousness when one is prepared to encounter, interpret, mentally record, and psychologically manage incoming stimuli of all types.

figure4.4

The six steps of the listening process

| Presence of stimuli | Reception of stimuli | Mental focus upon stimuli | Recognition of stimuli | Filling and indexing stimuli | Appreciation of stimuli |

1. **Presence of stimuli.** The first requirement for listening (under the hearing–listening model) is that auditory stimuli need to be present in the communication environment. For a stimulus to be present, it is necessary for some type of audible sound to be made. This can be voice, percussion, white noise, or any other type of vibration made within the overall stimulus environment.

2. **Physiological reception of stimuli.** The second requirement for listening presents in the human ability to properly sense and receive stimuli. Sometimes people cannot do this because they have physiological barriers or impediments (e.g., deafness). Sometimes people can do this with decreased ability because of partial damage to their hearing. Regardless, hearing is important to our listening ability and directly affects one's ability to be mentally aware of stimuli.

3. **Mental focus on stimuli.** The third requirement for proper listening comes in the human ability to remain mentally focused on a given desired stimulus. This is perhaps the most important psychological stage of the listening process because it is the one predominantly controlled by the receiver of the stimulus. To be able to concentrate on certain incoming stimuli and disregard other noise (unwanted stimuli) within the environment is a learned skill.

4. **Recognition and discrimination of stimuli.** Beyond merely taking in stimuli and not making sense of them, the human mind must be able to recognize what the stimuli are, or are not, through evaluation. This stage of appreciating stimuli is layered in the mind over years and decades of human experience with previous stimuli encounters. Significantly, stimuli can be either internal or external in orientation, which implies, of course, that these stimuli can present from outside or inside the human being. We

often refer to internal stimuli as thoughts or **psychological noise** because they either enhance the processing of incoming stimuli or, to the contrary, detract from them.

5. **Filing or indexing of stimuli.** The next step in the listening process is to record mentally what the stimuli are or are not. The mind is like an enormous encyclopedia of personalized information, and we file things away in our neural networks so that we can retrieve information whenever it is necessary. When we file or index said information, we are literally recording that information for future recall. Sometimes we decide to recall that information (like a song or a particular line from a favorite movie), and other times it is recalled in our cognition without our free volition or choice, almost by reflex. Filing and indexing are enormously important parts of the listening process because it is *how* we go about ordering our known information.

6. **Appreciation of stimuli.** The final step in the listening process is to evaluate and appreciate the various stimuli we encounter. This can be done in a number of ways. We can intellectually appreciate stimuli, we can emotionally appreciate stimuli, and we can simply *appreciate* stimuli for the sake of pleasure and enjoyment. But, regardless, at the end of the listening process enters (a) the human element of understanding, (b) appreciation, (c) the construction of meaning, and (d) even critique.

Our eye contact, facial expressions, and body language communicate along with our words.

© v.s.anandhakrishna/Shutterstock.com

As a result, you should now understand that *meaning* is constructed not only by the sender, but also by the receiver (or listener). We call this the co-creation of meaning. You see, there are many ways in which this meaning is conveyed, derived, and interpreted by the symbol-using and, indeed, misusing, human animal. For example, we communicate through verbal symbol systems (language). We also communicate nonverbally through motions, eye contact, facial expressions, body language, and paralinguistics (some of the things we do to our voice). Further, the listening process defines what meaning is derived by the receiver because it hinges upon the receiver's predefined psychological characteristics. For example, Listener A will hear, see, and interpret a given message from Speaker 1 in a completely different interpretive fashion than Listener B or Listener J. Sometimes this is done by human choice, and sometimes this is done through years of deep behavioral conditioning.

Meaning: A Voyage into Human Thought and Neural Networks

Have you ever wondered how, exactly, humans go about the process of *creating meaning* through communication? Have you ever wondered how human thought, itself, develops in the anatomy and physiology of the mind? It is an interesting puzzle and has been the subject of formal study through the ages. You see, humans create meaning through known language and symbol systems. What we see, hear, smell, taste, and feel are all stimuli data that give us pieces and bits of information that we store away for future recall and use with preexisting data to make decisions about our past, present, and future.

To begin the understanding of thought and neural networks, we must consider this textbook's definition of the word meaning. Meaning is a linguistic or symbolic mental value placed on the presence of some type of stimuli in the environment and is vested with the receiver. So in a very real sense, meaning is based within the receiver. To recap what has been covered in former chapters, senders are those persons or entities that create language and symbols and emit meaning. On the other hand, receivers are those persons who take in the stimuli of language and symbols and find or create meaning from them. Therefore, meaning resides within the receiver. It is a very complex process and requires a basic understanding of both anatomy and psychology to appreciate. Let us now peer into biological neural networks deep inside the brain to make sense of how we make meaning.

Without going into the chemistry of neural network transmission too deeply, you should know that neural networks uniquely develop within

Meaning: A linguistic or symbolic mental value that is placed on the presence of some type of stimuli in the environment and is vested with the receiver.

each and every one of us. In other words, imagine brain matter as being similar to a simple human fingerprint. The various stimuli that a brain is exposed to, and the reactions of the human governing that brain, literally shape human neural networks. The neural networks become trained to work in certain ways and therefore think and react similarly each time a message or symbol is presented. Have you ever smelled a perfume or cologne and had it remind you of a certain someone? Maybe you have heard that "special" song being played on the radio. This stimuli–response mechanism is built into each one of us and is etched into our minds physiologically because our neural networks become preset and laced with information about the past over time.

The external stimulus presents, and then in turn physiological–electrical connections called "synapses" are formed between axons (**Figure 4.5**) and dendrites through electrochemical impulses. But, apart from this discussion of the basic elements of brain function, you should also know that certain chemical neurotransmitters that chemically permeate the brain tissue are also critical in that they regulate the entire context of *how* synapse function occurs. These billions and billions of tiny brain cells work together in a magnificent concert to achieve a symphony of listening and thought patterns that are central to human meaning creation. More important, however, these brain cells are formed independently in each and every one of us. We are all unique, a fingerprint of one. No one human being's brain is physiologically the same as anyone else's. Now that you have a better understanding of what physiologically and psychologically happens within the hearing–listening link, let us examine ways in which we can all improve our listening habits and look at the benefits of doing so.

WHAT YOU CAN DO TO IMPROVE YOUR LISTENING SKILLS

With the knowledge we have gained so far, you should be aware of the fact that the hearing, listening, and meaning creation process is a highly complex human communication process. Accordingly, we need to look at some of the listening improvement suggestions prevalent in the communication literature. Grasping these proven listening techniques will help you understand *why* these skills are important and, furthermore, *why* you should apply them in your everyday communication practices. It is one thing to know what to do, after all, and another thing entirely to practice it. The sooner we move from theory to praxis, the better.

figure 4.5

A typical neuron, the building block of a neural network

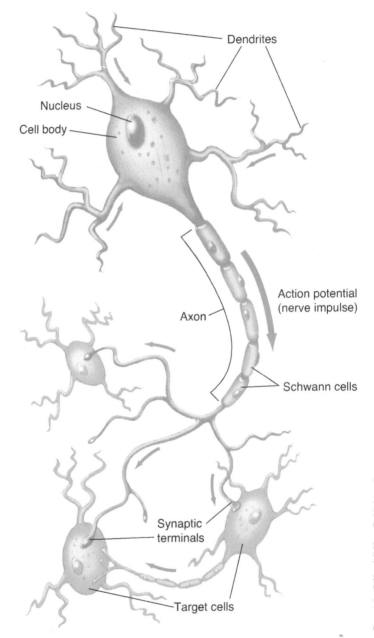

© wavebreakmedia/Shutterstock.com

Yet, before we begin listing these "top ten" suggestions, you should also know that effective listening is not simply a passive process. In other words, you cannot effectively listen by just sitting there, hoping that the information around you seeps into your consciousness by happenstance. Effective listening is very much an *active communication process*. It involves your constant attention and dutiful care. It involves you taking notes. It involves you being mindful of everything going on in the context. To put it another way, if you are not truly committed to becoming a better listener, then none of these suggestions listed here will help you. You have to want it, both personally and professionally. And moreover, you have to *work* at it constantly. Even the best listeners know that they have room for improvement.

Effective listening is an active process and involves taking notes and being mindful of the situation.

- **Begin your quest to become a more effective listener by observing what other "good listeners" are doing in the communication environment.** Although imitation is possibly the most sincere form of flattery, there is ample wisdom in the notion that mimicking the practices of those who have quality skills in place will help. What is their body posture like? What do their facial expressions reflect? Are they taking notes? How, exactly, are they taking notes? A good way to determine if someone is a good listener in your communication

How can you effectively listen when your attention is focused elsewhere?

class is to do an informal review of your classmates while someone (or even possibly yourself) is speaking. Ask yourself how it makes you feel as a speaker if your audience is genuinely listening and paying attention to you and your message. Likewise, ask yourself how you feel when someone is not paying attention to you while you are speaking. After all, we all want to be sincerely heard by our audience, don't we?

- **Understand when you are in listening mode.** One of the major problems that poor listeners have stems from this very issue. You see, some people simply do not understand the unwritten social norms of communication well at all. There is a time and place to talk, just like there is a time and place to listen. Some people want to talk and debate all the time and do not understand that they are monopolizing the conversation. We all know that communication is a two-way street. Similarly, some people like to chit-chat in the classroom with their friends or even spend time on their phones, laptops, and iPads, texting people around the world, instead of focusing on the information-specific task at hand. It is fundamentally imperative that you realize the contextual purpose or boundary defining the event you are attending—and act accordingly. It will only benefit you in the end.

- **Be patient with the speaker.** When someone is talking, they are trying to assemble meaning for us. They are working hard to encode their ideas, thoughts, logic, and arguments in a language-friendly and understandable fashion. This is a difficult process for anyone, but can be especially difficult for some. So, take the necessary time to allow the speaker to formulate their thoughts. Use your face and eyes strategically to let them know that you are, in fact, listening to them. Be there for them.

- **Put yourself in the other person's place.** Consider the fact that roles will likely be reversed at some point, and you will be communicating with the very same people to whom you are listening. A good way to do this is to empathize with the speaker, and recognize that truly effective communication is an enormously complex and challenging activity. By empathizing with the speaker, you make an emotional connection or bond with them that transcends the moment. Plus, doing so actually helps you take in the information being conveyed more efficiently.

- **Communicate silently with the speaker through facial expressions and eye contact.** One of the better ways to "connect" with your speaker is to engage them nonverbally. This means that you give them steady eye contact, sincere facial reactions to their comments, and even appropriate head nodding when in agreement with what they are saying. It does not take a lot of effort. And, more important, recognizing that you have to do this as a good listener will give you another solid reason to listen well. Being an active listener in the communication process not only helps you obtain all the information necessary from the message, but it also helps the speaker feel more secure.

- **Be ever vigilant about your presence of mind.** Another one of the pitfalls that people fall into is letting their mind simply wander. Controlling and allocating your consciousness is absolutely critical to the mission at hand. Do not look out the window of the room at a tree or passersby; make sure your attention is focused on the speaker, the message, and the context for the communication to which you are a participant.

- **At the appropriate time, do not be afraid to ask questions for clarification.** There comes a time when the speech or stream of communication is complete. Once it is, and you are certain that it is, if you need some information clarified pursue the sender with a

How do you make a connection with a speaker to show that you're engaged in the message?

© Rido/Shutterstock.com

series of friendly, nonthreatening questions. By doing so, you are not only showing the speaker that you have listened to their message, but you are also making certain that you are getting a clean read of the information that was presented. Always ask questions when you are left uncertain. That is the listener's job.

- **Always acknowledge the emotions, feelings, and affective displays of the person who is communicating with you.** If the speaker is sharing sensitive personal information with you, revealing a lot about their feelings, you should always acknowledge them. Again, you do not necessarily have to *agree* with the feelings being displayed, but you should seek to acknowledge said feelings. Doing so is a sign of respect, and furthermore, it shows that you are listening on many levels of meaning. Plus, it is common human courtesy.

- **Seek first to understand, then to be understood.** This sentence is an old maxim in the communication discipline, for sure. But the impetus of its meaning rings true. We should seek first to understand the message and the speaker *before* we seek to be understood as communicators ourselves. Why? It is a value-laden priority. By understanding, and having confirmed that we understand through questioning, we can

Always ask questions if you're uncertain about information that is presented.

© wavebreakmedia/Shutterstock.com

move on to trying to be understood ourselves. Keep listening in mind first and foremost, and your own messages will be understood better.

• **Always restate or paraphrase what you have heard to the speaker through reflective listening practices.** Good listeners always make sure they are getting the information that they need through repeating what they have heard to the speaker or communicator for verification and feedback. Commonly, listeners will ask the question: "Let me see if I understand you correctly. What you are saying is this, right?" Repeating what is said by the speaker shows that you have not only internalized their commentary and line of argument, but it also demonstrates that you are, in fact, listening. And, after all, that is what your speaker wants to know—that you are mindfully present for their message.

Taking Quality Notes

There are many systems and methods by which you can take quality notes. It really is something of a personalized art form that you develop and master over time. Following are some observations that will be helpful in developing your own personal note-taking style. Of course, you can mix and match these suggestions with your own style, as necessary. But, know that some of these methods are proven to increase not only your immediate knowledge of the subject matter you are notating, but also your long-term recall of the information.

1. **Set a three-inch margin to the left side of your paper, and draw a vertical line down the center of your page.** Most people do not do this when taking notes, but definitely should. Why? Well, imagine on the left side of the line all your hand-drawn figures, charts, and symbols that will be apart from the raw text notes, which will appear on the right side of the line. Simply put, all your graphics and drawings appear to the left and all your textual notes appear to the right. Believe it or not, this increases your memory of both the graphic representations (left) and textual information (right).

2. **Make sure to complete all outside readings, engage all textbook assignments, and reassess the previous lecture notes before you begin taking new notes.** If you keep in mind the fact that you need to be *prepared* before you walk into the room, then you are in the right frame of mind. Prepping for new information necessitates a complete and thorough understanding of the former information. Without having this understanding, you might be able to record the new information, but not understand it. And because understanding new material is key, why be unprepared?

3. **Have all the necessary tools at your disposal, so that you are not caught off guard.** The last thing you want to have happen is to run out of ink in your pen without a backup, or to not have enough paper, or to be without the necessary accoutrements required for taking notes on the lecture or address at hand. As the old adage goes, "Fail to plan, plan to fail." By ensuring that you have the right tools for the job, the rest becomes a responsibility of you and your awareness.

4. **Color coding by using different colored highlighters actually works!** Yes, it is true. Having three to four different colored highlighters nearby will help you color code information and also properly subordinate ideas when placing items in bulleted lists or classic outline structure. Our minds and eyes appreciate color, and it helps with short-term and long-term memory recall for classroom discussions and examinations. So, by all means, get a good set of highlighters, and keep them nearby.

5. **Use your own personal symbol systems to accentuate the importance of greater information over lesser information.** Clearly, when taking notes, some of the information you encounter will be of primary importance over other parts. You should develop your own system of identifying this information with underlines, stars, check marks, exclamation marks, and so forth to notate the significance of the data you are recording.

6. **Recall that the entire reason you attend a lecture is to take notes, so be responsible about the entire affair.** We do not go to lectures for grins and giggles. We go to lectures to extract important information that, hopefully, can be useful to our professional careers and personal development as human beings. To wit, you should also know that it is your responsibility to be highly organized with the notes you take. Keep them responsibly in one binder, and focus on reviewing that information on a daily basis to keep it fresh in your mind.

7. **In the age of computers and word processing, it is extremely smart to make a permanent copy of your notes.** Not only should you trade notes with a classmate to ensure that you both have the most accurate information possible from class, but you should also record your information in textual form on your personal computer. Making a permanent set of notes somewhere will prompt you to review the information periodically and also force you to have *complete* knowledge about missing parts. And frankly, doing so may mean the difference between an A and a B in a particularly challenging class.

Taking quality notes will help in both your short-term and long-term recall of the information.

SECTION 2: General Communication Competencies

Listening Contexts: Engaging Different Types of Listening

Beyond simply knowing some quick "tricks" to help you become a better listener, effective and engaging listeners pay careful attention to the *context* of the listening in which they are about to participate and act according to that specific communication context. If you are at work, there's a certain way you go about your listening. If you are at school, there's also a way you go about listening, there, too. The same can be said of church, interpersonal dialogue, reading/note taking, and even small-group discussions.

Every single communication context has different templates for listening, and being presciently aware of them will help you gauge and determine *how* you are about to listen. Accordingly, let's now review the various forms of listening:

Keep a permanent copy of your notes on your computer.

- **Discriminative listening.** Sometimes, we have the task of discriminating between sounds, symbols, and information. This is the most basic form of listening, and we practice it regularly without even realizing it. Believe it or not, in this mode of listening you are seeking to identify *differences* in sounds and symbols so that you can properly identify them. You are literally discriminating between things, so that you can readily understand and classify them. We discriminate between sounds, nonverbal cues, variations in someone's voice, and all kinds of human communication phenomena.

- **Comprehension listening.** Other times, communication contexts require us to comprehend the information being conveyed to us. These contexts do not require us to do anything else but *understand* what is being said. Obviously, to understand a given message, we must be able to engage that message with a shared sense of language, grammar, syntax, usage, and even pronunciation. Without these basic shared elements, comprehension cannot be attained. Interestingly, the same is true of nonverbal language. To understand the other, we must share a sense of body language, facial expression, hand gestures, and other important elements of the nonverbal realm. This form of listening is also known as *content* and *informative* listening in the communication literature.

- **Biased listening.** This form of listening occurs when the listener is filtering the entire message through a biased screen of information. Typically, the person will only hear what they wish to hear in these situations. Or worse, sometimes, they will hear things that the message sender never said or intended, completely misinterpreting what the other person meant. The use of *stereotypes* is frequently the root or basis of the problem in this scenario.
- **Evaluative listening.** This form of listening is also known as *critical listening*. In this context, we tend to make conclusions or judgments about what the other person is conveying while they are communicating. We assess what is being said "on the fly" by trying to determine the validity or worthiness of the message. This type of listening is principally important when someone is attempting to change our attitudes, beliefs, values, or even individual behaviors through persuasive communication. While doing this, we often try to look at the finer points of language and grasp the more intricate meanings of what is being said.
- **Appreciative listening.** This listening context is defined by isolating information or data that is of appreciative value to us. Whether this information is professionally or personally related depends on the individual; however, that is highly dependent on the person's life

Sympathetic listeners connect with the other person to share in their emotional state.

needs, goals, and desired life objectives. Appreciative listening can occur when we are reading a motivationally inspiring book, listening to a speech from a corporate leader, listening to music that we like, or even reading poetry.

- **Sympathetic listening.** This listening context is marked by our genuine concern for the other party. We typically engage in this form of listening when the other person is experiencing difficulty, turmoil, sadness, or even glee and joy. By and large, this is an affective form of listening in which we mildly "connect" with the other party to share in their emotional state.

- **Empathetic listening.** To listen empathetically we transcend the simple context of sympathetic listening to seek the true meaning about someone's feelings from a personal-involvement standpoint. Here, we must be critically aware and caring about the other person's emotional state. These types of contexts require painstaking awareness and a huge emotional energy investment because they are possibly the most heightened of all the listening contexts listed, in terms of emotional inquiry and deliberation. In this form of listening, a significant amount of self-disclosure takes place.

- **Dialogic listening.** Some people's learning styles are not conducive to the lecture-based format because of its high formality and rules orientation. There is another type of lecture format that is often used in communication courses called dialogic instruction. In this form of instruction, teachers open discussion to their classroom to demonstrate all the angles and perspectives that may bear on an issue. The word **dialogue** comes from the Greek and is a mixture of "dia" (meaning *through*) and "logos" (meaning *logic*). So, *through logic* we discuss issues until they are dissected well, and all perspectives are rendered identifiable. Of course, this type of instruction format is unique when compared to the traditional lecture format, and thus, it requires its own listening style. Here, we must be mindful that many opinions pertain to certain issues and our job is to try to understand them all *before* we critique them.

■■■■■■■■

Dialogue: Meaning "through logic"; discussing all issues until they are dissected well and all perspectives are rendered identifiable.

In sum, you should know that there are many forms of listening, just as there are many forms of communication. Accordingly, it not only becomes your job to acquire better listening skills for your professional future, but you also clearly need to know which *context* or *mode* of listening you will be engaging in, depending on the situation.

ACTIVE LISTENING: RELAYING THEORY INTO PRACTICE

Passive listening:
Occurs when the listener is not truly engaged in the moment or aware of the message coming from the sender or speaker.

Active listening:
Occurs when the listener is fully engaged in the moment, is aware of the message and sender, and is fully cognizant of the context of communication presently unfolding.

We have previously mentioned that there is an enormous difference between passive and active listening, although we have not really defined these two concepts well. Passive listening occurs when the listener is not truly engaged in the moment or aware of the message coming from the sender or speaker. You do this type of listening when you are watching a situation comedy on television, listening to the radio while driving your car, or having an ordinary conversation with a friend on campus. On the other hand, active listening occurs when the listener is fully engaged in the moment, is aware of the message and sender, and is fully cognizant of the context of communication presently unfolding. Obviously, it goes without saying that active listening is the desired state for all listeners, although we cannot maintain this active state all the time. Your task is to increase your moments of active listening and decrease those moments of passive listening.

When preparing for a communication event, it is a very good idea to review several questions in your mind beforehand. For example, are you giving the speaker your full, undivided attention? Are you properly consuming the information and details being presented? Are you taking good notes? Are you seeking to understand both the meaning of the words being presented *and* the feelings driving them? Are you *encouraging* the speaker to continue with their tack of communication through nonverbal reinforcement, eye contact, and proper facial expressions? And, overarching this, would you be able to restate what you have heard if asked to do so?

These questions are important, but turning ideas into actual skill sets that you can repeatedly use is far more relevant to your overall professional communication success. If you have read and understood the information presented in this chapter up until this point, then you should also know that it is vital for you to put theory into practice. After all, all the communication knowledge in the world is useless unless you transfer it into behaviors, skills, and finite practices. And let's face reality, your listening skills will make or break you in this increasingly fast-paced business world. They will affect your leadership potential, how you run and manage teams, your personal relationships with customers and clients, and your overall negotiation strategies. It does not matter whether you are a top executive, a middle-managerial professional, an independent entrepreneur, or on the front lines of business in sales, customer relations, or retail management. Listening in the business world is as critically important, if not more so, than being able to competently convey an argument or point of information. The next section of this chapter shows you how to put communication theory into practice. The focus of this section will bear on "active listening" generally, but will also be geared toward the business and professional communication context.

1. **Before you begin to listen, define the overall listening objective of the context.** Are you seeking to exchange information? Are you seeking to initiate or build on a personal relationship? Is persuasion being employed by the speaker? What is the true motive of the speaker? All these questions will signify to you the type of communication context in which you are actively engaging. What's more, *knowing* the context will shift all your listening skills accordingly.

2. **Try to avoid pre-judging what you will hear.** Let's face it: there are topics that interest us and topics we're sure we don't care about. When required to attend certain classes or a presentation, we see or hear about the topic and immediately decide that it will be boring or a waste of our time. The speaker begins, and without giving him or her a chance, you immediately disengage. You text a friend,

How can you increase your active listening time?

©g-stockstudio/Shutterstock.com

check your e-mail on your phone, or simply daydream. Next time, give the topic 15 minutes before making a decision about whether you will continue listening. You will probably be surprised at what you hear. There is usually something to be learned in every presentation. Every topic has the potential to impact your life. So, keep an open mind and practice your listening skills.

3. **Be aware of your right to remain silent and simply listen.** Just because you are involved in a communication situation does not mean that you have to talk. In fact, in many situations where high information and persuasion missives are being parleyed, it may be best not to say anything and just listen. Ultimately, you control the choice to communicate or not to communicate. Sometimes, it is smart not to say anything at all and simply be a "sponge" by absorbing everything that you possibly can.

4. **Plan what you have to say before you speak.** Effective business and professional communicators always *mentally prepare* their line of commentary or critique before they begin participating in any discussion. They do not speak simply to speak, and they do not speak without a purpose in mind. Through mental focus and clarity, these communicators learn and apply the art of brevity; being completely succinct in what they have to say in the minimal amount of time required to say it. Through attentive and active listening, you essentially learn when, what, and how to say *exactly* what you need to, depending on the communication context.

5. **Make sure to turn off the digital world.** In this almost insanely active digital communication environment, we are often tethered to the Internet and cellular sphere through a host of personal electronic equipment. Without question or fail, make certain that you do not miss out on a great listening opportunity because you are too engaged in cyberspace. Nothing turns a speaker off more (or sometimes even enrages them!) than people text messaging their friends in the same audience or, perhaps worse, quietly chatting away on a cell phone in a corner of the room. It is not "okay" to do this, and effective professionals turn their equipment off in advance of an important event. As well, if the equipment goes off, smart professionals realize that they should turn their equipment off until the live event is finished, and they are free to engage the electronic conversation.

6. **Practice reflective listening through speech.** Another one of the things that effective communicators do is to reiterate what

they have heard in an abbreviated fashion to the speaker when it is appropriate within the overall communication context. These listeners verbally abstract what has been said through a series of well-signposted information statements that consider the major planks or points that the speaker has conveyed. Repeating what you have heard proves two highly important things to the speaker: (a) you heard him or her correctly, and (b) you were being respectful by simply paying attention.

7. **Face those speaker distractions.** All of us have been to a class or a presentation where the speaker does something that distracts us. Perhaps the speaker's attire is different from what you expect: a tie is leftover from the 1970's and it is too short and too wide; a dress shirt clashes with a jacket; a skirt hem is just too short for a professional event; shoes have sky-high heels, and you wonder how the speaker walks in them; hair keeps falling into the speaker's eyes; or a dress or a suit is just unflattering on a speaker. Some speakers use filler words such as "ah," "um," or "like" so many times that you begin to keep score. Other speakers pace, clear their throats repeatedly, or even slap the podium without realizing what they are doing. It's hard, but try not to criticize the speaker. Instead, concentrate on the message. That is your focus.

8. **When the going gets tough...keep listening!** It's much easier to listen to music that you enjoy than to listen to a class lecture on a difficult subject. Effective communicators anticipate a complicated subject in advance and come prepared to listen. Keep an open mind, take notes, ask questions when appropriate, and listen carefully. It's too easy to just stop and make up an excuse for not listening. Challenge yourself to be an active listener in all situations.

9. **I know this already...** Parents often repeat information more times than you would like (I know not to text and drive, I know to watch my speed, I know to keep both hands on the wheel.) They tell you things, and you zone out. Sometimes a professor or other speaker will cover material that you have heard before. But, they need to make sure that you have the basics down to save you from getting behind later. Resist the temptation to stop listening because you think you "know it already." Once you convince yourself that you know more than the speaker, you cease to be an effective communicator or a good listener.

1. **Come prepared to listen.** Turn off phones, iPads, tablets, and computers. Just concentrate on listening.

2. **Take notes.** You can take notes on your electronic device, but you might try writing them on a piece of paper instead. You type so much during the day that it's easier to go into automatic mode as you type notes, not really paying attention to what you hear.

3. **Paraphrase in your mind as you listen.** Repeat to yourself the more difficult concepts, but put them in your own words.

4. **"Clear the decks."** It's hard to do, but minimize any distractions. If you use an electronic device for notes, don't also use it to check Facebook or post a picture on Instagram, place other books and notebooks out of sight, and tell yourself that for the next 75 minutes, you are just going to listen to the speaker.

5. **Test yourself.** At the end of the class or presentation, write down the five most significant things the speaker said. Add your reasons for why they are the most significant.

Of course, we have offered just a few of the major professional listening suggestions that can be used. So, if you have other well-developed ideas, make sure to share them with your instructor and classmates. We are all on this exciting journey of trying to become more competent and respectful listeners together. And, what is very clear to us, your authors, is that the most basic of all human needs and desires is to be heard, understood, and acknowledged. Working harder to demonstrate that you are an effective and caring listener will not only help you obtain more information from your communication environment, but it will also justly acknowledge the people who are trying to commune with you. In the business world, this is critical.

CONCLUSION

Cecilia Ramirez knew that she had a lot of work to do. It wasn't going to be easy, either. Not only was her attention span admittedly short, but she often missed all the nonverbal cues that other skilled communicators sent her way. However, following some online research of her own, and by executing a few simple suggestions from her friendly university communication professor, her attention span and nonverbal message reception began to pick up dramatically. And this made her excited and proud.

As a direct result, her clients became increasingly happy with her work performance. Some of them even officially requested to work with her exclusively instead of other attorneys at the office because they felt that "she acknowledged their presence" when discussing contract details. Of course, Cecilia Ramirez still has to work at her listening skills every day. They do not come automatically or by magic. But now, what is different in her communication approach is that she understands that listening is literally tied to effective leadership and even her own ability to communicate effectively. Why is this the case? Simple. Now, she seeks first to understand, then to be understood.

ACTIVITIES

1. In contemplating your listening skills and those of your friends, family, bosses, and coworkers, create a list of bad listening habits. How do you know when someone is not listening to you? What are the consequences of poor listening? How might these incompetent interpersonal behaviors translate to the workplace? Record your answers in the space provided.

2. Part of what makes listening a difficult task is that it takes great focus—especially if the speaker/sender isn't encoding a strong message. From the speaker's perspective, how might you structure your messages to assist your listeners in listening? Record your answers in the space provided.

3. Consider the six steps of the listening process described in Chapter 4. In the space that follows, develop a list of tips and techniques for improving your ability in each area. How might you polish your skills?

REFERENCES

[1] Bostrom, R. N. (1990). *Listening behavior: Measurement and application.* New York: Guilford.

[2] Brownell, J. (1996). *Listening: Attitudes, principles, and skills.* Needham Heights, MA: Allyn & Bacon.

[3] Sypher, B. D., Bostrom, R. N., & J. H. Siebert (1989). Listening, communication abilities, and success at work. *Journal of Business Communication, 26,* 292–303.

[4] Wolvin, A. D. (2010). *Listening and human communication in the 21st century.* West Sussex: Wiley-Blackwell.

chapter
five

Working with Text: Writing for Business and Professional Communication

After reading this chapter you will be able to:

- Describe the importance of the writing process in business and professional communication
- Understand how to properly use style, voice, grammar, and usage in business and professional writing
- Know how to properly construct your writing and citations according to the American Psychological Association style guide when conducting your research

CHAPTER OUTLINE

key words

INTRODUCTION

The beauty of human language is that each of us controls its construction and usage in accordance with our life needs, wants, and goals. As a direct result, language becomes an extension of human existence itself. We use language to relay information and foment change. Sometimes we use it well, and sometimes we use it poorly. After all, human beings are language using and misusing animals. When skillfully executed, language is nothing short of a powerful ally in our quest to understand and interact with the world around us. Poor language skills can also be a painful embarrassment—especially in a business and professional context. One of the most important things we, your authors, wish to impress on you in this chapter is that the proper use of style, grammar, and mechanics in your writing is not merely a "good skill" to possess; it is absolutely foundational to your survival in whatever career you pursue.

Good writing not only helps you obtain significant employment, but it also helps you advance and evolve as a personnel commodity, no matter the discipline you pursue. To be certain: you must know how to write—and write exceedingly well. If you cannot, you would be extremely smart to dedicate a noteworthy portion of your time toward learning the art and science of the writing craft. If you choose to just "let it slide," however, you might end up experiencing something similar to what Mr. Fred Marken encountered with Jefferson Capital Holdings (JCH) after 18 years of devoted employment.

Fred Marken was a top employee at JCH. He *always* knew the right moves required to advance the company's bottom line. He studied the commodities and worked late hours to maintain sound judgment over the ebb and flow of commodity indicators. He knew when to buy in on a bull run and, just as important, when to bail on the bear. In fact, he was considered a "financial genius" by all at JCH and was always called on for advice. To the detriment of his profession, however, Mr. Marken's writing skills were breathtakingly inadequate. The full truth be known, he didn't think it was all that important to know how to spell certain words, use commas well, or even properly write a basic office memo. That was the "useless stuff" for some "secretary." His job, as he defined it, was to make the company cold, hard, cash. Right? Yes and no. After giving what seemed like the better part of his adult life to the company for nearly two decades, a coveted vice president of commodity investments position was announced at the trading house (mainly due to his spectacular moves in agricultural markets). He wanted the job. Heck, he deserved the job! And, of course, you know what happened. Fred Marken was "passed over" for a less financially savvy junior associate, who could write and speak (communicate) with precision. Marken was bitter and infuriated. And if you put yourself in his place for a moment, you might be a little angry, too.

The proper use of style, grammar, and mechanics in your writing is essential for success.

What lesson can be learned here? Mr. Marken couldn't spell or write to save his life. Moreover, he didn't even care that he couldn't spell or write, which made matters worse. But upper management did care. They didn't want Fred Marken's administrative credibility to be called into question by his potential subordinates over a gross misspelling in a memo or from persistent subject-verb disagreement in e-mails, or due to a poorly crafted sticky note left on someone's office door. The JCH board of directors knew that his financial knowledge and experience were superior to anyone else's in the shop. Yet, they also knew that people would be silently laughing at him because he could not write well. It was a credibility play. And the employee who won the job made *her* case far more clearly, cleverly, and credibly than Mr. Marken did. How powerful can the written language be to you and your life? In a mere word: very.

THE WRITING PROCESS: ESTABLISHING YOUR CREDIBILITY THROUGH THE KEYBOARD

Writing is not something that just "happens" magically overnight. You need to know this before we begin to dissect the *metier*. Writing involves a lot of hard work, discipline, dedication, and screen time in front of a computer (nowadays). You really have to *give* yourself to the work. And, moreover, you also need to be able to *think originally*. True, some folks are far more versatile than others at writing. But this is because these persons have labored hard to acquire the rules and tricks of writing and have—for all intents and purposes—changed their way of being over time to become more skillful purveyors of text.

Good writers have learned how to write more efficiently and effectively. They write with brevity, saying exactly what they need to say as concisely as possible. They have become textual in all that they do, every minute of every day. They have transformed themselves into wordsmiths and equipped themselves with the tools of the trade: dictionaries, thesauruses, grammar and style guides, quality word-processing software, famous quotation books, desk reference materials, and a solid computer and quick Internet connection. Skilled writers clearly understand, as well, that they must constantly read challenging material. It isn't enough just to skim the business section of the newspaper; you must read everything, everywhere, of interest. Often, the best writers become the best writers because they are also the best readers. They discover how to write by mimicking the well-crafted examples of others. Your goal should be the same.

Are you ready to embrace the exciting world of text? If you are, you must realize that you are about to be changed forever. To what degree this change will occur is a personal decision. Some choose to acquire the basic skills necessary to stay in step with professional expectations. Others will choose to transcend the expected and add additional literacies and proficiencies to their skill sets. And then, there are the writing addicts who focus on text as a way of interacting and understanding life itself. We strongly believe that holding a vigilant, constant state of textual awareness is basic to any true leadership position in the businesses and professions, contemporarily speaking. Hence, if your professional expectations are rather high for yourself, your skill-acquisition goals should be equally high. Prepare accordingly.

Often, the best readers make the best writers.

figure5.1

The Writing Process

The Writing Process: Seven Basic Steps

Whenever doing any significant writing, keep the seven steps shown in **Figure 5.1** in mind: (a) the creation of a thesis statement, (b) the development of a writing outline, (c) the crafting of introduction and conclusion statements, (d) fleshing out the body of the work, (e) prewriting, (f) finished writing, and finally (g) proofreading and editing. This is the much-celebrated "writing process" endorsed by almost every major writing guide in print today. Some more advanced issues you should also keep in mind are (h) dealing with writer's block (sometimes known as writer's anxiety), (i) evidencing or sourcing, and (j) adapting your text to an appropriate presentational format, or template, for showcasing. Let's examine the seven-step process in motion first:

1. Creating a thesis statement can be a challenge, especially if you have not spent an adequate amount of time properly researching and selecting your topic. This section assumes that you have, indeed, selected a suitable topic for your writing. To create a thesis statement, you need to first determine what type of writing you will be conducting. Predominantly, there are three types of writing: (a) **investigative**, wherein you dissect an issue to its core elements; (b) **expository**, wherein you explain important concepts to your readers; and (c) **opinion-based** or **argumentative**, wherein you make a claim of some sort, backed with supportive evidence. Your thesis statement should be precise and unambiguous. It should be direct. More important, though, the thesis statement should

Investigative: A type of writing wherein you dissect an issue to its core elements.

Expository: A type of writing wherein you explain important concepts to your readers.

Opinion-based or argumentative: A type of writing wherein you make a claim of some sort, backed with supportive evidence.

fully canvass the scope of your writing agenda and must be front-loaded at the beginning of your work. Some writers believe that the thesis statement should immediately begin any essay, and some, alternatively, believe that it should conclude the introductory teaser paragraph of the work. Wherever you choose to deploy it, recognize that you may have to revisit the thesis topic a few times during your writing because your ideas will always shift as your writing unfolds.

An Investigative Thesis Statement Example

A thorough examination of the university's debate team recruiting process demonstrates that federally funded urban debate leagues significantly enhance the critical thinking skills of economically challenged high school students, typically to the level of sophomore collegiate competitors.

An Expository Thesis Statement

You may have to revisit the thesis topic during your writing because your ideas will shift as the writing unfolds.

Urban debate leagues successfully enhance economically challenged high school students' critical thinking skills, causing them to compete better at the collegiate level.

© wavebreakmedia/Shutterstock.com

All urban areas should seek federal funding to create urban debate leagues to assist lesser-privileged students who want to compete at the collegiate level.

2. Developing an outline to write from is also very important, given that no writing should ever be conducted without first knowing where you are headed. Each writer must keep three concepts in mind concerning the outline: (a) parallelism and balance in content structure, (b) the proper subordination of ideas, and (c) the proper symbolic division of concepts. Parallelism is when you ensure that no one particular segment of your outline overpowers or outweighs any of the other segments. There should be "balance" among your ideas on the outline in terms of an even distribution of information. Subordination of ideas deals with ensuring that all ideas contained within the subheading of an outline, in fact, bear some logical, associated meaning to the principal heading. In other words, if your main heading is "automobiles," then all the subordinated concepts should be logically related to automobiles. Symbolic division means that each heading under the outline tree *must* contain a minimum of at least two subheadings. And, it also means that the proper use of outline symbols should be used at all times.

Parallelism: When you ensure that no one particular segment of your outline overpowers or outweighs any of the other segments.

Subordination of ideas: Deals with ensuring that all ideas contained within the subheading of an outline bear some logical, associated meaning to the principal heading.

Symbolic division: Each heading under the outline tree must contain a minimum of at least two subheadings.

How to Outline for Writing and Presentations

Recall that the entire purpose of developing an outline is for you, yourself, to see the clarity and hierarchical relationship of your ideas in a concise, portable manner. Most writers find that constructing a clear outline before they begin writing their work helps them better understand, manage, and organize their thinking. So, if your outline is solidly constructed, your writing will also be of significant structure and impact. Always begin with the end in mind. What are you trying to accomplish in the bigger picture?

Basic Outline Structure
Title of Your Work

I. **Introduction**

    A. Seek to motivate your readers with a good quotation, anecdotal story, or personal experience relevant to your topic.

    B. State the reasons why you are writing the essay; present your justifications.

    C. Preview the main points of your work:

        1. First Main Point

        2. Second Main Point

        3. Third Main Point

II. **First Main Point:** Developing a Solid Outline

    A. Always make sure to begin an outline with symbolic structure in mind.

        1. Symbolic structure requires a strong sense of hierarchy of ideas.

            a. *Always subordinate your ideas well.*

                (1) No point should be disproportionately stronger than another point in your outline.

                (2) Make sure your ideas are nicely balanced, exhibiting parallelism.

            b. *Always keep the overall goal of your work in mind.*

                (1) Ensure that your work exudes a recognition of your specific thesis statement.

                (2) Use outline indentation to your advantage.

    B. At least two subpoints should always fall within an outline structure; no subpoint should be left hanging without a balanced secondary subpoint

III. **Second Main Point**

(Outline should flow according to the topic—see Section II above.)

IV. **Third Main Point**

(Outline should flow according to the topic—see Section II above.)

V. **Conclusion**

    A. Briefly review your three main points:

        1. First Main Point

        2. Second Main Point

        3. Third Main Point

    B. Summarize your ideas well by repeating the thesis statement of your work.

    C. Make sure to connect to the introductory quotation, anecdote, or story from your introduction when concluding to demonstrate balance and harmony in your work.

■ ■ ■ ■ ■ ■ ■ ■ ■

Introduction: The opening, which serves to entice and interest the reader in the writing.

3. Introductions are your way to entice and interest the reader in your writing. There are many ways in which introductions can be accomplished; as such, there is no real predetermined, standardized formula. There are, however, four good questions you should typically ask yourself when thinking about how to introduce your topic. First, what am I *really* writing about? What is the context surrounding the topic? Second, you should also keep in mind the main purpose, or function, of your writing. In other words, why should the reader continue reading your work? This is often called the "so-what test." Third, the introduction should be novel enough to completely

and totally captivate your reader. This means that the introduction should be unique and compelling. Is your introduction unique and compelling? And finally, your introduction should preview your topic. Have you adequately prepped the preview statement at the end of your introduction to signpost to the reader *where* you are headed in the overall body of the text? Conclusions do the same thing as an introduction, but in reverse progression. They let the reader know that the essay is drawing to a close and that the arguments have been adequately conveyed. Likewise, they also allow the reader to reflect on the ground that has been covered in the writing. Both introductions and conclusions are critically important components of any writing.

Conclusion: The closing, which lets the reader know the essay is ending and that the arguments have been adequately conveyed.

4. Developing the body of your work is step four of the writing process, and it occurs when you take the basic outline from a mere thought or keyword model to a full-sentence outline. Ordinarily, this step of the process is conducted on a computer with word-processing software. Here, writers take the basic outline and put significant thought to the arguments they are making, along with the corresponding evidence necessary to bolster their claims. This part of the process is where a lot of thought, detail, and attention are afforded to the text to develop it from seed ideas into actual positions and arguments. Similarly, this is the part of the process in which ideas are ordered, reordered, compacted, expanded, and adjusted until parallelism is perfected in balanced thought. The body of the work is complete when the full-sentence outline is ready for transfer into actual rough draft essay text.

Developing the body of the work takes a lot of thought, detail, and attention.

© Pressmaster/Shutterstock.com

5. **Prewriting** is also called rough draft writing. Here, your job is to transfer the sentence outline into a corpus of text. This includes all the necessary grammatical and structural elements of writing—including signposts, paragraph-ordered indentations, and proper punctuation. Sometimes, during this stage of the process, writers discover that their ideas require elaboration or more evidence to substantiate an argument. When this happens, prewriting seamlessly mutates into **finished writing**.

6. Recall again that prewriting is merely rough draft writing. Some people are "old school" and still prefer to do this on paper first, which works fine. On the other hand, some people are "new school" and prefer to do this on a screen with a good computer. Either way you accomplish this stage, know that once draft copy begins to gel and solidify, begging for more evidence and embellishment, you have entered the finished writing portion of the process. Finished writing thus begins where prewriting ends.

7. **Proofreading** and **editing** represent your final pass at writing before you are finished. Not only should you give this final stage of the writing process your all, but you should also enlist the help of friends who are writing veterans to review your final copy for passage. Never go it alone! It is always important to have a friend or colleague closely review your work and check it for clearance.

© Lisa F. Young/Shutterstock.com

STYLE, VOICE, GRAMMAR, AND USAGE

Style. Panache. Flair. It is what has made so many notable personalities throughout history both famous and infamous. It is the personality in Thomas Jefferson's signature on the Declaration of Independence. It is Carol Burnett's knowing wink and earring tug. It is Tiger Woods's power fist pump after clinching another green jacket at the Masters. It is Sarah Palin's designer spectacles. It is Mark Twain's coy Americana wit. And this precious aspect of humanity is within each and every one of us if we will set it free. It is called our humanity, and style is the vehicle that sets it free through our writing. This section of Chapter 5 first talks about how to find something called your "voice." Then, second, we consider the basics of grammar and mechanics.

Style

Simply put, a **writing style** is the method by which a writer conveys and shapes text, thereby revealing their personality or **voice**. Before we tell you how to find your voice, especially in the business and professional context, you need to know that often the form of writing you are involved with will dictate certain parameters. For example, what you are reading right now is a textbook. As a textbook, certain structural rules must be obeyed, or it wouldn't pass as a textbook. Textbooks should have a very scholarly writing style, be well researched, read intelligently, reinforce arguments and ideas with adequate theories and citations, and have an adequate amount of boldfaced definitions for the student to memorize for examinations. This represents the writing structure or **form**. Generally speaking, we must always ask the overarching question: To what extent is the writing a product of form or voice? The following poetic example illustrates this point well:

> Haikus are easy
> But, sometimes they don't make sense
> Refrigerator

The form of the poem is the shape and structure of the haiku itself. The voice is the author's unmistakable joke about and within the poetic form. Accordingly, you have to recognize what form (as a higher language) has become a consensual template on the type of writing you will conduct. There are all kinds of constraints placed on a given writer's style, and this is especially true when doing writing at the workplace. Certain words

Writing style: The method by which a writer conveys and shapes text, thereby revealing their personality.

Voice: The personality conveyed in writing.

Form: The writing structure.

can and cannot be used at work—for both relational and professional reasons. Certain sentence structures can and cannot be implemented as well because of workplace dynamics. In short, know that a given writer's style is dictated first by the form and guided second by voice.

Voice

Finding your writing voice cannot be done overnight. It takes years and years of practice and effort and resembles something of a personal campaign to cultivate. Some writers spend their entire lives in search of their "real" voice. In fact, numerous books have been written on the subject of trying to find one's actual voice. In the business and professional environment, finding one's voice in writing is not wholly difficult. For the most part, in this context, you will write résumés, curriculum vitae, cover letters, thank-you notes, memos, and standardized reports. So, why do we discuss voice at all in this chapter? Simply put, although business and professional writing is, indeed, often clinical and dry, the craft is not devoid entirely of personal voice. Certainly, you do not want to use emoticons (those little smiley faces we place in e-mails) in your writing, either on paper or in e-mails, when conducting professional writing. But you can let your personality be known to a certain extent; this is especially the case when the communication is of a less sensitive nature. Still, knowing when and when not to exercise your voice is central to smart writing because sometimes it is just not appropriate. Therefore, always be cautious about putting your voice in written business and professional communication. Be judicious.

Grammar and Usage

Grammar: The accepted structure of a language.

Usage: The conventions of both speech and writing that characterize particular groups of communicants.

Grammar deals with the accepted structure of a language. Usage, however, refers to the conventions of both speech and writing that characterize particular groups of communicants. Interestingly, a lot of people think that proper grammar has hard and fast rules that are clear, fixed, and absolute. In all actuality, nothing could be farther from the truth. Language morphs and changes over time according to our usage. Accordingly, then, so do the structural rules (grammar) for our language. This is also true in the business and professional context and is therefore highly dependent on what discipline or field we are discussing. Thus, not only should you purchase a current, respected grammar guide—and be exceedingly familiar with it—but you should also constantly keep in step with the contemporary shifts occurring in the English language.

© Ahmet Misirligul/Shutterstock.com

Sometimes using your own voice in your writing is not appropriate, so be cautious.

New words, new writing techniques, and new formats for writing evolve every day. Consequently, you need to be prepared to adapt with them over time. If you do not adapt, you will be writing in an obsolete mode.

You should also know that grammar is separate from punctuation and spelling. Grammar has more to do with the parts of speech and proper sentence structure than anything else. On the other hand, punctuation and spelling—although related components to grammar—have their own rules and principles. It would be very wise to consult a thorough grammar, punctuation, and spelling text for additional information.

BUSINESS AND PROFESSIONAL WRITING: CONSIDERING THE CONTEXT

Now that we have covered some of the basic elements of good writing in general, we must turn to focus on the business and professional environment, specifically. Of course, workplace writers need to be effective with their words, language, and grammar—there is no doubt about this. But, they also need to be aware of (a) who their readership is going to be, (b) the requirements of specific documents, and (c) the basics of a professional résumé or curriculum vitae (CV). These three essential issues represent the forthcoming three segments of this chapter's third section. Please note, however, that these "essentials" of business and professional writing are critical to developing yourself as a bona fide workplace commodity and also for simply functioning within the modern business world. They are not written simply for the sake of writing. They are critical to the workplace endeavor. In short, you cannot exist or advance within a profession without having a solid working knowledge of this information.

Audience Analysis

If you fail to analyze fully your probable readership and what they might be expecting from your writing, you have likely already missed the mark. In fact, all your informational and persuasive missives should be geared accordingly. Ask yourself a series of questions before you begin writing. First, who will be reading the document you are preparing? Second, what might that person really think of your document? Third, when will they be reading it, and how much time will they have to dedicate to the document? This simple three-question analysis will help you find your way with your words, arguments, goals, and objectives. When you stop for a moment to analyze *who* will be reading or perusing your work, you genuinely achieve a great deal. It helps you foment an understanding about the person and even project what they might be expecting of you.

Ask yourself who will be reading the document you are preparing and consider what they will expect.

© Pressmaster/Shutterstock.com

Beyond this simple projection, however, a readership-centered approach requires that you be persuasively aware on several levels: (a) your main purpose in writing, (b) the intended and unintended audiences who might read your work, (c) the affected stakeholders of your document, and (d) the context in which the document will be dissected.

First, you must follow the writing process defined at the beginning of this chapter quite religiously. It is important to build a solid document from the ground up, using outlines, rough drafts, advance copy, and final drafts that have been proofread by trusted and skilled eyes. It assumes a lot on your part not to go through this process. Very few writers are able to produce final-copy text on a first pass. While going through this tedious writing process, you should be able to see your values and goals develop in your writing. These values and goals, hinged together, represent your fundamental purpose for writing. It is always good to know, exactly, what you are trying to accomplish. If you do not know what you want to accomplish, you are, essentially, writing without aim or purpose. And, it will show in all that you do. So, always begin with the end result in mind. Know for certain what you want the person reading your document *to do* when they are finished. Unless your document is for informational purposes only, you should be writing with persuasion in mind with every keystroke. Rhetoric should exude from your fingers.

Second, you need to realize that sometimes our readers are not precisely who we think they are going to be. This is particularly important when considering the slippery nature of the modern electronic environment presented by the Internet. People forward e-mails and copies of documents all the time. Accordingly, you should not put anything of an incriminating or sensitive nature in an e-mail or attached document that could be used against you—or worse, have unintended consequences that reach far beyond the scope of anything that you could imagine. Consider the possibility of one of your secretive e-mails to a "friend" either intentionally or unintentionally falling into the hands of a rival coworker or being posted to a distribution listserv with thousands of users. For this reason, it is important to be aware of what you are writing in copy. The things that we say in writing are impossible to take back. Be cautious.

Think about all the places an e-mail could go before you send it.

Third, think about who will be affected by your written document. True, your excellent cost-cutting measures at the workplace may, in fact, save the company over $3.2 million in the long run. But, will doing so come at the expense of your fellow cubicle mate? Or maybe even yourself over time? When we are dealing with persuasion, we must recognize that we are dealing with a powerful craft that has the ability to make vast, paradigmatic changes among and throughout systems and people. Think before you argue. Consider the end-result scenario of your line of argument if, in fact, it actually takes root and gains credibility and compliance. Do you really want to change things that much? Is the status quo truly that bad? If so, think about the full implementation of the solutions, writ large. Remember, rhetoric is the art of persuasion beautiful and just. Consider all the angles of your advocacy, and act accordingly with prudence.

Fourth, and finally, the context in which your document will be reviewed is imperative. Context deals with the history, reasons, rationale, and background of both the document you are creating and also the environment in which it will be reviewed. In short, before you draft a single word, make sure that you are aware of the context in which all things, all arguments, and all positions will be weighed and appraised. Through this contextual awareness, business and professional communicators become more readership centered and, thus, more prone to make successful arguments. Whether you are writing a basic memo, a business report, a research paper for work, or a position paper, you must consider these four components in your writing.

Mandatory Workplace Documents: Application Cover Letters, Job Acceptance Letters, and the Résumé/ Curriculum Vitae

Two of the things you need to do before constructing your workplace documents (e.g., application cover letters, job acceptance letters, and professional statements) is to: (a) conduct a professional skills assessment of the talents and abilities you possess and, as a direct result, (b) identify and extract several key action words and phrases that you will typically use to describe yourself. Following is a skills assessment instrument. We urge you to complete this inventory, and determine what skills and specialties you possess. More information on constructing a résumé can be found in Chapter 8.

The Skills Assessment

Skills are developed through paid and unpaid work experiences, volunteerism, hobbies, classroom experiences, and everyday living. The following is only a partial sample of skills that by no means exhausts your own skills repertoire. You may use this list to initiate your skills assessment. Your goals should be to take an accurate inventory of your skills, to prioritize your skills according to level of interest, and then to assess your proficiencies.

To begin, follow these steps:
1. Photocopy this list.
2. Put a check mark by those skills you have used in the past.
3. Review your checked skills, and circle those that interest you the most.
4. Prioritize the circled skills according to your level of proficiency.

abstracting	acting	adapting	adjusting	administering
advertising	advising	analyzing	answering	anticipating
applying	approving	acquiring	arbitrating	arranging
assessing	assigning	assisting	assuring	attaining
auditing	bargaining	briefing	budgeting	building
calculating	charting	checking	classifying	coaching
collaborating	communicating	comparing	compiling	completing
composing	computing	constructing	consulting	coordinating
coping	copying	counseling	creating	deciding
decorating	defining	delegating	demonstrating	detailing
determining	developing	devising	diagnosing	directing
discovering	discussing	displaying	dissecting	distributing
drafting	dramatizing	drawing	editing	eliminating
empathizing	empowering	encouraging	enforcing	estimating
evaluating	examining	explaining	expressing	extracting
facilitating	filing	financing	following	gathering
guiding	handling	helping	hiring	hypothesizing
identifying	illustrating	imagining	implementing	improving
improvising	influencing	initiating	innovating	inspecting
inspiring	installing	instructing	integrating	interpreting
interviewing	inventing	inventorying	investigating	leading

learning	lecturing	listening	managing	manipulating
mediating	memorizing	mentoring	monitoring	motivating
navigating	negotiating	observing	operating	ordering
organizing	originating	participating	perceiving	performing
persuading	photographing	piloting	pinpointing	planning
predicting	preparing	prescribing	presenting	printing
problem solving	processing	producing	programming	promoting
proofreading	proposing	providing	publicizing	purchasing
reading	reasoning	receiving	recommending	reconciling
recording	recruiting	referring	rehabilitating	reinforcing
relating	reorganizing	repairing	reporting	researching
restoring	reviewing	revising	risking	scheduling
selecting	selling	separating	serving	setting up
sharing	simplifying	sketching	solving	speaking
sorting	sporting	studying	summarizing	supervising
supplying	synthesizing	talking	teaching	team building
telling	training	translating	traveling	treating
troubleshooting	tutoring	understanding	unifying	uniting
verbalizing	visualizing	writing		

Once you have assembled and prioritized your action words that you will use to describe yourself, begin crafting a professional overview of yourself. It is generally a good idea to use this overview on the long form of your professional résumé or curriculum vitae (CV). This would be a good time to distinguish between a professional résumé and a CV. The professional résumé comes in two forms: short and long. The short résumé is usually a one-page document that quickly canvasses your abilities and skills. The long résumé is a two- to five-page document that denotes your professional potential more fully. Ordinarily, the short résumé is submitted first, and then, when requested, the long résumé is presented. Curriculum vitae are very long résumé-like documents that detail all the activities of a professional over the course of a lifetime. You should begin your foray into the professional world by preparing a short résumé, then a long résumé, and eventually (once you have matured into a true professional) via a curriculum vitae. Please note that there are no set rules as to what an employer is or is not looking for, so always adapt to the audience by asking the potential employer what type of document they require for application submission.

CONCLUSION

Fred Marken knew, too, why he had been passed over for the promotion at Jefferson Capital Holdings. A lifetime of aliteracy (possessing basic literacy skills, but not exercising them) had finally caught up with him. And although he desperately wanted the new promotion and was angry and upset at first, he knew that top-line professionals had to communicate effectively in writing as well as speaking. It still did not make things easier to swallow, however. As expected, the news of the promotion choice was delivered to him gently. He had come to terms with his shortcomings, but personally vowed that it would never happen again. In fact, he told his employers as much and asked for official company support in taking some English and communication classes in rhetoric and composition to improve his skills at his community college. Little did he know that this request was all the superiors at JCH wanted to hear. They simply wanted to know that he was sincerely *willing* to work on his deficiencies. To wit, they granted his professional improvement request through the company's tuition repayment benefits program and conveyed their full support of his time away from work to meet with his class.

Mr. Marken knew that his skills would not change overnight. But learning some of the basics of writing helped a long way. He wasn't aware of the writing process whatsoever. And moreover, he did not know the difference between *voice* and *form*. Within two short years, the position opened up again, but this time he was rhetorically ready. His vocabulary had improved tremendously, his grammar and usage were evident not only in his writing but also in his speech, and he could even construct sentences with technical ease and aplomb. What a difference some desire and education makes, no?

Given that his predecessor in the position was not as financially savvy as he was, there was a lot of work to be done. However, not only could he command the market moves necessary to achieve market position for JCH, but he could also explain *why* and *how* he had done this to his subordinates. Soon after taking the VP position, uniquely because of his writing proficiencies in quarterly reports and e-mails, everyone could understand the "Marken Method" to futures investing. And sharing this knowledge well in writing opened up political and economic doors that Fred Marken never dreamed existed, as he was asked to be a guest interviewee on CNBC's investing show *Squawk Box* to explain JCH's skyrocketing performance. In two short years, his writing skills had helped him realize his true potential and made him a professional celebrity and commodity. That is how important writing can be to your career.

Short résumé: Usually a one-page document that quickly canvasses your abilities and skills.

Long résumé: A two- to five-page document that denotes your professional potential more fully.

Curriculum vitae: A very long résumé-like document that details all the activities of a professional over the course of a lifetime.

ACTIVITIES

1. Google a topic that interests you on the Internet. When you find a story that relates to your topic, take a few minutes to read the story carefully. Take a sheet of paper and see if you can identify the visible steps from the writing process detailed in this chapter. Can you identify the thesis statement? Do you see a clear introduction and conclusion? Do you see typos or grammatical errors, or did the author or editor clearly proofread and edit?

2. This chapter talks about the importance of the introduction in writing. If you had to write a brief story of your life, how would you write the introduction? Based on what you have learned from this chapter about the four questions to ask yourself when writing an effective introduction, what would your introduction look like? Please write the introduction to the story of your life and then ask someone to read it. Would they want to read the rest of the story? Does your introduction accomplish its purpose? If not, what needs to be changed?

REFERENCES

[1] Anderson, P. V. (2007). *Technical communication: A reader-centered approach, 6th edition.* Boston: Thomson-Wadsworth.

[2] Guffey, M. E. (2008). *Business communication: Process and product,* 6th edition. Mason, OH: South-Western.

[3] Johnson-Sheehan, R. (2005). *Technical communication today.* New York: Pearson-Longman.

[4] Katz, S. M. (1998). A newcomer gains power: An analysis of the role of rhetorical expertise. *Journal of Business Communication, 35*(4), 419–442.

section three

Social, Group, and Professional Competencies

chapter
SIX

Interpersonal Communication Skills at Work

After reading this chapter you will be able to:

- Understand the role of interpersonal communication in the workplace
- Describe the types and functions of relationships
- Identify different approaches to conflict
- Determine how certain conflict styles work in different situations
- Analyze and apply negotiation strategies that meet different objectives
- Provide and evaluate constructive feedback
- Identify and apply Gibb's framework for building positive climates

CHAPTER OUTLINE

key words

Interpersonal communication
Interdependence
Uniqueness
Mixed-status relationship
Leader-member exchange
   theory (LMX)
In-group
Out-group
Same-status relationship
Informational peer
Collegial peer
Special peer
Conflict
Avoiding

Accommodating
Compete
Compromise
Collaborate
Negotiation
Constructive feedback
Organizational climate
Descriptive message
Problem-focused message
Spontaneous communication
Empathetic message
Message of equality
Provisional message

INTRODUCTION

Cora Sims has worked at Kelpin Publishers as a project manager for five years. In this role she works with many different members of the organization to facilitate the publication of elementary school reading materials. From graphics to technology to accounting, she has developed relationships with many different departments. She reports directly to the senior publishing partner, Mac Feral. Although she feels that she has a strong relationship with Mac, she sometimes feels disappointed that he does not consult with her on big decisions. This is especially upsetting because she sees her coworker Sue having lunches and meetings with Mac where she gets to share her opinion and provide input. Many times, she'll filter messages for Mac through Sue because she feels as though Mac is more likely to listen. Sue encourages Cora to make more of an effort to work with Mac and not to be afraid of telling Mac when he's leaning toward making the wrong decision. Even though Cora feels that her relationship with Mac could be stronger, she feels more confident in the relationships she has developed with others in the organization. She considers Sue one of her best friends, and they even carpool daily, where they talk about work and their families. She plays on the company softball team, which in addition to being fun, provides a way for her to interact with people from different departments that she relies on for meeting publication deadlines. Although her relationships are strong, she has some fear about what the future might bring. Mac has informed her that a massive budget cut is in the works that will affect the entire company. He's holding the project managers directly responsible for decreasing costs by coordinating and monitoring the work from the different areas such as advertising, instructional technology, and graphics. She contemplates how she might handle the tough times ahead knowing that she'll have to be assertive in meeting the new budget goals.

The following sections offer Cora more to contemplate in the way of her relationships with her boss and coworkers and provide specific strategies for negotiating with others as well as working to keep the climate at Kelpin Publishers positive and supportive in the midst of budget cuts. Read on to see how these topics might help Cora.

DEFINING INTERPERSONAL COMMUNICATION

Interpersonal communication is critical to the basic functioning of any organization. **Interpersonal communication** is defined as communication of a relational nature between two or more people. These relationships are marked by **interdependence**, where people rely on each other equally for both personal and professional support, and **uniqueness**, which signifies the special quality of the communication between individuals. Relationships form between many individuals in the workplace and are marked by communication that is *task oriented* (focused on completing projects and duties) and *relationship oriented* (focused on supporting others or sharing personal information). We form relationships with coworkers, supervisors, and clients or customers. Our ability to communicate competently with people at work affects our job satisfaction, feeling of belongingness in an organization, and ability to complete tasks and projects successfully and in functional and rewarding ways. Many of the chapters in this book deal with issues of interpersonal communication, including nonverbal communication, language use, multiculturalism, diversity, and working with others in small groups. This chapter focuses on the different types of relationships you are likely to encounter, how to develop effective relationships through understanding the communication patterns of others, and learning how to manage relationships through negotiation, constructive feedback, and strategies for enhancing relational climates.

Interpersonal communication: Communication of a relational nature between two or more people marked by interdependence, uniqueness, and quality.

Interdependence: A characteristic of interpersonal relationships describing how people rely on each other equally for both personal and professional support.

Uniqueness: A characteristic of interpersonal communication signifying the special quality of the communication between individuals.

How does our ability to competently communicate at work affect our job satisfaction?

© wavebreakmedia/Shutterstock.com

TYPES OF WORKPLACE RELATIONSHIPS

You are likely to form many types of relationships at work. Contrary to traditional forms of organizational management, much more happens during a work shift than merely accomplishing tasks. Through completion of duties we come to know and interact with many different organizational members and form friendships. These relationships are often classified as same status or mixed status. These terms signify whether you work on the same organizational level or whether one person holds higher status or power, such as a supervisor. Let's begin by examining mixed-status relationships.

Mixed-Status Relationships

Mixed-status relationships refer to relationships employees have with people above or below their own position in the organization. Mixed-status relationships often are referred to as supervisor–subordinate or leader–member relationships. The nature of these relationships can vary significantly, depending on individuals and organizational structures.

Mixed-status relationship: The relationship an employee has with people above or below his/her own position in the organization.

One theory that describes outcomes of the quality of these types of relationships is leader–member exchange theory (LMX).[1] The basic premise of this theory explains how leaders typically have groups of employees who emerge as part of their in-group, middle-group, and out-group. Being in the in-group signifies a higher level of liking and higher-quality communication, which results in more support, resources, and even responsibility. Out-group membership means that an employee is not in the supervisor's inner circle and has lower-quality communication exchanges, resulting in less support, resources, and responsibilities. Quite a bit of research on this topic shows that members of the in-group often receive greater benefits than those of the out-group. Scholars recommend that managers work to include all their employees in the in-group and to promote equality among employees to reduce the perception that they show favoritism in distributing resources. The stronger, more positive the superior–subordinate relationship, the higher the performance and innovation levels among employees. Additionally, these relationships likely motivate employees to go above and beyond their role responsibilities for the organization.[2]

Same-Status Relationships

Same-status relationships include a wide variety of people in the organization, specifically at the same level of power and authority within or outside an employee's department or work group. These types of

©Rawpixel/Shutterstock.com

relationships provide a wide range of support, ranging from what Kram and Isabella describe as informational, collegial, and special peers.[3] **Informational peers** are coworkers with whom we primarily share information about work, whereas **collegial peers** are coworkers with whom we discuss work-related topics as well as family and personal issues. Finally, **special peers** are considered the most intimate peers with whom we share personal information and from whom we receive emotional and social support. Smooth working relationships with coworkers provide us many benefits, including an ability to complete our work efficiently and at higher quality levels. They also provide us with social support to cope with burnout and workplace stressors. Friendship enhances our interest and motivation at work and can help us to identify more with our organizations. After all, organizations are made up of people, so forming meaningful relationships can translate into meaningful work. A study by Bridge and Baxter[4] found that workplace friends decrease tension and increase cohesion, especially when employees face role conflicts. Of course, not all same-status relationships are classified as friendships, but cultivating strong same-status ties is important for organizational satisfaction, productivity, and commitment.

Learning specific skills such as how to negotiate conflict and offer constructive feedback are important ways to build positive working relationships with employees of higher or equal status. The following sections focus on these skills and ways you can frame your messages to maximize success.

Informational peer: Coworker with whom we primarily share information about work.

Collegial peer: Coworker with whom we discuss work-related topics as well as family and personal issues.

Special peer: Coworker who is considered the most intimate peer with whom we share personal information and from whom we receive emotional and social support.

Workplace friends decrease tension and increase cohesion.

© racorn/Shutterstock.com

The previous sections stressed the positive outcomes of strong organizational relationships, but there is growing research on the effects of dysfunctional relationships in the workplace. These relationships include incivility, emotional abuse, and bullying behaviors. The following excerpt written by Dr. Pamela Lutgen-Sandvik describes the prevalence and harmful nature of workplace bullying. For a full transcript of the story go to: http://www.communicationcurrents.com/index.asp?bid=15&issuepage=8

Workplace Bullying

Adult bullying at work is a shocking, terrifying, and at times shattering experience. What's more, bullying appears to be quite common, as one in ten U.S. workers report feeling bullied at work, and one in four report working in extremely hostile environments. Workplace bullying is repetitive, enduring abuse that escalates over time and results in serious harm to those targeted, to witnessing coworkers, and to the organizations that allow it to persist. Bullying runs the gamut of hostile communication and behavior and can consist of excluding and ignoring certain workers, throwing things and destroying work, public humiliation and embarrassment, screaming and swearing, and occasionally even physical assault. What makes workplace bullying so harmful is its persistent nature. Exposed workers report that bullying goes on and on, lasting for months and—in many cases—even years.[5]

DEALING WITH CONFLICT

Conflict is an inevitable part of life, especially work life, so learning how to deal with difficult people and situations is critical to maintaining relationships and being successful. In organizations conflicts arise over many different issues, including personal differences, budgets, resources, office space, methods, procedures, and policies. At the root of most conflict is the idea that we have differing goals and often different styles and values from other people. Learning your own tendencies in dealing with conflict and knowing the style of others is critical to managing situations. This next section reviews the basic conflict management styles with a focus on the pros and cons to each style.

Conflict, broadly defined, describes the verbalized tension that occurs between two or more people with differing goals or wants. Conflict is often characterized in terms of wins and losses, but you should examine these styles beyond the terms of a scoreboard because what might appear as a win or a loss in reality might not be successful or unsuccessful, depending on different situations. Five conflict styles are used based on different situations: avoiding, accommodating, competing, compromising, and collaborating. These styles were developed by Killman and Thomas,[6] who categorized a person's orientation to conflict based on their concern for people and their concern for task.

Conflict: The verbalized tension occurring between two or more people with differing goals or wants.

© bikeriderlondon/Shutterstock.com

Avoiding

The **avoiding** strategy is often referred to as the withdrawing style because instead of dealing with conflict directly, a person will avoid it altogether. The outcome of avoiding or withdrawing is that neither person gets what they want. The person who engages in an avoidance strategy either gives up their desires or they meet their desires by failing to engage in the conflict to begin with. Avoidance can be a sufficient strategy if the issue is not important or if engaging in the conflict would be detrimental to the relationship or if we could hurt someone by pursuing the conflict. The downside of overreliance on this strategy is that the person using avoidance will not have their needs met and the conflict may never be resolved. This can wear on a relationship over time. Many times people engage in rather bizarre behavior when avoiding conflict, such as reducing eye contact, ignoring phone calls, or going out of their way when walking to avoid crossing paths with someone. As you can see, these tactics do not facilitate solutions and more than likely postpone them.

In organizations conflicts arise over many different issues.

Avoiding:
Withdrawing from conflict resulting in neither party gaining what they want.

Accommodating

When we have a strong preference about something such as a policy or proposal, but instead decide to let the other person have their way, we are **accommodating**. In this situation, we don't withdraw from the conflict altogether, but we work at smoothing things over to allow the other person to get what they want. Smoothing is another term used to describe this conflict approach. Accommodating is a skillful tool when the other party is really passionate about a specific course of action and you do not feel as strongly. However, accommodating can be detrimental when you always use this specific strategy. In the workplace people may perceive you as lacking initiative, especially if you continually give up your power to persuade on courses of action by always allowing someone else to get their way. Always being accommodating can make you feel like a doormat.

Accommodating: Smoothing over conflict by allowing the other person to get what they want.

Competing

The word *competition* evokes a sense of winning and championship over another person, and that is exactly what this conflict strategy describes. When we **compete** with others in conflict, we seek to persuade others that our courses of action or desires are supported over another person's or another group's. When one person "wins" a conflict, then the other party loses. There are times in organizations where this is a highly valued skill, especially when negotiating for new business. Sometimes, organizations themselves set individuals and groups up to compete for resources, which is not always the best course of action for promoting strong interpersonal relationships. Losers may come out disappointed and hurt, which affects morale. If your primary style is to compete, you need to analyze each situation to see if the outcome is really worth potentially damaging relationships.

Compete: When one person "wins" a conflict, and the other party loses.

Compromise

Compromise is a useful tool because it allows both parties to gain a solution by each sacrificing a part of what they want. Although something must be given up, a reasonable solution can be arranged that makes both parties happy. Compromise is probably one of the more common ways of negotiating conflict. In the workplace, overreliance on this conflict strategy can promote more strategic bargaining from both parties. Situations can be manipulated in that if you know going in that you will have to give something up, you may fight to include something that's not all that important so that you can show a good faith effort at compromising by

Compromise: A conflict strategy that allows both parties to gain a solution by each sacrificing a part of what they want.

giving up this item later. It can result in a much more strategic conflict resolution than necessary. On the other hand, there are positive outcomes of compromise because everyone gets a little bit of what they want.

Collaboration

Ideally, when parties **collaborate**, they both come out with all their goals met. Perhaps, their goals are not met in the way they initially intended, but as two opposing groups or people collaborate, they can actually come up with joint solutions that meet all the needs, goals, or demands of the situation. Although collaboration is thought to be one of the healthiest conflict management approaches, it is not always possible or optimal in all situations, depending on money, relationships, and time pressure. Collaboration is more time consuming than other conflict approaches because it requires consensus and careful negotiation.

Collaborate: When two parties work together to develop a joint solution that meets all the needs, goals, or demands of the situation.

Negotiation

Regardless of the status of the other person, specific interpersonal skills are critical to smooth interpersonal relations. First, we must understand

Why is collaboration a useful tool in conflict?

© Pressmaster/Shutterstock.com

how to negotiate and deal with potential conflict. As a student of communication, you should take the time to assess the motivations and the communication styles of others, as this tells you a lot about which communication strategies will be most effective in dealing with others and in making sure both parties are able to have their goals and needs met. **Negotiation** is a means to reach mutual agreement through communication.[7]

According to Teresa Smith, business professor at the University of South Carolina, Sumpter, and organizational consultant, most organizational members make six common mistakes when negotiating.[8] They negotiate emotionally, take it personally, fail to ask for what they want, accept "no" too quickly, and lack knowledge and flexibility. To avoid these pitfalls, she recommends the following strategies:

1. Decide what you want.
2. Understand the other side's bargaining style.
3. Analyze the situation.
4. Structure the situation to your advantage.
5. Display confidence.

Any time you go into a negotiation, you need to have a goal in mind and know what you are willing to accept as an outcome. Typically, this means you should prepare to ask for something more than you are willing to settle for and then offer compromise solutions that move you closer to your desired goal. You also have to go into the situation knowing whom you're dealing with. Knowing a person's basic approach to conflict and negotiation helps you to plan your communication strategies accordingly. For example, if you know that your supervisor or another department manager hates small talk and likes to cut to the chase, then be prepared for that scenario. Sometimes the person will allow you to make your case, but other times they will want to begin by asking questions. Knowing what to anticipate from the other person helps you to construct the most persuasive arguments. This also suggests that you must be able to demonstrate your knowledge of the issue and to address different perspectives. Communicating in an informed, assertive way builds your competence and confidence and makes a positive outcome more likely. Arguing for your position takes persuasive skill, which requires practice. This does not come naturally for very many people, so it is a great idea to practice the negotiation with a colleague or family member.

Research suggests that when relationships are a priority in negotiation, higher relational capital can be an end result, even if the most economically

Negotiation: A means to reach mutual agreement through communication.

feasible solution is not reached.[9] Communication researchers also find that when employees perceive an open, task-oriented relationship with supervisors, they feel more confident in their ability to negotiate their work roles, resulting in higher job satisfaction and a reduction in role conflict.[10]

Negotiating is often affiliated with the concept of interpersonal persuasion or your ability to persuade others to hold a certain belief or take a specific action. Gaining compliance from others is an important skill. Another form of compliance gaining through the use of interpersonal persuasion is offering constructive feedback in an effort to get coworkers or supervisors to comply with your requests. More than likely, negotiating with supervisors and coworkers will involve constructive feedback. Employees need to determine specific ways to offer and receive constructive and sometimes not so constructive criticism as a natural part of work life, whether it is in negotiating, working in groups, or going through the performance appraisal process. The following section provides important advice for competently communicating constructive feedback.

Negotiating with supervisors and coworkers usually involves constructive feedback.

© imtmphoto/Shutterstock.com

GIVING CONSTRUCTIVE FEEDBACK

Although frequently termed constructive *criticism*, **constructive feedback** constitutes communication intended to motivate others to change a process, procedure, or even a belief. Constructive feedback need not be critical in a negative sense, but can focus specifically on helping others grow in their organizational roles or correct a process or procedure that is not leading to success for the individual or the organization. The ability to provide constructive feedback is an important skill in organizations.

Dealing with conflict or providing constructive criticism is tricky business. It is easy to offend someone or to escalate the conflict by using the wrong words or language. You can assert yourself and/or use effective communication by using "I" language instead if "You" language. "You" language places the blame on someone else. In fact, many people interpret "You" language as accusatory and then they become defensive in response.

Some examples of "You" language are:
- "You're always late for meetings. It is disruptive to everyone else."
- "Your report isn't done correctly. You'll have to do it over."
- "You made a stupid remark in today's staff meeting."

Can you see that these three statements are not examples of effective communication? Each statement is aggressive, offers no constructive criticism or helpful advice, and places the blame on the other person.

"I" language is also descriptive language. "I" language focuses on the speaker instead of on the other person. See these two examples of "I" language:
- "I need to emphasize that our weekly meetings begin promptly at 8 a.m. Everyone needs to be here on time."
- "I feel that your report contains some errors that will keep it from being taken seriously. Let's go over it together and edit it for mistakes."

Start out simply. Instead of saying to someone, "You are wrong about that issue," say instead, "I don't agree with your views on that issue." The other person still holds the same view, and you still disagree, but you are not accusing that person of being wrong. It is fine to disagree. You each are left with your own opinion and your self-worth.

Developing constructive messages takes care, planning, and empathy. Many situational factors come into play such as the nature of the problem as well as the personalities involved, but the following guidelines can be used in a variety of circumstances.

- **Prepare a structure for your approach.**

  If you are engaging in a formal feedback session such as a performance appraisal, make sure you prepare a structured approach for the process. This might involve forms that you and the other person prepare, as well as outlets for responding, especially in the case of a disagreement.

- **Be specific in describing the problem or behavior, including consequences.**

  When communicating with someone about a specific issue such as a mistake in a procedure or a personnel issue such as tardiness, be direct in delivering the message and be sure to provide examples of the behavior as well as the impact it has on other people or the business in general. Avoid directing the critique at the person, and instead describe the behavior. You can still promote a strong interpersonal relationship while also being direct. A study by Asmub[11] found that when supervisors avoid presenting constructive feedback as socially problematic, they are better able to communicate the issues directly and allow for more positive interaction with the other person.

- **Allow for two-way communication.**

  Competently and carefully resolving conflict involves two-way communication in which both parties are able to discuss the issue openly. How the recipient receives the feedback is often connected to how the supervisor feels about the social implications of delivering criticism. According to Asmub an "interview preparation form can be designed in a way that helps the supervisor produce negative feedback in an unproblematic way" (p. 425). This can be done by allowing both the supervisor and the employee to write down criticism prior to meeting.

- **Focus on solutions.**

  Another important element of providing constructive feedback is to work with the other employee on solutions for the problem. Many times feedback takes the form of growth feedback, in other words, a discussion of specific mechanisms or procedures can be developed to assist the employee and the organization to grow and improve. This also allows for two-way communication and becomes a negotiation of sorts geared toward growth, not necessarily correction. By focusing on solutions, all parties will feel empowered to resolve the issues and good will results.

- **Be concrete about expectations and goals.**

  Once solutions are developed, consider setting goals, time frames, and expectations about when the issue will be revisited. Formal performance interviews allow for scheduled follow-ups, but there are less formal strategies such as adding deadlines to joint calendars or planning to touch base with someone via e-mail.

Successfully delivering feedback is an important skill that requires a high degree of consideration in terms of how to construct the best messages to gain compliance. Strong interpersonal relationships and negotiation skills go a long way toward facilitating growth. Employees and supervisors should be vigilant at constructing supportive messages that help to create a positive work climate where all individuals strive to do their best work for the organization and for one another. The next section of this chapter provides specific types of messages you can use to create positive relational climates.

Supportive messages create a positive work environment where everyone strives to do their best.

© wavebreakmedia/Shutterstock.com

Receiving Constructive Criticism[12]

Receivers, too, must play a complementary role to the critic for criticism to be optimally useful. Receivers must resist being dogmatic, rigid, or overly ego involved with their work. Dogmatism includes characteristics of stubbornness and superiority. Rigidness is manifested by an unwillingness to change, adapt, or embrace flexibility. Superiority is seen when others' judgments are ignored, dismissed, or evaded based on the receiver's assumption that the person whose work is being critiqued knows better than any critic(s).

Too often, people instantly reject an idea, phrasing, or strategy without truly listening attentively to the entire comment. Sometimes, critical receivers hear what they want to hear or what they expect to hear, rather than what was, in fact, said. This is why tone and perceived critical motive are crucial: to allow greater opportunity to calmly listen to criticism.

Sometimes critical discourse results in statements like: "This is not what I want to do" when offered suggestions. All suggestions do not have to be followed; however, when the critic is a thoughtful, representative member of your eventual audience, it is wise to give added weight to implicit messages that your premise, intention, or strategy may be flawed. Remember, your work needs to be audience centered, and what you want to do or how you plan to do it will be ineffective if they are not consistent with audience needs, expectations, and abilities.

If one asks for criticism, that request needs to be honestly sought and graciously received. Receivers are never obliged to alter their beliefs, values, or behaviors; criticism is to be offered, not forced on receivers. Receivers, like critics, need to pay attention to the tone, timing, and context of the critical act.

Constructive criticism, in its best sense, is a way to solicit and provide others with measures of success, with ways to improve on past or future performances, and with affirmation, support, and encouragement. Quality constructive criticism implicitly recognizes worth in receivers' work; it also builds a positive goodwill bond when improvement assistance and support are offered; and it adds to performers' credibility by demonstrating willingness to adapt, to be flexible, and to be concerned with audience expectations and needs.

Criticism is vital to build a reciprocal, symbiotic, and respectful community. Critics need to be honest, direct, and civil; receivers need to be flexible, adaptable, and audience centered. When these qualities are present, idea sharing is indeed pleasurable and utilitarian.

From *College Student Journal*, 34(3), 2000. Reprinted by permission of the author, Ken Petress.

DEVELOPING SUPPORTIVE COMMUNICATION CLIMATES

Being a savvy negotiator and a skilled giver and receiver of constructive feedback are key elements in maintaining positive communication climates. Whereas an organizational climate is made up of many factors, it is simply the way things feel in an organization. Is your workplace welcoming and friendly, or formal and strict, or hostile and paranoid? Climate quite literally relates to the temperature and feel of a workplace, and it is said to be a shared perception by most people in the organization. In addition to organizational climates, each relationship also has a climate that can be positive or negative. The positive and negative nature of a climate is determined by the types of messages exchanged. In 1961, Gibb developed categories describing supportive and defensive organizational communication climates.[13]

Supportive climates are marked by descriptive, problem-focused, spontaneous, empathetic, equal, and provisional types of messages. On the other side of the spectrum, *defensive climates* are marked by messages that are evaluative, controlling, strategic, neutral, superior, and certain. Read the following descriptions for examples of each.

Descriptive Messages

Descriptive messages focus on describing issues that have occurred as opposed to stating an evaluation. Consider how this might fit within the relationship of a student and teacher. A teacher who uses descriptive communication when grading a paper will offer a student specific, constructive feedback on problems identified, whereas a teacher who uses evaluative communication might simply state, "This is poor work" or "Wrong answer." Clearly, describing the problem is more helpful for communicating areas for improvement.

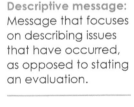

Organizational climate: Describes the way the communication environment feels in an organization.

Descriptive message: Message that focuses on describing issues that have occurred, as opposed to stating an evaluation.

Supportive Messages	Defensive Messages
Descriptive Consider making this report more formal by adding titles and section headings.	Evaluative This report reflects badly on you. You need to work on being more professional in your writing.
Problem Focused The deadline for this report has just been moved up to the end of the workday today, would you mind clearing your schedule to assist me?	Controlling Clear your schedule today, we have a new deadline that you need to meet.
Spontaneous We are sponsoring a table at the health fair this Saturday. Are you available to staff the table for a couple of hours?	Strategic Are you busy on Saturday?
Empathetic I understand why you feel frustrated when Sheila constantly complains about how much work she's doing, as if you have nothing to do.	Neutral Oh well, some people are more attention starved than others. That's life.
Equality You have great ideas for the marketing plan. Do you mind sharing them with the committee?	Superior Don't bother making suggestions for the marketing plan, the committee has a lot of training and it's really their project to be concerned with.
Provisional When we worked on this project three years ago, the vice president never approved our final draft.	Certain The vice president did not approve of our revision to the project.

Problem-Focused Messages

Second, positive communication climates are marked by **problem-focused messages**, as opposed to control-focused ones. Posing requests in a problem-focused way makes it clear to the other person that there is an issue that needs a resolution. Control messages serve to command others to act. If a supervisor needs assistance with a project, it is much more competent to say, "I have a deadline coming up on the expansion proposal, could you assist me?" as opposed to "You will help with this project, ASAP." Or, when a manager develops and distributes a new policy, it is more problem focused to provide a rationale and explain the problems it addresses. A control message would stipulate that the new policy must be followed, no questions asked.

Problem-focused message: Message that poses a request by focusing on how to solve problems together, as opposed to a message that communicates control over another person.

Why should you use a descriptive message rather than an evaluation of the problem?

© Jeanette Dietl/Shutterstock.com

Spontaneous Messages

Spontaneous communication: Communicating our thoughts and motivations in a way that indicates sincerity and objectivity and does not hide agendas.

Another interesting quality of supportive messages includes spontaneous communication as opposed to strategic communication. When we communicate spontaneously we seek to convey our thoughts and messages in a way that indicates sincerity and objectivity. When we plan messages in advance in an effort to manipulate others or when we carry hidden agendas, we speak in a way that intends to hide our motive. Many times, others will become suspicious of these messages and react negatively. You may experience this bluntly when a telemarketer calls you and asks, "How are you doing today?" when you know that there is another reason for the call. Another example is when a coworker asks if you will attend a meeting in his/her place, knowing that the meeting will be long and boring. Once you have experienced the true intention of the other person, you are likely to mistrust future requests. This is considered a very indirect form of communication.

Empathetic Messages

Empathetic message: Communicating in a way that identifies with others on an emotional level.

The fourth dimension of climate is communicating empathy as opposed to being neutral. Empathy is a very powerful skill that involves identifying with others on an emotional level. It is a way that we express caring for others and is a sign of our ability to see issues and events from other people's perspectives. When we remain neutral to certain topics or individuals, we are sending a message that we are indifferent to the needs of the other person. Consider the response you get from a coworker when you express frustration about having to work late for three days in a row. An empathetic response might sound something like this, "I know it's really difficult for you and your family when you have to work overtime" as opposed to a more neutral response such as, "Today's organizations expect employees to do what it takes. You win some, you lose some." Clearly, empathetic responses recognize the emotion and difficulty of a person's situation, whereas the neutral response does not tailor the message to the concerns of the coworker.

Messages of Equality

Gibb's next dimension is that of equality versus superiority. Treating others with equality is evidenced in the messages you receive from others. Speaking to others as equals involves recognizing the needs and rights of others. Speaking with an air of superiority sends the message that you are better than or more powerful than others. Even when employees do have more positional power and authority than others in the organization, it is not a license to treat others as such. Imagine that your boss is offering a critique of your work saying, "I know you thought your proposal was on track, but I've been here a lot longer than you, and it is not up to par." This type of message conveys a sense that one person is superior to another. A different way to frame this message in a way that communicates equality might sound like, "Your proposal is a great start, but there are a few suggestions I have that would appeal to the board, would you like to meet to work on this together?" This message conveys the value and worth of the other person while being direct in explaining that improvements could be made.

Message of equality: Message that recognizes the needs and rights of others.

Provisional Messages

Gibb's final category for supportive and defensive messages includes speaking provisionally as opposed to with certainty. So many topics in life and business are uncertain, so it makes sense that we would communicate messages in a way that is provisional, or that allows for alternative meanings. When we speak provisionally, we add on a provision or statement that says our opinion may not always be correct. Provisional tags we place on statements include, "As I recall" or "Last year" or "When we last spoke." When people speak with absolute certainty, they essentially claim to know all things, even when they are making an educated guess or an assumption. Phrases that communicate certainty send the message that you are right while others are wrong. For example, if a coworker says, "Jack is not in favor of your proposal,"

Provisional message: Message that acts as a provision or statement indicating that there are multiple meanings or that our assessment of a situation may not always be correct.

they sound absolutely certain of Jack's position. However, knowing another person's position is not always an easy thing to ascertain. A more appropriate, provisional statement might sound like this, "The last time I spoke with Jack about your proposal he raised several concerns" or "Jack may not like some of your options, but he's been known to change his mind."

By focusing on supportive messages, employees and managers work together in creating a positive climate. Positive climates focus not only on achieving goals but also on preserving relationships and making the workplace a meaningful place to spend your time.

CONCLUSION

This chapter focuses on a variety of interpersonal communication issues ranging from the types of relationships we have at work to specific ways we can navigate the interpersonal terrain through competent conflict negotiation, skillful use of constructive feedback, and genuine use of supportive messages. As discussed at the beginning of this chapter, Cora Sims has some food for thought as she debates how to develop a stronger relationship with her manager, while also maintaining strong relationships with her coworkers as they face severe budget cuts. Based on LMX theory, Cora needs to find ways to improve her communication and connections with her boss so that she can emerge as a member of his in-group. Doing so will allow her more input and

Giving Praise

Praise can be a powerful tool for motivating employees and coworkers and can go a long way toward creating positive communication climates. The following types of praise are described by Dr. Bob Nelson, president of Nelson Motivation, Inc.[14]

1. **Personal praise** is considered by employees to be the most important type of praise. It consists of being verbally thanked one-on-one for doing good work, being specifically sought out for such praise by one's manager, or being commended for good work in front of others. The best personal praise is timely, sincere, and specific.

2. **Written praise** is the next most valued type of praise by employees. It, too, comes in several varieties, from a letter of commendation being added to an employee's personnel file to a written thank-you note. In past years, I've taken the time to write an individual letter to each of my employees, specifically listing highlights of their performance that I was proud of over the past year.

3. **Electronic praise** lets you leverage positive communication as it occurs in your daily work. In a recent online survey that I conducted, 28 percent of employees reported it is "extremely important" to them to have positive e-mail messages forwarded to them, and 65 percent said it's "extremely or very important" to be copied on positive e-mail messages.

4. **Public praise** can come in many ways. You can post positive letters from customers on a "Good News Bulletin Board" or even bring some key customers in house to acknowledge employees. Or use the company newsletter to name top performers or to thank project teams. Many companies have a year-end awards banquet to recognize individuals and groups. Bring such ceremonies alive with stories about people's successes and the obstacles that they had to overcome to achieve their goals.

5. **Indirect praise** uses any of the preceding communication when employees are not present, knowing that word will get back to them. For some employees, this form of recognition is the most credible because it is done without any return expectation.

Reprinted by permission of the Dr. Bob Nelson, author of *1001 Ways to Reward Employees*.

flexibility in how she deals with the upcoming challenges. Furthermore, she has fostered strong relationships with her coworkers as informational, collegial, and special peers due in large part to the supportive communication climates she has developed through work projects but also through social events like the company softball team. All this provides her with more negotiating power when it comes to budget cuts. By knowing the personalities of different people in the organization and having perspective on the challenges, wants, and needs of different groups, Cora can develop specific strategies that can lead to more collaborative outcomes. The importance of interpersonal relationships at work cannot be overlooked by employees or managers.

ACTIVITIES

1. Describe the types of relationships you have experienced in a previous job. Identify which of these were mixed status and same status. What benefits did you gain from these relationships? Were there any problems or disadvantages that resulted? How would you describe strong coworker and supervisor relationships?

2. In reflecting on your relationship with a past or current supervisor, would you describe yourself as being a member of the supervisor's in-group or out-group? What advantages or disadvantages did you experience based on this?

3. Identify your primary conflict management style. Do you always use this style when dealing with conflict? Under what circumstances might you consider using different approaches to managing conflict in an organization? What characteristics of a conflict situation are likely to influence the strategy you use?

4. After three rounds of successful interviews, you have just been offered a position at a prestigious accounting firm. You are aware of the salary range for the junior accountant position, but the firm's offer comes in just under the low end of the range. How might you utilize the negotiation steps outlined in the chapter to obtain a higher salary?

5. Imagine that you are a supervisor preparing to give a performance appraisal to a high-performing and a low-performing employee. Develop a structure you would follow for providing feedback. What elements of constructive feedback would you incorporate? How might you prevent the appraisal from taking a negative turn?

6. Describe your experience in a toxic or a supportive communication climate at work. What types of messages were exchanged? Identify whether these messages were supportive or defensive. Provide a specific example of a memorable defensive message and rewrite the statement as more supportive according to Gibb's categories.

REFERENCES

1 Graen, G. B., & Uhl-Bien, M. (1995). Relationship-based approach to leadership. Development of leader-member exchange (LMX) theory of leadership over 25 years: Applying a multi-level multi-domain perspective. *Leadership Quarterly, 6*, 219–247.

2 Sias, P. M. (2009). *Organizing relationships: Traditional and emerging perspectives on workplace relationships*. Thousand Oaks, CA: Sage.

3 Kram, K. K., & Isabella, L. A., (1985). Mentoring alternatives: The role of peer relationships in career development. *Academy of Management Journal, 28,* 110–132.

4 Bridge, K., & Baxter, L.A. (1992). Blended relationships: Friends as work associates. *Western Journal of Communication, 56*(3), 200–225.

5 Lutgen-Sandvik, P. (2007). How employees fight back against workplace bullying. *Communication Currents.* Retrieved from http://www.communicationcurrents.com/index.asp?bid=15&issuepage=8

6 Killman, R., & Thomas, K. (1975). Interpersonal conflict handling behavior as reflections of Jungian personality dimensions. *Psychological Reports, 37,* 971–980.

7 Downs, L. J. (2008). *Negotiation skills training*. East Peoria, IL: ASTD/Versa Press.

8 Smith, T. L. (2007, October-December). Let's make a deal: A guide to successful workplace negotiations. *Business & Economic Review*, 11–14.

9 Curhan, J. R., Neale, M. A., Ross, L., & Rosencranz-Engelmann, J. (2008). Relational accommodation in negotiation: Effects of egalitarianism and gender on economic efficiency and relational capital. *Organizational Behavior & Human Decision Processes, 107*(2), 192–205.

10 Miller, V. D., Johnson, J. R., Hart, Z., Peterson, D. L. (1999). A test of antecedents and outcomes of employee role negotiation ability. *Journal of Applied Communication Research, 27*, 24–48.

11 Asmub, B. (2008). Performance appraisal interviews: Performance organization in assessment sequences. *Journal of Business Communication, 45*(4), 408–429.

12 Petress, K. (2000). Constructive criticism: A tool for improvement. *College Student Journal, 34*(3), 475–477.

13 Gibb, J. (1961). Defensive communication. *Journal of Communication, 11,* 141–148.

14 Nelson, B. (2002). Motivation matters: Five ways to praise your employees. *Corporate Meetings & Incentives, 21*(12), 30.

chapter seven

Working in Small Groups, Team Building, and Running a Successful Meeting

After reading this chapter you will be able to:

- Define small group communication
- Know the advantages and disadvantages of working in a group
- Understand the lifecycle of groups
- Understand how individual roles function within groups
- Understand several steps involved in conducting a successful business meeting

CHAPTER OUTLINE

key words

Small group
Groupthink
Forming
Primary tension
Storming
Secondary tension
Norming
Explicit norms
Implied norms
Conformity
Group roles

Task roles
Group building and
    maintenance roles
Individual roles
Performing
Adjourning
Meeting
Scheduled gathering
Structured discussion
Designated chairperson

INTRODUCTION

Lydia Jackson works for the University of San Angelo in the admissions office and has been charged with leading a group to create a new admissions/marketing campaign designed to increase enrollment by ten percent over the next five years. While she has worked with groups in her department for years, this particular group is an ad hoc committee formed with many different people throughout the university. The committee is charged with creating a comprehensive plan including advertising material, programs, and events for increasing new student enrollment. As Lydia sits down to plan this process she considers the composition of the group. She'll need representatives from student affairs, accounting, student retention and advising, and many other areas of the university. How should she plan to convene this diverse group that will remain intact for the better part of a year? What types of activities should she plan for the first meeting? With tight schedules and large workloads, what is the best way to facilitate these meetings?

The material in this chapter will assist Lydia as she begins this process. Specifically, it will describe the advantages and disadvantages of group work, the steps of group formation, how to deal with conflict between the group members tied to their diverse perspectives, and specific steps for planning and facilitating meetings. As you read, formulate a plan for how she can successfully chair the committee.

Working in groups is not simple; it is in fact overwhelmingly complicated. The communication conundrums that groups face are many and varied. And the fact that not everyone within the group may have the same expectations of what should occur when the group gets together only adds to the confusion.

Furthermore, what specific rules govern the communication process within a group setting? What we do know comes from preconceived notions of what group behavior should be like. Making matters more complicated is the fact that the person that we expect to be the leader, the boss, the person who likely called the meeting, is no more apt to be an expert communicator than you are. Most managers are people who have worked hard to achieve technical expertise in their given field and been rewarded with a promotion. However, as a manager, their time is not likely to be spent further honing the skills that got them their promotion, but rather the managers are thrown into a new world of bringing people together, of moderating, of delivering good and bad news; in other words, they are now expected to be experts in communication, and it is a world that they are likely unprepared for.

The leader of the group is no more apt to be an expert communicator than you are.

And so the appropriate first step to understanding group work in a professional setting is to rid ourselves of the notion that this process is

© Andresr/Shutterstock.com

simple. Get rid of the idea that meetings are always efficient. Lose the belief that there will always be an agenda, and that the agenda will be followed. Not everyone is going to participate equally, and some people's contributions will not necessarily be valuable or even on topic. Because here is the truth: meetings that have clearly written agendas that are followed point by point, and allow everyone the opportunity to offer an insightful comment and provide for a group vote to approve are not only fictional but would be a tremendous waste of time.

The value of working within a group does not lie in the ability to quickly rubber-stamp an agenda, nor does the value lie in coming up with only one solution. Group work, when operating at its best, can be messy, it can be long, and it can be tedious. But it can also produce new information, improve performance, bring people together, improve cultural understanding and aid everyone involved in learning.

DEFINING AND UNDERSTANDING SMALL GROUPS

We often find ourselves communicating in groups. Although we do communicate intrapersonally (communicating with yourself) or in dyads (communicating in pairs), people are by nature social creatures. We are raised often in a family, our first groups, and then continue to join other groups as our lives progress. But to get a firmer grasp of what is meant by small group in terms of business communication, certain terms will need to be understood.

A small group is a *collection of people*, working together, *interacting* with the *interdependent* purpose of accomplishing some *common goal*. Breaking down the definition further, the following section defines several important terms: collection of people, interaction, interdependent, and common goal.

Small group: A collection of people, working together, interacting with the interdependent purpose of accomplishing some common goal.

Collection of People

Small groups require, at a minimum, three people. When working in dyads, the communication process is very different. While interacting with only one other person, the communication process, although not easy, is greatly simplified. Breaks in the conversation naturally occur. Turn-taking only makes sense. But a third person will alter the dynamic greatly. Roles are suddenly redefined. What would once be a cordial

A third person changes
the communication
process dramatically.

conversation, even if the conversation is an attempt to persuade, can now be decided with a majority vote. The third person acts as an intermediary, both parties speaking to him or her as they judge the situation. The third person takes sides immediately, making the conversation a bullying session as opposed to an honest contest.

The more people who are in the group, the more the dynamics change. Three is the minimum number, and although there is no hard and fast rule for a maximum number of people in a small group, there seems to be a consensus that five to seven people make the ideal small-group size. The odd number is preferable, so that, like the Supreme Court, ties can be avoided if a vote is required. If the number of members is smaller than five, the group may not have the diversity needed to produce new and different ideas, perhaps even leading to **groupthink**. If the group is larger than seven, then there are some new dangers to face: (a) Members may feel that their role is reduced to the point that their presence is useless. They may become disenfranchised with the group, and if this happens, their presence may serve as a distraction rather than a contributing force. (b) The group may splinter—not just into two different factions but several.

© Matthias G. Ziegler/Shutterstock.com

Multiple competing factions within the same group will only make it harder for the group to operate efficiently and effectively.

Now, five or seven is not a hard and fast rule. Clearly there are small groups out there of more than five to seven people such as PTA groups or even unions. But five to seven people are typically enough to offer diversity while still encouraging all involved to participate fully.

Interaction

Interaction between group members is key to any group's success. As discussed in Chapter 6, creating an open and supportive communication climate is essential to high functioning group interaction. Whether the group is meeting in person, via phone, e-mail, or Skyping, the way group members communicate with one another, verbally and nonverbally, will define the relationships within the group. Traditionally group roles have been defined in large part by their face-to-face interaction. Through this interaction, roles will be defined and behaviors will be accepted or rejected. The close contact also allows for nonverbal signals to be more easily interpreted. However, as technology improves, the interaction between members will become more delicate. If not meeting face-to-face, the challenge in interpreting silence and tone becomes even more important. If communicating via e-mail or text message, as is becoming more and more common, you will need to be aware that you often forfeit any intricacy in the language. As Mehrabian pointed out in *Silent Messages*,[1] anywhere from 65 to 93 percent of all communication is done through

Typically five to seven members make the ideal small-group size.

© Monkey Business Images/Shutterstock.com

nonverbals. If you were joking in a very sarcastic manner during a meeting that the latest idea that your colleague suggested was a really "great idea," you might all have a good laugh. However, if this same message were typed and sent to a group via e-mail, that "great idea," which is really a very poor one, might be seen to be gathering support. These contextual elements have a critical impact on group interaction, so the development of appropriate and effective messages that are appropriate for face-to-face and computer-mediated channels are critical to group success.

Interdependence

It is a cliché to say that a team is only as strong as its weakest link, but that does not make it any less true. Members of good teams and strong groups rely on each other, knowing that if one person is to fail, it is likely that the entire group will fail as well. To use a sports metaphor, if the offensive line fails to block for the quarterback, it does not matter how talented the quarterback is, for he will soon be crushed by an onslaught of defenders. To use an academic metaphor, if a group of five students decides to get together to plan a study session before a final and divides a ten-chapter textbook into five sections so that each member will have two chapters

If any member of the small group fails to do his or her job, everyone's grade will suffer.

© Ammentorp Photography/Shutterstock.com

SECTION 3: Social, Group, and Professional Competencies

to read and report back on, only to have one member of the study group come to the meeting unprepared, the group will be unable to answer any of the questions concerning those two chapters. That means, at best, that the A that the group could have gotten is now likely to be a B−. If two people do not pull their weight, the best that a group can expect to achieve on the final is a D−. Finally, in a business setting, if your small group has put together a presentation for potential investors and one of your members has failed to create the PowerPoint presentation as assigned, your small band of venture capitalists is not likely to get your funding, and the great idea that you had will go undeveloped.

The point of all of these examples listed is that all members of the group are interdependent. They rely on each other for success. Working in groups is an inevitable part of worklife. This may not always be the popular sentiment, for many people feel that they work best alone. But this is unrealistic in any walk of life. One person cannot possibly play 11 positions on the football field or thoroughly read 10 textbook chapters in a night and hope to comprehend all of the information presented, or put together a comprehensive presentation for a group of investors as well as any group possibly could.

Common Goal

The previous examples also serve to illustrate another feature of group work. Each group has a common goal that they are trying to achieve. The football team is aiming to score a touchdown and win the game. The study group wants to pass the final; not just pass but excel. The entrepreneurs need to secure investors to begin working in earnest on their dream. Every group that you are in will have a common goal.

It is appropriate to note at this point that each of these groups is working toward achieving this common goal. There are lots of collections of people who just get together with no greater purpose than being together. These people may be your friends or your family, which in a different textbook may constitute a group. However, within a business context, the group should be working toward achieving a specific goal.

Now depending on the type of group, you may or may not have the freedom to choose your own goals. As students you will often be assigned to work in groups with little to no say about the actual activity. However, other times you will participate in a small group and have much control over the aims of the group. For example, if you decide to form a committee to fundraise for any number of activities, you are in charge of your own destiny.

Whether your group's goal was assigned or of your own choosing, the goal is perhaps the critical feature of group work. For without a goal, your group will languish in futility. Having a clear goal that is understood by all members will be crucial to group success. A goal will serve to set measurable bars of success and motivate members to attain that success. If the goal is not understood by all, then it will be even easier for the group to lose focus and get off task.

ADVANTAGES AND DISADVANTAGES OF GROUP WORK

Working in teams or groups can be a double-edged sword. Many of you, no doubt, shudder at the thought of working in teams. These fears do not automatically leave once you have left school. The same fears exist in business settings. You may be worried that members of your team will not fulfill their responsibilities, leaving the lion's share of a project for you. You may worry that your contribution will go unnoticed, lost in a sea of other paperwork. You may worry that your voice will be drowned out by overeager yet underqualified cohorts. However, when a group works together efficiently and effectively, the advantages will greatly outweigh any potential setbacks that you and your team may encounter.

Advantages of Group Work

GROUP PRODUCTION

There is a reason why so many people work in groups. And the reason is simple. As a group, we can accomplish far more than any one individual can. Tedious work (data entry, etc.) can be handled by a group minimizing the amount, time, and effort that any one person has to put in. Groups trying to do creative work (problem solving, etc.) are better off than any individual, for they have each other to bounce ideas off of and people to double-, triple-, and quadruple-check their work. Think of any television show that is airing today, even reality television shows. All of them have a team of creative writers so that no one person will have the entire burden of creating a new show by themselves every week.

© Rawpixel/Shutterstock.com

Even though groups can have high levels of productivity, not all tasks are best handled by a group. After all, a smart and capable person who is qualified may not need others to perform a simple task. Other people might actually be a hindrance if the job is to write a memo or answer a relatively simple question. If one person already knows the answer, calling together a committee to attempt to answer that same question would only serve as a waste of resources. However, more often than not, groups will have an advantage over the individual.

Why is it advantageous to do creative work within a group?

Team and Individual Satisfaction

Working in groups has many benefits associated with it, and not all of them have to do with productivity. Group work is just as often a chance to do some social networking. The group structure provides an opportunity for members to meet not only at school or in the office, but also outside these formal environments. The more opportunity the group has to become friendly with one another and the more chances they have to chat and communicate with one another, the more likely they are to profess themselves satisfied with the group. The more satisfied with the group, it logically follows that the members will be more satisfied with their overall work experience.

DECISION-MAKING AND COMMITMENT

A small group is ideally constructed for decision-making. This may seem counterintuitive, as one person can easily make a decision, and adding more people to that mix will inevitably complicate the process. However, complication in this instance may turn out to be a good thing. Decision-making needs to be a collaborative process. When several people examine the situation, they may spot wrinkles that the original "decider" did not. However, if the group, after serious consideration of the problem, can come up with no better solution, you now have something more than you would have had originally. If only the "decider" reaches one conclusion, other group members may feel resentment at not being included in the decision-making process. When all members are allowed to participate and reach a joint decision, they are far more likely to be committed to the decision being made and more willing to support the decision if it later comes under fire.

How do other members feel if a lone "decider" determines the outcome?

OWNERSHIP

The concept of ownership is intertwined with individual satisfaction and commitment. Ownership is the idea that people will have some control

© Monkey Business Images/Shutterstock.com

over their product. This is easily seen in an artist's work—a person who is allowed to create or express whatever he or she chooses. The business world conversely can be a place where little freedom is offered. It would not be unusual for an employee to be given an assignment in which they have little choice in how or why they are doing what they are doing. However, small groups can be a place where this sort of control is given to employees. When the group members are allowed to make their own decisions and exercise some control over what they are doing, they will feel a greater commitment to the product. That greater commitment can lead to a greater sense of satisfaction within the workplace.

SUCCESS

Success breeds success. If group members think of themselves as successful, as having achieved some intermediate or long-term goals that they have set for themselves, they will become more satisfied and cohesive than they previously were. Even members who have actually had little to do with the success the group has achieved will still feel that same sense of satisfaction. Think of the backup center on last year's championship football team. This is a person who never saw the field and yet still ends up with the championship ring and a head covered with Gatorade and champagne. That person is now glowing in the warmth of victory and will have a renewed commitment to coming back the following year. Furthermore, others will wish to join the group because of the success, and those who are in the group will become more committed. In simplest terms, the more success the group has, the more committed to success the group will become.

Disadvantages of Group Work

THE RINGLEMANN EFFECT

Although the overall production will be greater for a group than it would be for the individual, studies indicate that the productivity level for each individual group member will be lessened by the mere fact that they are working in groups. This is known as the *Ringlemann effect* or as social loafing. Group members, knowing that they have others to rely on to pick up the slack, might be less motivated.[2]

Ringlemann noticed this phenomenon and decided to test it using experimental methods. He had subjects pull a rope individually to see how hard they pulled. He then teamed up one subject with another and then another and so on. He found that when a person is working alone, they obviously pulled the rope using 100 percent of their maximum force. If a second person is added, each person pulled with an average of 93 percent of their maximum force. Add a third person to the group, and the effort drops to an average of 85 percent of their maximum force. If you add as many as eight people, each person exerted on average 49 percent of their maximum effort. Furthermore, the eight people demonstrated no more productivity than seven people. These results have been attributed to difficulties in both coordination between members and motivation among individuals.

Despite the drop in individual member productivity, the team is still more productive than the individual. Even if members are not giving their best efforts, more people working together are able to achieve more. The key to overcoming the Ringlemann effect is to be constantly vigilant. Be on guard. All members will need constant encouragement from all other members. This does not have to be destructive, harassing, never-ceasing criticism. If the group is going to run efficiently, respectful reminders, deadlines, and constructive feedback will need to be put in place.

TIME

Working in groups will never be an easy thing. If you are still in school and are assigned group work, finding the time to get together outside class may be next to impossible, given the amount of outside responsibilities that many students are now shouldering. If you are working in a professional environment and are given the time to conduct meetings, that is no guarantee that your time will be well spent. A 2005 survey done by Microsoft found that employees spend on average 5.6 hours per week, or 14 percent of the workweek, in meetings.[4] Of the employees surveyed, 71 percent said their time spent in those meetings was wasted. Furthermore, 39 percent of people said that meetings were a "productivity pitfall."

Getting together as a group is going to take time, and you are not always going to walk away feeling that something major has been accomplished. But this is one of the stereotypes that you are going to need to get away from if your group work is going to be successful. Time is what you need to invest for greater results in the long run. However, do not expect every meeting to be dynamic and fruitful.

DISHARMONY

If you are asking seven people to sit in a room and come up with solutions to complex problems that not everyone agrees on, you are going to have

Many people feel much of the time they spend in meetings is wasted.

© BlueSkyImage/Shutterstock.com

to expect some feathers to get ruffled. The group, which hopefully is invested in the product that they are creating, will disagree about the best way to get things done. What's more, you are going to want employees who will stand up and say what they believe is right. If you do have this, you need to be aware that conflict is inevitable. The key to overcoming this disharmony is to realize that just because someone does disagree with you is no reason to lose your temper and begin berating your colleagues. You will need to strive to be respectful of your group members and the different perspectives that they bring to the table. Argue points on their merit; argue tenaciously, but do not lessen yourself and your group by resorting to profanity or even worse. The ability to manage conflict and provide constructive feedback is critical for group functioning.

GROUPTHINK

Groupthink is even worse than disharmony. Groups excel because so many different perspectives come together searching for a solution to a problem. But when group members give up their unique perspective to be only one voice, it can be very problematic. This process is known as groupthink, and it can happen for a number of reasons: (a) Group members may be very intimidated by an overwhelming personality within the group. If one group member, particularly a member in a leadership role, has strong feelings regarding a particular subject, then other members may not feel comfortable standing up to the leader. However, if the group is only there to rubber-stamp the opinions of one person, the group has already lost its function. Each person must be willing to speak their mind if the group is going to operate as effectively as possible. (b) Conversely, members may feel that they have little to contribute, that they do not offer any new solutions or perspectives, and so they best serve the group by supporting the more experienced and seasoned opinions. If this happens, then no alternate perspective can or will be offered, and the group is likely to continue to make the same decisions ending with similar results. (c) It is possible, especially considering the Ringlemann effect, that members may not want to give their all to a particular project. They may view the group meeting as a chance to slack off while others do the hard work. If this is the case, then low-performing members may happily support the first solution offered.

Although presenting a unanimous front can be a powerful statement to the organization, you should be aware that if only one solution/opinion is being discussed in the group, your group is failing in its job of coming up with the best possible option/solution. Even if the solution decided on by the group is the best solution for this particular problem, how would you know that if no other solutions were discussed? It is difficult to altogether avoid the problem of groupthink, but in an effort to do so, your group may want to implement several of the following suggestions: (a) Create and follow an organized procedure that encourages all members to freely and easily participate in the decision-making process. (b) Before any decision is made, discuss the potential negative consequences of that decision. Do not just think short term but examine the long-term effects of your decision. (c) Make sure that all members who have doubts about the proposed solution have ample opportunity to express these doubts. (d) All members should be able to justify the rational reasons for taking a particular position. (e) Ask questions. Do not be afraid to delve into the reasons that people have taken a certain stance. Without questions, there will likely be no understanding of the problem or the solution.

Myths Surrounding the Small Group

To further aid you as you begin to participate within small groups, several myths should be dispelled. These are all notions that people bring with them to the process of small-group work. If you do away with some of these false premises, then you will likely be better off.

Myth 1: There Is Always One Right Answer

See if you can solve this old riddle. "A man and his son are going out for a drive when all of a sudden, another car runs a light and crashes into the man and his son. An ambulance arrives shortly, and the man and son are rushed to the hospital. The father is bruised and worried sick because his son has been knocked unconscious. When the pair reaches the hospital, the boy is wheeled into surgery. The surgeon looks down at the boy and says, 'I can't operate on this boy. He's my son.'" How is this possible? Usually the riddle is told to test how deeply entrenched our preconceived notions about gender roles are set. For the answer usually is the surgeon is the boy's mother. But why would it not be acceptable for the answer to be the surgeon is gay and the boy is his adopted son? Or perhaps the boy is his stepson, his new wife's child from a previous marriage. The latter two answers are every bit as correct as the first, and yet most people will assume that there is just one correct answer. The truth is there is not just one answer to every question. In fact, sometimes there are several options. And the more solutions your group can come up with, the more options you will have, which can never hurt you.

MYTH 2: THE SOLUTION YOU REACH MUST BE "THE BEST SOLUTION"

People often agonize over group decisions. The more people who are in the group, the more likely that the solution will have been tested and retested, poked and prodded until you as a group feel that the solution you have reached is the best solution out there. However, just because you put a great deal of effort into finding your solution does not mean that it is the best solution. If the group becomes convinced that it cannot be wrong and refuses to listen to any more suggestions, then they will have fallen into another trap. Better to think that your solution is best now but be open to more possibilities. Once you become so committed to your answer that you cannot even entertain other options you have seriously erred.

MYTH 3: YOU MUST FIND "THE ULTIMATE SOLUTION"

Somewhere between the second and fourth grades, you were asked to master your multiplication tables. And so when the teacher asked you what seven times eight was, the whole class could respond in unison, "56." And there was a right answer and a wrong answer. Later, when you got to college, your professors likely asked you to engage in critical thinking exercises—seeing if you could determine long-term consequences to your actions. Although there may not have been a perfectly clear answer at first, given time, you would reasonably determine what the correct path should be. But you will reach a point in your professional career when your group is going to be asked to solve a problem that perhaps has no good answer.

The group is going to feel pressure to come up with a solution and not just a solution but the absolute right answer. If this is the case, you are in an impossible situation because not every problem has an ultimate solution. Many times, there is no easy fix, and problems can become overwhelming. Your group may not have been given the appropriate resources (money or technology) or have enough time to really get to the depth of any problem. And yet you will still feel compelled to give an answer because that is what you were asked to do. But you need to realize that not every problem has an answer or an answer that you are capable of reaching within the parameters given. If you are forming a neighborhood watch program to combat a rise in local crime, you may have several solutions: faster police response times, neighborhood alerts, and so on. But these ideas are not new, and crime still may continue to rise. The easy solution does not exist. Your group, despite its best efforts, may simply have encountered a problem to which there is no solution.

TEAM BUILDING

Listed among the positive aspects of working in small groups is the sense of commitment and personal satisfaction that comes when the group is working effectively and efficiently. In an effort to further encourage those same behaviors, it is essential to establish some guidelines for team building. The first necessity in team building is to establish the purpose of the group. What are your team's goals? Why are you getting together to work? Depending on the nature of your problem, this will in many ways help to shape what kind of team you will be building. Is the goal to create policy? Is the goal to improve performance in one particular department? Is your goal project specific? The answer to any one of these questions will help determine which sort of team you are building.

Types of Teams

One-Time Teams

The one-time team is a unique communication experience. Without the benefit of long-term planning, the group is forced to rely on an existing power structure that may not be to everyone's liking. The group should know going into this process that not everyone will get equal time in this meeting. This is not an opportunity to get together and discuss long-term plans. This group is called together to discuss a specific issue—an

© Pressmaster/Shutterstock.com

issue that can likely be handled in a relatively short time. Given the time constraints, team members must be willing to do away with a certain amount of ceremony and speak their minds quickly.

For a one-time team, all members must be willing to reach a conclusion at the end of the meeting. The point is to reach a conclusion, and so all members of the team need to be well aware of the issues being discussed before they get to the meeting. They should all be invested in the outcome of the meeting but willing to compromise to reach a satisfactory conclusion.

Establish some guidelines for the team so it can work more effectively and efficiently.

Ad Hoc Committees

Ad hoc committees have a few things in common with the one-time team; both are coming together for the first time with no previous history, and both are there to focus on one core problem. However, unlike one-time teams, ad hoc committees have the potential benefit of long-term planning. These meetings will progress in a much calmer, slower way than one-time teams. All members will informally be tested by other members to help determine leadership, social norms, and points of procedure for future meetings.

The unique aspect of the ad hoc committee is the focus on one core problem. The problem may be so large that it takes months or even years of meetings, but once the problem is solved, or the situation is improved, the group will disband. Take, for example, the Ad Hoc Committee on an International Convention against the Reproductive Cloning of Human Beings. The General Assembly of the United Nations called together this ad hoc committee "for the purpose of considering the elaboration of an international convention against the reproductive cloning of human beings."[3] The committee formed in 2002, and it took three years of meetings and consulting before they were able to attach three Annexes to Resolution 59/280 in 2005. The resolution passed overwhelmingly and the United Nations officially discouraged its members from conducting research or funding or encouraging experimentation resulting in human cloning. Once the resolution was passed, the group disbanded.

NEGOTIATING GROUPS

Situations arise in many walks of life that require people to take contrary sides on any number of issues. To better confront these daunting situations, small groups are often formed. These groups may be a small contingent of a larger group; take for example the Teamsters Union or the United Auto Workers Union. When there is cause for negotiation, the small group responsible for the negotiation meets, even though they speak for the larger group as a whole.

Negotiating groups do not just meet in massive labor disputes. They take place often in smaller everyday situations. A pedestrian event that often requires a negotiating group is the purchase of a new car. This is a situation in which customers finds themselves faced with potentially spending thousands of dollars unnecessarily, for few people really have any idea about the value of a car, especially first-time buyers. And so customers are confronted with an array of experiences strategically designed to get them excited about a potential new vehicle, all in an effort to produce the maximum amount of profit for the dealership and commission for the salesperson. And after you smell the new car, go for a ride, and dream a little about what this car can mean to you, you will be confronted by a group of people. There will be the original salesperson, the salesperson's team leader, and a finance expert, as well as an insurance salesperson. The sales negotiating team is practiced and ready to deal.

Meanwhile, a savvy customer will perhaps feign indifference to a car they may actually be excited about, refuse to hand over the keys to their trade-in, and scoff at the first, second, or even third offer the dealer presents all in an effort to get themselves a better price. And faced with a seasoned team of salespeople, it is wise to at least consult with others who have been through the experience of buying a new car before. Bring in experts whom you trust, people to keep you sane during what could be a long negotiation.

Bear in mind that, within a negotiation session, it might appear likely that all sides are working amicably together. When studying communication, you should be aware that these negotiating sessions are fraught with misinformation and misleading nonverbal communication by both sides. Your team or group needs to be on the lookout for this and needs to remember that the goal is to get yourself or your team the best deal available.

CREATIVE TEAMS

One of the benefits of teamwork is the creative output that is often produced. "Brainstorming" sessions are a fundamental aspect of the creative process and is a term that was coined in 1953 by Alex Osborn, a partner in an advertising firm.[5] The goal of these brainstorming sessions

How is brainstorming fundamental in the creative process?

© Monkey Business Images/Shutterstock.com

was to produce as many ideas as possible. Members were encouraged not only to shout out any idea but also to add on suggestions to other group members' ideas. No idea was too radical or too impractical. No one in the group was allowed to be critical of others' ideas. The time for that would come later. The goal was to produce as much information as possible.

While in a professional setting, you will find yourself in a situation where you may have need for any one of the previously mentioned groups. And although this list of group types is not exhaustive, it should give a good overview of some of the specific challenges and problems that groups are expected to overcome. Once the group has its goal, its purpose, the group may begin to come together and go through its own lifecycle.

Phases of Small-Group Communication

Although several theories exist describing the development stages of group work, this text will primarily focus on Bruce Tuckman's "Stages of Small Group Development Revisited," which is generally well accepted and easily demonstrated.[6] According to Tuckman, a group's lifecycle will go through five distinct stages: forming, storming, norming, performing, and adjourning. These five stages are called a lifecycle because they take the group from its infancy through its death and explain what behaviors are expected at each stage in its life. The lifecycle metaphor is also apt because a group's measure of success is likely dependent on the group being able to grow into adulthood. If the group fails to reach adulthood and is stuck in its adolescent years, it is likely that the group will never achieve its primary purpose.

FORMING

The initial stage of group development, **forming**, is marked by members cautiously feeling their way into a new and potentially frightening situation. It is akin to a person sticking their toe into the water—testing the temperature before they dive into the pool. Members will have to balance individual and group goals as they meet new members. All members are likely to avoid conflict within this stage, for they do not wish to seem combative. Ernest Bormann describes primary tensions that may exist during the forming stage.[7] The **primary tensions** (which are perfectly normal) are feelings of unease as a group begins. People will "not know what to say or how to begin. The first meeting is tense and cold and must be warmed up. When groups experience primary tension, the people speak very softly; they sigh, and they are very polite" (p. 133).

Forming: The initial stage of group development, marked by apprehension by its members and an overall tension throughout the group. The group must break this tension before it can proceed.

Primary tension: Ernest Bormann's term for the feelings of unease that group members feel when they initially meet. Members are unsure of social interaction rules and so are not sure how to act when first encountering a new group.

SECTION 3: Social, Group, and Professional Competencies

Although group members may appear disinterested in the early process, this is in all likelihood a facade. Group work marks a real opportunity for most people to prove their abilities and be recognized by both their peers and superiors. But until the primary tension is broken, the group will be unable to progress. The group will need to laugh and will need to socialize. And so time spent at the beginning of the initial meeting goofing around, laughing, or participating in icebreaker activities is not time wasted but time spent building toward something better. When they are done warming up, or participating in icebreaker activities, the group should have oriented itself, have begun to think about a common goal, and be ready to get to work.

STORMING

Work will actually begin during the secondary stage of **storming**; it is then that the group will experience some discomfort because members will be asserting their personalities and trying to push their own agendas. When this happens, conflict is likely, and members' feelings might get hurt. Group members' roles will also be determined during this stage, and any push for a group goal is likely to also be a push for individual status within the group. Some groups will be eager to skip over this stage for fear of conflict; however, this would be a mistake. To avoid a passionate discussion for fear of conflict is to defeat the purpose of

Storming: The second stage of group development. It is marked by actual work beginning, members trying to assert themselves, feelings perhaps getting hurt by other members pushing specific agendas.

Time spent laughing and joking is time spent toward building a better team.

©wavebreakmedia/Shutterstock.com

Secondary tension:
Ernest Bormann's term for the struggle that group members go through while trying to find their identity within the group. As opposed to primary tensions, secondary tensions are likely to be more aggressive in nature and lead toward open hostility.

the group and to give into what Bormann calls **secondary tensions**. Secondary tensions are strains that the group experiences when members struggle in finding their role within the group, disagree about ideas, and have personality conflicts.[7] "Secondary tensions are louder than primary ones. People speak rapidly, they interrupt one another and are impatient to get to the floor and have their say; they may get up and pace the room or pound the table" (p. 135). These tensions need to be addressed and hopefully released or else the group will flounder, never progressing past the storming stage.

But conflict is important in creating an environment in which members feel comfortable expressing their opinions. This may seem counterintuitive in suggesting that conflict leads to an open environment where conversation is encouraged, but as Wheelan[8] and Wheelan and Danganan[9] explain, if a group is able to get past the conflict, they will realize that each member is more committed to the group and that just because there is a disagreement, it does not mean the group will break apart. This will create a more secure feeling, and people will know that they can honestly offer their opinion in this environment.

To overcome these tensions, members must be able to fall back on the habits and relationships created during the forming phase of group development. Laughter is a good way to break tension, and social roles enacted during the norming stage may help break the tension simply by commenting on them. If humor does not work, the group will be forced to confront the problem head on. This may mean a rational discussion during the meeting or a private discussion between the conflicting group members after the meeting.

NORMING

Norming: The third stage of group development. It is marked by the group coming together and beginning to be productive. Rules for behavior will be firmly established during this point.

"Norms are the group's rules."[10] It is during the **norming** stage that the group begins to feel comfortable working together. They have established through their interaction a set of rules that will determine how they should behave during any given situation. The group will have learned how to deal with conflict and so should feel more comfortable expressing individual opinions. The group will have learned how to reach decisions, and so voting rituals will likely have been set. If the group chooses another method of decision-making besides a voting majority, then etiquette will have been created to allow differing opinions to be heard, and all sides to be granted the opportunity to present their point of view.

Norms will govern all behavior, not just decision-making processes. That is why it is important to establish the difference between **explicit** norms and implied norms. Explicit norms are rules that have been clearly stated and/or written and are agreed on by all involved parties. These may be rules handed down by an authority figure such as your teacher saying that you are not allowed to use your cell phone during class. Or they may be rules that the group has agreed to such as the procedure for reviewing the minutes of a previous meeting. Implied norms are rules that have not been discussed or written out but are still agreed on by the group through nonverbal interaction. As these rules are unwritten and unspoken, new members are going to break them unknowingly. When this happens, conflict will arise, and the new member will be confused as to what the problem is. For example, if you find a person sitting in your seat during class, you might stare and wonder how that person could be so insensitive. Or if a student breaks the implied dress code by wearing a tuxedo or formal cocktail dress to class, you could reasonably ask what the student had planned. This uncertainty can lead to stress, anger, or even conflict.

Once the norms have been established, the group can begin to work in harmony. However, a heavy premium is going to be placed on conformity to the norms. Conformity is choosing to adhere to the already socially accepted behavior or majority behavior. In our society, conformity is expected. If you choose not to conform to the social norms, you risk being alienated by your peers. An acceptable level of nonconformity is healthy for the group.

Explicit norms:
Rules that have been clearly stated or written, and all members are expected to know them.

Implied norms:
Rules that have not been written or clearly stated, and all members are expected to know them.

Conformity:
Adherence to the socially accepted behavior rules or the majority behavior rules.

An acceptable level of nonconformity is healthy for the group.

© Frank Gaertner/Shutterstock.com

According to Dentler and Erikson[11] and Pavitt and Curtis,[12] deviant behavior by some members serves as a release for tension, a reminder of what acceptable behavior is, a basis for comparison that conforming members can be rewarded for, and last that the deviant member gives the conformists a problem to solve (p. 177).

Also, although it would be easy to assume that the group would want all members to conform to its ideals, it is in fact advantageous to have some members who are nonconformists. If all members of the group have gelled and are in constant agreement, the group will have succumbed to groupthink and will no longer be able to function effectively. Bear in mind that constant nonconformity will serve to disrupt the group, but occasional nonconformity is what every group needs. If the group is going to continue to be efficient, certain norms will need to be questioned from time to time. For example, if there is a standing weekly meeting scheduled with your group, but there has been no progress made from one week to the next, then there is no reason to have the meeting. At least one nonconformist in the group needs to have the courage to say that this is an issue.

Discussion of conformists and nonconformists transitions very naturally into a discussion of group roles in general. At this point in the group development lifecycle, social roles will have been set, and members will begin to expect certain behaviors of each other. Like an actor cast in a supporting role, no one expects that person to show up one day and play the lead.

In 1948, Kenneth D. Beene and Paul Sheats compiled a list of 25 roles that members are likely to take on when interacting in a group situation.[13] The roles have been broken down into three different categories: Task roles, which are roles that are focused on goal completion; group building and maintenance roles, which focus on interpersonal relationships and group harmony; and individual roles, which focus on personal agenda to the possible detriment of the group. **Table 7.1** provides a list of all 25 roles and a sample message that would come from each.

Bear in mind that that members of Table 7.1 are usually not relegated to only one role. A person who is an encourager can also be a gatekeeper or an information seeker. A harmonizer who often uses comedy may also be a follower when it comes to decision-making. Each of these parts has the potential to play an important role in group development, whether that role is a task role, a group building role, or an individual role. However, this list is far from exhaustive. Over the years as business has changed, so have the roles people play in small-group communication. McCann and Margerison,[14] in studying high-

Group roles: Certain behavior is expected from all group members. Once a behavior is expected from an individual member, that member has officially been assigned the role.

Task roles: A specific category of group roles that focus on the goal completion.

Group building and maintenance roles: A specific category of group roles that focuses on interpersonal relationships and group harmony.

Individual roles: A specific category of group roles that focus on personal agendas to the possible detriment of the team.

performance groups, have observed that members are often assigned roles or assume roles because they are already proficient in a certain area. For example "organizers," people who are naturally good at making plans, will work to make sure people stay on top of their deadlines. "Advisors," people good at researching, will compile information for the group and be able to disseminate that information to help direct future plans. Once roles and norms have been established, then the group may proceed to the next stage.

Table 7.1: Group Roles	
Role/Definition	**Sample Message**
1. Task Roles	
Initiator–Contributor	Constantly pushing new ideas, always looking for a new direction for the group. *"Let's examine the effects of President Obama's new public option for health care."*
Information Seeker	This person is a researcher, constantly searching for new information and better information for the group. *"Has anyone found evidence that supports our premise that is not from Wikipedia?"*
Opinion Seeker	Always seeking the opinion of other group members and checking for potential disagreements among members and looking to address them as soon as possible. *"What do you think about the direction we are going?"*
Information Giver	Perhaps not a researcher but able to synthesize information and distribute it to the group. *"Sacramento State University has increased its tuition 60 percent in the last three years."*
Elaborator	Expands on and clarifies the ideas of other members. *"I want to make sure the rest of the group understands exactly what you are getting at."*
Coordinator	Connects the hypothetical to the real world. Tries to make the problem something tangible. *"You cannot compare public transportation in New York and Los Angeles because the cities, although both big, are so different in so many ways."*
Orienter	This person's role is to keep the group on task. *"That was very funny but we should really be focusing on the task at hand."*

Evaluator–Critic	Attacks the argument that the group is presenting. This is not done in a negative way but with the intent of pointing out flaws in the plan so that it may be adjusted. *"The governor may want to legalize marijuana, but he does not have the support of key congressmen."*
Energizer	Needs to keep the group moving and will exert extra effort when the group is beginning to drag. *"I will be happy to do this research but who is going to work on the presentation?"*
Procedural Technician	This person will act as a type of coordinator between the group members, making sure that meetings are scheduled when people can attend, that the location is adequately stocked, etc. *"The meeting is going to be held at Karen's house next Thursday. Who can bring some snacks?"*
Recorder	People may also think of this as the secretary. Recorder will take the minutes, detailed notes. *"It was agreed at last week's meeting that all parties would have their assignments ready tonight."*

2. Group Building and Maintenance Roles

Encourager	Constantly building up the self-esteem of other members—the cheerleader of the group in some ways. *"Way to go Clara. That was a great idea."*
Harmonizer:	Peacekeeper. Will work with other members to help settle differences, often using humor. *"Why don't you tell us how you really feel?"* (sarcastic remark following an argument)
Compromiser	Is looking for everyone to be happy and will try to modify ideas/plans to please all. *"I know that you might be too busy to finish your assignment so how about we all divide up your section?"*
Gatekeeper and Expediter	Ensures that everyone in the group has an equal chance to participate in the conversation. *"We have not heard from John in a while."*
Group Observer	Provides a running commentary about the group's actions. *"We are really making progress here."*
Follower	A person who goes with the flow. Will not volunteer a new opinion. *"That sounds great—what you guys are talking about."*

3. Individual Roles

Aggressor	Unlike the evaluator–critic, this person attacks ideas with the intention of aggrandizing themselves, not with the interest of the group in mind. *"I think this plan is a bad one. Why aren't we doing this the way I suggested?"*
Blocker	Tries to veto any idea that comes forward without offering any alternative. *"I don't like any of these ideas."*
Recognition Seeker	Tries to enhance individual status, not by working, but by citing past accomplishments. *"The last three group projects I led all got A's."*
Self-Confessor	Makes him or herself the center of attention by constantly talking about him or herself while not necessarily talking about work. *"The other night, I was out way too late. Do you know what I mean? I am always out too late."*
Playboy	Incapable of being serious. Is constantly is making jokes and distracting others. *"Why don't we knock off early? We can pick this up tomorrow."*
Dominator	Monopolizes the conversation with attempts to prove his/her own brilliance. Characterized with long speeches and excessive opinion giving. *"It is my opinion that we should…"*
Help Seeker	Expresses insecurity often. Turns that into a cry for help. *"I am really not very good at this…. Would you help me make this presentation?"*
Special-Interest Pleader	Has a private agenda that he/she puts above the group's interest. Will continue to push special agenda to the detriment of the team. *"Why don't we re-explore my earlier ideas? I really think that is the way to go."*

PERFORMING

When a group has reached the **performing** stage, they have firmly set their goals, found out what accepted behaviors are, and know what their roles should be. The group is focused and firing on all cylinders. This stage is defined by its productivity. But because of the high level of productivity, it is also at this point that those roles and norms may need to be violated. With so much focus on the final goal and such a push to reach that goal in a hurry, new problems may arise. When last-minute details pop up, a member who is primarily a harmonizer may need to

Performing: The fourth stage of group development. It is marked by extreme productivity and the slight breakdown of group roles.

© Zurijeta/Shutterstock.com

In the performing state, the group maximizes its productivity.

quickly change gears and become a coordinator or an information giver. The key to success here is to be flexible. Do not be locked into playing one role. Efficient groups are able to adjust on the fly, and this becomes critical during this phase.

This phase is also marked by high enthusiasm with group members and high loyalty to the group. As discussed earlier, success breeds success. As the group becomes more productive, the members will feel more excited about how much they have achieved and will be eager to achieve more. And because of that success, they will want to be more loyal to the group. The performing stage is very exciting because, if for no other reason, the goal is nearly at hand.

Adjourning: The final stage of group development. It is marked by a sense of pride at having accomplished the group's goal and a sense of loss at the disbandment of the group.

ADJOURNING

Once the goal has been accomplished, the group may begin to disband, or **adjourn**. When people leave an effective team, they will simultaneously feel both a sense of pride at having accomplished something meaningful and a sense of loss at having to walk away from newfound friends and colleagues. Keeping up personal relationships is difficult when people meet regularly, but that challenge is compounded when members no longer see each other on a regular basis. This last stage is truly why the metaphor of the lifecycle of the group works because when a group metaphorically "dies," naturally there will be a sense of loss. When the group breaks up, people will miss each other.

Table 7.2: Stages of Group Development	
Stage	**Definition**
1. Forming	Initial stage of group/team development. Marked by members feeling their way into a new and potentially frightening situation. Members balance individual and group goals as they meet new members. All members likely to avoid conflict to seem non-combative.
2. Storming	Secondary stage of group/team development. Members assert their personalities and try to push their own agendas. Conflict is likely and members' feelings might get hurt. Group members' roles will be established at this point.
3. Norming	Group begins to feel comfortable at this point. Have established a set of rules (norms) to determine how they should behave in a given situation. Group will have learned to deal with conflict, and can express individual opinions. Voting rituals will be set.
4. Performing	Group has firmly set their goals, found out what accepted behaviors are, and what their roles should be. Group is focused and firing on all cylinders. This stage is defined by its productivity. At this stage, roles and norms may need to be violated. The key to success is to be flexible. Efficient groups are able to adjust on the fly.
5. Adjourning	The final stage of group development. It is marked by a sense of pride at having accomplished the group's goal and a sense of loss at the disbandment of the group.

RUNNING A SUCCESSFUL MEETING

On an average workday, 11 million meetings occur. And many employees wish that they had that time back. Meetings that have so much potential to be productive and successful are so often dismal failures. Employees dread a daily drain on their productivity, and they view meetings as one of the primary drains.

Meetings fail for a number of reasons:
- The meeting was unnecessary in the first place.
- There was no purpose to the meeting.

What are the three elements of a meeting?

Meeting: A scheduled gathering of group members for a structured discussion guided by a designated chairperson.

Scheduled gathering: A purposefully held meeting that was prearranged.

- There was no time to prepare for the meeting.
- People who needed to attend the meeting were absent.
- Ineffective leadership.

This list is far from exhaustive, but these are all problems that are easily remedied and, if solved, can lead to greater job satisfaction, better economic decisions, and less wasted resources. The first step in having a successful meeting is to define what a meeting is because a meeting is more than people sitting in a room together. A **meeting**, as defined by Engelberg and Wynn,[10] is "a scheduled gathering of group members for a structured discussion guided by a designated chairperson" (p. 327). Keep in mind the critical elements of this definition: (a) **scheduled gathering**, (b) **structured discussion**, and (c) **designated chairperson**. All three of these elements are important and call for further elaboration. Obviously, the meeting needs to be scheduled because an unscheduled meeting is not a meeting at all but rather a collection of random people sitting in a room together. The second element of the definition is slightly more complicated. The term *structure* implies different things to different people. Structure may mean highly rigid and controlled to some people

© bikeriderlondon/Shutterstock.com

but that is not the intent in this definition. Although some meetings may take on a highly structured discussion in which each person is allowed one minute to offer their opinion on a particular subject, other meetings may have a minimally structured discussion—one where a general idea is kicked around for an hour or two. Brainstorming sessions, although they do have some particular rules, would have to be considered minimally structured. But there is still a structure to guide the discussion. Without this structure, there will be no basis for discussion on any particular topic. Finally, the idea of a designated chairperson needs to be briefly explained. The chairperson may not be the group "leader" but may act more as a moderator does during a presidential debate. The person is there to make sure the group stays on task and that the group keeps going in an agreed-on direction. This person may be elected or appointed, but it is necessary that someone is there to guide the discussion. Now that a definition for a meeting has been established, all incidental gatherings may be eliminated from the discussion, and the focus can be turned to eliminating the aforementioned problems from meetings.

Structured discussion: Unlike idle chatter, structured discussion is a guided conversation with a specific purpose.

Designated chairperson: The person who is there to make sure the group stays on task and that the group keeps going in an agreed-on direction.

Steps for Planning Successful Meetings

The first step in having a successful meeting is planning. And the first question that you need to ask yourself as you plan a meeting is this: "Do we even need to meet in the first place?" If the answer to that question is no, then stop creating the agenda. The meeting is not necessary. But if the answer is yes, then you have another question to ask yourself: "Do we need to meet face-to-face?" This question may appear simple, but it has great financial ramifications. Suppose a face-to-face meeting is necessary and that the meeting will last approximately 3 hours. If 10 people will attend the meeting, all of whom make 10 dollars per hour (an amazingly low figure, even in today's economic climate), the meeting has already cost you or your employer 300 dollars, not including the time it took to gather information and put the presentation together. And nothing is guaranteed to be accomplished at the end of the 3 hours. So think carefully about whether you need to meet face-to-face. If you need to make a major decision and gather information, or provide training, or need immediate feedback, then call the meeting. Otherwise postpone or cancel altogether. Other means are available to you to gather simple answers or to pass on a new social norm.

If you still decide that a meeting is necessary, then it is incumbent on the person who has called the meeting to do some serious planning. Not only will planning need to take place, but also more critical questions

MEETINGS AND TECHNOLOGY

In the workplace, individuals have a variety of technologies readily available for communication or meetings. These technologies range from the most commonplace and affordable, such as telephones and e-mail, to newer technologies, such as virtual conferencing and even robotics. Portable digital phones are now capable of video conferencing in addition to sending and receiving text messages, shared applications, and standard voice communication. A number of emerging media are designed to provide individuals with a more immersive communication or conferencing experience, characterized broadly as *telepresence*. Traditional media such as the telephone, radio, and others offer a degree of presence as well. Specifically telepresence occurs through the use of technology and creates within the user a psychological state where the actual media used becomes transparent in the interaction.[a] These definitions suggest at least two aspects of telepresence that are important for this section. First, telepresence is an experience that occurs when the conveyance of information in an environment is perceived to be non-mediated. This is felt as a sort of being a part of the environment that is presented through some technology. Second, telepresence is thought of as psychological state (one that is experienced) which exists along a continuum—meaning that one can experience more or less presence.[b] Stated differently people can be more or less aware that their communication is mediated. Therefore an immersive environment is created not only from the technology used but also through the psychological state of the individual.

You might wonder why it is important to reduce the appearance of mediation. As noted by Matthew Lombard, telepresence in business offers the advantages of saving the time and emotional labor involved with traveling for a business meeting in addition to the costs associated with business travel. Telepresence has implications for several other aspects of business communication such as persuasion, social learning, task enjoyment, and attention.[c] One of the most common effects of telepresence is enjoyment; however, there is little research on the relationship between telepresence and enjoyment because we tend to take this effect for granted.[d] Intuitively, if we enjoy the mediated experience more as if it were real, that should also create other positive outcomes for the organization and employees. Additionally, involvement is also associated with telepresence, which too has obvious benefits for the workplace.

The most common business application involving telepresence is its use for meetings. Cisco, for example, markets a line of products under the description of telepresence solutions. They promote high definition video and enhanced audio, in addition to sharing of multimedia applications. Cisco offers options from dedicated telepresence rooms to mobile device solutions all with the goal of creating a more immersive environment to enhance outcomes of meetings and collaborations. However, the company does compete with similar technologies which are not being marketed as telepresence, but offer many of the same features. Issues of cost, mobile technologies, and advantages in the cloud are allowing more companies the ability to have the look and feel of being in the same place as other meeting attendees along with all the benefits.[e] Although most individuals using such technologies to create immersive environments may not use the term telepresence, the idea of using technologies to reduce the appearance of mediation is attractive to a variety of organizations.

Another promising use for telepresence involves training, and is an area of considerable research. If a person can complete a training seminar without having to fly to a central location and has similar outcomes as a face-to-face training session, there are cost and time savings for the organization. Studies have shown that telepresence is beneficial to learning and teaching, to an extent that it is being used in medicine as well as business.

Telepresence robots are also being used in business. Companies such as Suitable Technologies are marketing these devices with the goal of making meetings and telecommuting more immersive. The ability to move around a physical business environment and facilitate scheduled or impromptu meetings are advantages that telepresence robots have compared to immersive videoconferencing technologies. Such telepresence devices give more autonomy to the user and reduce the restrictions of being confined to one room. It is uncertain how commonplace telepresence robots will be. Currently they have a novel use while offering many if not more of the benefits of traditional telepresence systems.

Therefore technologies in the workplace will continue to evolve, not only to transmit messages, but also to provide a sense of "being there" or "being there with others." As they do, the possibility for higher levels of satisfaction in mediated workplace communication will become more focused in addition to the cost and access of such technologies becoming more attainable.

[a] Bracken, C. C., Pettey, G., Guha, T., & Rubenking, B. (2008, May). Sounding out presence: The impact of screen size, pace and sound. Paper at the annual conference of the International Communication Association, Montreal, Canada.

[b] Westerman, D., Spence, P. R., & Lachlan, K. A. (2009). Telepresence and the exemplification effects of disaster news. *Communication Studies*, 60(5), 542-557. doi: 10.1080/10510970903260376

[c] Bracken, C. C., & Skalski, P. D. (2009). *Immersed in media: Telepresence in everyday life*. New York: Routledge.

[d] Savitz, E. (2012). 5 Reasons Cisco And Polycom Are In Trouble In Telepresence. Retrieved from http://www.forbes.com/sites/ciocentral/2012/05/03/5-reasons-cisco-and-polycom-are-in-trouble-in-telepresence/

[e] Lombard, M (2010). The promise and peril of telepresence. In Bracken C., & Skalski, P. (Eds). *Immersed in media: Telepresence in everyday life*. New York: Routledge.

will need to be asked. For example, what is the purpose of the meeting? If the purpose is distribution of information, you may not need to have a meeting. If the information can be e-mailed to colleagues and you will be available and are willing to answer any queries via e-mail, then do not hold the meeting. However, if the purpose of the meeting is to create a new product line or ad campaign, then the face-to-face meeting will need to be called. Determining the purpose of the meeting will go a long way in helping the moderator of the meeting keep the group on task and focused. If the goal of the meeting is unclear, then the moderator is likely to be confused as well.

If you know the purpose of the meeting, then you will find yourself asking another important question. Who should attend this meeting? Are specific people already familiar with the product line that you are trying to launch? Do company accountants need to be present to discuss financial limits of the ad campaign? If certain people need to be at your meeting and they find themselves unable to attend, you need to postpone the meeting. There is no point in calling a meeting if the key players cannot be in attendance. It would be akin to a graduate student calling a thesis defense meeting when his or her thesis committee could not attend. Time is always going to be one of the difficult aspects of teamwork, but it is one that needs to be dealt with realistically.

Now let's suppose that the necessary players can meet tomorrow morning or three weeks from now. Given the choice between meeting sooner rather than later, people may often feel overeager and decide to meet the next day. This can be a crucial mistake that leads to an ineffective meeting. All sides need a chance to prepare for the meeting. To call a last-minute meeting is not only unfair to the people attending the meeting but it is also unfair to you, the person calling the meeting. As has been previously pointed out, many people will spend their days counting the minutes in a meeting rather than actively participating. Give yourself the greatest chance for success, and that means taking the appropriate amount of time to prepare a well-thought-out agenda and to distribute that agenda to all members attending the meeting at least a week in advance to give those group members a chance to prepare any necessary materials. Make sure the members know why they are there. If they feel they are there just to sit back and be spectators, then they "should stay at their desks and do their work."[15]

Pandexter Nail Company
Executive Board Meeting Agenda
Wednesday June 25, 2016
8:00 a.m. Board Room

I. Approval of Minutes

II. Old Business
  A. Conflict of interest forms
  B. Travel request forms
  C. Dress code revisions

III. New Business
  A. New product line—timeline for installation
  B. Sales team initiative—where are we now?
  C. International conference—reservations needed ASAP

IV. CEO's Report
  A. Budget
  B. Marketing campaign
  C. Future goals

V. Adjournment

SAMPLE AGENDA II

Speech Communication Department
Faculty Meeting Agenda
Wednesday, April 16, 2015
3:00 p.m. Center Hall 100

I. Approval of Minutes

II. New Business
  A. Committee reports
  B. Faculty senate
  C. Curriculum
  D. Calendar committee

III. Director's Report
   A. End of the year party
   B. Global studies—study abroad proposals due by May 1
   C. Budget—expect a 4.2% cut for 2016
   D. New grant proposals due now
   E. Office updates take place next week

IV. Administrative Reports
   A. Coordinator, Undergraduate Studies
   B. Director, Speech Communication Center
   C. Advisors

SAMPLE MEETING MINUTES

Speech Communication Department
Faculty Meeting Minutes

March 5, 2016

The Speech Communication Department met on Wednesday March 5, 2016 in Center Hall 100.

Call to Order: Dr. Mitch Blake called the meeting to order at 3:00 p.m.

Faculty/Staff Present: Suzanne Brown, William Thomas, Mathew Davis, Andrea Lee, Mitch Blake, Britanny Connor, Danielle Streeter, Brian Richards, Eric Murphy, Todd Thompson, Barbara Turner, Cindy Russell, Teresa Joan, and Glenn Putnam.

I. Approval of Minutes
Dr. Barbara Turner motioned to approve the minutes from the January 22nd faculty meeting and Dr. Cindy Russell seconded the motion.

II. New Business
   A. Committee Reports
         1. Faculty Senate (Teresa Joan)
               a. New student center approved.
               b. Budget cuts—4.5% approved by chancellor
               c. School of the Arts has been approved

   d. Faculty Assembly is discussing post tenure review process

  2. Assessment (Cindy Russell)

   a. Assessment survey has been implemented and data will be collected next month. Watch for e-mails.

  3. PRSSA (Cindy Russell)

   a. Group has two field trips to NYC planned. There will be workshops and networking opportunities. Panel discussions regarding job interviewing available as well as a networking lunch.

III. Director's Report

 A. Budget

  1. $100K in lapse salary (adjuncts, overloads, DE summer classes, etc.)

  2. $124K Operating Budget (faculty travel, office supplies, maintenance agreements, postage, student employees, part-time employees).

  3. Possibilities

   a. Eliminate DE classes

   b. Raise undergraduate admission standards

   c. Eliminate master's program

 B. Cancelled classes and make-up days

  1. April 29th make-up day for January 30th.

  2. April 30th make-up day for January 29th.

  3. E-mail sent from Chancellor regarding these make-up days.

 C. Global Studies

  1. Study abroad—proposals due by May 1.

  2. Be thinking ahead to summer 2015. If interested, please let Director know.

IV. Administrative reports

 A. Assistant Director: Summer I and II schedules are done. These will be printed out and placed in your mailbox next week. Please read and sign to show your approval.

 B. Summer GA assignments are still being done.

Meeting adjourned at 4:55 p.m.

Chairing a Meeting

If you have clarified the purpose of the meeting and created an agenda, determined where and when it should be held and who should be attending, and received confirmation that those group members will be there, then you, acting as chairperson, have accomplished a great deal. But there is still a major obstacle to overcome. That is the actual running of the meeting. As the acting chairperson, you will have several responsibilities to deal with: You will need to open and close the meeting, you will need to deal with difficulties within the discussion, you will need to be conscious of meeting logistics, and ideally you will follow the agenda while still being flexible and smart enough to allow discussion to flow off the charted agenda if it is still productive. These separate duties all need to be elaborated on.

The logistics of running a meeting are daunting. Even a task as simple as getting started on time can be challenging. If several of your group members tend to tardiness, you may need to provide the group members with a recommended arrival time and a hard meeting time. This will simultaneously send the message that there is an exact time when this meeting will occur, but also provide some time to get the social networking aspects of group work out of the way. Members who wish to chat may show up early to do so, but once the meeting begins, it is all business.

When opening the meeting, the chairperson needs to be considerate of time constraints and quickly get to the point. Thank the group members for coming and being on time, introduce the purpose for the day's meeting, and either hand over the reins to the first presenter or, if there is no presenter, throw out the first discussion question—something that will get group members involved. Please be aware that some members may not be eager to volunteer. If that is the case, the chairperson may have to delicately pass the question to an individual instead of asking for volunteers. This may save time compared to waiting for the next person to jump up and answer. Closing the meeting is just as important. You will be able to sense when the group is getting fidgety, losing their patience and productivity. As the chairperson, you should briefly review the information covered during the meeting; discuss whether any assignments, duties, or responsibilities were assigned during the meeting; and if another meeting is necessary, ask the members while you have them all in the same room when the next time is that they are all available. Once that information is attained, thank everyone for their contributions and adjourn.

©Dragon Images/Shutterstock.com

One of the major responsibilities of running a meeting is to make sure that you stay on the agenda. To use our earlier financial example, if a meeting starts 15 minutes late because some members are tardy and runs 45 minutes long because people tended to wander off point, that is another 100 dollars just in salary costs. You as chairperson need to balance the cost of these delays against the information that is being produced. If group members are creating new ideas in a new direction, but you find that you are slightly off the agenda, then ask yourself what the relative worth is of the ideas being produced. Perhaps a group member is telling a humorous story that has nothing to do with the agenda items but is serving to unite the group and bring them closer together. What is the value of that bond? As chairperson you will have to answer those types of questions in real time as they occur. Be aware that this situation may happen; do not be afraid to interrupt and say that we need to get back on track, but do not do so just for the sake of finishing the meeting right on time.

Perhaps the most difficult task that the chairperson takes on is trying to deal with difficult group members. You will certainly need to wear the gatekeeper hat while acting as chairperson. Certain group members will not want to participate, and you will need to try to prod answers out of

The meeting chairperson should open the discussion and quickly get to the point.

them. Other members may wish to dominate the floor, thinking of you as competition rather than a helpful moderator. A smart moderator may assign the dominant member another job that will not allow that person the time to participate, such as the role of recorder. Side conversations that arise during the meeting may prove especially distracting. People who are content to text during the meeting rather than participate will also be an issue. As an effective moderator, you may attempt to address these problems before they occur. However, a warning may not be enough. If that is the case, the whole group may have to use nonverbals to get the deviant members to comply. A silent room that has all eyes glaring at one person who is playing solitaire on their phone may be enough to shame that group member into putting away their phone.

Meetings that are ineffective are nothing but a drain on company resources, both time and money. But effective meetings will produce a greater quantity of work as well as a higher quality. Although this chapter offers several hints on how to run a successful meeting, you must also remember the information presented at the beginning of the chapter. Group work is difficult; it is messy and a potential waste of resources. Not every member will give their all because they are working in a group. But efficient and effective groups will lead to greater productivity, which will lead to greater success, which will lead to greater employee loyalty, which will end with greater employee satisfaction.

CONCLUSION

As mentioned at the beginning of the chapter, Lydia Jackson has a big job ahead of her as she convenes an ad hoc committee at her university to develop a new admissions campaign. Based on the information in this chapter, Lydia can expect the group to progress through the stages of team formation including forming, storming, norming, performing, and adjourning. Because she's at the beginning of the process, she should plan activities that will allow the group members to get to know one another and also allow the group to determine its own goals and objectives. During these processes, Lydia will not be surprised by the roles and conflict that emerge. However, she now understands that conflict can be a constructive form of dialogue and a way for new ideas to come to the forefront and avoid groupthink. Even more importantly, Lydia recognizes the important role she will play in planning for their meetings. Specifically, she will prepare agendas and material in advance and provide committee members with adequate time to prepare for meetings, and she will only call face-to-face meetings when appropriate. She has also decided to appoint a process observer, a person who will make sure that the meeting is staying on track with the agenda and within the set time limits. Finally, she understands that the group needs to come together on a social as well as a task basis, so she will work to incorporate some unstructured activities in the meetings that will help bring people together, while tapping into their creative potential.

Group work and meetings can be extremely productive, but before you convene a group or call a meeting, be sure that this is the appropriate step to take. Meetings and group work are seen as a drain because they are often used ineffectively. Meetings and group work are opportunities for members to contribute to the overall success of the company in a real way. These events are opportunities to form lasting social relationships with coworkers leading to greater job satisfaction. Despite all of these benefits from group work and meetings, people still see the majority of this time as a waste. And so before the meeting is called, before the group is convened, think. Ask yourself: Is the meeting is really necessary? What is the purpose of the group? If you know the purpose of the group, and the meeting is necessary, you are well on your way to creating a positive work environment in which your team will thrive.

ACTIVITIES

1. Considering the advantages and disadvantages of group work, make a list of the special benefits or challenges of working with the following types of groups:
    - Ad hoc committee/task force with members of different departments set to review an organization's benefits plans
    - Volunteer group formed to determine ways to make local neighborhoods more safe
    - Volunteer group formed to construct a Habitat for Humanity house
    - Department committee set up to create a new policy for scheduling vacation days
    - Quality circle group created to identify ways to improve safety procedures on a manufacturing line
    - Student group for completing a final research project (paper and oral presentation) for a communication course

2. Recognizing the importance of icebreakers in the forming stage for groups, brainstorm a list of activities that will work to familiarize the group members with one another, while not feeling like a waste of precious time. Have you participated in an icebreaker that you felt was particularly effective? If so, describe the activity.

3. What techniques could be used in a group to make sure that all ideas are heard, even if they are controversial? Develop a list of structured approaches that could be used.

4. Reflect on your previous group experiences and see if you can identify the task, relational, and individual roles that were present. Describe these roles and share with a classmate. What roles do you have a tendency to play? Are your roles helpful or hurtful to group functioning?

5. Imagine you are planning a five-minute informative presentation with a small group in your class. What specific steps should you take for leading the group through the project? Develop a sample agenda for your first meeting and share the agenda with a classmate. How should the work be accomplished and what timeline should the group follow? What would you do in the event that one or more group members were failing to perform? How would you expect your professor to intervene in this conflict and/or how might the professor construct the assignment in a way that diminishes the likelihood of social loafing? Can this type of intervention/structure be replicated in a business setting?

REFERENCES

[1] Mehrabian, A. (1981). *Silent messages: Implicit communication of emotion and attitudes* (2nd ed.). Belmont, CA: Wadsworth.

[2] Ingham, A. G., Levinger, G., Graves, J., & Peckham, V. (1974). The Ringlemann effect: Studies of group size and group performance. *Journal of Experimental Social Psychology, 10*, 371–384.

[3] United Nations General Assembly, Ad Hoc Committee on an International Convention against Reproductive Cloning of Human Beings. (2005). *United Nations declaration on human cloning*. New York: Office of Legal Affairs United Nations. Retrieved from http://www.un.org/law/cloning/index.html

[4] Microsoft Press Release. (2005). *Survey finds workers average only three productive days per week*. Redmond, WA: Author.

[5] Osborn, A. F. (1953). *Applied imagination: Principles and procedures of creative problem-solving*. New York: Scribner's.

[6] Tuckman, B. W., & Jensen, M. A. C. (1977). Stages of small group development revisited. *Group and Organizational Studies, 2*, 419–427.

[7] Bormann, E. G., & Bormann, N. C. (1996). *Effective small group communication* (6th ed.). Minneapolis, MN: Gordon Press.

[8] Wheelan, S. A. (1994).

[9] Wheelan, S. A., & Danganan, N. B. (2003). The relationship between the internal dynamics of student affairs leadership teams and campus leaders' perceptions of the effectiveness of student affairs divisions. *NASPA Journal, 40*, 93–112.

[10] Engleberg, I. N., & Wynn, D. R. (2007). *Working in groups*. Boston: Houghton Mifflin.

[11] Dentler, R. A., & Erikson, K. T. (1959). The functions of deviance in groups. *Social Problems, 7*, 98–107.

[12] Pavitt, C., & Curtis, E. (1990). *Small group discussion: A theoretical approach*. Scottsdale, AZ: Gorsuch Scarisbrick, Publishers.

[13] Beene, K. D., & Sheats, P. (1948). Functional roles of group members. *Journal of Social Issues, 4*, 41–49.

[14] McCann, D. J., & Margerison, C. J. (1989).

[15] Henkel, S. L. (2007). *Successful meetings: How to plan, prepare and execute top-notch business meetings*. Ocala, FL: Atlantic Publishing Group.

ADDITIONAL SOURCES

Cathcart, R. S., Samovar, L. A., & Henman, L. D. (1996) *Small group communication: Theory & practice* (7th ed.). Dubuque, IA: Brown & Benchmark Publishers.

Fujishin, R. (2007). *Creating effective groups: The art of small group communication* (2nd ed.). Plymouth, UK: Rowman & Littlefield.

Snow, H. (1997). *Indoor outdoor team-building games for trainers: Powerful activities from the world of adventure-based team-building & ropes courses*. New York: McGraw-Hill.

chapter
eight

Résumé Building and Social Media Strategies

After reading this chapter you will be able to:

- Choose the right type of résumé for yourself
- Construct the best résumé to get the job you want
- Construct a scannable résumé
- Understand the implications of social media as a pre-screening tool during the employment process
- Develop a professional networking profile

CHAPTER OUTLINE

key words

Brainstorming
Traditional résumé style
Skills résumé style
Scannable résumé
Social information
    processing theory

Context collapse
User-generated cues
Other-generated cues
System-generated cues

INTRODUCTION

Ethan Jordan is starting his senior year at Mideast State University finishing up his bachelor's degree in Communication Studies with a concentration in Organizational Communication. He's been thinking quite a bit about his future career and has decided that he would like to work in the pharmaceutical industry for a company such as Pfizer or in the health insurance field with a company like Humana. He keeps a close watch on both of these organizations' employment Web sites and is realistic in knowing that he'll need an entry-level position in order to work his way up and ultimately secure a position in employee training and development. While Ethan feels confident in his part-time work experiences and his extra-curricular activities, he's not exactly sure of how to begin preparing his employment materials and he's even less confident about the interview process. Is it time for him to remove all of his high school awards from his résumé? How can he communicate to future employers that his dream job is in the area of training? What if there aren't any openings at his two targeted organizations? These questions reflect a high level of critical thinking on Ethan's part. Preparing your application materials and building your confidence in the interview process takes time and focus, but the effort you put forth on the front-end will pay off when you get that first job offer. This chapter and the next focus exclusively on the job search process including résumé building, impression management through social media, and interviewing.

RÉSUMÉS

Before you can even think about the interview, you have to apply for the job, and that means a résumé! It is important to remember that résumés don't get jobs—they get interviews. The purpose of a résumé is to let a potential employer know that you are interested in a position within their organization. Just as there are lists and lists of job interview questions out there, there are also many different forms of résumés out there. The important thing to do is to make your résumé your own; don't be tempted to follow a résumé template. The point of a résumé is to make you stand out from the crowd, and the definition of a template *is* going with the crowd. Use a format that fits your skills, the job you are applying for, and the company as well. In this chapter are some general guidelines; be sure to put your own spin on them! Your résumé should convey your own unique abilities and skills that relate to the specific position you are applying for, but at the same time should not include every detail about you. That is what the interview is for. The résumé should just highlight the specifics that make you a great candidate for the job you are applying for.

Think About Your Life: Brainstorm!

Brainstorming:
An approach to idea generation that encourages free thinking and minimizes conformity.

The first step in résumé creation is to sit down and really think about your life. **Brainstorm.** What have you done? And not just when it comes to work. There can be a lot of changes just when it comes to the work part of your life. According to the U.S. Department of Labor, workers between the ages of 18 and 38 change jobs an average of 10 times! That's a lot! What about the rest of your accomplishments outside work? The Résumé Inventory Worksheet is a good way to start writing the details of your life down on paper. At this point, you shouldn't leave anything out. Think about volunteer experience, military training, extracurricular activities, study abroad experiences, hobbies, and other life experiences. Everything is fair game because you don't know what will work best for what position you will be applying for. Write everything down and don't limit yourself!

Grouping your skills into categories or headings can help you to generate ideas about information to include on your résumé. Some potential categories could include the following:

1. **Personal achievements**. Paying for your education yourself, first in your family to graduate from college, overcoming obstacles
2. **Education.** Universities graduated from, classes related to the job you are applying for, certifications, or other special training

3. **Activities and honors**. Student organizations, professional associations, scholarships, academic achievements, sororities or fraternities
4. **Volunteer experience**. Church, civic groups, tutoring
5. **Experience**. Paid/unpaid, part/full time, internships, military
6. **Important career-related skills.** Computer proficiency, foreign languages, problem solving, critical thinking, communication skills
7. **Hobbies and interests.** Planning trips, sports, managing personal investments

Wow, I've Done a Lot!

Second, narrow down your list to the job you are applying for. You need to identify just the information that you will use in the résumé that you are creating for the specific job you are applying for. This means figuring out what the employer's needs are and tailoring your skills toward those needs. Rex Irwin, manager of operations of Westar Energy, says résumés that come across his desk that don't utilize the terms from the job description are given less regard. This is just an example of how you want to make sure you turn your experience and skills into what the employer is looking

Include any volunteer experience on your résumé.

© michaeljung/Shutterstock.com

for. An employer has spent a lot of time crafting the job description into stating exactly what they are looking for in an employee; therefore, you need to make sure you take special care to use those words in both your résumé and cover letter.

Time to Write

Remember that applicability, brevity, and clarity are vital. That's how you get the interview and really show potential employers what you have to offer. Above all, it is recommended that you write your own résumé and not have someone else do it for you. This task will accomplish several things for you. First, it will help you become aware of your qualifications and the best ways to present them to employers. Knowing your qualifications in this way will help your self-confidence for the interview process. Second, writing your résumé will give you a chance to recognize your weaknesses. Of course, you wouldn't put these down on your résumé, but this would give you a chance to identify them and grow. Now, regardless of what kind of résumé you put together, make sure that it passes the 10-second glance test. When hiring, an employer looks at stacks on stacks of résumés, so you need to make sure that yours is the one that stands out and is the easiest to read of the bunch. Using clearly labeled headings and a consistent format throughout is key to making your résumé easy to read and a standout over the rest. Choose a format and headings that allow you to communicate effectively the combination of skills and abilities that highlight your qualifications for the position and provide insight into you as a unique candidate.

Résumé Formats

Traditional résumé style is set up in a reverse chronological order, meaning the most current events go first. Most résumés are set up in this fashion, and most employers will be looking for this type of résumé. Use this type of résumé when your experience shows a logical progression toward the preparation for the position. It works best when you have experience in the field you are applying for, you can demonstrate some sort of measurable result from your work activities (e.g., "Increased sales by 10 percent"), and you have held impressive titles or worked for big-name companies.

Skills résumé style emphasizes the skills you've used rather than the job or the date when you used them. These résumés are often useful for older workers and those returning to the workforce because it minimizes dates, and for those who are changing careers because it outlines transferable work skills.

Traditional résumé style: Set up in a reverse chronological order, meaning the most current events go first.

Skills résumé style: Emphasizes the skills you've used rather than the job or the date when you used them.

Résumé Formatting and Writing Tips

- Make it easy to skim using bullet points, short declarative sentences, and an easy-to-read font (10–12 pts.), and avoid abbreviations.
- Use no more than two fonts throughout the résumé, and avoid script fonts.
- Do not use graphics, shadowing, or clip art and no photographs (unless you are in creative field such as graphic design).
- Do not use a résumé template.
- Use bold or underlining appropriately, but sparingly, to highlight your strengths.
- Put your materials in order of importance and relevance.
- Begin phrases with action verbs.
- Avoid generalities, and focus on specifics about experience, projects, products, etc.
- Quantify experiences when possible (sales quotas met, customer satisfaction ratings, etc.).
- Be clear about what position you are seeking.

Résumé Possible Headings

- Objective
- Summary of Qualifications
- Profile
- Awards and Recognitions
- Honors
- Honors and Awards
- Education
- Specialized Training
- Accomplishments
- Activities
- Relevant Experience
- Related Experience
- Work Experience
- Internships
- Employment History
- Work Authorization
- International Experience
- Volunteer Experience
- Professional Experience
- Additional Experience
- Study Abroad Experience
- Other Experience
- Relevant Skills
- Computer Skills
- Technical Skills
- Computer Software
- Certification
- Licensure
- Languages
- Professional Memberships
- Professional Affiliations
- Additional Information

Absolute Must-Haves on Any Résumé

1. **Contact information.** An employer should be able to figure out instantly how to get in touch with you. In the header of the document of your résumé, you should include your name (which must be the biggest item on the whole page), your address, phone number, and e-mail address. Make sure that all your information is current and that you can be reached easily. If you put down your cell phone number, listen to your outgoing message and

make sure that it is professional and easy to understand. Also, ensure that your e-mail address is professional. An e-mail tag of sugarlips@hotone.com is not appropriate. There are lots of free e-mail services out there, so setting up one just for job searching is a good idea. Setting up one that has some form of your name is the best idea, such as first.lastname@email.com.

2. **Career objective.** An objective should convey useful information. It is preferable to omit the objective rather than include something "fluffy" or vague. You do not need an objective when handing out résumés at a career fair. Fit the objective to the job description, and use the employer's name and the name of the position for which you are applying.

   Ineffective: "To obtain an entry-level sales position in the pharmaceutical sales industry."

   Effective: "To obtain an account executive position with Pfizer Pharmaceutical."

3. **Education.** This section should clearly communicate that you have the needed education required for the job. If you have just graduated from college or if education is required for the position that you are applying for, then list your education directly below your career objective. In this area include both credit-based higher education degrees and certifications as well as noncredit learning. Your information should include the degree (e.g., Bachelor of Arts), area of study, graduation date including month and year, the name of the university including location with city and state, as well as any minor areas of study, concentrations, or emphasis. Be sure to list your most recent degree first (Ph.D., Master's, Bachelor's). You should list the universities that you actually completed a degree at and every one where you happened to take one course. Once you are in college, high school doesn't matter any longer; therefore, no high school information should be included on your résumé unless you need to include a national award that you earned during high school.

4. **Work experience.** It is important to consider the tasks that you completed when working in your previous jobs from someone else's perspective. Remember that when a prospective employer is reading your résumé, they don't know what you did on a daily basis at your last job. Explain things clearly and concisely with good details about what you've done in this area. Be sure to include the following for each job, paid, unpaid, or self-employment: the position or job title, name of organization, city and state location,

dates of employment, and other details such as full or part time, job duties, special responsibilities, or promotions. When listing employment, go back no further than the summer after high school. Quantify where you can, as people like numbers, and the proof of evidence comes across clearly in this manner.

THE DEVIL IS IN THE DETAILS

Too vague: Sales Manager, *The State Hornet*, Sacramento, CA, 20101-2014. Supervised staff; promoted ad sales.

Better: Sales Manager, *The State Hornet*, Sacramento, CA, 20101-2014.

- Supervised 22-member sales staff.
- Helped recruit, interview, and select staff.
- Assigned duties and scheduled work; recommended best performer for promotion.
- Motivated staff to increase paid ad inches 10 percent over previous year's sales.

Explain things clearly and concisely regarding your work experience on your résumé.

© Andrey_Popov/Shutterstock.com

figure 8.1

SHANE BLAKEMAN

123 Oak Crest Drive ~ Chicago, Illinois 60678
312-555-1234 ~ sblakeman@gmail.com

SUMMARY OF QUALIFICATIONS

A sales-driven, team-oriented Sales Professional with more than 10 years of experience in the highly competitive field of office supply products.

Proficient as a sales trainer as well as salesperson, a highly motivated leader with the flexibility and experience required to adjust to the changing demands of the industry.

Efficiently manages many projects at one time as well as delivering quality results on strict time lines because of strong organizational skills and creative problem solving.

PROFESSIONAL EXPERIENCE

Management Experience
- Promoted to team leader of the sales group, responsible for the weekly, monthly, and annual reports for the group.
- Maintained a working knowledge of the various product lines sold throughout the five different company divisions.
- Provided ongoing training and supervisory oversight to a sales group of 25 employees who managed and maintained a banquet hall.
- Prepares summary reports including monthly invoice summaries for more than 300 clients.
- Extensive educational background in business management with a *Bachelor of Science degree in Business Administration* as well as several graduate level accounting courses.

Training Experience
- Successfully organized and implemented training program for all new company sales hires for the past three years.
- Provide comprehensive training materials for all members of sales team.
- Remain current in all business computer skills by successfully completing courses in Microsoft Office Professional and Windows XP.

EDUCATION

Iowa State University – Ames, Iowa
Bachelor of Science in Business Administration (2002)

WORK HISTORY

Top Office Supplies – Iowa City, Iowa   2004-Present
Sales Manager

Memorial Hall - Davenport, Iowa   2002-2004
Events Manager

figure **8.2**

Isabelle Ima Singer

Campus Address:	617-111-0000	Permanent Address:
Potter Campus Center Box 1111	isinger@harvard.edu	54 East Post Street
Cambridge, MA 02138		Boston, MA 02159

EDUCATION

Harvard University, Cambridge, MA — June 2015
A.B. in Business, Certificate in Vocal Music — GPA: 3.1
Coursework includes: Vocal Music, Topics in Music, History of Music
The University of Queensland, Brisbane, Australia — Summer 2013
Eight-week summer study abroad in business

EXPERIENCE

Get Up and Move, online exercise blog, Boston, MA — April 2012-present
Editorial Intern
- Research fitness topics ranging from nutrition to exercise tips and give story ideas to editors
- Contribute to online stories and write a daily blog for the Exercise Tip section
- Post responses to the editorial page
- Use social media outlets such as Twitter, Facebook, and Pinterest to help generate interest among college students for the blog

Simon Gallery, Boston, MA — May-Aug. 2011
Intern
- Researched historical events to include in displays
- Reorganized gallery shop
- Performed administrative tasks such as updating inventory spreadsheets

Harvard University Outreach Program — Sept. 2010-May 2011
Volunteer
- Worked in several elementary schools throughout the Boston area
- Mentored three children during the school year
- Helped with in-class special activities when needed

CAMPUS ACTIVITIES

The Blaze — Sept. 2012-present
Staff Writer for Entertainment Section
- Write weekly stories previewing upcoming events in the area

Treble Choir — Sept. 2011-present
Soprano
- Sang with the choir in all performances

HONORS

Harvard University: Outstanding Freshman Vocal Performance, June 2012
High School: Member of the National Honor Society

SKILLS

Proficient in Microsoft Word and Excel; Conversational in French

5. **Honors and awards or activities and honors.** This is a place to make your résumé one of a kind. Anything is fair game, so make a heading that is all your own. List recognitions in books such as any "Who's Who in America" books, any academic honor societies, fellowships and scholarships, any awards given by professional societies, major awards given by civic groups such as the Rotary Club or the Lions Club, college varsity sport letters, and anything else you can think of. Remember that this is just post–high school activities, with the only exception being a national award such as being a National Merit Finalist. This is an area that can start conversations with the employer, as the interviewer could share the same interests as you.

6. **References.** Do *not* say "References available upon request." It is redundant; you are going to give them your references or you won't get the job. Either give the employer your references right off the bat or don't. It is the opinion of the authors to send the references anyway, as the employer will be requesting them, and you will be saving them a step along the way. Use three to five references. If you have recently graduated from college, include at least one professor and one previous employer or supervisor. Do not include personal references; these should be people who can comment on your professional abilities. Remember to ask for permission before you write down anyone's name as a reference. You don't want them to be surprised when they get a phone call asking about you.

Things to Always Do on Your Résumé

1. Create a file and prepare your résumé as a Word file.

2. Use consistent, standard format and style.
   a. Be consistent throughout.
   b. Keep it brief, concise, and to the point.
   c. Use conventional English, and avoid jargon.
   d. Use high-quality paper in a conservative, professional color.
   e. Use a high-quality printer.
   f. Include your name on the second page and mark it page 2.

3. PROOFREAD.

4. Point the reader to key elements.

5. Lead with your strengths.

Things to *Never* Do on Your Résumé

1. Don't list personal information such as age, marital status, health status, religious or political affiliations—no photos.

2. Never tell everything—that is what the interview is for.

3. Never use complete sentences and personal pronouns such as I, me, and my.

4. Never include salary information.

5. Never send it without a cover letter.

6. Never present information that is false.

7. Never give reasons for leaving a job.

8. Never send a résumé that is not your best effort.

The Résumé Checklist

1. Does the text visually fit the page?

2. Is your name easy to read? Is it in a large font, surrounded by white space?

3. Are the headings and text easy to skim? Bold, rather than underlined, using bullet points?

4. Does a summary of qualifications or keywords highlight your skills and knowledge?

5. Do recent, relevant, and substantive details show that you are qualified for the job?

6. Do details interest the reader and set you apart from other applicants?

7. Are details quantifiable where possible?

8. Does the text omit the word "I"?

9. Is the writing clear and concise?

10. Is everything listed in reverse chronological order (most recent first)?

11. If there is a second page, does it contain your name and "page 2"?

12. Is the résumé free from typos and other errors?

CREATING SCANNABLE RÉSUMÉS

It is not always the case that the first eyes to examine a résumé are human. Companies use software programs to scan and screen résumés. Such programs are often known as Applicant Tracking Systems (ATS). These are common for larger firms and an applicant should be aware of their existence. Therefore an applicant needs to think about at least two rounds in their résumé review. Round 1 is the machine, and Round 2 is a human. The applicant must appeal to both.

There are several advantages for the organization in automating the search process. The first is the number of applicants for a position; some report that there are 70 applicants for each job vacancy, while others report the number as high as 250.[1] During the recession many human resource jobs were cut and in subsequent years those jobs were not replaced. This creates conditions where it is difficult for hiring managers to carefully examine each résumé. Another advantage of using software to examine applicants' materials is the absence of bias. People consider automated processes as more fair because a machine is absent of bias.

One survey found that recruiters spend about 6 seconds scanning résumés to decide if the candidate fits the position.[2] Therefore, for some positions the applicant must first get the résumé through the ATS before it will be reviewed by a human. Thus an important aspect of preparing a résumé to meet the discrimination of the ATS and the needs of the human recruiter is first to ensure the formatted résumé is simple, not embedded with pictures, graphics and logos, or unique fonts which can't easily be processed by the ATS software. Also, for many Applicant Tracking Systems, a PDF is not searchable. Therefore read the instructions closely before uploading a résumé. If you are e-mailing a résumé, don't be afraid to e-mail it in both a txt and PDF format.

One way to make a résumé stand out through the ATS software is using appropriate keywords. For example, use keywords from the position announcement itself in the résumé. Moreover, examine the Web site and mission statement of the organization and look for repetitive words or keywords that identify the organizational culture. However, don't make the mistake of replacing content and description with keywords. The applicant must still explain the skills, successes, and qualifications possessed. Some positions require certifications or other prerequisites to be hired. If these are not asked for within the system, then the ATS is probably programed to find them in the résumé. The applicants must ensure these are included. The applicant is balancing the résumé between the ATS (Round 1) and the human recruiter (Round 2). Remember that length doesn't matter to the ATS. Therefore don't be brief for the sake of saving space; the applicant should provide all the necessary information needed to sell themselves. ATS systems are becoming more advanced and learn from information obtained from both applicants and decisions made by the organization. Therefore if an applicant knows someone who has been recently hired, or an employee of the organization has posted his/her résumé online, this is a good resource to obtain information from. Applicant Tracking Systems are always evolving to best meet the needs of the organization. Use the information in this chapter as a starting point for résumé creation and tailoring, then search well known career and job placement sites to learn the most recent information on these technologies.

Some recruiters and career coaches argue that an applicant should have two versions of their résumé. The first is often called a **scannable résumé** and is designed to cut through the clutter and requirements of an ATS. This is the version an applicant would send when applying for a position online. These are created with all the keyword recommendations expressed earlier. Additionally such a résumé uses a standard font, ensuring that the font size is never less than 10 point. The scannable résumé avoids stylistics such as bold font, italics, and lines that cover the width of an entire page. It is also popular to e-mail a scannable résumé as an attachment in addition to placing it in the body of an e-mail. The applicant is then encouraged to have another version of their résumé that the applicant will carry with them to provide at the interview. This résumé will include more stylistics, and follow many of the popular recommendations outlined in this chapter.

The truth is that there is no longer one right way to create a résumé; rather it's important to think of stronger and weaker approaches. The applicant has to research the organization and the process. He/she needs to know who may be reviewing the résumé and tailor it specifically to the hiring manager, interviewer, automated system, and the position. Preferences, technologies, and expectations change, and change often. The résumé is no longer a document that an applicant perfects and adds to throughout their career. The process, format, and other characteristics change rapidly. Creating a résumé requires research, revision, and flexibility. If you are reading this textbook, there is a strong probability that you are a university student. The university you attend probably has a career center and it would be wise to use their resources. According to Sally Foster, the Director of the Graham Office of Career Management at the University of Kentucky, students underutilize the resources of the career center. The career center should not be viewed as a place to visit in your senior year. Rather you should develop a relationship with a career center counselor and use their expertise throughout your college experience, particularly developing the relationship during your freshman year. This will aid in clarifying your career goal and gaining relevant internships while in school.

Scannable résumé: A type of résumé focused on key words that is designed to cut through the clutter and requirements of an Applicant Tracking System. This is the version an applicant would send when applying for a position online.

figure 8.3

Joan M. Beck

PERMANENT ADDRESS

987 Evergreen Street, Reston, VA 20191

CURRENT ADDRESS

6743 Applegate Drive, Chicago, IL 60876

HOME PHONE: (312) 555-xxxx

CELL PHONE: (703) 555-xxxx

RESEARCH INTERESTS: Software Engineering

EDUCATION:

Master of Science Degree, Computer Science, June 20xx, GPA 3.3

Loyola University, Chicago

Bachelor of Science Degree, Business, May 20xx, GPA 3.6

Columbia College, Chicago

SKILLS: UNIX, C Programming, VRX; conversational in French

EXPERIENCE:

Software Engineer, April 20xx-June 20xx

AAA Computer Software, Chicago, IL

Created software for database management. Provided technical support to clients who installed various company software.

Associate Software Engineer, January 20xx-March 20xx

CompuServe, Reston, VA

Maintained company's current software programs and monitored client accounts.

HONORS:

Dean's List

Outstanding Programmer Award 20xx

MISCELLANEOUS:

Intramural Volleyball

Enjoy running, music, reading

figure 8.4

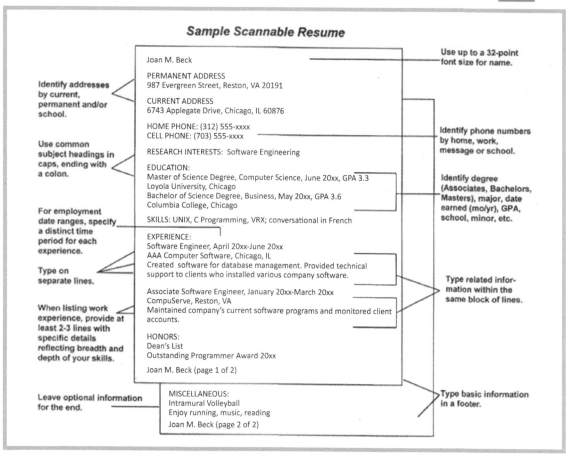

Sample Scannable Resume

Joan M. Beck

PERMANENT ADDRESS
987 Evergreen Street, Reston, VA 20191

CURRENT ADDRESS
6743 Applegate Drive, Chicago, IL 60876

HOME PHONE: (312) 555-xxxx
CELL PHONE: (703) 555-xxxx

RESEARCH INTERESTS: Software Engineering

EDUCATION:
Master of Science Degree, Computer Science, June 20xx, GPA 3.3
Loyola University, Chicago
Bachelor of Science Degree, Business, May 20xx, GPA 3.6
Columbia College, Chicago

SKILLS: UNIX, C Programming, VRX; conversational in French

EXPERIENCE:
Software Engineer, April 20xx-June 20xx
AAA Computer Software, Chicago, IL
Created software for database management. Provided technical
support to clients who installed various company software.

Associate Software Engineer, January 20xx-March 20xx
CompuServe, Reston, VA
Maintained company's current software programs and monitored client
accounts.

HONORS:
Dean's List
Outstanding Programmer Award 20xx

Joan M. Beck (page 1 of 2)

MISCELLANEOUS:
Intramural Volleyball
Enjoy running, music, reading

Joan M. Beck (page 2 of 2)

Annotations:
- Use up to a 32-point font size for name.
- Identify addresses by current, permanent and/or school.
- Use common subject headings in caps, ending with a colon.
- Identify phone numbers by home, work, message or school.
- Identify degree (Associates, Bachelors, Masters), major, date earned (mo/yr), GPA, school, minor, etc.
- For employment date ranges, specify a distinct time period for each experience.
- Type on separate lines.
- When listing work experience, provide at least 2-3 lines with specific details reflecting breadth and depth of your skills.
- Type related information within the same block of lines.
- Leave optional information for the end.
- Type basic information in a footer.

SOCIAL MEDIA AND NETWORKING: CONSIDERATIONS FOR THE PRE-EMPLOYMENT PROCESS

In addition to preparing your résumé for the job search, you should also consider how social media is used as a screening and a networking tool. Today's employers use different forms of mediated communication tools to connect with potential employees. According to **social information processing theory**, in face-to-face communication and through mediated communication, individuals have the same overarching motivation: to reduce uncertainty in initial interactions by forming impressions of others.[3]

Social information processing theory: Describes how perceptions and relationships are formed in the on-line environment.

Many people believe that face-to-face communication is the "best type" of communication, and that all other communication interactions should be measured against this archetype. However, such a view is limited; it limits the scope of human communication, the improvements of technology, and the ability of humans to meet their communication goals. Moreover, it ignores the fact that some things can be conducted better through mediated communication. Because there are fewer available cues which exist online, individuals use whatever cues a channel affords them to form impressions/make judgments about another—this creates opportunity and innovation.[3] All media, but particularly social media, are often viewed negatively in the workplace. Media such as social media can be seen as a distraction, a means of slowing down work or information or simply as unnecessary and unprofessional. Rather, media and social media are tools. They don't possess a negative or positive characteristic; the user is responsible for the proper/improper uses or functions of the tool.

Social Media and Impression Management in the Job Search

For employers engaged in the hiring process, information acquired during the pre-interview stage can be particularly salient because there is a wealth of additional resources that can be analyzed outside of the traditional résumé and cover letter. Due to the availability and popular use of social media sites, such as Facebook, Twitter, and LinkedIn, an employer can utilize these sites as potential tools to determine whom to interview and this information can impact hiring decisions both positively and negatively.

Social media provides opportunities for networking that can be advantageous when looking for a first job, or when attempting to change jobs. However, the social media user must be aware of their online presence and promote a presence that will be attractive to a potential employer. Human resources departments and hiring managers often use social media as an applicant screening tool. This can be considered as part of the pre-interview and hiring process.[4] A CareerBuilder survey with a sample of 2,303 human resources and hiring professionals found that more than a third of companies indicated that they use social media to assess potential candidates.[5] The most prevalent reasons hiring managers gave for using social media were to assess the candidate's professionalism; to determine if the candidate would fit in with the culture of the company; to better educate themselves on the candidate's qualifications; and to uncover information that would prevent the candidate from being hired. Furthermore, 34% of those surveyed who used social media as a part of the screening process indicated they found information that resulted in a decision not to hire an individual. This type of information ranged from a candidate whose social media contained inappropriate content/photos, instances of drinking alcohol and drug use, negative comments about previous employers, and similar other issues.

Social media can also be a potential advantage for job candidates whose online presence demonstrates a professional image, strong communication skills, attractive personality characteristics, and varied interests. These were some of the reasons employers in this survey gave as to why they hired a candidate based on his/her social media presence. It appears likely that because of the prevalence of social media and emphasis on utilizing new technology, more companies and recruiters will start to access and assess a potential candidate's social media site(s) to inform hiring decisions. Of employers that indicated they did not utilize social media, 11 percent said they intended to start doing so.[5]

Based on the results of this survey, social media can and does play an integral part in the pre-interview and hiring process. In addition, the finding that some employers based their decision not to hire an individual on his/her social media presence demonstrates the significance of this

Employers may base their decision to hire you on the way you represent yourself on social media.

© scythe5/Shutterstock.com

topic. Other research findings are consistent with results indicated in the CareerBuilder survey; particularly some of the reasons individuals gave that would prevent a candidate from being hired.[5]

For example, researchers Bohnert and Ross conducted an experiment in which participants were given a Web page and résumé that had been altered to reflect a candidate who was somewhat or well-qualified, and a Web page that reflected a person whose interests were drinking alcohol, their career, or their family (a control group did not receive a Web page).[6] Similar to hiring managers in the previous survey, participants in this experiment assigned the lowest ratings to the individual who reflected an affinity for drinking, and additionally, recommended the individual in the alcohol-oriented condition be paid less money than the person reflected in the family-centered condition. Similar results were found in another experimental study by communication researcher Joe Walther and colleagues.[7] They found that participants rated individuals whose Facebook profiles indicated excessive drinking and sexuality less favorably than those who did not. Although the Walther and colleagues study did not examine ratings in regard to hiring decisions, factors such as drinking, negatively influenced perception ratings in both studies. A phenomenon labeled context collapse is used to describe how information posted on social media networks intended to reach a particular group appears for unintended groups.[8]

A popular way to think about promoting oneself in social media is to consider it as a form of impression management. Specifically consider how system, user, and other generated cues work to promote an image or online presence of a person. In examining one's own profile, the question should be asked, "does my online presence communicate someone worth hiring?"

A person's first reaction is usually to change the privacy settings on their social media account, and this is a good first step. However, previous information could be reposted or accessible because of comments or reposts from other individuals (context collapse). Moreover, a person without a social media presence is often considered suspicious; thus there are many disadvantages to becoming social media invisible.[9] Therefore the best course of action is to work to create an appropriate and professional online presence. The first thing to think about are user-generated cues, these are the cues that the profile owner has the most control of. For example, consider the profile picture and profile name used for the account. Also, go back to Facebook and Twitter and any other account and ensure that the user-generated content communicates an image that is appropriate

Context collapse: The term used to describe how information posted on social media networks intended to reach a particular group appears for unintended groups.

User-generated cues: Pieces of information that social media profile owners have the most control over.

for the field in which you are applying. Remember, the user-generated content will be persuasive because it is content you have control over. Even check your YouTube.com account. If you use your name or e-mail address as your user name, an organization could stumble across it when examining your online presence. Ask yourself if the type of videos you have posted support the identity you have created in your other social media accounts. One of the authors of this textbook knew a member of a search committee examining applicant materials. The member of the committee stumbled across the YouTube.com account of an applicant. The organization was a charitable non-profit and was concerned about its members promoting the mission. The videos associated with the account, although not offensive, did not seem congruent with the mission of the organization, and the candidate, although qualified, was not interviewed.

Next, critically examine the other-generated cues which appear on your social media feed. Think of **other-generated cues** as information, or communication, created by someone who is not the owner of a social media page (someone other than you). These cues have the potential to be particularly influential. A profile owner has the ability to promote any impression they wish; however, if posts or comments left behind by others are not supportive of that image, it can harm the profile owner's credibility. Examples of other-generated cues which could undermine an image you want to present include inappropriate comments about images, offensive language, or links to sites with questionable content. These types of cues can include posts to a wall, retweets or directed tweets, frequent tags on pictures, or conversations on social media that should not be public. Such other-generated cues not only undermine the image you are attempting to manage but will allow the hiring manager or recruiter to question your image, your social network (which is a reflection on you), and it will raise the question "why wasn't this content removed?" which then impacts your credibility because obvious answers to this question include:

- the applicant does not realize this is inappropriate
- the applicant does not believe it is inappropriate
- the applicant does not know how to use social media

Other-generated content can be quite persuasive, so you want to ensure such content bolsters the image you present rather than negatively impacting that image or promoting a different image.[10]

System-generated cues also are pieces of information people can use to make attributions about an individual through social media, such as the number of followers on twitter, or friends on Facebook.[11] Cues left by the system often are given much credibility by individuals. This is because

Other-generated cues: Pieces of information, or communication, created by someone who is not the owner of a social media page (someone other than you).

System-generated cues: Pieces of information people can use to make attributions about an individual through social media.

a system-generated cue is difficult for an individual to manipulate. For example, the time stamp on a tweet, or image posted to Instagram are system-generated cues. If your time stamps consistently show someone who is active in the early hours of the morning (after midnight), employers may attribute this to negative characteristics about the individual. A person up late may be believed to be inattentive in the morning and therefore their application materials may not receive full attention.

System-generated cues also outline your public displays of connection.[12] Social network sites allow you, the user, easier access to your network, but also allow others to evaluate your network and who you are connected with. As with any other tool, there are positive and negative features, and guilt by association, although unfair, is a potential consequence of social network sites.

Think of social media as a tool to sell yourself and make connections during the pre-employment process. As outlined earlier, this is the time to straighten your online presence. At the very least many hiring managers will do a basic online search of their job candidate. See what emerges when a search is done with your name and school, or name and current employer. If there are comments and images which don't help communicate the impression you wish to promote, take them down or ask your friends to remove them. If you have social media sites which you no longer use or update, consider deleting or disabling your account. Additionally if you are active on several social media sites, consider eliminating some of the accounts. If you appear too active, a potential employer may question how seriously you will take your position. Some companies will ask you to turn over your social media passwords or to "friend" the organization for an initial check; however, the legality of this practice is state and situation specific. It's much easier to clean up your account before you have an interview or start a job search than after.

Professional Networking Sites: Creating a Professional Profile

If you are planning to look for a job, or change positions, consider the following suggestions as a starting point to create a better online presence. The first thing you should do is set up a LinkedIn account for your job search; most career experts agree that a public persona gives you an advantage when looking for a job. LinkedIn is the largest professional social network site and will allow you to best create a professional network. When creating your profile, start with good photo (a user-generated cue). According to an article titled "10 LinkedIn Blunders That Make You Look Like An Amateur," "all headshots are not created equal."[13] Therefore the photograph should be professional and pleasant, remember to smile. He also suggests considering having a professional take the photograph. You can hire someone to take it; however, you probably have a friend who can take it and enhance the image through photo editing software.

An article in *Business Insider* outlines the importance of the 120-character headline.[14] Rather than simply putting your official job title, use that space to describe what it is you do. Most importantly, complete your profile. LinkedIn can be a powerful tool if you use it to communicate, build, and maintain relationships. Use all of your social media to create a synergistic impression of yourself. Post your thoughts on industry trends or issues, post links to articles and other professional topics on your main page to share them with your network, and then comment on them. Attempt to lead the conversation and outline your expertise. Finally follow or connect with companies and individuals within the industry you hope to begin a career in. Use social media not only to connect and have conversations but to learn from these individuals and organizations.

It is also wise to be mindful of your conduct while you are considering a job offer. Employers not only will check your social media before an interview, but also will follow up after an offer is made.

CONCLUSION

As this chapter demonstrates, the quality of your résumé, application material, and social media profiles is paramount to obtaining a job interview and landing a position. Spend time with your résumé and tailor it to each individual company where you apply. Also, invest in sending the right message via your social media accounts.

Ethan Jordan, the college senior mentioned at the beginning of this chapter is off to a good start on his job search in that he has identified two specific industries and organizations as potential career options. He should begin conducting research on both and develop a résumé that demonstrates how he is a fit for each individual company. Specifically, Ethan will want to make an inventory of his skills, abilities, coursework, and personal interests that he can highlight in his résumé. This includes his participation in and leadership roles with different campus organizations, and leaving out high school information. He also plans to take a draft of his résumé to a couple of trusted professors and the campus career placement center for feedback. He intends to have two versions of his résumé available, one for mail and one that is scannable, and, he has already started setting up a LinkedIn profile that conveys his skills, interests, and professionalism. Ethan realizes that getting ready for the job market is time-consuming project, but he's confident that once his gets his first job, it will be time well spent.

ACTIVITIES

1. With a partner, brainstorm your experiences and come up with the best approach to present them in a résumé.

2. How would a chronological résumé be different for the job you are applying for than a skills résumé? Under what circumstances would you use the different formats?

3. Search the Internet for copies of scannable résumés. What are the similarities and differences between the samples? Which elements do you think would work best for creating this type of résumé?

4. Login to your Facebook or Twitter account. Analyze your entire account including your photos, comments, and newsfeed. What user, other, or system-generated content do you see? How would you evaluate the impression you might be giving to a potential employer? What types of strategies might you employ to edit and adapt your social media accounts to reflect the image you want to portray?

REFERENCES

[1] Vasagar, J. (2010, July 5). Graduates warned of record 70 applicants for every job. *The Guardian*. Retrieved on October 14, 2014, from http://www.theguardian.com/education/2010/jul/06/graduates-face-tougher-jobs-fight

[2] *Keeping an Eye On Recruiter Behavior*, Retrieved on October 14, 2014, from http://cdn.theladders.net/static/images/basicSite/pdfs/TheLadders-EyeTracking-StudyC2.pdf

[3] Walther, J. B. (1992). Interpersonal effects in computer-mediated interaction: A relational perspective. *Communication Research 19* (1): 52–90.

[4] Smith, W. P. & Kidder, D. L. (2010). You've been tagged! (Then again, maybe not): employers and Facebook. *Business Horizons, 53*(5), 491–499.

[5] Hunt, R. (2012). Thirty-seven percent of companies use social networks to research potential job candidates, according to new CareerBuilder Survey. Retrieved from http://www.careerbuilder.com/share/aboutus/pressreleasesdetail.aspx?id=pr691&sd=4%2f18%2f2012&ed=4%2f18%2f2099

[6] Bohnert, D., & Ross, W.H. (2010). The influence of social networking websites on the evaluation of job candidates. *Cyberpsychology, Behavior, and Social Networking, 13*(3), 341-347.

[7] Walther, J. B., Van Der Heide, B., Kim, S-Y., Westerman, D., & Tong, S. T. (2008). The role of friends' appearance and behavior on evaluations of individuals on Facebook: Are we known by the company we keep? *Human Communication Research, 34*, 28-49.

[8] Vitak, J. (2012). The impact of context collapse and privacy on social network site disclosures. *Journal of Broadcasting and Electronic Media, 56*, 451–470.

[9] White, M. C. (2012). Does not having a Facebook page make you 'suspicous' to employers? *Time magazine*. Retrieved http://business.time.com/2012/08/08/does-not-having-a-facebook-page-make-you-suspicious-to-employers/

[10] Spence, P. R., Lachlan, K. A., Spates, S. A., Lin, X., Shelton, A. K., & Gentile, C. J. (2013). Exploring the impact of ethnic identity through other-generated cues on perceptions of spokesperson credibility. *Computers in Human Behaviour, 29*, A3-11.

[11] Westerman, D. W., Spence, P. R., & Van Der Heide B. (2012). A social network as information: The effect of system generated reports of connectedness on credibility and health care information on Twitter. *Computers in Human Behavior, 28*, 199-206.

[12] Donath, J., & Boyd, D. (2004). Public displays of connection. *BT Technology Journal, 22*(4), 71.

[13] Arruda, W. (2014). 10 LinkedIn Blunders That Make You Look Like An Amateur. Retrieved from http://www.forbes.com/sites/williamarruda/2014/01/27/10-linkedin-blunders-that-make-you-look-like-an-amateur/

[14] Lumiere, H. F. (2013). 8 Steps To Creating A Powerful LinkedIn Profile. Retrieved from http://www.businessinsider.com/8-steps-to-creating-a-powerful-linkedin-profile-2013-12

ADDITIONAL SOURCES

Bukharian Entertainment and News. (2005, March 31). *What employers look for in applicants*. Retrieved May 10, 2008, from http://www.boojle.com/forums/showthread.php?t=180

Department of Labor. (2008, Spring/Summer). *The Labor Advocate*. Retrieved May 15, 2008, from http://www.dol.gov/

Isaacs, K. (n.d.). *Declutter your résumé in 5 steps*. Retrieved May 30, 2008, from http://career-advice.monster.com/resume-writing-basics/Declutter-Your-Resume-in-5-Steps/home.aspx

Isaacs, K. (n.d.). *Résumé critique checklist*. Retrieved May 30, 2008, from http://career-advice.monster.com/resume-critique/Resume-Critique-Checklist/home.aspx

Isaacs, K. (n.d.). *Résumé dilemma: Career change*. Retrieved May 30, 2008, from http://career-advice.monster.com/resume-writing-basics/career-changers/Resume-Dilemma-Career-Change/home.aspx

Isaacs, K. (n.d.). *What's your objective?* Retrieved May 30, 2008, from http://career-advice.monster.com/resume-writing-basics/Whats-Your-Objective/home.aspx

Oregon Employment Department. (2006, November 29). *What do employers look for in a job applicant?* Retrieved May 10, 2008, from http://www.qualityinfo.org/olmisj/ArticleReader?itemid=00004747

University of Wisconsin–River Falls. (n.d.). *What employers seek*. Retrieved May 10, 2008, from http://www.uwrf.edu/career/assets/documents/handouts/what_employers_seek.PDF

Vogt, P. (n.d.). *Avoid the top 10 résumé mistakes*. Retrieved May 30, 2008, from http://career-advice.monster.com/resume-writing-basics/entry-level-jobs/Avoid-the-Top-10-Resume-Mistakes/home.aspx

chapter nine

Interviewing: Processes and Best Practices

After reading this chapter you will be able to:

- Understand the types of interviewing questions
- Prepare yourself for a successful interview
- Have questions to ask of a potential employer
- Compose an appropriate follow-up message after an interview
- Prepare for phone or mediated interviews

CHAPTER OUTLINE

key words

Job interview
Behavioral interview

INTRODUCTION

Remember Ethan Jordan from the beginning of Chapter 8 who was worried about putting together a strong résumé to secure a job interview in his chosen field? Now that his résumé is ready to send out to potential employers, he plans to focus on obtaining and preparing for an actual job interview. His first stop is his university's career advising center. Not only do they provide job listings with potential employers, but they also supply much needed support for getting prepared for interviews including participating in a mock interview. After his first mock interview appointment, Ethan is left feeling a bit overwhelmed. He realizes there are many interpersonal processes at play and he wants to make sure he's ready to make a persuasive case that he's the right person for any job. This chapter spotlights the employment interview as an interpersonal mechanism for obtaining a new job. Read ahead and see how this information can assist Ethan Jordan in creating a well-thought-out plan for securing a position upon graduation.

SUCCESSFUL INTERVIEWING

Preparation is the key to a successful job interview. One of Ben Franklin's well-known sayings is that "Failing to prepare is preparing to fail." This fits well with the adage of getting it together for a job interview.

What is a **job interview**? Very simply put, a job, or employment, interview is just a conversation with a specific purpose. Whether you are the interviewer or the job candidate, trying to view this sometimes-intimidating experience as a simple conversation between people may take some of the pressure off. The job interview is a conversation between two people who both have a specific purpose in mind. Now, what are those purposes?

Job interview:
A conversation between two people who both have a specific purpose in mind.

For the job candidate, the purpose of a job interview is to make the most favorable impression possible, while gathering enough information about an employer to decide if you would like to work for them. It is important to keep in mind that the employer is not just interviewing you. You need to remember to use this time to interview them and decide whether or not you even want to work for them. This is why it is important for you to have questions prepared to ask the interviewer toward the end of the interview. Some examples of these questions will be posed later in the chapter.

For the employer, the purpose of a job interview is to gather enough of the right kind of information about you (the job candidate) to make a reliable prediction of how well you can do the job and fit into the organization. It is vital for the employer to be able not only to estimate how well you can perform the tasks of the job, but also how well you can work with the other people in the organization. This "fit" is probably even more important than how well the tasks of the job can be performed. In today's society people are working longer and longer workweeks averaging around 55 hours in 2007,[1] and frankly, you are going to have to spend a lot of time together!

Each person in a job interview has a specific purpose in the conversation.

© Kzenon/Shutterstock.com

SECTION 3: Social, Group, and Professional Competencies

How Do You Prepare for an Interview?

First, you need to give some serious thought to the following items:

1. **Your education, experience, and training, which will show your value to the employer.** You may think that this is material that you already know because you've already gathered it for your résumé and lived it, but it is important to really know what you've put down on your résumé, as the employer will have just read it, and it may have been a while since you put it together. You also need to strongly consider exactly what the organization is looking for and figure out how to turn your specific experience into exactly what they need. Make sure you know the terms and keywords or jargon of the organization that you are interviewing with and use those terms to describe your own experience.

Make sure to show off your personality!

2. **Personal traits, values, interests, and skills that will support your ability to make a contribution to the employer.** It may seem at first that the only thing an interviewer would need to know about your background would be your education and experience, but remember that the other part of an interview is how you will "fit" with the organization. Your personal traits and values will help you not only show the interviewer how you can fit into the organizational culture, but will also show them how you are different from the other people who are interviewing for this position. Make sure to show off your personality!

3. **Accomplishments, awards, acknowledgments of personal excellence that will make you a desirable candidate.** Now is the time for you to think outside of the box beyond your straight career goals or personality traits. Remember that if you are a recent college graduate, a good deal of other recent college graduates are competing with you for the job that you are interviewing for, so think about what really makes you different and what sets you apart

from the crowd. Whether it is passing the Jeopardy exam to be on the television show or appearing in the *Guinness Book of World Records* for making the world's largest burrito while in college, these are things that set you apart from the other applicants and give you and the interviewer something different to talk about. Highlighting your other interests such as snowboarding or sailing is another way to make a connection with the interviewer.

4. **Evidence of having well-thought-out career goals and following an intentional plan toward those goals.** If you are a recent college graduate, then the idea of having a plan for what you want to do for the rest of your life is incredibly daunting. When it comes to a job interview, if you really want the job, then you need to show the interviewer that you have a long-range goal that also includes them. This is not the time to talk about your personal life, so resist the urge to talk about your upcoming marriage or home purchase. Focus on the job that you are interviewing for and the company. Show them that you want to be with them for some time.

5. **Entry-level knowledge of your chosen field.** When starting a new job, employers don't expect you to know absolutely everything about everything nor to be able to run the place on your first day. They *do* expect you to know the basics of your area of work.

Now that we know how to prepare for our "conversation with a purpose," what are employers *really* looking for in job applicants? A quick search of the Internet will give you lists upon lists of topics, but here are just a few of those compiled into categories:

What Do Employers Look for in Applicants?

1. **Appearance.** First on the list is appearance because the age-old adage applies more to job interviews than anywhere else: "You never get a second chance to make a first impression." Many authors on this subject, including Cathie Garnier,[2] list appearance at the top of their lists of what employers look for because you won't get through the door if you don't have the visual appearance to match what the organization is looking for. More specifics on this topic will be discussed later in the chapter.

2. **Personality/style.** It may sound funny to say, but you have to have a personality! Make yourself stand out by really showing who you are and not who you think the interviewer *wants* you to be. This won't help you get the job because you aren't being yourself, they aren't

getting to know the real you, and you won't be able to see if you fit within the organization's culture. Showing your own personal style is a great way to get people to see your true personal self.

3. **Articulate/fluent expression.** This strongly fits under the category of communication, but being articulate is something that is getting lost in modern American English. Remember the movie *Miss Congeniality* with Sandra Bullock? Michael Caine, who plays the beauty pageant coach, tells Bullock's character "It's 'yes' not 'yeah.'" Remember to speak clearly and slowly, which can be difficult when you are nervous. Try to be conscious of your speech.

4. **Energy, drive, ambition.** You can overcome any weaknesses in your background or résumé by showing your interviewer some energy, drive, and ambition. A willingness to work is something that can't be taught in any school or gained by any experience; therefore, demonstrating your energy to work for their organization in particular will definitely give you a leg up on the competition.

5. **Positive attitude.** Having a positive attitude is something that may be difficult to accomplish. Even if this is not your favorite company to interview for, or you have been on a string of interviews, keeping up a happy face is key to getting that job.

6. **Thoughtful answers.** There are many places and sources for finding the answers for the typical interview questions (including this chapter), but you have to make sure that you take the time to think about how you are going to answer those questions. Spouting back the same answer that you read on the Internet isn't what will get you the job. Remember that those answers are just strategies, and you need to be sure to be thoughtful and place both yourself and the organization into the answer that you provide.

7. **Composure/confidence.** A job interview can be one of the most nerve-wracking experiences that you will have to go through, but maintaining a strong sense of composure while also appearing confident in yourself and your abilities is what will get you through it. Confidence is not arrogance, but remember that a job interview is a conversation with a purpose, and it is about selling yourself.

8. **Leadership.** Whether you are the captain of the community softball team or the president of any student group on campus, leadership is yet another thing to set you apart from the crowd and it is what will make you different. If you want to get ahead in today's work world, leadership is the key skill you need, and you need to demonstrate it from the beginning in your interview.

What do employers look for in future employees?
Ten key attributes that successful candidates of the future will bring to job interviews:
1. The ability to use information
2. An emphasis on interpersonal skills
3. Marketing skills—sell your ideas
4. Knowing when to act and when to respond to direction
5. Involvement—know how to participate with others
6. Change experience
7. Time management
8. The ability to be a team player
9. Personal accountability
10. Computer literacy

What do you want your appearance to say about you?

"You Never Get a Second Chance to Make a First Impression"

Your appearance says it all in an interview. There are several key steps that apply to all fields of business and professional life when it comes to the "professional" appearance. First, do your research and know your industry or field and what is considered appropriate to wear. More conservative fields such as accounting or finance demand more conservative dress, whereas more creative industries such as design areas will allow for more leeway. For the most part, dress conservatively. You want an employer to remember you, not your clothing. There is a reason that most of America tunes into *American Idol* for the initial auditions. Yes, one part is the bad singing, but the other is to see the crazy outfits! You want to be known for your experience and for what you will be able to do to help the organization, and not for the crazy suit you wore!

Think of your first interview suit as an investment in your career, not an extravagance. A quality suit says a lot about you without you saying anything. Make sure that it fits well and also feels comfortable to you. You don't want to have to spend several hours in a jacket that is several sizes too small or show up in a suit several sizes too big which makes you look like you are wearing your father's old suit. Another consideration is to think about your shoes. If you have not had to wear dress shoes at all or for long periods of time, wearing a new pair of shoes to a long interview can be murder. Make sure that you break in your shoes prior to your interview, and this goes for both men and women!

Above all, remember the details. That goes for matching shoes (brown shoes go with a brown belt, yes, people notice these things), a good haircut, tasteful jewelry and/or watch, and an overall professional image, no matter the industry you are going into.

Body Language Can Be Revealing

Actions speak louder than words. First impressions are extremely important. Your initial meeting forms a lasting impression on the employer, but your appearance is just part of this initial meeting impression. There are a few tricks to keep your first impression on the right track. First, remember to use good eye contact. When we get nervous, it may be easier to look at the floor or around the room, but direct your attention at the person to whom you are speaking. Try to control your nervousness, as looking overly anxious makes you seem unprepared. We all have different means of expressing nervous energy, but be careful to not play with your hair or jewelry, tap your fingers on the table, or jingle the change in your pocket. A strong handshake is expected, but don't overdo or underdo it. The "crusher" and "cold fish" handshakes don't leave the lasting impression you want with the interviewer. Be firm and leave it at that. Remember that smiling is an important nonverbal behavior, as it shows interest. You may be tired or uninterested, but if you want to get the job, remember to smile! A quick way to look engaged in the conversation is to lean forward. When sitting in a chair, sit toward the edge of it with your back away from the back of the chair to avoid slouching. When standing, lean forward slightly onto the balls of your feet. This slight angle will give the nonverbal signal that you are interested in the person speaking to you. Above all, remember to look and act interested and excited about the position!

Researching Employers: "What in the World Am I Looking For?"

It is equally or even more important for you to recognize what you yourself want from a job and an employer. There are several things to consider

© Kzenon/Shutterstock.com

Pay attention to your nonverbal communication so it sends the right message.

about an organization that will help you determine if you would like to work for them.

1. **Size of the organization.** A large multinational corporation or a small family-owned company will have a different feeling and a different work environment. The number of people that you would be working with may seem like a small fact, but the interpersonal dimensions that come from that are huge.

2. **Projected growth.** If you have decided that you would rather work for a smaller company, and then they develop a new product and shoot to the top of the *Fortune* 500 list, there goes your best-laid plan. Do your research and know where the companies you are interviewing with are headed in the near future.

3. **Product lines and services.** What do they make and who do they serve? This sounds like a basic question, but sometimes large companies or information-based companies can have clouded or hazy visions; therefore, doing your research and knowing what goes on in an organization on a day-to-day basis will help you make your decision.

4. **Projected new markets and services.** In addition to what they make and who they serve, knowing what they plan on making and who they plan on serving will help you predict the future of the company and yours with them as well.

5. **Type of training available.** When starting a new job, there is always a learning process. Finding out what kind of training is available may determine whether or not you want to work for a company or their competitor. If there is a 6-month training period, finding out if that time is paid or if that training is done in the location where you will be working or across the country may help you make your decision. Also, be sure to ask who is responsible for expenses when you are in training. If you have to go across the country, does the organization pay for your housing or do you?

6. **Who is the competition?** Find out who the competition is because you may want to work for them!

7. **Location of headquarters and branch offices.** If your goal is to stay in your local community, knowing where the other branch offices and the headquarters of the company are located is important. If, for some reason, the branch you are placed in closes, where would you and your family be moved? Perhaps this could be the deciding factor in selecting an organization to work for.

8. **Current news items.** Even a quick Google search can tell you what is happening publicly with an organization. Awards or board

Ask questions about the company's training for your position.

© Pressmaster/Shutterstock.com

of trustees' indictments can be found in the media and tell you a lot about what is going on within an organization.

9. **Promotion opportunities.** Assuming that you don't want to stay with the same entry-level job the rest of your life, a promotion is what you should be looking for. Do some research about how quickly you can get promoted and how that process occurs.

What Are They Going to Ask Me? Questions Asked by Employers

There are lists upon lists of questions that could be asked at a job interview and the following are just a few that are either more common or more thought provoking.

- Tell me about yourself.
- Why are you interested in this position?
- What are your greatest strengths?
- What is your greatest weakness?
- What accomplishment are you most proud of?
- How does your education and work experience relate to this job?
- What job-related skills have you developed?
- How would a past supervisor describe you?
- Do you work well under pressure?
- Where do you want to be in your career in 5 years?

"So Do You Have Any Questions for Us?" Questions to Ask Them

It is important to have a few questions planned to ask the employers at the end of the interview. Without a doubt there will be a time when the interviewer asks you for questions, and it is a good plan to have some questions prepared in advance just so your mind doesn't go blank at that moment. Following are just a few examples.

- What are the opportunities for personal and professional growth?
- How is an employee evaluated and promoted?
- Describe a typical workday.
- What makes your organization different from its competitors?
- What qualities are you looking for in your new employees?
- What are the organization's plans for future growth?
- What is the retention rate of people in the position for which I am interviewing?

What Is Behavioral Interviewing?

Behavioral interviewing is a structured interviewing strategy built on the premise that past behavior is the best predictor of future performance in similar circumstances. These are the "Tell me about a time when" questions. This is a way for the interviewer to try to figure out how you will react to situations that may come up in their organization. Following are a few that will both get you thinking and put you in an organizational setting. The trick to answering these is to remember to think of an organizational setting (or even a group project that you worked on while in school) that you were once in and apply that to the question.

Examples of behavioral based interview questions:

- Tell me about a time when things didn't work out the way you wanted them to.
- Tell me about the most difficult customer you have run into recently.
- Tell me about a recent project that you've found challenging.
- Tell me about a situation where you had to do creative problem solving.
- Tell me about a time you were assertive and it backfired on you.
- Tell me about the coworker you get along with the least.

Quick Tips for a Positive Interview

1. **Use the interviewer's name during the interview.** Even if you are bad with names, repeating the name of the interviewer is an important detail to pay attention to.
2. **Phrase questions so that you sound sure of yourself, "What would be my duties?" rather than "What are the duties of the job?"** This is a way to place yourself into the job even while you are in the interview. You demonstrate confidence at the same time.
3. **Use good grammar and diction.** It's yes, not yeah.
4. **Don't talk too fast; moderate your speech.** This can be very difficult

© wavebreakmedia/Shutterstock.com

when you are nervous or when you start talking about yourself, but try to be conscious of your rate of speech.

5. **Don't fill pauses with "um," "you know," "like," or "OK."** Verbal fillers are just a part of everyday speech, but they can become even more prevalent when you are nervous. Be careful of filling verbal space just to avoid silence.

6. **Be animated rather than monotone when speaking.** A job interview can become monotonous, but remember to show them your energy and positive attitude.

7. **Use active verbs.** Active verbs are verbs that show action. Using active verbs such as writing, showing, or presenting show the interviewer your action and energy.

8. **Talk about your skills with positive words; avoid indecisive phrases such as "pretty good" or "I guess."** Women have a tendency to do this more than men: "I'm pretty good at that" instead of "I am good at that." Show your confidence and your knowledge by clearly stating your skills.

9. **Watch your voice tone—don't end sentences with a higher tone of voice, making them sound like questions.** This is called cadence in speech delivery, the rising of pitch at the end of a declarative sentence, which in turn makes it sound like a question. Because of this, it makes you sound unsure of yourself.

10. **Offer examples of your accomplishments; use stories and illustrations to support your claims.** Be sure to not just answer "yes" or "no" to any questions asked of you. Use stories to illustrate your answers clearly, and remember to stay on target with your answers.

11. **Don't be afraid to acknowledge that you might not have all of the answers.** If you don't know that answer to something, acknowledge what you don't know, but then formulate your answer highlighting what you do know.

12. **Find a balance in the length of your responses.** Focus on not saying too much or too little. Knowing when to stop talking and when to keep talking are important interpersonal communication skills that involve self-monitoring. Don't ramble.

13. **When responding, take your time.** It's better to pause and collect your thoughts than to ramble on until you come up with the right answer

14. **Don't worry about being judged, just stay calm** and focus on integrating your personality, skills, and experiences with what the company is looking for.

15. **Be yourself, and be personal while at the same time tailoring your responses**. Work to frame your answers in a way that fits the position and the needs of the organization

Above all try to be yourself. Being successful in a job interview does not mean being inauthentic or trying to give the interviewer all the answers that you think he or she wants to hear. It's about showing your personality while at the same time discussing your experiences and accomplishments in a way that showcases how you can meet the needs of the employer. If you have spent time preparing your application materials, researching the industry and organization, and practicing interviewing with friends or family or your university's career services center, then you'll be ready to respond with thoughtful answers to any question that might come up.

Interviewing Do's and Don'ts
DO
1. Do know all you can about the organization beforehand.
2. Do arrive at least 5 minutes before the interview.
3. Do greet the employer with a firm handshake.
4. Do present yourself positively, with enthusiasm for the organization and the position.
5. Do sell yourself effectively.
6. Do be yourself—let them get to know you.
7. Do ask appropriate questions.
8. Do thank them for the interview and follow up with a letter.
DON'T
1. Don't arrive late.
2. Don't bring up negative information.
3. Don't act like the kind of person you think they want.
4. Don't act unsure about your career goals.
5. Don't bring up salary.
6. Don't smoke or chew gum.
7. Don't answer only "yes" or "no" without further explanation.

8. Don't "undersell" yourself.

9. Don't expect perfection—mistakes are OK; you're human.

10. Don't expect to be hired on the spot.

The Night Before the Interview

Remember that preparation is key. The night before an interview is like the night before an exam like the SATs or ACTs. Basically, just remember to take it easy, review your research, and relax.

1. Get a good night's sleep.
2. Make decisions about your wardrobe.
3. Determine how long it will take to arrive at the interview and where to park.
4. Review how you will greet the interviewer.
5. Examine your files on the organization and review notes on the position.
6. Practice the most important questions and answers.
7. Use stress-reduction techniques.
8. Review the content of your résumé.

After the Interview: Follow-Up Letters

The employment interview process doesn't end with the last handshake, many employers expect a follow-up message. Sending a follow-up letter or a thank you note after an interview is a common practice and often considered a professional courtesy. These follow-up letters are promoted because they not only demonstrate good manners, but also provide the applicant another opportunity to present a positive image to the interviewer. Little research has been conducted on the best type, content, or time frame for follow-up letters. However, it appears that an applicant should send one because everyone else applying for the position will most likely be sending a follow up or thank you message.

Most career centers, blogs, or popular press articles indicate that follow-up letters should include an expression of appreciation for the time and information provided by the interviewer. The applicant should also restate the position he/she interviewed for, the interview date, and place.

Other suggestions for follow up letters include

- restating interest in the position,
- specific references to the conversation,

- any additional qualifications or work experience not included on the résumé
- the applicant's availability for additional interviews

There is no agreed-upon format for the follow-up letter. Some suggest that an e-mail 2-5 days after the interview is appropriate, whereas others suggest that it should be a handwritten note or a purchased thank you card. Regardless, with research on this topic being absent, and many recommending the use of a follow-up message, it is sound advice for an applicant to follow an interview up with some type of thank you card, phone message, or note.

Phone Interviews in the Pre-Employment Process

Now that we have covered what to expect and how to prepare for a face-to-face interview, it is also important to know how to navigate phone and Skype interviews. Often the use of phone interviews occurs in the pre-employment process. These are sometimes used as a screening tool, or when circumstances don't allow a face-to-face interview to happen. It is also becoming more common to use Skype or some type of video chat software in the screening interview process. These are both inexpensive tools to assess candidates early in the recruitment process. The phone interview as a screening interview may be the first verbal contact a person has with a prospective employer. It is common for this to be conducted by a member of human resources, the position supervisor or a company hired to conduct the screening interview. At this point the prospective applicant's materials have been reviewed and the employer and the individual making a hiring decision believe the applicant possesses the minimum qualifications for the job. The interview process is used to find the right person for the position and learn more about the applicant's characteristics and previous experience. The phone interview may create anxiety in the applicant, especially with the absence of nonverbal cues used in face-to-face communication; however, handling the phone interview is necessary to get to the next step of the process.

If the screening interview is being conducted by a professional company, it will be highly structured. The interviewer will not be interested in small talk or getting to know the applicant. For this type of interview it is important to be relaxed and give honest straightforward answers. Such highly structured phone interviews vary in length, but an applicant should expect them to consist of 30-60 minutes of questions.

There are several suggestions an applicant can follow to improve the phone interview. The first is to find a quiet place. Any distraction such as loud roommates or noise from a coffee shop will reflect poorly on the applicant. The interviewer will probably internalize negative attributes associated with the call, and also has other people interested in the job. Also, an applicant should have their résumé and the position announcement nearby during the interview, making it easier to refer to that information. If the interviewer calls without notice and asks to conduct an interview at that moment, it's best for the applicant to ask if he/she can call the interviewer back in 10-15 minutes. The applicant should simply indicate that they are in the middle of something and can quickly finish it. This allows the applicant time to collect relevant materials, relax, and to remove any distractions which may emerge.

If the interview is conducted using Skype, remember to use a clean room, remove any questionable photographs from the walls and make sure all pets (and family members) are in another room and quiet. One of the authors of the current text was interviewing a person over Skype and the applicant had a cat which kept jumping on the keyboard of the laptop and obstructing the view of the camera. This was a continued distraction which reduced the credibility and professional image of the applicant.

According to several corporate recruiters and career counselors the applicant should also dress professionally for the phone interview. Although the interviewer can't see the applicant, the act of dressing professionally can make the applicant feel more confident, this will be reflected in their voice. Also, when taking part in a phone interview, the applicant should smile and consider standing; this is noticeable and also makes a difference. Don't chew gum or snack during the interview. Finally, as with any other interview, remember to ask questions. The applicant should ask specific questions about the job, organizational culture, day-to-day expectations, and anything else that will help him/her make an informed decision. Also, the applicant should ask about the next step in the interview process, including when the applicant should expect to hear back from the company.

Many Web sites and books suggest that an applicant should use a landline for the phone interview. Although this is ideal, many individuals no longer use a landline or have access to one in a quiet place. Because of this, make sure you are in a location with strong and reliable cell phone service and make sure your battery is fully charged.

If an applicant is confident they are speaking to a member of the company such as a hiring manager or supervisor and not a professional interviewing company, it is important to approach the phone interview the same way as one would a face-to-face interview. This includes being able to explain all information presented on the résumé. Answers should be honest and to the point providing as much detail as necessary. The applicant should also remember that the interviewer will attempt to make attributions about characteristics such as self-confidence, personality, communication ability, and emotional intelligence through the phone interview.[3] Therefore the applicant has to answer the questions and build rapport. Also, because the interview may not be as structured as one conducted by a professional interviewing company, it is appropriate to ask how much time the interviewer has to talk. This will allow the applicant to have some control concerning how much information is covered and allow the applicant to prioritize what information they believe they need to cover. Other common suggestions include being slow to answer, ensuring that the applicant does not interrupt the interviewer. This is best accomplished by listening carefully. The box below highlights other important tips to remember when preparing for and participating in a phone or Skype interview.

Bill Smitley, a Human Resource specialist with DP Fox Ventures, headquartered in Grand Rapids Michigan, knows the ins and outs of interviews. He conducts phone and in-person interviews on a daily basis. Bill states that there are many ways a candidate can win a position or lose a position during the interview. He outlines these pointers for the applicant to remember during the phone interview:

Things to Remember and Enact (Phone Interview–Do's)
- Prepare for the phone interview by compiling a list of your strengths and weaknesses, accomplishments, and answers to typical questions.
- Have a copy of your résumé in front of you to refer to when speaking about your work experience.
- Talk slowly (pace) and deliberately, be relaxed and confident
- Have a pen and paper (or tablet) available to take notes during the interview and questions to ask at the end.
- Be in a quiet place **alone**—turn off the radio, television, and any other background noise that might be distracting.
- Take a moment to think about the question (don't be afraid of a second of silence), and, then, respond with a slow and deliberate pace.
- Smile during the phone interview to project a positive tone in your voice and your image.
- Ask well-thought-out, relevant questions about the job, company, market, and industry.
- Send a thank you note after the phone interview to reiterate your interest in the position.

Things to Remember and Avoid (Phone Interview–Dont's)
- Smoke, eat, or chew gum or candy during the interview. A quiet sip of water when the interviewer is talking is not a problem.
- Ramble—make sure that your answers are direct and to the point.
- Interrupt the interviewer when he or she is speaking.
- Provide too much information—keep your answers short and to the point; however, make sure to answer the questions fully.
- Repeat the question to the interviewer, just answer it.
- Speak negatively "bad-mouth" former employers.

Mr. Smitley can be found on LinkedIn.com/in/williamsmitley or on twitter @billsmitley

CONCLUSION

As this chapter demonstrates, your ability to communicate interpersonally is critical to securing employment and advancing within any organization. Never underestimate the power of these tools. Not only is face-to-face communication important, but how you navigate mediated channels in the interview process has critical implications for your job search.

Ethan Jordan, the college senior mentioned at the beginning of this chapter has a well-developed résumé and is ready to prepare for the interview process. When he gets an interview, he'll practice with a friend first, answering questions and incorporating lots of examples from his life which relate appropriately. With a new conservative business suit, his notes on the organization, a list of questions for potential employers, and a positive attitude, Ethan is already in a better position than many of his competitors. More than anything else, he wants to be himself, and let others see his personality and his potential.

ACTIVITIES

1. With a partner, role-play interviewing each other with standard interviewing questions, such as, "What is your greatest weakness?" and "Tell me about yourself."

2. With a partner, role-play interviewing each other by Skype. Prepare just as you would for a face-to-face interview. What did you observe when interviewing your partner? Did the mediated channel present any unexpected challenges for you as the interviewer or interviewee? Debrief the activity and discuss ways to improve with your partner.

3. Watch clips from television shows that interview different types of people (e.g., *The View, Nancy Grace*). What do you notice about how questions are asked and answered? How might these types of interviews inform your own approach to an employment interview?

REFERENCES

[1] Wax, D. (2007, September 3). *Labor Day meditation*. Retrieved May 10, 2008, from http://www.lifehack.org/articles/lifestyle/labor-day-meditation.html

[2] Garnier, C. (2006, September 22). *Top 10 qualities employers look for in teen job applicants*. Retrieved May 10, 2008, from http://www.associatedcontent.com/article/61622/top_10_qualities_employers_look_for.html

[3] Fertig, A. (2014). 7 Tips to ace a phone interview. What you need to know to impress during a phone screen interview. Retrieved from http://money.usnews.com/money/blogs/outside-voices-careers/2014/02/18/7-tips-to-ace-a-phone-interview

ADDITIONAL SOURCES

Bukharian Entertainment and News. (2005, March 31). *What employers look for in applicants*. Retrieved May 10, 2008, from http://www.boojle.com/forums/showthread.php?t=180

Department of Labor. (2008, Spring/Summer). *The Labor Advocate*. Retrieved May 15, 2008, from http://www.dol.gov/

Hardy, D. (n.d.). *What if your interview is tomorrow?* Retrieved May 10, 2008, from http://career-advice.monster.com/interview-preparation/What-If-Your-Interview-Is-Tomorrow/home.aspx

Levchuck, C. (n.d.). *How to answer the toughest interview questions*. Retrieved May 12, 2008, from http://hotjobs.yahoo.com/interview/How_To_Answer_The_Toughest_Interview_Questions___2003915-1702.html?subtopic=Interview+Preparation

Levchuck, C. (n.d.). *How to deal with interview stress*. Retrieved May 12, 2008, from http://hotjobs.yahoo.com/interview/How_to_Deal_With_Interview_Stress__20050126-011331.html?subtopic=Interview+Preparation

Martin, C. (n.d.). *Assessing your skills: What makes you different from all the others?* Retrieved May 10, 2008, from http://career-advice.monster.com/selfassessment/Assessing-Your-Skills/home.aspx

Martin, C. (n.d.). *Nonverbal communications: Escape the pitfalls*. Retrieved May 10, 2008, from http://career-advice.monster.com/at-the-interview/Nonverbal-Communications-Escape-the/home.aspx

Martin, C. (n.d.). *Ten interview fashion blunders: What not to wear to the interview*. Retrieved May 10, 2008, from http://career-advice.monster.com/interview-preparation/Ten-Interview-Fashion-Blunders/home.aspx

Oregon Employment Department. (2006, November 29). *What do employers look for in a job applicant?* Retrieved May 10, 2008, from http://www.qualityinfo.org/olmisj/ArticleReader?itemid=00004747

Peterson, T. (n.d.). *100 potential interview questions*. Retrieved May 10, 2008 from http://career-advice.monster.com/job-interview-practice/100-Potential-Interview-Questions/home.aspx

Peterson, T. (n.d.). *Job interview pointers: Get advice and insight from Waggener Edstrom's staffing partner.* Retrieved May 10, 2008, from http://career-advice.monster.com/interview-preparation/Job-Interview-Pointers/home.aspx

Rossheim, J. (n.d.). *Do your homework before the big interview.* Retrieved May 10, 2008, from http://career-advice.monster.com/interview-preparation/Do-Your-Homework-Before-the-Big-Int/home.aspx

Turner, J. (n.d.). *An interview strategy: Telling stories.* Retrieved May 12, 2008, from http://hotjobs.yahoo.com/interview/An_Interview_Strategy_Telling_Stories__20061128-041625.html?subtopic=Interview+Preparation

University of Wisconsin–River Falls. (n.d.). *What employers seek.* Retrieved May 10, 2008, from http://www.uwrf.edu/career/assets/documents/handouts/what_employers_seek.PDF

Vogt, P. (n.d.). *Dressing for the interview by industry.* Retrieved May 10, 2008, from http://career-advice.monster.com/interview-preparation/Dressing-for-the-Interview-by-Indus/home.aspx

Vogt, P. (n.d.). *Six answers interviewers need to hire you.* Retrieved May 10, 2008, from http://career-advice.monster.com/job-interview-practice/Six-Answers-Interviewers-Need-to-Hi/home.aspx

section
four

Presentation Preparation Issues

chapter
ten

Audience Analysis and Delivery Dynamics

After reading this chapter you will be able to:

- Describe how to analyze your audience
- Explain the importance of audience adaptation
- Delineate the four delivery methods
- Describe techniques for a successful presentation

CHAPTER OUTLINE

- Introduction
- Audience Analysis
- Delivery Dynamics
- Conclusion
- Activities
- References

key words

Audience analysis	Audience adaptation
Situational analysis	Delivery
Audience oriented	Manuscript
Egocentric	Memorized
Demographic data	Impromptu
Ethnocentrism	Extemporaneous

INTRODUCTION

William Mathews, an investment broker, is employed by a well-known bank that has just opened a branch in a large city in the Midwest. Being the "new kid in town," the bank administrators decided on a PR campaign that included sending employees out to speak to various groups in the community. The administrators felt that this exposure would help bring business to the bank. They chose their top brokers, telling them that their presentations to various community groups were crucial to the bank's success. The brokers boned up on their knowledge of successful mutual funds, annuities, and other stock offerings. They also reviewed their knowledge of the history of the bank and its operating success in other communities. The brokers knew their information inside and out and were excited about speaking to many members of the community about the opportunities for investing that the bank could provide.

William's first presentation was made to a group of graduating seniors from a local college. As William delivered his prepared comments to the group, he noticed restless movement, lack of eye contact, and silence. At the end of his presentation, he asked if there were any questions. There weren't any, and the group seemed eager to leave. The next group he addressed was a mixture of people who worked in various professions outside banking and investments. He delivered the same comments and again noticed a lack of interest. Driving back to the bank at the end of the day, he thought that his audience members must not be very bright because they obviously couldn't see how useful the bank could be to them. He had three more groups to address the next day. Certainly, they would see the benefits of using his services. His next thought was that he couldn't wait to get back to his condominium and spend some time relaxing. After all, his work was essentially done. He had his remarks prepared and ready to go. All he had to do was deliver them.

The next day, things didn't go much better. His audiences were polite, but there were no questions at the end of his comments, and the people didn't really seem to be listening. He couldn't understand it. He had PowerPoint slides loaded with numbers and percentages and great examples filled with lots of statistics to impress his listeners.

He also used lots of investment jargon to impress his listeners: put, call, stock option, margin, annuity, mutual fund, and leverage. He couldn't understand why his listeners weren't jumping out of their seats, eager to open up accounts with him.

William Mathews knew all about the world of investments, but he had no idea how to communicate what he knew to his audience. He had done his homework on the investment end. But he failed in one crucial area. He didn't analyze his audience. He had no idea who was in his audience, why they were there, and what they knew about his topic. He gave the same remarks to five different audiences. No wonder his communication failed. The other problem William had was that he didn't think about his delivery skills. Mostly, he read his prepared comments from his PowerPoint slides or from his very detailed notes. He didn't recognize the importance of eye contact or vocal variety or sounding enthusiastic about the material

Why is it essential to know your audience before you present?

he presented. After all, he thought it was exciting. He figured that was enough. William failed to communicate because he didn't understand the importance of audience analysis and dynamic delivery skills.

Could this happen to you? It could, and it will happen to you if you don't understand how important your audience is in the communication process. If you don't know who is sitting in your audience, their purpose for being there, where they come from, and other important factors such as their age, income level, educational background, religious affiliation, political affiliation, how many men and how many women, and their knowledge about the topic, then you cannot tailor your remarks to meet the needs of your particular audience. If you read from your PowerPoint slides or from a manuscript, never establishing eye contact with your audience, then you will fail to communicate with your audience because they will stop listening to you. On the other hand, you can be a successful communicator if you are aware of two aspects of successful communication: audience analysis and dynamic delivery.

AUDIENCE ANALYSIS

Audience analysis refers to knowing as much as you can about the audience to whom you will be speaking. No two audiences are the same, and no two presentations that you do should be the same either.

It is vital to know where your audience is coming from—their understanding of the subject matter, background, interests, and reasons for being there. Clearly, you would not deliver the same message to a high school graduating class that you would to your board of directors or your stockholders.[1]

■ ■ ■ ■ ■ ■ ■ ■

Audience analysis: Knowing as much as you can about the audience to whom you will be speaking.

An apocryphal story tells how a speaker once was going to address the handicapped bowlers' league. He never called his host to check on the audience because he assumed that the name said it all. He carefully prepared his remarks to focus on issues related to disabled athletes. He was prepared to commend them on their tenacity and courage in pursuing athletic activities in the face of physical disabilities. As he stood at the lectern and looked across the audience, he suddenly noticed that there was not a wheelchair in the house. Handicap referred to their bowling scores. The only thing disabled was his speech.[1]

Audience analysis is not hard, but it does take effort on your part. Whenever you are asked to do a presentation, you are usually informed about the date, the time, and the topic. This is when *your* real work begins. When you agree to do the presentation, ask questions. The event organizer or the contact person will not mind answering your questions, so don't be shy. If you have to ask 18 questions before you are confident that you know all you can about the audience, ask the 18 questions with no apology. The event organizer might not understand that you need information about who will be in the audience. The event organizer is not the speaker and may have never given a presentation. If not, then they have no idea how important this knowledge is to you.

Audience analysis has two parts: the situation and the audience. Both of these are equally important.

Situational Analysis

Situational analysis includes knowing about the room size, the arrangement of the chairs and the tables, whether there is a microphone, whether there will be a stage or a dais, whether the situation is formal or informal, and whether it is a serious or a more humorous event. All these aspects will determine how you structure and deliver your speech.

The components of situational analysis include:

1. **Room size.** Any presentation needs to be more formal as the room gets bigger. A large audience usually means that you will need to use a microphone to be heard. You will usually need to stand in

Situational analysis: Knowing about the room size, the arrangement of the chairs and the tables, whether there is a microphone, whether there will be a stage or a dais, whether the situation is formal or informal, and whether it is a serious or a more humorous event

What do you look for when you conduct a situational analysis?

© August_0802/Shutterstock.com

front of the group rather than walking around. It will probably be more lecture style than interactive.

2. **Arrangement.** The way that the chairs and tables are set up is important for you to know. If this is a breakfast, lunch, or dinner meeting, then people might be seated at round tables, which means some people will have their backs to you. If this is a conference style presentation, people might be seated at round tables or square tables, but there still might be people sitting with their backs to the speaker. You need to know if the chairs will be set up in rows, in a U-shape, or in some other configuration.

3. **Microphone.** Are you comfortable using a microphone? Have you ever used one? Keep in mind that there are different kinds of microphones. One type is a stationary microphone, which is attached to a lecture or podium and limits your movement. You need to stay in front of this microphone, or your words will be lost. You might also have a handheld microphone, either wireless or attached by a long cord. This is also somewhat limiting because even though you can carry the microphone with you, you need to watch how far you turn your head away from the microphone. A wireless lapel microphone is convenient because the microphone clips to a collar or a jacket lapel, and the battery pack clips to your waistband. This microphone is quite mobile, but if you turn your head too far away from the microphone, some words will still be lost. The other thing to remember about a microphone is that you need to speak slowly and clearly so that your voice is not distorted. Whenever possible, do a microphone check well before your presentation. This will help you figure out how far away or how close to the microphone you need to stand. Some microphones are extremely sensitive, whereas others require that you stand very close.

4. **Stage or dais.** Where will you be seated? Will you be on a stage or seated on a dais? How far is it between you and the lectern? Find out beforehand where you'll be seated so you know whether you have to climb stairs to get up to the stage or dais or if you need to modify your attire because you will be sitting in front of and above your audience.

5. **Type of event.** Is your event formal, informal, humorous, or serious? Don't make the mistake of not finding out this information. If you don't ask, the organizer of the event might not think to tell you. The type of event will determine your personal appearance, your delivery method, and the type of remarks you make.

President Lincoln knew the importance of tailoring his remarks to his audience and the situation.

One example of excellent audience analysis is the "Gettysburg Address," delivered by President Abraham Lincoln on November 19, 1863. Do you remember the circumstances surrounding the delivery of the "Gettysburg Address"? The nation was engaged in the Civil War. President Lincoln was the sitting president. He was asked to give remarks at the cemetery at Gettysburg, but he was not the featured speaker. A man named Edward Everett, a noted orator, was to be the featured speaker. The event would be held outside in Pennsylvania in November. President Lincoln knew all these things as he prepared his remarks. Mr. Everett spoke for two hours. Mr. Lincoln spoke for less than three minutes. Whose words did you study in middle school and high school? Whose words have been recorded in our history books? Mr. Lincoln spent time thinking about the audience and the situation and then he tailored his remarks to that situation and to those listeners.

You may never give a speech of such historic nature, but your speeches will be important. Don't set yourself up for failure because you neglect to find out ahead of time about the situation. If you live nearby, ask the organizer of the event if you can make arrangements to spend a few minutes looking over the room where you will be speaking. Ask how the chairs and tables will be arranged for your event. If there is a microphone, ask that the sound be turned on so that you can practice your remarks using the microphone. If there are stairs leading up to the stage, practice walking up those stairs, preferably in the shoes you will be wearing at the event. If you will be seated on the stage or a dais, find out how far away from the lectern or podium your seat will be. If you will be using technology, make sure you practice your presentation with that technology. Be familiar with how to activate projectors and computers and overheads. Make sure you know how to pull down screens or access the button that will raise and lower the screen or close the blinds for you. Walk to the back of the room and look toward the lectern. This will give you the audience's view of *you*. Can they see you? Can they see the screen? Can they see any other visual aids that you will use? Practice your entire presentation complete with visual aids in the room where you will be speaking whenever possible.

The Gettysburg Address

Four score and seven years ago our forefathers brought forth on this continent, a new nation, conceived in liberty, and dedicated to the proposition that all men are created equal.

Now we are engaged in a great civil war, testing whether that nation, or any nation so conceived and so dedicated, can long endure. We are met on a great battlefield of that war. We have come to dedicate a portion of that field, as a final resting place for those who here gave their lives that that nation might live. It is altogether fitting and proper that we should do this.

But in a larger sense, we cannot dedicate—we cannot consecrate—we cannot hallow this ground. The brave men, living and dead, who struggled here, have consecrated it, far above our poor power to add or detract. The world will little note, nor long remember, what we say here, but it can never forget what they did here. It is for us the living, rather, to be dedicated here to the unfinished work which they who fought here have thus far so nobly advanced. It is rather for us to be here dedicated to the great task remaining before us—that from these honored dead we take increased devotion to that cause for which they gave the last full measure of devotion—that we here highly resolve that these dead shall not have died in vain—that this nation, under God, shall have a new birth of freedom—and that government of the people, by the people, for the people, shall not perish from the earth.

If you don't live nearby, arrange to arrive at your speaking destination early so that you have access to the room where you will be speaking. Go in before anyone arrives and check out the room arrangements and the microphone so that you feel comfortable when it's time for you to speak. There is no worse feeling than walking into a speaking situation and not knowing how to use the technology, not knowing how sensitive the microphone is, and being frustrated at how the chairs are arranged. Do yourself a favor and ask questions ahead of time. If you want the room to be set up in a specific way, make that clear to the organizers of the event. If you need certain technology, make sure that it is available and in working order. Practice as much of your presentation as time allows. You will be grateful that you did this preparation.

The Audience

Audience-oriented: Keeping your audience first in mind as you plan, write, and deliver your presentation

Check out the room arrangement and microphone before anyone arrives so you feel comfortable when it's time to speak.

As hard as it may be to believe, successful communication depends on you, but it is really all about your audience. That statement might seem contradictory when you first read it. What it means is that you are responsible for your communication being successful, and the only way to do that is to concentrate on communicating with your audience. Many new speakers mistakenly believe that they need to think primarily about themselves: their clothing, their hair, their makeup, their knowledge, and the list continues. These things are important, but they become secondary when you need to communicate successfully. As a speaker, you need to be **audience-oriented**, which simply means that you keep your audience first in mind as you plan, write, and deliver your presentation.

One advantage of being in a public speaking or a business and professional communication class is that your audience is the same every time. Don't make the mistake of thinking that you know all that you need to know about your audience just by looking at them. You don't. This is a great time to start sharpening your audience analysis skills. Maybe your first speaking assignment is to write and deliver an informative speech, and you choose to speak about the rising cost of college tuition. One way to be audience oriented is to show your audience how the rising tuition costs will affect each of them directly. Ask questions. Find out how many students are paying for college themselves, how many students are on scholarship, how many receive financial aid, how many are having their college paid for by their parents, and how many classmates hold down a job. This allows you to discover what your audience needs to hear in your speech. One essential piece of information for you to always remember about any audience is that they are **egocentric**, which means that they are primarily concerned about themselves. You've heard the expression, "Looking out for number one." That's what audience members are doing. They are looking out for number one—themselves. So, how can you make your speech on the rising cost of college tuition affect your audience? Give them specific, clear examples of how the rising tuition will affect them specifically. If the amount of the increase is $800 a year, one tactic you can use is to break that $800 down.

Egocentric: Being primarily concerned about yourself

Carrie Benning chose to do her first informative speech on changes in the airline industry, specifically detailing the changes in food available during flights. She knew from speaking to her classmates that some of them had never flown before and some had not been on a plane in several years. Spring break was coming up, and many of her classmates were flying to choice destinations in Florida, Jamaica, and the Caribbean. One of her main points focused on the option of passengers taking food on the flight. Instead of making general comments about the Transportation Security Administration restrictions, she did her research in advance and then gave specifics that she thought were applicable to college students. She reminded them that any beverages brought from home or purchased before passing through security in containers larger than 3 oz. could not be carried on the plane, but could be put into checked baggage. Beverages in containers larger than 3 oz. could be purchased after going through security and could be brought on the plane. If passengers wanted to take food on the flight, food could be purchased at restaurants found in the boarding area and taken on board. Snacks like Jell-O, pudding, and yogurt could be brought on board as long as they were in containers that were 3 oz. or smaller. Finally, she referred her audience to the TSA Web site at http://www.tsa.gov/travelers/prohibited/permitted-prohibited-items.shtm#10 for more information.

You could compare that to the number of pizzas a college student could buy over the year, how many gallons of gas that money would buy for their car, how many textbooks that money might purchase, or the amount of groceries that money could buy. If students have jobs, show them how many additional hours they will need to work in a week to offset the increase in tuition. If students live far away, show them how the increase in tuition will affect their travel home if they also have to pay for the gas in their vehicles. In this way, your audience members see that the tuition hike will directly affect them, and then they will become connected to your speech. Instead of them tuning you out, they will tune your information in.

Demographic Audience Analysis

Demographic data: The selected characteristics of a certain population

How does the demographic data of the audience affect your presentation?

Demographic data refers to the selected characteristics of a certain population. Demographic factors include gender; age; income; sexual orientation; racial, ethnic, and cultural background; religious affiliation; political affiliation; and even geographical origin. Knowledge of these factors, when obtained, will tell you who makes up an audience. And depending on the information that you obtain, your presentation will

© Monkey Business Images/Shutterstock.com

be reshaped for each audience that you address. Remember William Matthews, our investment broker from the beginning of this chapter? He addressed five different groups in two days, using the exact same presentation for each group.

That was a problem because each of his audiences was different. He gave the same speech about investment options to a group of graduating college seniors, a group of 40-year-old businesspeople, and a group of retirees. The college seniors needed some introductory comments about future opportunities for investing. The businesspeople would need to hear about retirement options as well as long-term investment opportunities. The retirees would need information about short-term investments.

Listed next are some of the demographic aspects that you should consider whenever you are asked to give a presentation:

1. **Gender.** How many men and how many women are in your audience? You might not think it matters, but it does. If you are a male speaker delivering a speech on professional baseball and say something like, "I know that this won't interest you women, but you guys will love it," you will immediately alienate the females in your audience. On the other hand, if you are a female speaker and want to talk about the three stages of pregnancy, you are going to have a tough time getting the men in your audience interested, simply because they are not capable of being pregnant. You might think that one way to be audience oriented would be to say, "All you women will be pregnant at some point in your lives…" or, "You guys will be married and your wives will be pregnant some day…" These are weak attempts at audience orientation because some of the women in your audience will choose to not have children, some of them will not be able to have children, and some of the men will choose never to marry or have children themselves. Broad generalizations are not effective audience orientation. You need to do your homework about your audience before you deliver your speech. Never make assumptions. You might be asked to speak to the PTA at your child's school, and you assume that your audience will be all mothers. That may have been the case years ago, but today, both moms and dads are involved parents.

   The movie industry has noticed the importance of the gender factor as well. The summer 2008 release of the movie *Sex and the City* had some executives wondering how well a movie geared heavily to women could possible do at the box office. They needn't have spent time worrying. In its opening weekend, the movie earned $55.7 million.

Senator Barack Obama's speech in Minneapolis, Minnesota, on June 3, 2008, when he declared victory as the Democratic nominee for the 2008 presidential election, is another example of knowing your audience in terms of gender. His speech capped a historic primary season in which he battled for delegates with Senator Hillary Clinton. In giving his speech, he knew that he couldn't afford to alienate those people who had voted for Mrs. Clinton during the primaries, many of whom were women. He smartly spent the opening of his speech praising Senator Clinton and her campaign. The text of this speech is available at http:www.nytimes.com/2008/06/03/us/politics/03text-obama.html?_r=1&oref=slogin.

2. Age. How old are the members of your audience? If your classmates are traditional college students, they could range in age from 17 to 25 years of age. If you have some nontraditional students in your class, then you will have some students in their 30s, 40s, 50s and even older. With the age demographic, you as the speaker need to keep in mind that not all your audience has shared the same experiences. For example, you may only be familiar with the current war in Iraq, but some members of your audience might be just as familiar with the Vietnam War, the Korean War, the first conflict in the Gulf, or even World War II.

A younger college student might read about the Vietnam War or watch a movie depicting that war and think it's amazing that anyone survived, but a Vietnam veteran sitting in the audience will have a much different appreciation of that conflict. Some of your audience may have voted for the first time in the 2008 presidential election, whereas others may have voted several times. Some people in your audience may actually remember growing up without the Internet. Age determines what people know, and even what people want to know. A band or musical group popular with college-age students may just seem like noise to someone who grew up listening to Elvis Presley. On the other hand, the rock 'n' roll popular in the 1980s might bore traditional college students in their early 20s. A businessperson who remembers the days of handwritten memos will have a much different appreciation of the efficiency of e-mails than someone who has grown up with a computer in their bedroom. Once again, do your homework and find out about the age of your audience so you can tailor your remarks to each listener.

SECTION 4: Presentation Preparation Issues

The 2013 release of the movie *Nebraska* featured Bruce Dern at age 77. The success of that movie shows that an older Bruce Dern still appeals to a broad audience. The movies *Iron Man* and *The Avengers* featured Robert Downey, Jr., a middle-aged superhero. Hollywood executives realized that there is a market for movies geared toward older audiences. At 78 million strong, the generation born between 1946 and 1964 is showing its economic clout once again by defining what's sexy and sellable in Hollywood.[2]

3. **Racial, ethnic, and cultural background.** How do you communicate effectively when you have a culturally, ethnically, and racially diverse audience? The answer is that once again, you do your homework and find out who is in your audience.

   Ethnocentrism is the habit of observing situations and events from your own cultural perspective and making the judgment that your own culture is superior. Remember that what works in the United States doesn't always work overseas. For example, Europeans tend to want more detail than Americans. Their attention spans aren't quite as short. So your key points may require more explanation, numbers, and background than you would include in a typical

Those who lived through certain periods of history, such as the Vietnam War, view it differently than others.

Ethnocentrism: The habit of observing situations and events from your own cultural perspective and making the judgment that your own culture is superior.

presentation back home. [3] Colors can give different messages to different cultures. In Japan, white symbolizes death. In Venezuela, yellow often has negative meaning. Do some research if you are using slides so that you use culture-friendly colors.[3] Remember that not all members of your audience speak English, and those who don't will need a translator. It will take people longer to process information when it's being translated. Build in pauses so that the translators can keep up with you and translate your words and your inflection, emphasis, and tone.[3]

From 1990 to 2005, minority group market share and purchasing power doubled and in some cases tripled. According to Jeff Humphreys, director of the Selig Center, one-sixth of the U.S. population claims Hispanic origin. "The $1.3 trillion 2014 Hispanic market shows a gain of 155% since 2000--far greater than the 71% increase in non-Hispanic buying power."[4]

Racial and ethnic minorities, who currently represent one quarter of all U.S. households, will contribute to the majority of household growth over the next decade. By 2010, nearly 3 in 10,000 households will be headed by minorities. [5]

4. Religion. Don't just assume that the people in your audience share the same religious beliefs that you do. Businesses across the country have recognized the importance of embracing religious diversity. When you speak to an audience, you should be aware that some of your listeners may belong to a variety of religions, and some may not have any religious beliefs at all. Christians observe Sunday as the holy day, although many Catholic churches have mass late on Saturday afternoons. For Muslims, Friday is the holy day, and Jews observe the Sabbath on Saturday. If your presentation focuses on food, remember that Jews are not allowed to eat pork products or shellfish or to mix milk and meat, Hindus are forbidden to ingest beef, and Muslims cannot consume alcohol. [6]

5. Sexual orientation. In today's society, sexual orientation is an important demographic factor. If you give a speech about financial planning for the future and mention that your audience members and their spouses need to look for jobs with companies that have great benefit packages, you could potentially exclude audience members who have or will have same sex partners but who cannot marry in some states. You can simply change your language to, "… you and your spouse or partner …"

The label "homosexual" is considered derogatory by lesbians and gay men.[7] So are references to a gay or lesbian "lifestyle."[7] These references imply that all gays and lesbians live the same way. There is no single heterosexual lifestyle, and there is no single gay or lesbian lifestyle.[7] Even if you don't agree with a lifestyle that is different from your own, your speech is not the place for derogatory comments, abusive language, or name calling. Two Web sites that are worth looking at are the American Civil Liberty Union's Lesbian and Gay Rights Site (www.aclu.org/LesbianGayRights/LesbianGayRightsMain.cfm) and Gay/Lesbian Politics and Law (www.indiana.edu/~glbtpol).

Audience adaptation should occur before, during, and after the speech.

What Now?

How do you find out all this information about your audience members? If your speech is for your class, your job becomes a lot easier. During the semester, you will get to know many of your classmates through casual conversation and listening to them give their own speeches. You will also have the opportunity to ask questions and find out what your audience knows about your topic and if they have any type of attitude about your topic area. Remember that your goal isn't to find out whether or not your audience will be interested in your topic. Your goal is to gain knowledge that will help you tailor your message to your audience. In addition to informally asking questions, you can put together a short questionnaire or survey to distribute to class members as well. Once you are out of college, you will need to continue to use your knowledge of audience analysis: ask questions, do your research, and use short questionnaires and surveys. This preparation will allow you to find out who your audience members are and what they need so that you can tailor your remarks to your listeners.

© Stuart Jenner/Shutterstock.com

Audience adaptation: Adapting your speech to the needs of your audience before, during, and after the speech

Audience adaptation refers to adapting your speech to the needs of your audience before, during, and after the speech. Before the speech, you do your homework, analyzing the situation and the audience. Now you know where the presentation will be, how the room will be arranged, whether you'll be using a microphone, how many people will be in the audience, and whether they are listening to you out of choice or because they are required to attend. In addition, you'll know how much knowledge they have about your topic, their attitudes toward the subject matter, and what they need and expect from your presentation. It's not enough just to know this information, however. You use what you know to prepare and deliver your speech.

Many speakers mistakenly believe that audience adaptation ends with speech preparation. In fact, you should be adapting your speech throughout its delivery. You always need to have a Plan B for glitches that may occur. If, for example, the PowerPoint projector doesn't work or stops working during your speech, what will you do? If the room location is changed at the last minute, how will you adapt? If the air conditioning stops working and the room becomes uncomfortably warm, are you prepared? If your listeners look confused at your explanation of an important concept, how can you clarify the material for them?

After you complete your speech, take a few minutes to mentally review how the presentation went. What could you have done different to better reach your audience? What did you miss this time? How comfortable were you during the question-and-answer session? What would you change for the next speech? What parts of your speech worked well, and which parts needed more clarification? Where did your audience seem most responsive? Where did they seem most confused? Knowing the answers to these questions will help you as you prepare and deliver your next speech.

Always be prepared to adapt your speech to your audience before, during, and after your presentation. Stay audience oriented as you research, write, and deliver the speech and even after your presentation is finished. With every presentation, you will learn a little more about the importance of audience analysis and audience adaptation.

DELIVERY DYNAMICS

Delivery: Bringing the words of your speech to life.

Delivery refers to bringing the words of your speech to life. It's not enough to just read the words on the page. Your job is to make those words meaningful to your audience. Your goal is to communicate with your audience. If you choose to read the words in a monotone voice without establishing eye contact with your listeners, be prepared for your listeners to doodle, look around the room, sleep, read a book, or finish homework. If you choose instead to deliver your speech using vocal variety, emphasis, strong volume, engaged eye contact, and clear language, be prepared for your audience members to maintain eye contact with you, lean forward in their seats, nod their heads as your speak, and applaud enthusiastically when you finish. Which of these would you prefer?

Each speaker will develop his or her own delivery style. What works for your classmate may not work for you. What works for one audience may not work for another audience. Your delivery might need to be a little more energetic for an 8 a.m. presentation than it does for an 11 a.m. presentation. The best delivery is all about communication. The only way to refine the art of good delivery is to practice and practice and practice.

Methods of Delivery

The four methods of speech delivery are:
1. Manuscript
2. Memorized
3. Impromptu
4. Extemporaneous

Manuscript

Manuscript delivery means writing down every word of your speech and then reading those words verbatim. The potential pitfalls of manuscript delivery are obvious: no eye contact, mumbling, lack of enthusiasm, and lack of communication in general. Manuscript delivery, however, can be done well. Sometimes it's even necessary. When the president of the United States delivers the State of the Union Address, it is viewed live, recorded to be shown later on television, uploaded to YouTube, and beamed by satellite around the world for a global audience. This will be a manuscript speech because the president cannot afford to misspeak or to be misquoted. Other people who will depend on manuscript delivery include anyone with a time constraint, anyone dealing with sensitive information, anyone who knows that sound bites from their remarks will appear on television, radio, and the Internet, or anyone who wants to make sure they don't forget what they need to say. The key to great manuscript delivery is practice. It's not enough to just practice by reading the words silently to yourself. You need to practice reading the words out loud. This way you'll hear the speech the same way that your audience will. As you practice, you can figure out where you need to pause, what words you need to emphasize, where you might need to make your volume stronger or softer, and where you can look up to establish eye contact with your

Manuscript: Writing down every word of your speech and then reading those words verbatim.

audience. You also may need to make sure that you can see the words on the page or the words on the Teleprompter. Whenever possible, practice with the Teleprompter or with the final manuscript.

Memorized

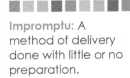

Manuscript: Writing your speech out word for word and committing the entire speech to your memory.

Memorized delivery is similar to manuscript delivery in that you write your speech out word for word. The difference is that with memorized delivery, you commit the entire speech to your memory. The potential pitfall here is obvious: forgetting the words. The other possible problem with memorized delivery is that the words can sound stilted and mechanical. You might be so intent on remembering your words that you forget to communicate with your audience. It's perfectly acceptable to memorize a quotation or statistic, your attention-getting statement or your concluding comments, but memorizing your entire speech should only be done if absolutely necessary. You should still practice your speech out loud in a setting that closely resembles where you will be speaking. If you do memorize your speech, you should be able to recite your speech in your sleep so that you can concentrate on communicating with your audience rather than on trying to remember what comes next. Always remember that your goal is to effectively get your ideas across to your audience.

Impromptu

Impromptu: A method of delivery done with little or no preparation.

Impromptu delivery can be scary because this method of delivery is done with little or no preparation. Toastmasters International, an organization devoted to improving the communication skills of its members, makes impromptu speaking a part of their meetings. They call this portion of the meeting "Table Topics." One person introduces a topic or a theme, and then asks various club members questions relating to that theme. The club members do not know in advance who will be called on, so everyone has to carefully listen to the question. Members try to speak on the topic for 1 to 2 minutes. This is a great example of impromptu speaking. You might think you'll never have to do this type of speaking, but you're wrong. Any time a professor calls on you to answer a question in class, and you are not prepared to answer that question, then you have participated in impromptu speaking.

If you are called on to address a group and you haven't had time to prepare, don't panic. Remember that this isn't going to be a lengthy speech, but you still want to sound as organized as possible. You can begin by

© Blend Images/Shutterstock.com

repeating the question to remind yourself and everybody else of the topic. You can preview the two to three quick points that you will cover. You can then develop those points briefly, adding some examples and other clarification for support. Finally, you can summarize the points you've made. These points will help you stay organized, and you will appear much more prepared than you really are. You also should take a second to gather your thoughts before you speak. If you are seated when asked the question, take a few seconds as you stand up and push back your chair to gather your thoughts. If you choose to remain seated, remember that you don't have to start speaking immediately. You can still take a few seconds for a pause while you think through what you want to say. If you are expected to walk to the podium or lectern, use that time to gather your thoughts. No one will expect perfection with an impromptu speech. If you act as though you are confident, establish eye contact with your listeners, and speak clearly, then you will come across as an accomplished impromptu speaker. Welcome opportunities to speak with little or no preparation. The more you do this type of speaking, the better and more comfortable you will get with impromptu delivery.

If you're called on for an impromptu speech, give yourself a few moments to organize your thoughts.

Extemporaneous

■■■■■■■■

Extemporaneous:
Speech that is
prepared and
practiced ahead
of time, but the
exact wording of
every sentence is
determined at the
time of delivery.

Extemporaneous speaking is prepared and practiced ahead of time, but the exact wording of every sentence is determined at the time of delivery. To be specific, although you write your notes out and practice your speech, the exact wording can change slightly each time you practice your speech. The ideas and the organization will stay the same, but the words you choose may vary from one practice session to the next. This allows extemporaneous delivery to sound fresh, more conversational, and more spontaneous than the other three methods of delivery. This is the most user-friendly method of delivery. This method of delivery allows you to speak to the audience rather than at the audience. You can concentrate on eye contact, vocal variety, clear articulation and pronunciation, and natural gestures—all the elements that contribute to excellent delivery. In the 2008 Democratic presidential primaries, many listeners were impressed by Senator Obama's oratory because he seemed to be speaking to each listener. He often used no notes or teleprompter, and this made audiences feel that he was knowledgeable about his topic and that he was enthusiastic about getting his message across.

The Speaker

You are the person responsible for your delivery. Many factors play a part in excellent delivery skills: your voice, volume, pitch, rate, use of the pause, vocal variety, correct pronunciation, clear articulation, dialect, personal appearance, posture, movement, gestures, and eye contact.

Voice

Your voice is unique. No one else will sound exactly the same as you do. If you aren't sure what your voice sounds like, record it and play it back. You might be surprised at what you hear. If your voice sounds wispy or breathless, you might try making sure that you are breathing from your diaphragm so that your voice is supported. Maybe you will hear yourself racing through what you say, mispronouncing words, and mangling articulation. Once you know what mistakes you are making, then you can work to correct these mistakes. Great speakers are not always the speakers with the natural, deep, resonant voices. Those aspects help, of course, but you need to learn to work with the voice that you have. Lou Holtz, noted coach, speaker, author, and ESPN commentator, acknowledges that he has a lisp, but he continues to be a successful speaker regardless of this impediment. Many celebrities are hired to do voice-overs for commercials because of the pleasing quality of their voices. Other celebrities are known for their unique voices: Melanie Griffin, Rosie O'Donnell, Clint Eastwood, James Earl Jones, and Jack Nicholson. You may not be able to change the voice you have, but you can learn to work with it and to control other aspects of your verbal delivery such as volume, pitch, rate, articulation, pronunciation, gestures, and vocal variety. These are all aspects of delivery that you can control.

Body

Personal appearance—speakers dress professionally. Audience members will make judgments based on your appearance. Your job is to look the part of the speaker. You also want to minimize distractions. Conservative dress is usually the best option. Unless you have specifically been told to dress more casually by an event organizer, you should dress professionally. For men, this can include a suit and tie, khaki pants, a blazer and a tie, or other colors of dress pants, with appropriate blazer and tie. For women, this could include a pantsuit, skirt suit, a dress, skirt, or pants with a jacket. A jacket for women is important because it equalizes them in terms of dress to the men. Take a look at successful women in the corporate world, and you'll understand that a jacket for women in a must. Retail consultant Susan Rolontz of the Tobe Report believes that to look professional and to be taken seriously, you need to wear a jacket.[8] It is difficult to recall an instance when one of the women of Capitol Hill appeared in public during the day wearing a dress without a blazer. Members of the House of Representatives do not wear dresses. They wear suits. So do senators, lawyers, and the secretary of state.[8] Strapless tops or dresses; halter tops; miniskirts; tight pants, skirts, or tops; see-through anything; and low-cut tops are not appropriate in the business setting for women. Jeans, athletic shoes, baseball caps, workout gear, and shorts are not acceptable for either gender as business attire. You would never want your audience members to be dressed more professionally than you are dressed. You always want to be clean, your clothes should be pressed, and your shoes should be shined. Jewelry for both genders should be conservative. Ties for men should not be distracting. Facial hair for men should be neat. Hair shouldn't hang in your eyes so that you repeatedly have to brush it back as you speak. Remember, your goal is to communicate with your audience. You might question the validity of having to dress up to give a presentation, especially with popular celebrities appearing on talk shows in jeans and pushing the envelope with fashion trends on television shows. So, even though *Modern Family* star Sofia Vergara wears outrageously high heels and short, tight dresses and tops on the show, remember that she is a celebrity playing a character who does not work in an office. If your listeners are too busy looking at your appearance, they will not be listening to your words. [9, 10]

Movement

Many classroom speeches are recorded so that students can watch themselves as they give their presentation. This may not sound like a fun activity, but watching yourself can be an excellent learning tool. In your mind, you will have a picture of yourself as you speak. When you see yourself, that mental picture may change. Watching your recorded self will help you see nervous habits and other mannerisms that can be a distraction for your listeners. Unnecessary movement or awkward movement can betray your nervousness.

Begin at the beginning. After you've been introduced, stand up and walk with confidence to the lectern or podium. Take a few seconds and situate your note cards where you can see them easily, put your visual aid where you can access it easily, turn on or adjust any electronic equipment you'll be using, and prepare yourself to deliver your speech. Stand up straight, look at your audience, take a good deep breath, and begin only

Professional dress enhances your image as a successful speaker.

© El Nariz/Shutterstock.com

when you're ready. One common mistake made by many beginning speakers is to rush up to the lectern and to rush preparation. Own your space. Your audience will wait for you. The few seconds you take to get ready to speak will pay off during your speech.

During your speech, control unnecessary movement. Place your hands comfortably on the lectern or podium or let them hang at your sides. Don't drum your fingers on the lectern, hold on to the podium in a "death grip," jingle change that you find in your pockets, or play with your hair, glasses, or jewelry. The best way to avoid unnecessary movement is to practice your speech ahead of time. Plan some gestures and plan on moving out from behind the lectern at certain points in your speech. Don't pace behind or in front of the lectern. Don't talk as you move, and never turn your back on your audience.

After you finish speaking, pause and gather your note cards and visuals before moving back to your seat. Make sure that you finish speaking before you begin to gather you things. If there is a question-and-answer session, move to the side of the lectern or remain behind it. Maintain eye contact with your listeners.

Eye Contact

Maintaining engaged eye contact is crucial to successful communication. If you've heard somewhere that you will be less nervous if you look over the heads of your listeners or if you look at their shoulder or at their nose, you need to file that information under your "useless" folder. Look at your audience. You should do this first before you actually begin to speak. Establishing eye contact prior to speaking will send the signal to your listeners that you are comfortable and confident. It will also make them feel as though they are a part of your presentation. If you are doing business in other cultures, do your homework. Eye contact is influenced by culture. When engaged in conversation, Arabs, Latin Americans, and Southern Europeans tend to look directly at the person with whom they are talking. People from Asian countries and parts of Africa tend to engage in less eye contact. In Kenya a discussion between a woman and her son-in-law may well be conducted with each person turning his or her back on the other.[11] In the United States, eye contact is expected. This does not mean long, lingering glances at each person sitting in your audience. It does mean 2 to 3 seconds of eye contact with as many listeners as possible. In your speech class, don't just look at your professor. This will make the rest of the class feel left out of the communication. Try not to look at just those people in the front rows or on the right or left side, or those you know. Try

© Andreser/Shutterstock.com

Establishing eye contact shows that you are confident.

to establish eye contact with all your listeners. Eye contact will help you establish a bond with your listeners. It will show that you are confident and comfortable, and it will help put your audience members at ease.

Anxiety

Feeling nervous about giving a speech is quite normal. Even CEOs, top executives, and business owners feel apprehensive when they have to give a speech in public. Anxiety should be looked at as excess energy that needs to be used. Put anxiety in perspective: You also feel nervous or anxious when you do exciting activities such as snow skiing, riding a roller coaster at an amusement park, parasailing, bungee jumping, skydiving, or white-water rafting, but you are looking forward to that activity, so you look at your feelings as excitement instead of anxiety. When you have to do a speech, you are not looking forward to it, and so you view your nervousness as a negative thing rather than as excitement. You often fill yourself with negative thoughts such as, "I can't do this, I'm not prepared, everybody else is a better speaker than I am, I'm going to fail." Why do this to yourself? Instead, fill yourself with realistic, positive thoughts. Realism is the key here. Thoughts such as, "I can do this, I don't have to be perfect, I am well prepared, and I am ready to do this," will set you up to be successful. Your goal is never to be flawless. Your goal is to be a successful communicator. Change your thinking. Try looking at your speech as an opportunity to communicate about a topic you enjoy. Look at this opportunity to develop a skill you will need for the rest of your professional life.

One approach to lessening your anxiety level is to be prepared and to practice. That might sound obvious, but many people think they can just "wing it" on the day of their presentation. Careful preparation, using what you know about audience analysis, and practicing your presentation out loud over and over again will set you up to be successful. When you know you are prepared, and when you have rehearsed your speech carefully, then your anxiety level will decrease. Other things that you can do to help manage the anxiety include watching your consumption of caffeine, not speaking on an empty stomach, engaging in some type of exercise to help use up the excess energy that is causing your anxiety, mentally visualizing yourself delivering your presentation successfully, and deep breathing. If you are sitting at your desk and feel your self getting panicky, try breathing in slowly to the count of four and then exhaling to the count of four. Do this several times, and you'll feel your anxiety level decrease.

> Two books that tackle the issues of panic and anxiety and how to manage them are *From Panic to Power* by Lucinda Bassett and *Feel the Fear and Do It Anyway* by Dr. Susan Jeffers. These books explain where the anxiety comes from, why we have anxiety, and how to move beyond the anxious feelings.

Practice, Practice, Practice...

Once the writing of your speech is completed, it's time to practice your speech. You might think that you can just read your speech to yourself silently several times and be ready for your presentation. You won't be. The only successful way to practice or to rehearse your speech is to stand up and say the words out loud with the visual aids that you will use. You want your rehearsal to be as close to the real thing as possible. If you can rehearse in the room where you will be speaking, that is the ideal situation. If you can't rehearse in the room where you will speak, practice in a room where you won't be interrupted. If you don't have a lectern, use a music stand or a piece of furniture that is high enough to put your note cards. Use a stopwatch to see how long your presentation is. Don't just guess because chances are you'll be wrong. If your speech is too long, you'll have to edit it down to meet time requirements designated by your instructor or by the organizer of the event. Time limits are not just suggestions.

There is a reason why your speech has time constraints. In the business world, time is money, and your supervisor or boss will expect you to stay within the time limits you've been given. If you are one of several speakers at an evening or lunchtime event, your disregard of the time limits will mean that another speaker will not have their allotted time to speak. At some meetings, participants will simply get up and leave at the designated ending time, even if you're still speaking. Finally, it's just rude to speak for longer than the time you've been given. When you actually deliver your speech, you won't worry about your time constraints because you will know that you are comfortably within the time limits. If your speech is supposed to be between five and six minutes, each time you practice it is should fall comfortably within that time range. If, when you practice it, it comes in at six minutes exactly each time, then you probably want to cut something out. Don't think that if you just speak really fast you'll get it all in and be okay. The problem here is that you might speak so fast that your audience can't understand what you say. So even though your time may be okay, your communication will fail. Be cautious about giving your speech for your best friend or your significant other. These people don't want to hurt your feelings, so they may tell you that your speech is great, even if it's not. If you do plan a dress rehearsal, choose audience members that will be brutally honest.

Bringing the Words to Life

How do you bring the words to life? How do you successfully deliver a speech? The answer is that you use your voice, your gestures, your eyes, and your body language to have great delivery. Remember the elements of vocal delivery from Chapter 3? These include vocal variety, rate, pitch, inflection, the pause, and volume. All these are vocal aspects that you can use to have effective delivery. If you've never heard yourself speak, you might try recording yourself and playing it back so that you can hear how you sound. Do you tend to sound tired as you speak? Do you have trouble understanding some of the words you use? Is your volume too soft? Is your pitch too high? Do you speak too fast?

As you rehearse your speech, you can work on all these elements of vocal delivery. One important reason for saying the words out loud, ahead of time, is so you hear the words in the same way the audience does. To make your communication effective, you need to emphasize certain words, speed up at certain spots or slow down, and get louder or softer, and even pause. One tool you can use to help with your vocal delivery is to read poetry out loud. As you read poetry, you become the interpreter. You can read poetry by Emily Dickinson, Robert Frost, or Shel Silverstein. If you have younger brothers and sisters, children of your own, or nieces or nephews, you can also read children's books out loud to them. When you read children's books to children, they won't sit still for you to just stumble through the words. You have to bring those words to life using all the vocal aspects that are mentioned in this chapter. It's great practice for delivering speeches.

Audience Questions

Because of time constraints in the classroom, your instructor might not be able to allow the audience to ask questions at the end of your speech. There will come a time, however, when you will need to entertain question from your audience that relate to your speech. This can make some speakers nervous because they are afraid that they will not be able to answer the questions asked of them. Once again, preparation is the key here. The more familiar you are with your topic, the easier it will be to answer questions.

It can be distracting to be interrupted during your speech with audience members asking questions. It is perfectly acceptable to let the audience know that they will have an opportunity at the end of your speech to ask questions. This way, they'll hold their questions until you are done speaking.

During the question-and-answer period, these tips will be helpful:

1. Listen to the question. Some speakers are nervous about answering questions, and so they forget to listen to the question. Listen to the question carefully and repeat it back to the questioner. You can say, "So, you're asking me… Is that correct?" This will help you clarify what they need from you. It will also ensure that each person in the room hears the question so that the audience stays involved. If the Q&A session can't be heard by all, you will lose control of the audience as they begin conversations with each other.

2. If you don't know the answer to a question, don't try to make up an answer. Be honest and tell them that you don't know. Don't apologize or try to evade the question. Then always follow up with a sincere statement such as, "I will find out that information and get back to you. Can you leave me your card?" Of course, you then need to find the answer and contact the questioner with the answer. Some speakers keep a list of e-mail addresses for participants. Once you find the answer to that listener's question, send your information to that listener and copy it to all the

audience members so that all see your answer and know that you followed up as promised.

3. Even if you are nervous, try to be enthusiastic and positive. Most people are asking questions because they are genuinely interested in your answers. They want to know more about your topic. Look at your answers as a way of helping them further understand your message. The question-and-answer period can be a time of clarification and a time for you to show the audience that you don't just know the information in your speech, but you are very knowledgeable on your subject.

4. Stay in control of the situation. It's easy to get diverted or to allow one person to dominate the conversation. You are in charge. Try to let as many people as possible ask questions. If one person has asked two or more questions and still has a hand up, tell them that you two can chat after other questions have been answered. Just politely tell them that you want to answer as many questions as possible, so you need to let someone else have a turn.

5. If you've been given a time limit for your entire presentation, keep your eye on the clock. As you get close to your limit, let the audience know that you can only take a couple more questions because your time is almost up. It's okay to tell them that the organizers of the event have asked you to be done by a certain time. That lets your listeners know that you are simply following the rules and you are not being rude. After you've answered questions, wrap up and conclude by thanking your listeners for their time.

CONCLUSION

William Mathews, the investment broker from the beginning of this chapter, failed to communicate his message to his various audiences because he neglected to analyze his audience and the situation, and he didn't know about the importance of dynamic delivery. He assumed that because *he* knew about the importance of investments and because he had great, detailed notes, that his audience would understand why they should do business with his bank. He didn't understand why he had failed to excite his listeners with his presentations. Fortunately for William, his coworkers had better luck with their presentations. William sat down and asked them how they had been successful and where he had failed. After talking with several fellow brokers, William learned about the importance of knowing who is in his audience and how to bring excitement to his presentation with his delivery. He decided to contact the audiences that he had addressed and ask them for a second chance at successfully communicating. He also lined up additional groups to address in the future. He felt confident that this time he would know how best to communicate his message.

After reading this chapter, you should now have a clear understanding of the importance of audience analysis, audience adaptation, and dynamic delivery skills. With audience analysis, you've learned that it's important to know the characteristics of your listeners, their knowledge level about your topic, and what they need from your speech. You've also learned how important it is to find out about the room where you will be speaking, the size of the audience, whether or not you'll be using a microphone, the arrangement of the chairs and tables, and whether the event is formal or informal. This chapter also looked at the four delivery methods, the aspects of great delivery that the speaker can control, anxiety about speaking, the importance of practicing your presentation, and how to have a successful question-and-answer session.

ACTIVITIES

1. To work on vocal variety, choose two different types of poems and practice reading them out loud. Pretend you have an audience of children. What would you do with your voice to keep their attention? How would you phrase each line? Where would you pause? Where would you get louder or softer? Faster or slower? Would you change your inflection on certain words? For even more practice, record yourself as you read and listen to the tape. Would you listen to yourself? Two poems that you might try include "The Road Not Taken" by Robert Frost and "The Walrus and the Carpenter" by Lewis Carroll .

2. Get a book on tongue twisters or access a Web site devoted to tongue twisters and practice saying these out loud. Once you can say all the words clearly, practice your vocal variety by making some of the tongue twisters into questions, some into exclamations, and so on.

3. Watch television at various times over the next several days. Be sure to watch the advertisements as well as the programs offered. Think about who the networks had in mind when deciding what to air at certain times of the day or night. What demographics did they consider as they scheduled their shows and ads? Are there ads that you don't watch normally because the products are not anything that interests you? Are there shows you don't watch because you are not interested? Think about why you are not interested. Why are you not the intended audience? What demographic factors are important here?

4. If anxiety about giving a presentation is a problem for you, consider reading some books that target anxiety. Two examples are *From Panic to Power* by Lucinda Bassett and *Feel the Fear and Do It Anyway* by Dr. Susan Jeffers.

5. Audience and situational analysis is too important to ignore. Two sources that address audience analysis and adaptation are:

    *   In 1990, Mrs. Barbara Bush gave a commencement speech at Wellesley College that shows her excellent preparation and adaptation to her situation, audience, and occasion. This is available at http:www.wellesley.edu/PublicAffairs/Commencement/1990/bush.html

    *   Elizabeth Urech is the author of *Speaking globally: Effective presentations across international and cultural boundaries* (2nd ed.). Rollingsford, NH: Book Network International, 2004.

REFERENCES

[1] Klepper, M. M. (with Gunther, R.). (1994). *I'd rather die than give a speech.* Burr Ridge, IL: Irwin.

[2] Hinds, J. (2008, June 3). Gray means green: Mature stars score at the box office. *Free Press.* Retrieved from http://freep.com/apps/pbcs.dll/article?AID=/20080603/ENT01/806030358

[3] Friedman, K. (2005). *Culture club: Tips for speaking with international audiences.* Blue Bell, PA: Karen Friedman Enterprises. Retrieved from http://www.karenfriedman.com/headlines/InternationalCultureClub.pdf

[4] Weeks, M. (2014, September 30). *Minorities energize U.S. consumer market, according to UGA Multicultural Economy report.* Athens, GA. Retrieved from http://news.uga.edu/releases/article/multicultural-economy-report-2014/

[5] National Association of Realtors. (n.d.). *Diversity is good business.* Retrieved from http://www.realtor.org/government_affairs/diversity/divgood

[6] Veit, L. (2002, February). Religious diversity. *Contracting Profits.* Retrieved from www.cleanlink.com/cp/article.asp?id=117

[7] Lucas, S. E. (2007). *The art of public speaking* (9th ed.). Boston: McGraw-Hill.

[8] Givhan, R. (2006, December 22). Dressed for work? For women, suits still wield power. *Washington Post.* Retrieved from www.washingtonpost.com/wp-dyn/content/article/2006/12/21/AR2006122101852.html

[9] Cullen, L. T. (2008, May 29). What (not) to wear to work. *Time,* p. 49.

[10] Patcher, B. (2007, May 7). Short skirts, cleavage and your job: 8 ways not to undermine professional image during the summer. *ExpertClick.* Retrieved from www.expertclick.com/NewsReleaseWire/ReleaseDetails.aspx?ID=16396&CFID= 2135569&CFTOKEN=40368707

[11] Knapp, M., & Hall, J. (2009). *Nonverbal communication in human interaction* (7th ed.). Belmont, CA: Wadsworth.

chapter
eleven

Information-Seeking and Traditional Library Skills

After reading this chapter you will be able to:

- Understand what the research process is and how it can apply to your coursework and presentations
- Find information that you need for assignments by understanding the concepts behind information organization
- Understand the importance of proper source documentation
- Be able to document sources properly

CHAPTER OUTLINE

key words

Dewey Decimal System
Library of Congress
    Classification System
U.S. Superintendent of
    Documents (SuDocs)
Search engines

Search tools
Reference material
Periodical
Peer-reviewed journal
Database

INTRODUCTION

This semester Dylan Green is enrolled in Business and Professional Communication and English 101, so he's planning to spend quality time in the library as he prepares presentations and writes papers for both courses. While he has had a tour of the university library and a quick review of the databases, he's feeling a bit overwhelmed by the massive amount of information available and he's unsure of how to begin his search. He just received his first speech assignment and intends to focus on informing his audience about how to find a summer internship. Given that his audience is primarily made up of college students, he knows he can do a good job of relating the topic; however, he would really like to get some data to back up the importance of obtaining an internship as well as the steps involved. He decides to jot down some notes in order to make a research plan so that he doesn't waste too much time wandering around in the stacks. This chapter provides many tips Dylan should follow as he proceeds with his research including: a description of the research process; an introduction to different library classification systems, search engines, and databases; and a discussion of credible sources, plagiarism, and appropriate formats for citing sources within documents and presentations. As you read determine how Dylan should proceed with his research project.

GETTING ORGANIZED

What Kind of Research Do I Need to Do?

The first thing you need to do when starting to research for a paper or presentation is to decide what kind of research you need to be doing. Starting a search for anything without a plan will lead to frustration and many difficulties. Not only is it important to know your audience prior to planning your speech, but also to have some idea of what information the audience already knows. What information do they need to know to understand your speech? Start from the audience and work your way back to the speech. You'll know what kind of sources to find when you are clear about what your audience needs to know. For example, if you were to deliver an informative speech on Roth IRAs, your audience would determine your sources. If you are delivering that speech to a group of people in their 50s, then focusing on short-term planning for upcoming retirement would be best. But if you were to deliver that same speech to a group of college students, why would you talk about retirement? Instead, you should focus on how investing a small amount of money when you are young leads to a lot of money in the long run. Young people are not thinking of retirement planning; therefore, hitting your audience where it matters most to them (in their pocketbooks) is key to your success. Know what you need to find before you start out to find it. Know your audience and research will be a snap.

Keep your audience in mind as you do your research so you deliver the right information in your speech.

© g-stockstudio/Shutterstock.com

Organization of Information

Information is simply ideas that have been communicated, but the organization of that information is key to your being able to understand, process, and use that information. It is valuable to organize information from a cognitive approach so that you will not be overwhelmed by it. For example, have you ever done a search for the word *communication* in Google? How many hits did you get? Probably millions, if not billions. Being able to search the Internet for information is an invaluable resource, but only if you know how to search and how that information is organized in the first place.

Organization in and of itself implies a system. That system is what makes rules or guidelines for arranging the information, and the key is that those rules are applied the same way over and over again. A couple major ways of organizing information are by content and by medium. Outside a library, the main focus of organization is by content. An old version of this type of organization is the yellow pages. You pick a topic such as "car wash" and under that heading is a list of all the car washes in that area. To organize by medium, think of walking into a bookstore. There are areas for fiction and nonfiction books, but there are also areas for CDs, DVDs, audio books, magazines, and many other categories. This is done as the customer is looking for a particular item, and they know that if they head to the big sign saying "DVDs" that they will find the new DVD they are looking for. Another medium is not a physical format, but also includes the information you find on the Internet, and this is why there are computer terminals in libraries today. The following classification systems will help you find the information most relevant to your research.

Classification Systems

DEWEY DECIMAL CLASSIFICATION

A common type of classification that many are familiar with is the **Dewey Decimal System**. This is the system of organization found in most public libraries along with libraries in grade and high schools. This type of organization takes the subject matter of the book, assigns a specific number to that subject (i.e., a call number), and places the books in order according to that number. This process means that all the books in that library on a particular subject (e.g., biology) are grouped together in one location. One benefit to this type of organization is that once you find a

Dewey Decimal System: A library classification system which assigns a call number to materials based on subject areas. All library materials dedicated to certain subjects are placed together on the shelves.

The Dewey Decimal System is the system of organization found in most public libraries.

© DavidPinoPhotography/Shutterstock.com

book on your topic, the other books around it are going to be useful to you as well. The Dewey Decimal System has 10 major subject divisions.

LIBRARY OF CONGRESS CLASSIFICATION

The type of classification used in the majority of college and university libraries is called the **Library of Congress Classification System**. This differs from the Dewey Decimal System in that the Library of Congress uses letters as well as numbers to generate call numbers. This combination of letters and numbers allows for many, many more subject divisions, but the broadest groupings are for the sciences, the social sciences, the humanities, and miscellaneous. Because you are studying communication, the majority of your materials will be in two of those broad sections: the social sciences and the humanities. Because of the virtually endless number of subject divisions in the Library of Congress system, items that relate to your topic may have different call numbers. Make sure that after searching on the online catalog, you write down all the numbers associated with the items you want, as you may have to go to several different areas of the library to find them.

Library of Congress Classification System: A library classification system which assigns all materials with a letter and call number based on subject areas. Using letters and numbers allows for more subject divisions.

U.S. SUPERINTENDENT OF DOCUMENTS (SUDOCS)

Many libraries have items that are from the federal government, and they are usually placed in their own area (or even their own building) of the library and use their own type of classification system. Instead of grouping items by subject as in the Library of Congress and Dewey Decimal systems, the **U.S. Superintendent of Documents (SuDocs)** groups them by cabinet-level agency. This is almost a subject-based system, as the cabinets that produce the documents are subject-themed, such as the Department of Education or the Department of Homeland Security. Most libraries include these documents in the general search of their online catalogs, but make sure that you find the physical location of these documents, as they will not be found in the general stacks.

U.S. Superintendent of Documents (SuDocs): A classification system which groups government documents by cabinet-level agency.

Organization on the Web

Most will say that there *is* no organization on the Web. This is all too true, but the Internet is developing every day into a more useable and accessible resource. The basics of Web organization is that Web designers create Web sites and then place them on a large computer called a server, either one that they own themselves or by uploading the pages to their Internet Service Provider (ISP). The main issue with being able to organize the Internet is that those who create and post Web sites do not have to provide search terms so that their pages can be found among the trillions upon trillions of pages out on the World Wide Web. The task of finding that page out there is done by **search engines** that scan the content of the pages for common terms, but the key is that you must type those specific words into the search engine to find that particular page. Sounds complicated, huh? It is, but what you need to know as a researcher is that using the Web takes time and a critical eye. Don't assume that everything you see and read is true, and make sure that you validate the credibility of all information you find online.

Search engines: Software programs designed to search Web sites for information based on search terms provided by the Web site owners.

Why Do I Need a Variety of Sources?

Let's say that you are doing a speech on an organization, and your goal is to persuade your audience to go to work for that organization. For this example, let's use Google as your selected organization. On the Google corporate Web site, you can find a list of the top 10 reasons why you should work for Google, along with many, many other documents that explain why Google is such a great company to work for. Why would it not be appropriate just to use the information that Google puts out about itself in your speech? I mean, they even make a list for you! The reason is that companies don't say bad things about themselves. You need a variety of sources in order to write a balanced speech. You could just go read the company Web site instead, and then what would the audience learn? Citing sources such as *The Wall Street Journal* and *Forbes* magazine, along with

Surfing the Web may be easiest, but you need a variety of sources to present a balanced speech.

quotations from current employees or from other organizations that work with Google, would be a much better (and more accurate) speech. In order to find an adequate variety of sources, you will need to use appropriate search tools.

Information Sources

WHAT ARE SEARCH TOOLS?

Search tools: Tools such as catalogs, bibliographic databases, Internet search engines, and bibliographies designed to assist researchers in obtaining information.

A **search tool** is what you are going to use to get to the actual information you will use in your speech. The major types of search tools are catalogs, bibliographic databases, Internet search engines, and bibliographies. A catalog is a file of records for all the information found in a library. A bibliographic database, often just called a database, is found through your library's Web site, as your school will subscribe to these services. A common database for communication studies is called "Communication and Mass Media Complete," but there are thousands of others run by indexing companies such as EBSCO Host and JStor. You may be able to find just a citation, an abstract, or even a complete full-text version of an article through a database. An Internet search engine, such as Google or Yahoo, will bring you a lot of information, but will not bring you everything on your topic. Remember that a search engine just looks at what is directly on the Web page; therefore, you must type in exactly what is on that page to find it. Also remember that the majority of what you'll find online isn't relevant information, so be critical. Finally, bibliographies are a great way to find information when you've found a good article or book on your topic. You may either look at the references at the end of your article to find other relevant sources or you may find a complete book of citations on a particular subject.

CREDIBILITY IN SOURCES

With the advent of the Internet, information flows at us so quickly that it is easy to both become overwhelmed and be taken advantage of. Therefore, being a critical thinker and absorbing information in a way that makes you the determining factor on its credibility is vital to your success as a researcher. The majority of information out there is not appropriate for your particular project and is not credible in the first place.

With the variety of types of media available, including everything from books to Web sites, it can be difficult to determine where the credibility lies, but this is by far one of the most important skills you must develop.

THE INTERNET

When evaluating the credibility of sources found on the Internet, there are some obvious signs, and it is important to listen to your gut. Spelling mistakes, blinking type, black backgrounds with white type, bad grammar, and formatting issues are just a few things to look for. Basically, if you wouldn't feel comfortable putting your credit card information on that page, then the information on it probably isn't credible. Beyond the basics, look for an author's name on the page and look for references to the author's background. If the author of the page is an organization, then what is the reputation of that organization? Does the page list its sources so you can follow up on where the information originated? If you can't find the original cited source, then you most likely wouldn't want to use that, as you weren't able to check its validity. Where did the Web site originate? You can generally tell this by looking at the URL address. The most common URL forms are .com (commercial), .edu (educational), and .gov (governmental). Some countries outside the United States use their own originating codes, such as .ca for Canada and .uk for the United Kingdom.

REFERENCE MATERIALS

Reference material:
Resources which
provide information
on primary sources;
material which refers
you to something
else.

Have you ever wondered why there is a separate section for reference materials in the library? That is because they are classified differently than the broader source information areas such as nonfiction or periodicals. **Reference materials** provide the most general approach to information in that you would be able to find anything from a brief timeline of the Vietnam War to a statistic on how many American cars are bought each year. The most important thing to remember with reference materials is that they are more of a resource than a source, and this concept applies to reference materials found on CDs, DVDs, or the Internet. This means that to ensure the validity of the information in the reference material, you must look to other sources to support it. Remember that a reference is just that—a referral to something else. A prime example of this is *The World Book Encyclopedia*, where you can find lots of suggestions for further reading directing you toward other sources to find more information outside the set of books.

Reference materials
are classified
differently and in a
separate space in the
library.

© connel/Shutterstock.com

PERIODICALS

The word **periodical** is used commonly to refer to magazines, journals, and occasionally newspapers. For the most part, anything that is published at regular intervals could be considered a periodical, as they are periodically published. The best thing about using periodicals for your research is that they can contain a more accurate snapshot of what the public may be thinking or feeling about an issue or event. Let's say you were studying the Vietnam War and were interested in what the American public thought about President Richard Nixon after his first 100 days in office. You could look to a newspaper published as close to that time as possible and find either an opinion poll or letters to the editor that show public opinion. Beyond that, you need to consider what type of periodical it is: popular, scholarly, or trade/professional. The main differences are that scholarly periodicals are published through some sort of evaluation process, whereas the others are not. Also, scholars or professionals in the field write the information found in scholarly or trade periodicals, whereas those that write in popular periodicals are paid to write for that periodical.

Periodical: Source which is periodically published such as magazines, journals, and some newspapers.

PEER-REVIEWED JOURNALS

Your professor may indicate that you must only use **peer-reviewed journals** for your project. This indicates that there was a selection process for the articles that appear in that journal. As previously discussed, scholarly periodicals are published through some sort of evaluation process, and that process could be a peer-reviewed process. Peer reviewing means that experts in that particular field are selected to be on the editorial board for that journal. Then when scholars wish to have their writing published in that journal, they must submit their article to the editorial board, and then those experts (peers to the author) determine whether or not the article should be published in that particular journal. These types of journals are important when you are studying a specific subject matter, such as communication.

Peer-reviewed journal: A journal which uses a more rigorous selection process involving review from professionals in a particular field.

Peer-reviewed journals are important when you are studying a specific subject matter.

© Carlos Caetano/Shutterstock.com

Examples of peer-reviewed journals in the study of communication are:

Journal of Applied Communication Research
Quarterly Journal of Speech
Communication Studies
Communication and Critical/Cultural Studies
Communication Education
Communication Monographs
Critical Studies in Media Studies
Journal of International and Intercultural Communication
Management Communication Quarterly

GOVERNMENT AND LEGAL DOCUMENTS

You can find a good source of U.S. governmental statistics at Statistical Abstracts (http://www.census.gov/compendia/statab/).

The fundamental basic principle of democracy is that the government is open to its citizens. This means that anyone can have access to the processes and procedures of their government. The drawback is that in the United States, our government produces a lot of information. This is why former presidents and some other public service figures such as senators have their own libraries just to house all the papers associated with their lives and time in office in service to their country. Most of the time, these documents are readily available, are the primary sources for most other information, and are the only source of information on many topics. If you are studying something in the social sciences, then governmental documents may be the sources for you, as statistics on just about anything can be found through the government. The U.S. Census produces a multitude of descriptive statistics on our population. Granted, searching through all that information can be tedious, but there is just so much information.

Searching Electronic Sources

When sitting down to start searching in an electronic information database, you should first break your topic down into its basic parts (e.g., What are the main issues I should talk about? What are the issues that my audience needs to know? What do they already know?) along with synonyms or any other terms that might be similar to the topic that you are using. For example, if your topic is about business, then think of other words such as finance, corporation, or organization. When words are interchangeable such as these, you need to search for all of them, as the electronic search engine will only pick up on the words that you type into the field. Becoming savvy at search terms is key to becoming a good researcher. Be creative! Think "outside the box!"

As the basis for all electronic processes, Boolean logic is used by database search programs and search programming on the Internet through a technique known as Boolean searching. This is a complicated mathematical equation that works to retrieve information as your computer scans for patterns of information that match what you put into the box. Basically, it groups information into smaller and smaller categories so that you can find exactly what you are looking for. For example, if you type just the word "*apple*" into a search engine, you will get millions of hits. But if you type "recipe for Washington red apple pie" you will get a more direct and specific search for what you are looking for by eliminating all the information on the apple farmers, types of apples, or Apple computer products.

Databases

There are several different types of information databases, including open (those available to the public), commercial (those produced to make money), and those that require a subscription to use. Most likely the types of information databases at your college or university are subscription based, but this does not mean that you yourself have to subscribe to them. This means that your university has paid for you to be able to use those particular databases. Most of the time this is achieved by your going through the Web site of your college or university to the Web site of your school's specific library and then logging in with a university-issued login and password. In today's modern age, this can be done both on campus and off campus. From the login point, the databases are organized by subject that they search (e.g., business, art, child development, sociology, women's studies). Then within those broader topics are links to the specific databases. Some of the more common ones used in communication studies research are Communication & Mass Media Complete (EBSCO), JSTOR (All Subjects), LexisNexis Academic, Academic Search Premier (EBSCO), and SAGE Journals Online (Sage), but there are many, many more.

Database: Online information storage systems, including EBSCO, JSTOR, and LexisNexis.

Databases are organized by the subject that they search.

©Sergey Nivens/Shutterstock.com

PLAGIARISM AND CHEATING

Whenever taking the step from research to writing, you must understand the issues associated with plagiarism and cheating. As plainly as possible, plagiarism is a form of cheating. Each college or university will have their own specific language for these terms, but generally speaking plagiarism is the use of distinctive ideas or other works belonging to someone else without providing adequate acknowledgment of that person's contribution. Regardless of the means of appropriation, incorporation of another's work into one's own requires adequate identification and acknowledgment. Plagiarism is doubly unethical because it deprives the author of rightful credit and gives credit to someone who has not earned it.

Plagiarism includes but is not limited to:
(http://www.csus.edu/admbus/umanual/UMA00150.htm)
1. The act of incorporating into one's own work the ideas, words, sentences, paragraphs, or parts thereof, or the specific substance of another's work without giving appropriate credit thereby representing the product as entirely one's own. Examples include not only word-for-word copying, but also the "mosaic" (e.g., interspersing a few of one's own words while, in essence, copying another's work), the paraphrase (e.g., rewriting another's work while still using the other's fundamental idea or theory), fabrication (e.g., inventing or counterfeiting sources), ghost-writing (e.g., submitting another's work as one's own), and failure to include quotation marks on material that is otherwise acknowledged.
2. Representing as one's own another's artistic or scholarly works such as musical compositions, computer programs, photographs, paintings, drawing, sculptures, or similar works.

Cheating is the act of obtaining or attempting to obtain credit for academic work through the use of any dishonest, deceptive, or fraudulent means. Cheating includes but is not limited to:
1. Copying, in part or in whole, from another's test or other evaluation instrument
2. Using crib notes, "cheat sheets," or any other device, including electronic devices, not permitted by the instructor in aid of writing an exam

3. Submitting work previously graded in another course, unless doing so has been approved by the course instructor or by department policy
4. Submitting work simultaneously presented in more than one course, unless doing so has been approved by the respective course instructors or by the department policies of the respective departments
5. Altering or interfering with grading or grading instructions
6. Sitting for an examination by a surrogate, or as a surrogate
7. Any other act committed by a student in the course of his or her academic work that defrauds or misrepresents, including aiding or abetting in any of the actions defined earlier.

Documenting Sources
Here are some quick guides to writing and citing:
1. University of Kansas—Student Success a. Writing Resources by Topic—http://www.writing.ku.edu/~writing/guides/
2. Research and Documentation Guide: a. Bedford/St. Martin's—http://www.dianahacker.com/resdoc/
3. Citing Internet Resources a. Georgetown University Library—http://www.library.georgetown.edu/internet/cite.htm
4. The Columbia Guide to Online Style a. Columbia University Press—http://cup.columbia.edu/book/978-0-231-13210-7/the-columbia-guide-to-online-style

CITATION FORMATS

Elements Necessary in Any Citation Format

In order to avoid plagiarism and provide an easy way for your readers or listeners to find your sources, it is important to follow an appropriate citation format. Any citation format includes several basic elements. These are the author's name, the date of publication, the title of the work, the location of publication, and the publisher's name. Here is an example of the American Psychological Association (APA) format for a book by a single author:

> Bernstein, T. M. (1965). *The careful writer: A modern guide to English usage*. New York: Atheneum.

If any of the required elements are missing (e.g., in a Web citation, sometimes a date or an author's name is missing), cite with as much information as you have available.

The most common citation formats are the American Psychological Association (APA) and the Modern Language Association (MLA) with Chicago/Turabian coming in a close third. For more information on Chicago/Turabian Style, please see:

http://library.osu.edu/sites/guides/chicagogd.php.

Here is a list of other citation styles. Examples of APA and MLA citations are in the following sections.

> Other citation styles: (see http://www.writing.ku.edu/~writing/guides/)
> American Chemical Society (ACS) Style
> American Institute of Physics (AIP) Style
> American Medical Association (AMA) Style
> American Physical Society (APS) Style
> American Political Science Association (APSA) Style
> American Sociological Association (ASA) Style
> Council of Science Editors (CSE) Style
> Harvard Style
> Institute of Electrical and Electronics Engineers (IEEE) Style
> Linguistic Society of America (LSA) Style
> Medicine (Vancouver) Citation Style

MLA Format
(http://www.writing.ku.edu/~writing/guides/mla.shtml)

This guide is intended as a quick reference to citing in a works cited list some of the most common types of materials using the Modern Language Association format for research papers. For citations in the text, you should consult the *MLA Handbook for Writers of Research Papers* directly. Check with your instructor to learn more about the citation style required for the course/discipline.

Book by a single author:

> Bernstein, Theodore M. *The Careful Writer: A Modern Guide to English Usage*. New York: Atheneum, 1965.

Book by two authors:

> Strunk, William, Jr., and E. B. White. *The Elements of Style*. 3rd ed. New York: Macmillan, 1979.

Edited book:

> Gibbs, Jewelle Taylor, and Larke Namhe Huang, eds. *Children of Color: Psychological Interventions with Minority Youth.* San Francisco: Jossey-Bass, 1991.

Anonymous book:

> *Encyclopedia of Photography.* New York: Crown, 1984.

Multivolume edited work:

> Koch, Sigmund, ed. *Psychology: A Study of Science.* 6 vols. New York: McGraw-Hill, 1959. 63.

Work in an anthology:

> Allende, Isabel. "Toad's Mouth." Trans. Margaret Sayers Peden. *A Hammock Beneath the Mangoes: Stories from Latin America.* Ed. Thomas Colchie. New York: Plume, 1992. 83–88.

An edition (of a work previously prepared for publication by another author):

> Twain, Mark. *Roughing It.* Ed. Harriet E. Smith and Edgar M. Branch. Berkeley: U. of California P, 1993.

Journal article:

> Craner, Paul M. "New Tool for an Ancient Art: The Computer and Music." *Computers and the Humanities* 25 (1991): 303–13.

Magazine article:

> Posner, Michael I. "Seeing the Mind." *Science* 29 Oct. 1993: 673–74.

Newspaper article, no author:

> "New Drug Appears to Sharply Cut Risk of Death from Heart Failure." *Washington Post* 15 July 1993: A12.

Article in a reference book:

> Brakeley, Theresa C. "Mourning Songs." *Funk and Wagnalls Standard Dictionary of Folklore, Mythology, and Legend.* Ed. Maria Leach and Jerome Fried. 2 vols. New York: Crowell, 1950.

NOTE: For familiar reference works give only edition and year of publication, not full publication information.

World Wide Web site:

> Taylor, Todd. *Basic CGOS Style.* 1 Sept. 1998. Columbia University Press. 20 March 2000.
> <http://www.columbia.edu/cu/cup/cgos/idx_basic.html>.

NOTE: The first date is the date of last update or copyright (if available), and the second date is the date the site was accessed.

Journal article from full-text database:

> Jacobson, Marjorie. "Note: Pregnancy and Employment: Three Approaches to Equal Opportunity." *Boston University Law Review* 68 (Nov. 1988): 1019+. *Academic Universe.* LEXIS-NEXIS. U. of Kansas, Lawrence. 16 March 2000 <http://www.lexis-nexis.com/universe>.

APA Format
(http://www.writing.ku.edu/~writing/guides/apa.shtml)

This guide is intended as a quick reference to citing in a reference list some of the most common types of materials using the American Psychological Association publication format. For citations in the text, you should consult the *Publication Manual of the American Psychological Association* directly. NOTE: Hanging indents (the second line is indented) are acceptable even though first-line indents are shown in the most recent edition of the manual. Check with your instructor to learn more about the citation style required for the course/discipline.

Book by a single author:

> Bernstein, T. M. (1965). *The careful writer: A modern guide to English usage.* New York: Atheneum.

Book by two authors:

> Strunk, W., Jr., & White, E. B. (1979). *The elements of style* (3rd ed.). New York: Macmillan.

Edited book:

> Gibbs, J. T., & Huang, L. N. (Eds.). (1991). *Children of color: Psychological interventions with minority youth.* San Francisco: Jossey-Bass.

Book, no author or editor:

> *Encyclopedia of photography.* (1984). New York: Crown.

Multivolume edited work:

> Koch, S. (Ed.). (1959–1963). *Psychology: A study of science* (Vols. 1–6). New York: McGraw-Hill.

Article or chapter in edited book:

> Bjork, R. A. (1989). Retrieval inhibition as an adaptive mechanism in human memory. In H. L. Rodeiger III & F. I. M. Craik (Eds.),

Varieties of memory & consciousness (pp. 309–330). Hillsdale, NJ: Erlbaum.

Chapter in a volume in a series:

Maccoby, E. E., & Martin, J. (1983). Socialization in the context of the family: Parent-child interaction. In P. H. Mussen (Series Ed.) & E. M. Hetherington (Vol. Ed.), *Handbook of child psychology: Vol. 4. Socialization, personality, and social development* (4th ed., pp. 1–101). New York: Wiley.

Journal article:

Craner, P. M. (1991). New tool for an ancient art: The computer and music. *Computers and the Humanities*, 25, 303–313.

Magazine article:

Posner, M. I. (1993, October 29). Seeing the mind. *Science*, 262, 673–674.

Newspaper article:

New drug appears to sharply cut risk of death from heart failure. (1993, July 15). *The Washington Post*, p. A12.

Article in a reference book:

Brakeley, T. C. (1950). Mourning songs. In M. Leach & J. Fried (Eds.), *Funk and Wagnalls standard dictionary of folklore, mythology, and legend* (Vol. 2, pp. 755–757). New York: Crowell.

World Wide Web site:

Taylor, T. (1998, September 1). *Basic CGOS style*. Retrieved March 26, 2000, from http://www.columbia.edu/cu/cup/cgos/idx_basic.html

NOTE: The date in parentheses is the date of last update or copyright (if available).

Journal article from full-text database:

Jacobson, M. (1988). Note: Pregnancy and employment: Three approaches to equal opportunity. *Boston University Law Review*, 68, 1019+. Retrieved March 16, 2000, from LEXIS-NEXIS Academic Universe.

CONCLUSION

This chapter reviews the basics of conducting research for your presentations and writing projects with emphasis on appropriately incorporating information sources. By correctly citing sources you give credit to authors for their work and you make it possible for your listeners and readers to access your sources as needed. An additional bonus is that proper citation builds your credibility as a writer and a speaker by demonstrating your knowledge and effort.

Dylan Green, the student from the beginning of the chapter, is off to a good start in that he is already developing a research plan on gathering information on internships. He could use many different types of sources to support his work including books and periodicals. More than likely, he'll use technology in some way to access and obtain both types of sources. His university uses the Library of Congress classification system so if he uses the library's online search tool, he can locate all books on employment, jobs, and internships. Chances are good that if he finds the correct section of books in the library holdings, he'll find the one source he's looking for, and many more that are related. Additionally, Dylan can use the library's online databases to search business periodicals for tips, and he can probably access many articles in full-text. Finally, the reference librarian will more than likely point him in the direction of the career placement office on his campus where he'll find a wealth of resources and could potentially conduct an interview with an expert to use as a source. Once he has narrowed to the best sources, he can begin compiling his citation list using APA format, as required by his communication professor. He should also feel confident in his ability to correctly cite them and can use the textbook to double check his format. The importance of research to your speaking and writing cannot be overstated. Read ahead to Chapter 11 to learn how to incorporate research to enhance the structure and content of your presentations.

ACTIVITIES

1. Take the source information for this book and cite it using APA, MLA, and Chicago style. How are these three styles different?

2. Using your university library's Web site, what databases are available? What variety of sources do you have access to? Why is using a variety of sources vital to the success of your research?

REFERENCES

[1] Colby, Bates, and Bowdoin (CBB) Plagiarism Resource Site: https://ats.bates.edu/cbb/

[2] KU Writing Center: APA Guide: http://www.writing.ku.edu/~writing/guides/apa.shtml

[3] KU Writing Center: MLA Guide: http://www.writing.ku.edu/~writing/guides/mla.shtml

[4] KU Writing Guides: http://www.writing.ku.edu/~writing/guides/

[5] The Ohio State University: Chicago Manual of Style Citation Guide: http://library.osu.edu/sites/guides/chicagogd.php

[6] The Columbia Guide to Online Style: http://cup.columbia.edu/book/978-0-231-13210-7/the-columbia-guide-to-online-style

chapter twelve

Presentation Development

After reading this chapter you will be able to:

- Explain the importance of choosing a topic and having a clear general purpose, specific purpose, and central idea
- Describe how to organize your speech into a clear introduction, body, and conclusion
- Recognize the patterns of organization used in informative and persuasive speaking
- Create a speech outline
- Demonstrate the correct usage of connectives, main points, supporting material, and citing sources

CHAPTER OUTLINE

key words

General purpose
Specific purpose
Central idea or thesis
    statement
Goodwill
Preview statement
Pattern of organization
Attention-getting statement
Transition

Signpost
Internal preview
Internal summary
Statistics
Testimony
Expert testimony
Peer testimony
Example

INTRODUCTION

Will Thomas has been asked to give a presentation to his service fraternity on an upcoming fundraising project. He doesn't have much experience with giving speeches, and he feels intimidated by the task. Will hasn't yet taken a public speaking class, so he doesn't have any background in giving presentations. He's been given the material that he needs to cover in his presentation, but no guidelines on how to organize it. He really doesn't know where to start.

Matt Davis is active in his church youth group made up of college students. He enjoys the weekly meetings, weekend retreats, service projects, and special presentations where people from around the country speak to their group on various topics. As with many nonprofit organizations, the youth group depends on fundraisers for their various activities. The organizer of their group has asked Matt to speak at the next church service about the need for funds so that they can continue their service projects. Matt doesn't have much experience as a speaker, and he's never given a speech about the need for money. He feels overwhelmed.

Will and Matt lack knowledge about the basics of presentation development. They each understand the importance of successful public speaking, but they don't yet have the tools they need to develop and deliver those presentations. How about you? If you were faced with a similar scenario, would you know how to put together a presentation?

Many people have no idea how to organize or develop a presentation. They mistakenly believe that public speaking means standing up and talking about a subject with no real organizational pattern and very little preparation. You may have witnessed somebody doing this type of public speaking yourself. If you have, then you know that their presentation was hard to follow, and you may not have understood the point they were trying to get across. You may have left feeling frustrated about your wasted time. You may have wondered why the speaker couldn't have been more organized.

Presentation development is not hard, but the knowledge surrounding presentation development is essential to successful public speaking. Can you imagine a restaurant opening at 5 o'clock on a Friday afternoon for dinner without a plan of how to feed the hungry diners who will be there that night? Can you imagine that restaurant opening without the correct amount of food, waitstaff, and cooks? That probably sounds ridiculous to you. You probably know that running a restaurant takes lots of planning and organization. The same thing is true of public speaking. Excellent public speaking takes lots of planning and organization. You wouldn't attend your college classes without the textbook, a pen and paper, or your laptop, and you should never give a speech without careful planning and development.

If you want to be successful at giving speeches, you need to begin at the beginning and know how to get to the end. You need to be aware of your overall purpose, your audience, organizational skills, supporting materials, outlining basics, language, and time constraints. You'll be on your way to having a successful presentation if you take the time to develop it correctly.

If you speak about a hobby of yours, the audience will find it interesting because of your enthusiastic attitude.

© Soultkd/Shutterstock.com

CHOOSING A TOPIC

The first step in developing a speech is choosing your topic. In the classroom, your topic might be assigned to you, but often it will be your choice. Outside the classroom, you will be asked to speak on your area of expertise.

You might think that choosing a topic is easy. Surprisingly, this can be one of the most difficult parts of speech development. Students seem to struggle when choosing a topic because they are afraid that the topic they choose will be boring to their listeners, or they start researching the topic and decide they are no longer interested. Here are some guidelines to choosing your speech topic:

1. **Choose something that you are interested in.** This might sound obvious, but some speakers try to choose a topic that they think their audience will find interesting. Remember that if you are interested in your topic, you will be excited about sharing information, your enthusiasm will be evident to your audience, and you will both benefit.

2. **Choose something that you are familiar with.** If you choose a topic that you know nothing about, you will have to first research the material, then work to understand what you have read, and then talk about it to other people. This is not recommended because your lack of knowledge will be obvious to your audience, and you will surely lose interest in the topic yourself. If you already have knowledge about your topic, then your research will be easier to conduct because you will be finding material that supports your points instead of starting from scratch.

3. **Choose something that you can make relevant to your audience.** You don't need to worry about choosing a topic that will interest your listeners. If you show your audience how your information will affect them, they will become interested. Work hard to show your audience the relevance of your material. While so far we have discussed topic selection within a course, the same ideas apply in the business context. Sometimes you will have a choice on your topic and other times you won't. The key is clearly organizing your business presentations with a clear purpose.

If a topic does not come to mind immediately, you can try reading magazines or newspapers or glancing at the news headlines on your Internet server. You don't want to choose something that has been the hot news story for the last 2 weeks because then many of your audience members will also be overly familiar with your topic. But, you might get an idea for a topic from something you read or hear. Another way to choose a topic is to brainstorm. Take a blank piece of paper and write down your hobbies, favorite bands, movies you love, books you've read, vacations you've taken, memorable experiences you've had, or a job you've held. Look over your list several times and see what comes to mind as a possible topic. Think novelty when it comes to your topic. Any audience loves to learn something new. Expand your boundaries. Don't choose the

Try brainstorming to make a list of possible topics for your speech.

same topic you wrote your biology paper on last semester or the same topic that your roommate chose last semester for her speech. The whole idea behind speechmaking is to communicate with your audience. When you choose a topic that you are familiar with, that you are interested in, and that you can make relevant to your audience, they will thank you by listening to your speech and remembering your information.[1]

WHY ARE YOU SPEAKING?

General Purpose

General purpose: Your overall reason for speaking.

Whenever you speak, you need to be aware of why you are speaking. What is the goal of your presentation, and what is your goal as a speaker? You always want to have a **general purpose**. The general purpose is your overall reason for speaking. You can speak *to inform, to persuade, to motivate,* or *to entertain.* Some speakers are never clear on what their overall goal is, and therefore, the audience gets confused as well.

Your general purpose should be one of the first things you think about when you are asked to do a presentation.

When your overall goal is to inform, your job becomes that of an information giver. You want to communicate information as clearly and accurately as possible. Your information can be presented in an entertaining or more lighthearted manner if you like, but your overall goal remains informative. If you tell your audience about opportunities to study abroad, the benefits of adopting a vegetarian diet, or the steps involved in starting a new club on campus, you are speaking to inform. You want to add to the knowledge of your listeners and give them information that they don't already have.

When your overall goal is to persuade, your job is to influence the members of your audience to think or feel or act in a certain way. You will give them information, but you will organize that information into arguments that will, hopefully, *change* or *reinforce* the attitudes and actions of your audience members. You can persuade your audience members to continue their exercise program, or to reduce their trips to fast-food restaurants, or to believe that one candidate is better qualified for office than another.

When your goal is to motivate, you want to move your audience to take an action. You can motivate them to begin walking instead of driving to the nearest grocery store because it will help cut down on pollution in the environment. You can motivate your audience to join a support group for people who want to lose weight, or you can motivate your audience members to volunteer at the nearest hospital.

When your goal is to entertain, your job is to inform, persuade, or motivate in a way that makes the audience have fun while you accomplish your goal. After-dinner speaking is usually entertaining because people are full and expect more lighthearted presentations. This does not mean you become a stand-up comic or just give a bunch of one-liners. Your speech always makes a point, and it is always well organized.

Specific Purpose

The second objective you need to be clear about is what you want to accomplish with your presentation. This is called your specific purpose. With the general purpose, you know what your goal is as the speaker. With the specific purpose, you decide what your goals are for the audience. Do you want them to understand the steps involved in applying for the study-abroad program? Do you want them to believe that they can help prevent global warming? Do you want your audience members to join a new club on campus? These are examples of goals you have for your listeners after they hear your speech. Remember that a specific purpose

Specific purpose: What you want to accomplish with your presentation; your goal for the audience.

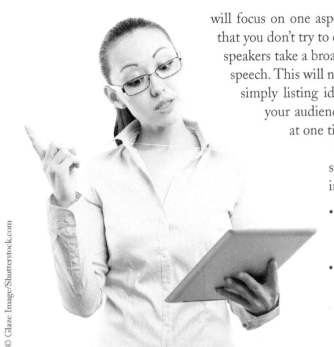

will focus on one aspect of your topic. It will also help ensure that you don't try to cover too many ideas in one speech. Some speakers take a broad topic and try to cover all of it in a short speech. This will never be successful because you will end up simply listing ideas and not developing those ideas, and your audience can only process so much information at one time.

The most effective way to formulate a specific purpose statement is in a single infinitive phrase such as:

- To inform my audience that there are four steps in the process of applying for the Alumni Scholarship;
- To persuade my audience that they must support the ban on smoking in restaurants because of the increase in cases of lung cancer.

Remember to limit your focus so your speech doesn't run over time.

A specific purpose will help you as the speaker narrow the focus of your presentation so that it will fit into the time you've been allotted. Most classroom speeches need to be relatively short so that all students have a chance to speak. Therefore, you have to limit your ideas and focus so that your speech doesn't run over time. But, what if you're asked to speak for an hour? The same principle applies: narrow down your topic and formulate your specific purpose so that it focuses on your topic only.

Guidelines for Specific Purpose Statements

1. Limit your specific purpose so that it has only **one clear idea**. There should not be any "ands," "buts," or "ors" in a specific purpose statement because that sets up more than one clear idea. Instead of: to inform my audience that there are three stages of road rage and road rage is on the increase, try this instead: to inform my audience that there are three stages of road rage OR to inform my audience that there are three reasons why road rage has increased over the last 5 years.

2. Make sure that your specific purpose is **written as a statement** and not as a question. "Can we stop pollution?" is an ineffective specific purpose. "To inform my audience that they can help reduce air pollution in our town through three simple steps" is much more effective.

3. Make your specific purpose as **focused as possible**. Instead of: to inform my audience about job interviews, it is much more effective to say: to inform my audience about four winning strategies for having a successful job interview.

4. **Avoid abstract or figurative language** in your specific purpose. Instead of saying: to inform my audience that NASCAR racing is great, try: to inform my audience that NASCAR racing has evolved from cars racing on the beach at Daytona to an organized sport that appeals to a wide audience.

Central Idea

The third thing you need to have is a central idea or thesis statement. The central idea should sum up your speech in a single sentence. Once again, this is a component that helps you and your speech stay focused. It is more focused than your specific purpose, and it is written as a single declarative statement. If your specific purpose is "to inform my audience that there are four steps in the process of applying for the Alumni Scholarship," then your central idea would be, "There are four steps in applying for the Alumni Scholarship" OR "The four steps involved in applying for the Alumni Scholarship include completing the application, obtaining your high school and current college transcripts, obtaining three letters of reference, and mailing all your information to the graduate office on campus."

Andrea Lee is a sophomore at a large university, and she is ready to give her first speech in her communication class. She has listened to the lecture about topic, general purpose, specific purpose, and central idea, and she is ready to write these down. Here is what she has developed so far:

Central idea or thesis statement: Sums up your speech in a single statement.

Topic:	Benefits of reading
General purpose:	To inform
Specific purpose:	To inform my audience that there are three benefits of reading
Central idea:	Reading is beneficial because it's educational, fun, and healthy.

From this, we can see that Andrea will show her audience how reading is educational, how reading is fun, and how reading is healthy. We know that these three aspects will be the content of her speech. In fact, they will be the main points that Andrea will cover in her speech. These should also be the ideas that remain in the minds of the audience after the speech is completed.

The general purpose, the specific purpose, and the central idea are three essential aspects of getting organized before you start writing your speech. Mastering these three components will help you stay organized as you write and then deliver your presentation.

ORGANIZING THE SPEECH

Every speech or presentation that you do should be organized with an opening, a middle, and an end. These are usually referred to as the introduction, the body, and the conclusion. Each of these parts of the speech requires important components described below.

The Introduction

In the introduction you want to accomplish five things:

1. Grab the attention of your audience
2. State your topic
3. Establish your credibility
4. Connect with your audience
5. Preview your main points.

GRAB THE ATTENTION OF YOUR AUDIENCE

How do you begin your presentation? You need to spend a lot of time deciding how to begin because this is where your audience decides whether or not they will continue to listen to you. If you begin with an apology for not being sufficiently prepared or for not getting enough sleep and feeling tired, or if you tell your audience that you put your presentation together the night before, or if you explain that your presentation won't be very good because you are not feeling well, then your audience will disengage immediately because they will assume (and they are probably correct) that you will waste their time. Don't *ever* begin your presentation with an apology or with a disclaimer. The reason so many students and other speakers make this mistake is because they feel that these statements will garner sympathy in case their presentation is not as good as it should be. This tactic will not work! Instead of feeling sympathetic, listeners will feel angry and irritated that you didn't take the assignment seriously. In business, this is a surefire way to diminish your credibility.

Now that you know what *not* to do at the beginning of your speech, here are some tips for great beginnings:

- Walk to the lectern with confidence, even if you are nervous. You know that expression, "Never let them see you sweat?" Well, now is the time to use it. Fake confidence if you have to. It will have a positive impact on you, and your audience will feel better about listening to you. Look your listeners in the eye and smile before you begin to show them that you are in control of your presentation and you are ready to begin communicating.
- There is usually no need to introduce yourself at the beginning of your speech. Most of the time, you will have been introduced or your name will be printed in the program. In class, other students know your name, and some instructors ask that student speakers place their names on the board at the beginning of class. To introduce yourself is redundant and is not an exciting way to grab the attention of the audience.

Here are some examples of ways you can successfully get the attention of your audience. Keep in mind that whichever method you choose, it should relate to your topic. For example, you wouldn't want to trick your audience by saying loudly, "Free gas available now!" and then give a speech on the

Whatever you use to grab your listener's attention should always tie into your topic.

© Africa Studio/Shutterstock.com

three stages in the development of a tornado. Whatever you use to grab your listener's attention should always tie into your topic.

1. **Ask a question.** This can be a rhetorical question or a question that you want answered. If you ask either type of question, give your audience several seconds to answer you or to raise their hands or to think about what you've asked. If you don't, your question will lose its impact. You will also have to guide your listeners as to whether you want them to verbally answer, raise their hands or indicate their answer in another way, or to simply think about their answer. For example, if you want them to respond to you, say something like, "By a show of hands, how many of you would like to increase your sales in the next two months?" If you just want them to think about your question, say something like, "Think about this scenario: You are walking across campus after studying at the library late one evening when you suddenly hear footsteps behind you. You increase your pace just a bit and glance behind you. All you can see is a dark figure because the lighting isn't very good. The footsteps behind you increase, matching your stride. You glance around for a fellow student or an emergency phone,

"Who wants a big sales increase?" Ask a question to get your audience involved.

© wavebreakmedia/Shutterstock.com

but you don't see anyone, and there are no emergency phones in sight. Your heart starts to pound and your mind races with scary thoughts about the person who could be following you and what they might do to you. With no other resources present, you are on your own. What will you do? How will you defend yourself?" Now, your listeners have the opportunity to think about the scenario you have set up, but they will not verbally respond.

2. **Make a startling statement.** In a speech on the rising price of gas in the United States, one student began this way: "Quit whining over gas prices! If you lived in Paris, you'd be paying $9.85 a gallon for gas, and in London, you'd pay $8.96. Americans pay much lower prices at the pump than do many people who don't make nearly as much money!" Of course, the student then continued by explaining three methods for getting more efficient gas mileage. But, his goal was to make his audience want to listen to his speech, so he began by startling them with his statement about whining and then his statistics about gas prices in other countries.

3. **Begin with a quotation.** There are books of quotations to be found at your college library, public libraries, bookstores, and even on the Internet. You can find a quotation that matches almost any topic. For example, a student choosing to deliver a speech on world hunger began with words from Psalm 59: "They that die by famine die by inches." In a speech on time management, another student began with a quote from Horace Mann: "Lost yesterday, somewhere between sunrise and sunset, two golden hours, each set with sixty diamond minutes. No reward is offered, for they are gone forever." Quotations can be from famous people, but you can also use quotes from people who are not well known.

4. **Tell a brief story or anecdote.** These have to be brief because you have a time limit for each speech, but you can still relate an effective story or anecdote that is funny, provocative, dramatic, or interesting. One student chose to deliver her informative speech on the topic of living life to its fullest and talked about a recent first-time skydiving experience, which left her both excited and terrified as the plane took off. She began her speech with a description of her feelings as the plane began its ascent, and she knew there was no turning back: "I can't believe I'm in this plane with 5 other people that I've never met before. I am going to jump out of this plane in 15 minutes, and I am more afraid than I've ever been in my life. I can't catch my breath, and I can hear

my frantic heartbeat in my ears. I want to tell them to turn the plane around and to take me back because I cannot do this! Why did I ever agree to come on this trip? Just as I thought my heart would explode out of my chest from fear, the person in front of me turned and shouted in my ear, 'Are you as excited as I am? I can't wait to do this. I want to know what it's like to fly. I don't want to die not knowing what that feels like!' I realized at that moment that I wanted to know that feeling as well. I was looking at this situation as something negative while my partner was looking at this as a great adventure. He had discovered how to live life to the fullest, and I wanted to follow in his footsteps."

STATE YOUR TOPIC

Find a good quotation to start off your speech.

One mistake that some speakers make is never clarifying their topic. They assume that because they know what their topic is, it will be obvious to their audience. Don't ever assume. It's better to clarify this in the introduction of your speech so that your audience isn't confused. If they are, they won't be listening to your speech. You don't have to say, "My topic today is saving time in the kitchen." You can be a little more

© michaeljung/Shutterstock.com

subtle if you like, but you do want to be clear. If you begin by talking about how much college students love to eat, but mostly eat fast food or packaged convenience food, chances are your audience will think your speech is about eliminating fast food from your diet. Be clear. You could start this way instead: "What are you having for dinner tonight? Fast food again? Is that because you truly love a Big Mac or is it because you think you don't have time to cook something you'd like to eat? Rachael Ray, a noted Food Network star, has made herself famous by cooking 30-minute meals. Some of you might be skeptical, convinced that no meal can really be prepared in 30 minutes and taste good. I'm going to show you that good-tasting, healthy, and economical meals can be yours … in 30 minutes!" After gaining the attention of your audience and clearly stating your purpose, you need to establish your credibility.

ESTABLISH YOUR CREDIBILITY

Credibility in a speech refers to believability. Why should your audience members believe what you say? Remember that credibility lies in the eyes of your listeners. They are the ones who decide whether or not to believe you. Therefore, one way to establish credibility is to explain to your listeners why you are giving your speech. What is your background with this topic or your experience or your knowledge? You first establish your credibility in the introduction of your speech, and then you continue to support your credibility throughout your speech with your clear organization, use of supporting materials, dynamic delivery, and adherence to your time limits. Here are some examples of how to establish your credibility in the speech introduction:

- I have had a part-time job as a literacy tutor for the past 2 years, and I have decided that this is an area I would like to pursue after graduation.
- I became interested in this topic after taking my International Studies class, and I have done some research in the area on my own.
- My parents died when I was young, and I have been raised by my grandparents, who now live on a fixed income. They never had much money. So I have learned how to live frugally but without going without the necessities of life. Using my own knowledge, and that of my grandparents, I will explain to you how to live on less money than you ever thought possible.

ESTABLISH YOUR GOODWILL

Goodwill means showing your audience that you have their best interests in mind. All audiences want a reason to listen to your information. If you can show them that your speech will benefit them in some way, they will be more likely to listen. That doesn't mean that your speech has to show them how to get rich quickly or to suddenly become an "A" student. Goodwill simply shows the audience that you have written and structured your speech with them in mind. In the previous example about the student who has learned to live frugally, he could establish his goodwill with a statement such as: "With the rising cost of gas prices, food prices, and textbook prices, I'm sure that all of you have made some changes in the way you live and spend money. Today, I'll show you how to pinch more pennies without pinching your way of life."

PREVIEW YOUR MAIN POINTS

The last component of the introduction is the **preview statement**. Here is where you tell the audience exactly what you will cover in the body of

©Stuart Jenner/Shutterstock.com

your speech by previewing each main point. You preview the main points that will be contained in the body of your speech. For example, you could say, "Today we'll see that reading is educational, fun, and healthy." Or if your speech is on learning new vocabulary words, you could state: "Today we'll look at two benefits of having great vocabulary skills: scoring higher on standardized tests and performing better in college English classes." If you are doing a speech on saving our national parks, you could say, "All our national parks are in trouble. You all must help save our national parks by visiting them and supporting the National Parks Conservation Association."

The preview statement provides the transition needed between the introduction and the body of the speech. But, once you state your preview, know that your audience will expect you to cover only the main points that you promise and no more. If you then add in more points, you will lose your audience's attention. Also, if you neglect to cover one of the main points that you previewed, your audience will feel cheated.

The Body

The *body* of the speech is where the majority of your information is found. This is where your main points, supporting points, evidence, arguments, examples, descriptions, and transitions all go. How do you decide what goes in the body of your speech? It all depends on organization.

First, you will need to decide on which main points of your topic you will cover. You can't cover every aspect of your topic in the time you've been given, and your audience can't remember all that information. Choose the specific areas you want to talk about. A good rule of thumb is to stick with three main points. This number of main points should fit comfortably into the time you are allotted for classroom speeches. You also want to keep your audience in mind. They can only process and remember a certain amount of information. If you try to cover six or seven main points, you will end up listing the points with no time to develop them, and your audience will forget most of what you say. After you graduate from college, when you are given a longer time to speak, you will still want to limit the number of main points in your speech. You might have as many as five or six in a 45-minute presentation, but more than that will be too many for your audience and for you. The key to a well-developed presentation is that you state your main point, develop that main point, and then move on. You don't want to end up with a grocery list of points with no development.

Next, you will need to do some research. You already know something about your topic. Now, you need to find examples, testimony, statistics, descriptions—all of which support the points you will cover.

Third, you will decide on the order of your main points. You will need to choose a **pattern of organization**. Your speech purpose will help determine which pattern of organization will work best. You can choose from the following patterns of organization.

CHRONOLOGICAL PATTERN OF ORGANIZATION. You use this pattern of organization when your topic refers to the steps in a process, the development of something over time, or a demonstration. Your main points will follow a time pattern.

Pattern of organization: The order of your main points.

For example:

Topic: Process of applying to graduate school

Specific purpose: To inform my audience that there are three steps in the process of applying to graduate school.

Main points:

  I. The first step in applying to graduate school is to complete the application.

  II. The second step in applying to graduate school is to obtain three letters of recommendation.

  III. The third step is to mail all materials to the graduate office at your school of choice.

Topic: Growing apples

Specific purpose: To inform my audience about the four stages of apple growing.

Main points:

  I. First, in the spring, the orchards are prepared by pruning and getting ready for the sprayers.

  II. Second, in the summer the orchards are sprayed for bug and disease control.

  III. Third, in the fall, the fruit is harvested and stored.

  IV. Finally, in the winter, the orchards are pruned.

TOPICAL ORDER. This pattern is used when your main points do not have to be in a specific order. Topical order is used when your topic naturally subdivides into subtopics. Each of the subtopics becomes a main point.

For example:

Topic: Three aspects of vocal variety

Specific purpose: To inform my audience about three aspects of vocal variety.

Main points:

  I. One aspect of vocal variety is rate.

  II. The second aspect of vocal variety is expressiveness.

  III. The third aspect of vocal variety is the pause.

Topic: It's not too late to learn new things.

Specific purpose: To inform my audience that it's never too late to learn something new.

Main points:

I. It's never too late to start a new hobby.
II. It's never too late to start a new friendship.
III. It's never too late to change a bad habit.

SPATIAL ORDER. You use this pattern of organization when your main points need to follow a directional pattern. This is not the same as chronological pattern because, in that pattern, you have to talk about your main points in a specific order. If you don't, the steps in the process won't work, or the development of an idea or theory or event won't happen. With spatial order, your points follow a directional pattern, but *you* decide on which direction. Directional patterns include from left to right, from right to left, east to west, west to east, north to south, south to north, top to bottom, from bottom to top, from outside in or inside out. Don't be intimidated by this pattern. It sounds tricky, but the directional pattern of the main points will help your audience picture what you are talking about.

Topic:	Three national parks
Specific purpose:	To inform my audience about three of the most well-known national parks in the Unites States.

Main points:

I. Cape Hatteras National Seashore is located along the coast of eastern North Carolina.
II. Yellowstone National Park is located in the northwest corner of Wyoming and the southeast corner of Montana.
III. Yosemite National Park is located east of San Francisco in California.

The directional order that the speaker has chosen is east to west. He/she could have just as easily started with Yosemite National Park and moved to Yellowstone National Park and then to Cape Hatteras National Seashore.

These three patterns of organization—chronological, topical, and spatial—are most often used in informative speeches. Following is a sample outline format that shows the use of topical order.

Sample Informative Speech Outline in Topical Order

Introduction

I. Your attention-getting statement goes here—you can ask a question; make a startling statement; tell a short, related anecdote; etc. Whatever you use here *must* relate to your topic.

II. This is where you *reveal the topic* of your speech: "Today we will look at three types of wood used in the building industry."

III. Establish your credibility and goodwill. Credibility is your believability—why we should listen to you give this speech. Goodwill shows your listeners what's in it for them. You give your audience a reason to listen to your information. Let them know how they will benefit from listening. (Credibility and goodwill can also be separate steps.)

IV. Preview statement: "Today we will look at the three types of wood used in building: cherry, oak, and walnut." (You forecast the main points you will cover in this speech.)

Body

I. Statement of your first main point. "One type of wood used in the building industry is cherry." (This should be a full sentence. It is never a source.)

   A. This is where you put your subpoint: "Cherry can be used in making beautiful and durable doors for homes.

      1. The detail or supporting point goes here. "According to the November 2006 edition of *Tree* magazine,…"

      2. You add more supporting detail here.

      3. You might need a third supporting detail here.

   B. This is where your second subpoint goes. "Cherry can also be used for building doors on sailing yachts."

      1. "As stated by Captain John W. Hughes of the American Yachting Company…"

      2. A supporting point here.

      3. A supporting point here.

Transition. Now that we've looked at the uses of cherry wood, let's move on to another type of wood used in building.

II. The second type of wood used in building is oak.

   A. This is your subpoint. You can talk about one place that oak is used—maybe in furniture of some kind?

1. This is supporting detail. It can be an example, testimony in quotation form, or a statistic.
   2. This is a supporting detail.
   B. This is your second subpoint.
      1. Supporting detail.
      2. Supporting detail.

Transition. Now that we've seen how both cherry and oak are used in building, let's move on to our final type of wood.

III. Walnut is the third type of wood used in building.
   A. Many top executives choose walnut for their desks.
      1. Supporting material here. It could be an example, a quotation or a statistic.
      2. Supporting material here.
      3. Supporting material here.
   B. Second subpoint.
      1. Supporting material.
      2. Supporting material.
      3. Supporting material.

Conclusion

   I. **Restate your main points.** "In conclusion, we've seen that cherry, oak, and walnut are three types of wood used in building."
   II. **Close with impact.** This can be a startling statement, a question, an anecdote, etc.

Let's now look at some patterns of organization that would work better for persuasive speeches.

CAUSE–EFFECT. This persuasive pattern organizes your main points to show a cause and an effect. With this pattern of organization, there are only two main points. Your first main point can show the cause and the second can show the effect or you can decide to use your first main point to show the effect and the second main point to show the cause. Your topic will help you decide which order to follow.

For example:
Topic: Slow down!
Specific purpose: To persuade my audience that their fast-paced lifestyle is causing two problems.

Main points:

I. We all have a lifestyle that is much too hectic (cause).
II. We are missing out on the good things in life, and our stress level is too high (effect).

Topic: Self-defense
Specific purpose: To inform my audience that self-defense knowledge is a necessary tool for personal safety.

Main points:

I. You will feel safer if you know you can defend yourself (effect).
II. You can learn three basic self-defense moves that will help you feel safer (cause).

PROBLEM–SOLUTION. This pattern of organization is used when you want to present a problem and then you present a solution to solve that problem. With this pattern, you will have only two main points: The first main point will show the need or the problem, and the second main point will show a plausible solution to the problem.

Transitions let your audience know you're moving from the problem to the solution.

For example:

Topic: Our national parks are in trouble.

Specific purpose: To inform my audience that our national parks need help.

Main points:

I. Our national park system is in trouble.

II. You must support our park system by supporting the National Parks Conservation Association.

Following is a sample outline format for a persuasive speech using the problem–solution pattern of organization:

Sample Persuasive Speech Outline in Problem-Solution Order

Introduction

I. Open with impact/attention-getting statement.

II. Reveal your topic.

III. Establish credibility—show your audience you are qualified to give this speech; and goodwill—show your audience why they should listen.

IV. Preview statement—clearly preview your main points.

Body

I. Statement of first main point. This should be a clear statement that states the problem. Remember that main points are not sources. First you state the point and then you support the point.

  A. This is your subpoint. It adds support to your main point. Each main point should be fully developed with at least two subpoints. These can be examples, quotations, statistics, descriptions, etc.

    1. This is a supporting point. It gives even more clarity to your main point.

    2. Another supporting point here. Use emotional appeal.

    3. Perhaps one more supporting point. You might have only two supporting points—depends on your topic and time limits.

  B. This is your second subpoint. It continues to back up or strengthen your main point. It might even be a counterargument. A *counterargument* states a possible objection to your claim and then (with sources and other material) shows why your argument is stronger. Counterarguments are very important to use in persuasive speaking because your audience WILL have objections in mind. You as the speaker need to anticipate the strongest objection and show why your point is stronger. Remember that you don't want your objection to be a main point because that would give it too much importance. You really just want to show your audience that you are aware that there are other sides to the story, but that your claim is the strongest.

1. Supporting point here that backs up your main point and subpoints.
2. Another supporting point here—use emotional appeal. Emotional appeal can be used throughout the speech. This is just an example of where you might put it.
3. Another supporting point.

Transition. This lets your audience know that you are done talking about the problem and are moving on to the solution.

II. This is your second main point—it should clearly state the solution you propose.
   A. This is a subpoint that backs up your main point.
      1. A supporting point goes here. Again, don't forget emotional appeal.
      2. Another supporting point here—perhaps a counterargument.
      3. If you like, a third supporting point.
   B. Your second subpoint that clearly adds support to your main point.
      1. Supporting point here—use emotional appeal.
      2. Supporting point here—use emotional appeal.
      3. Third supporting point.

Conclusion

   I. Restate main points—problem and solution.
   II. Close with impact.

Monroe's motivated sequence. This pattern of organization is used when you want to move your audience to take an action. This pattern was developed by Purdue University professor Alan Monroe in the 1930s. Monroe's motivated sequence has five steps.

1. **Attention step.** This step is found in the introduction of your speech. You can use any of the things already talked about in this chapter to capture the attention of your audience.
2. **Need step.** With Monroe's motivated sequence, your goal is to show your audience that there is a problem that needs to be solved. Many times, your audience will not be aware of the need to change, so you will have to persuade them in this step that there is an existing need.
3. **Satisfaction step.** In the previous step, you persuaded your audience that there is a problem that needs to be solved. In the satisfaction step, you present your solution to the problem. Your solution needs to be a workable plan. You will need to offer a detailed plan here, not just a general solution.
4. **Visualization step.** Here is where you show your audience the results of adopting your solution. You've persuaded them that your solution will solve the problem. You presented a detailed plan. In the visualization step, you show your audience the benefits of adopting your solution. Use vivid language that will help your listeners see those benefits. It is always best if you can show your audience how they will directly benefit from adopting your plan.
5. **Action step**. This step comes in the conclusion of your speech. Be specific about the action you want your audience to take. Don't be vague here and say: "So, the next time you have a test, try to use your study time more efficiently." Instead, try this: "The next time you have a test, remember that efficiently using your study time will lead to a better grade. Try allotting a certain time to studying, minimize your distractions by turning off the TV, iPod, and cell phone, and take a 10-minute break each hour." See how specific that action step is?

In your speech, follow the same rules as for any speech—have a clear introduction, body, and conclusion. In the introduction, you will grab the attention of your listeners, reveal your topic, establish your credibility and goodwill, and state your preview sentence. In the body of your speech, the need step, satisfaction step, and visualization steps become your main points. In the conclusion, you restate your main points, state the action you want the audience to take, and close with impact.

If you want to see Monroe's motivated sequence in action, watch television for about 30 minutes, paying close attention to the commercials. Many advertisements use this sequence in their ads.

Monroe's Motivated Sequence

Introduction

    I. **Attention**—really work to make the audience sit up and listen to your speech

    II. **Reveal topic**—tell us what your speech will be about

    III. **Goodwill** and **credibility**—tell us why you are giving this speech and then tell us why we should listen. What's in it for us?

    IV. **Preview statement**—preview your main points exactly as you will discuss them

Body

    I. **Need**—describes problem in a way that motivates the audience to see a need for change

        A. Statement of problem—details, description

            1. Stories, examples, statistics

            2. Support

            3. More support if necessary

        B. Ramification—what are the consequences of this problem?

            1. Supporting material

            2. Support

            3. More support if necessary

        C. Pointing—make it clear to the audience how they are directly affected by this problem and why they should care.

            1. Support

            2. Support

            3. Support

Transition—now that…

    II. **Satisfaction**—presents a specific solution

        A. Statement of proposed solution

            1. Support

            2. Support

        B. Explanation of solution

            1. Support

            2. Support

            3. Support

   C. Meeting objections—anticipate objections, address and refute them
     1. Support
     2. Support

Transition—now that we…

  III. Visualization—paint a mental picture for your audience
    A. Positive—how things will change for the better if your plan is adopted
     1. Support
     2. Support
    B. Negative—what will the negative consequences be if your plan is not adopted?
     1. Support
     2. Support
    C. Comparison of the positive and the negative
     1. Examples and support
     2. Examples and support

Conclusion

  I. Action—provide a call to action
    A. Summarize main points
    B. Statement of desired action or attitude change
    C. Close with impact

  Works Cited

Main Points
When you are writing your main points, remember a few guidelines:
1. Keep the main points simple. You should have only one idea per main point. That means no conjunctions such as *and, or,* and *but.*
2. Keep the main points balanced. You should have equal amounts of information in each main point. An easy way to keep up with this is to look over your outline. You should have roughly the same number of sub- and supporting points for each main point.
3. Make sure the main points look similar. The wording of the main points should be parallel in structure whenever possible.

Connectives

Transition: A word or phrase that lets the audience know you are done talking about one idea and are moving on to the next idea.

Signpost: A key word or phrase that points to what the speaker is covering.

Transitions and signposts both serve as bridges between your main points and between the parts of your speech. These function to help you get smoothly from one point to the next, and they help your audience move with you. That way, both you and your audience arrive at the end of your speech together.

A transition can be a word or a phrase. A transition lets the audience know that you are done talking about one idea and you are moving on to the next idea.

Here are some examples of transitions:

- Now that we've seen the problem with our national park system, let's look at what can be done.
- Now that we've seen how our hectic lifestyle causes health problems, let's look at another disadvantage of always being in a hurry.
- You've seen that building your vocabulary will help you recognize words in many documents; now let's look at a second advantage of building your vocabulary knowledge.

Signposts also serve as bridges, but they are identified as key words or phrases that point to what the speaker is covering. You can use words like, "first, second, third, finally," or "one, two, three," or "to conclude, to summarize, to sum it up, to review."

Here are some examples of signposts:

- The first reason you must support our national parks is because they are part of our nation's heritage.
- The second reason you must support our national parks is because their beauty is priceless.
- The third reason you must support our national parks is because the parks are home to endangered wildlife.

One easy way to signal that you are at the end of your speech is to use a signpost such as "in conclusion" or "to summarize." These signposts leave no doubt in your listeners' minds as to where you are in the speech.

Internal preview: Tells your audience what will be coming next.

Internal previews tell your audience what will be coming next. The most prominent place to use a preview is in your introduction. The preview statement should be the last thing your audience hears before you move into the body of your speech. The preview serves as a forecast of what's to come. An internal preview is usually used in a longer speech that will contain more ideas. You can give a preview of each section to let the audience know what is coming next.

Here are several examples of preview statements:

- Today we'll look at three aspects of kudzu: its origin, benefits, and termination.
- We'll examine two benefits of having great vocabulary skills.
- In this speech we'll look at three aspects of vocal variety in speaking.
- In this speech, we'll see that it's never too late to start a new hobby, redeem an old friendship, or change a bad habit.

Internal summaries are great tools to use in longer presentations to help your audience keep pace with your speech. Internal summaries allow you to review the information you have already covered before you move on to the next part of your speech. If you are persuading your audience that poor customer service hurts business production, you might want to use an internal summary after you fully explain the causes of poor customer service. This way, your audience is reminded of those causes before you move into the second portion of your speech, which will cover the effects of poor customer service. Here's an example of an internal summary:

> So far we've seen that employees provide poor customer service for four reasons: lack of education, lack of interest in the company, lack of training during orientation, and lack of leadership by management. Now let's move on and see how your business productivity will be damaged as a result of poor customer service.

Supporting Material

You should think of your main points as claims or assertions that you make. They may be perfectly valid, but you need to back up your claim or assertion with supporting material. The use of supporting material adds credibility to your speech. Supporting material comes from your research. It can include statistics, definitions, examples, explanations, testimony in the form of quotations or paraphrased material, and even brief stories. Carefully select your supporting materials, checking for accuracy, relevancy, and reliability. Don't go overboard on using all the numbers you can find; this can overwhelm and confuse your audience.

The three most common kinds of supporting material are *statistics, testimony,* and *example.*

1. **Statistics.** Some people love numbers. Some speakers throw in all the statistics they can find in hopes of impressing their audience. Instead of being impressed, listeners tune out, feeling

Internal summary: A review of the information you have already covered before you move on to the next part of your speech.

Statistics: A collection of quantitative data.

overwhelmed and confused. Using statistics is fine if you follow these guidelines:

- Use statistics sparingly
- Make the numbers relevant
- Explain any statistics you use
- Make sure your statistics come from a reliable source
- Identify the source of your statistics
- Round off complicated numbers
- Use a visual to help explain or clarify your statistics

2. **Testimony.** You can use direct quotes or you can paraphrase what someone says to support a main point. Either way, you must state where you got your information. Some people mistakenly believe that if they put someone else's words into their own words (paraphrasing) that they do not have to cite the source. There are two kinds of testimony available to you:

- **Expert testimony.** Comes from someone who is a recognized expert or authority in their field. You might have the opportunity to interview them and use their words in your speech, you might read something that they've said in another source, or you might read something they have written. Using expert testimony adds credibility to your speech because it shows that someone with a great deal of knowledge and experience supports what you say.

- **Peer testimony.** Comes from people who have knowledge or an opinion on a subject, but they are not a recognized expert in the field. If you were delivering a speech on our national park system, you would certainly get expert testimony from a park ranger or other official. But you could also talk to your neighbor who has been to many national parks and seen firsthand some of the issues you talk about.

3. **Examples.** This form of supporting material can add richness, relevancy, and a personal touch to your speech. Examples are a great tool for clarifying information. You actually use examples every day as you communicate, but you might not be aware of their frequency or their impact. When you return to your dorm room at the end of a long day, your roommate might remark that you look tired. You might reply, "It's been a horrible day. I forgot about a test in my Biology class this morning, and then my Political Science professor gave us an extra assignment.

Testimony: Using direct quotes or paraphrasing what someone says to support a main point.

Expert Testimony: Information from someone who is a recognized expert or authority in their field.

Peer Testimony: Information that comes from people who have knowledge or an opinion on a subject, but they are not recognized experts in the field.

Example: Form of supporting material that can add richness, relevancy, and a personal touch to your speech.

On the way to get some lunch, I realized I forgot my wallet, and I didn't have time to come back here and get it before my lab. I am exhausted and starving. That's why this day has been so bad." Your example helps show your roommate why your day was truly horrible. Examples help statements become specific. In a classroom speech where time is limited, you will need to use *brief examples*. When you do have more time to speak, you can use longer or *extended examples*. Another type of example is the *hypothetical example*—one that describes a situation that is not real or has not happened. You can ask your listeners to place themselves in a situation that has not happened to them to get them involved with your topic. For example, if you want to speak about the surgical nightmare some patients have faced of not being fully unconscious during surgery, you could use an example like this:

> *Put yourself in this situation. You are being prepped for knee surgery to repair your torn meniscus. You feel a little nervous but also confident that all will go well. You have a great surgeon, you are young and healthy, and you expect a full recovery. And, the surgery will be painless. After all, you'll be sound asleep.*

You can talk to an expert in order to get testimony for your speech.

But, what if you actually aren't sound asleep? What if somehow you wake up during the surgery and are able to feel every slice of the extremely sharp scalpels? And, what if nobody else knows? What if no one but you knows the excruciating pain and the terror you are feeling and no one helps you? What if this nightmare becomes a reality for you? What if you are "locked in"?

This hypothetical example sets the stage for the listeners to begin imagining how horrific this situation would be. It draws them into your speech. Using statistics, testimony, and examples helps bring your presentation to life and engage your listeners.

Citing Sources

Whenever you use material that is not your own original knowledge, or is not common, public knowledge, you must cite your source. This means that you tell you audience the source of your information. The best method is to state the source before you state the material. This shows the credibility of the upcoming quotation or example or statistic before you state that information.

Here are some examples of citing sources:

- According to the National Parks Conservation Association, the world's first national park, Yellowstone, was created by an act of Congress in 1872 as a "way to protect for all time this outstanding natural area."

- According to the *Moon Guidebook* by Don Pitcher,[2] "Yellowstone and Grand Tetons are famous not just for their geologic features, but also as places to view wildlife in their natural habitat."

- According to an article from *Science and Technology News* by Everett Worthington, Jr., "Twenty years ago, the major killers in the U.S. were diseases. Today, almost all the major killers are the lifestyle-related problems exacerbated by modern lifestyles."

- As stated in the book *Word Power*, children age 10 learn new words at the rate of many hundreds a year from the age of 4, while adults who are no longer in school learn only 25–50 words each year.

- Stephen Covey, author of the book *The Seven Habits of Highly Effective People*,[3] compares the making and breaking of habits to the launching of the spacecraft. As he said, "To get to the moon, the astronauts literally had to break out of the tremendous gravity pull of the earth."

In your works cited page at the end of your outline, you would then give the full citation of each source that you used in your speech. Your instructor will specify whether to use APA, MLA, or another style on your works cited page.

PUTTING IT TOGETHER

Once you have your topic, general purpose, specific purpose, central idea, main points, pattern of organization, and supporting material, you are ready to write your speech in outline form. You may already have your main points in outline form, and now the time has come to fill in the subpoints, supporting points, and transitions. Once you have your basic outline, begin practicing your speech out loud, making necessary adjustments as you go. Stand up to practice because you will be standing when you actually deliver your speech. Standing will also help you breathe from your diaphragm, which will help support your voice. Use a stopwatch or timer on your phone so that you can time your speech. You may have to edit your speech, cutting out some material to fit into the time limits you've been given. If your speech is too short, you will need to add some material. As you practice, be aware of your volume, rate, articulation, and pronunciation. Also, listen to the language of your speech. Do your ideas flow? Do certain words need to be changed to be clearer? Can you cut out jargon or unnecessary technical terms? Practicing your speech is a step that you don't want to skip. If you are using visual aids in your speech, practice with them as well.

BUSINESS PRESENTATIONS

The words *speech* and *presentation* are often used to refer to the same thing. Some people will argue that a speech is more formal than a presentation. Most people argue that they are the same thing. Whichever term you use, know that both a speech and a presentation require excellent organization, credible support, clear transitions, dynamic delivery, and visual aids that aid in the clarification and retention of your material. Remember that even if you are delivering a technical briefing, a proposal, a sales pitch, or a report, they are each organized with an introduction, a body, and a conclusion. Your outline should include main points, supporting points, sources, and transitions. Just because it's called a presentation and is done in the business world, you still want to follow the rules of presentation development found in this chapter.

Don't make the mistake of thinking that a business presentation means that you go overboard on PowerPoint. You should still use PowerPoint slides—or any visual aids—to supplement your material, not to replace it.

With a business presentation—as with any presentation—be culturally prepared. Know who is in your audience, so that you communicate clearly to all, rather than offending someone from another culture with your material. Failing to recognize and adapt to these differences can mean the difference between a done deal and a faceless failure.[4] Review Chapter 2 on intercultural communication for a reminder about the importance of adapting your presentation to diverse audiences.

Be sure your visual aids are a supplement to your material, not a replacement.

© Peter Bernick/Shutterstock.com

CONCLUSION

Will Thomas and Matt Davis were each faced with a challenge at the beginning of this chapter. They had been asked to write and deliver a presentation to different groups. Will and Matt understood that excellent public speaking was necessary for their success, but they did not possess the knowledge they needed to be successful speakers.

Will knew that he was in over his head, so he called an instructor at the university who teaches public speaking and asked if they could meet so that he could ask questions about his upcoming presentation. The instructor gave Will enough information and guidance so that he could do the presentation, and then Will registered for a public speaking class the next semester so that he could learn and practice even more. Matt also recognized that he was in over his head. He decided that the only way he could make the presentation was to sit down with the leader of their group and explain his predicament. He thought that the group leader would want to replace him once he learned of Matt's inexperience. Instead, the group leader told Matt that they could work on the presentation together and suggested that Matt take a class in public speaking so that he could get that much-needed experience and knowledge.

How about you? Do you now feel that you have the knowledge you need to develop a speech or presentation? After reading this chapter, you should understand the importance of choosing a topic and having a clear general purpose, specific purpose, and central idea. You should also understand how to organize your speech into a clear introduction, body, and conclusion, and know what to include in each part of your speech. You should understand the various patterns of organization used in informative and persuasive speaking, and you should be familiar with how to outline your speeches. Finally, keep in mind the importance of using connectives, main points, supporting material, and citing sources.

ACTIVITIES

1. Start brainstorming for topic ideas. Take a blank sheet of paper and divide it into columns. Label each column. Hobbies, travel, work, major, career, television, movies, and books are examples of column heading ideas. Read each heading and write down anything that comes to mind. Do this for each column. When you are done, you should have lists of words under each heading. Read through these and see if they spark your memory or your interest. They might make you think of a topic that becomes a great speech.

2. Practice writing specific purpose statements for informative and persuasive speeches. Read the following topics and write a specific purpose that could be used for an informative speech and a specific purpose that could be used for a persuasive speech.

> **Topic:** Improving workplace communication
> **Specific purpose** (informative):
>
>
>
>
> **Specific purpose** (persuasive):
>
>
>
>
> **Topic:** Effective use of technology in the workplace
> **Specific purpose** (informative):
>
>
>
>
> **Specific purpose** (persuasive):

Topic: Use of social media in networking
Specific purpose (informative):

Specific purpose (persuasive):

3. Listed here are central idea statements that could be used for informative or persuasive speeches. Read each one and decide which pattern of organization it sets up.

    a. There are three types of affordable digital cameras on the market.

    b. Excessive salt consumption leads to a variety of health problems.

    c. There are four beaches in the United States that have surfing, smooth sand, and an active nightlife.

    d. Four cities in the Unites States have family-friendly vacation activities: San Antonio, Gatlinburg, Baltimore, and New York.

    e. Identity theft is on the rise; therefore, you must take steps to reduce your potential as a victim.

    f. There are three major stages in making bread at home.

4. Please identify the following as:
A. Attention getting statement; **B.** Reveal the topic statement; **C.** Credibility statement; **D.** Goodwill statement; or **E.** Preview statement.

    _____ 1. My family has owned a small newspaper for over 20 years, and I have worked in various departments there for the past two summers.

    _____ 2. In this speech, we'll look at three methods for lowering your utility bill each month.

    _____ 3. Please think about this statement: "The Book of Lists ranks public speaking as the number one fear, above the fear of dying!"

_____ 4. You, too, can start getting a better night's sleep after listening to the suggestions I have to share.

_____ 5. Vocal variety can make or break a speech. We use our voices every day, but did you ever stop and think, "Is my voice pleasing? Can people hear me? Is my articulation clear? Is my rate too fast or too slow? Is my voice expressive enough?"

5. Think of three possible business-related speech topics. You might already have several in mind for your next speech assignment in class. Think of an effective attention-getting statement for each of those topics. Next, think of a way that you could establish your credibility with each topic and a way to show goodwill to your audience.

6. Take one of the topics you used in the previous activity. Using what you already have (attention getter, credibility, and goodwill), complete your introduction in outline form. Then, practice it out loud. Do the components flow together? Does the language sound powerful? Do you make the listener want to hear more?

REFERENCES

[1] Hopkins, P. D. (2007). *A guide to effective public speaking*. Dubuque, IA: Kendall Hunt.

[2] Pitcher, D. (2006). *Yellowstone and Grand Tetons* (3rd ed.). Emeryville, CA: Avalon Travel Publishing.

[3] Covey, S. (2004). *The seven habits of highly effective people*. New York: Free Press.

[4] Lee, H. (2005, October). Communicating across cultures. *Toastmaster*, p. 21.

chapter
thirteen

Visual Aids and Electronic-Enhanced Presentations

After reading this chapter you will be able to:

- Understand the role of visuals in public presentations
- Select the most appropriate visual aid for your presentation
- Understand the parts to creating the most effective visuals
- Types of visual aids

CHAPTER OUTLINE

key words

Bar chart
Line graph
Pictogram
Flip chart
Transparency

Contrast
Repetition
Alignment
Proximity

INTRODUCTION

The necessity, preparation, and vitality of visuals in speech delivery can be both demanding and rewarding. In the summer of 2010, master speech deliverer, Steve Jobs, then CEO of Apple, found out how much preparation is needed when it comes to visuals while attempting to demonstrate the iPhone 4's Wi-Fi capabilities in front of the world. Needless to say, when Jobs was unable to connect the new iPhone 4 to the building's Wi-Fi, Apple's credibility was at stake with the new, hot, and highly anticipated product. Jobs recovered from the blunder by saying that it must have been the building's Wi-Fi being overloaded and not the product being faulty. When it comes to preparing for your own presentations, preparation is key. After reading this chapter, you'll come to understand the role of visuals in public presentations, how to select the most appropriate visual aid for your presentation, the parts to creating the most effective visuals, and the types of visual aids.

VISUAL AIDS AND VISUAL PRESENTATIONS

As society has become more technologically driven, presentations are more dominated by images. However, competent business communicators understand the importance of the *message* and carefully craft visual support in a way that enhances the spoken word. In other words, effective presenters do not allow PowerPoint to become the presentation; they simply use it to strengthen their ideas.

The best speakers know that they need just a few visuals to assist them in their presentations. For example, Louis Gerstner, who was the chairman of the board and chief executive officer of IBM from 1993 until

2002 when he retired, is known for his speaking ability. During his time with IBM, Gerstner would regularly speak to investors and shareholders without a single visual aid. It is just Gerstner onstage, sitting on a stool, with a glass of water beside him. As one analyst commented, "It's a performance worth seeing," especially in the age of the dominant visual and for a company that furthers the use of the visual in everyday life.

It is important to note that visuals can and do assist a presentation, but they shouldn't be the focus of the presentation: You as the speaker should be. Developing visual aids is an integral part of your preparation for your speech, as many studies show that an audience can remember more of a presentation when they both hear and see the information, as opposed to something that they only hear. Because of this, it is vital to the success of your presentation that you do several things in preparation for your speech and for your visual aids:

1. Examine your audience's visual aid needs.
2. Evaluate the speaking setting and how your visuals will work within that setting.
3. Determine what is the best visual for your presentation.
4. Determine how the visuals will fit into your delivery.

Visuals can assist a presentation, but the speaker is always the focus.

© racom/Shutterstock.com

Examine Your Audience's Visual Aid Needs

The first step is to ask yourself what your audience needs to learn from your presentation, or what you want them to take away from your presentation. More than likely, this is information you have collected and considered through the audience analysis stage of your speech presentation. Readdressing the information that you know about your audience when preparing your visual aids will help you ensure that your audience leaves with the details from your speech that you want them to. You can begin this process by asking the following questions:

- Would my audience learn better by using a visual aid?
- Would an object or a video be more effective as a visual aid for this audience than a graph?
- How could using a visual aid hinder my presentation?
- Why do I need a visual aid for this presentation?

It is important to remember that a visual aid should be used only when you can make the point better with a visual than you can without it. Remember that the visual aid is not a crutch and will not make up for a poorly constructed speech. You are the speaker—not your visual.

The visual aid is used in the formation of the presentation to support the arguments and claims formed within the speech. If you don't want to be remembered by the audience, turn on the projector, turn your back to the audience, and read the slides to them. The audience is sure to tune out. To make an impact and have the audience remember your presentation, use as few visuals as possible. In this case, less really is more.

Evaluate the Speaking Setting and How Your Visuals Will Work Within That Setting

The second step in preparing for your visual aids is to analyze your speaking setting. Chances are you have seen a presentation where the speaker says something to the effect of "I know you can't see this in the back, but. . . ." Knowing the size of the room, the number of people attending, and the equipment available is the key to putting together a good visual aid. Asking yourself the following questions will assist you in choosing the correct visual:

- How large or small is the room in which I will be speaking?
- How many people will be attending my presentation?
- If there is no electronic equipment available, how can I ensure that my audience can see my visual aid?
- How can I use any electronic equipment to fit the speaking setting?

© Matej Kastelic/Shutterstock.com

Properly analyzing the speaking setting is vital to preparing your visual aids.

To be sure, you will be upset if you spend most of your speech preparation time creating PowerPoint slides, only to find out when you get to the place where you are supposed to deliver your speech that there is no media projector. Because of very likely situations such as this, you always need a backup plan, whether that be transparencies of your PowerPoint slides available so that you can speak from an overhead or even just being prepared to speak without any visuals if the equipment just isn't there or isn't working. This can be very frustrating, but don't let the speaking environment dictate the success or failure of your speech. Stay calm, and know that you are prepared to speak.

Determine What Is the Best Visual for Your Presentation

There are many types of visual aids for you to pick from when preparing your presentation. It is important that you recognize what visual would work best for your specific presentation. Select the visual aid that will enhance your presentation and not distract your audience.

Keep in mind that a visual aid functions to:

1. **Show what things look like.** A photograph or a model of a building's renovation can help the audience feel more connected to a space and therefore help them visualize that space.

2. **Explain how things function.** A diagram can help show the audience how to do a simple task such as putting together your new desk.
3. **Demonstrate how things are structured.** A flowchart can show the audience the steps to complete a task or the hierarchical structure of your organization.
4. **Emphasize key points.** Sometimes a chart can more easily show the audience complicated material or data that involves a good deal of numbers.

Types of visual aids for you to pick from include objects and models, photographs or videos, pie charts, diagrams, pictograms, or bar and line graphs. The most commonly used visual in the age of PowerPoint is bullet points.

OBJECTS/MODELS. Sometimes simply showing the audience the thing that you are discussing can help them to grasp the concept more easily. Be sure that the object is big enough so that the audience can easily see it, but it is generally a bad idea to pass anything around for the audience to view. Passing things around means that the audience is focused on the object being given to them and not on your presentation.

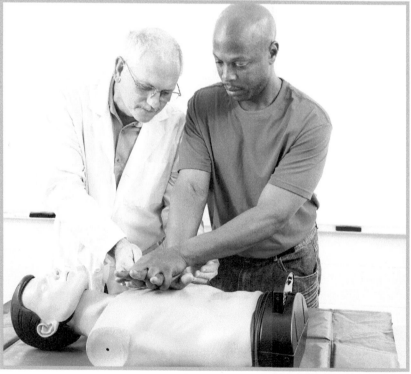

If you are speaking about how to do CPR, you will want to be able to demonstrate it to the audience.

© Lisa F. Young/Shutterstock.com

A good example of when to use an object would be for a demonstration speech when you are unable to physically do the act you wish to demonstrate. For instance, if you wanted to show the audience how to change the oil in a car it would be very difficult to show the audience, in most speaking situations, how to do this on an actual car. An alternative would be to show the parts involved on a model or toy car and this would still allow the audience to visualize what you are discussing.

Another reason that models work well is that sometimes it is difficult for people to conceptualize things that are three-dimensional. This is the reason architects spend so much time learning how to build models in addition to drawing blueprints of their designs. For most people, it is difficult to look at a blueprint and see a building, but a model of the building gives people a sense of space that they can't get from a flat drawing.

PHOTOGRAPHS/VIDEOS. A great way to show the emotive quality in anything is through a photograph. The realism of a photograph grounds the audience into the emotion of the image and, hence, the topic. A video can do the same thing, but one should remember that a video should not be your entire presentation. For even a 10-minute speech, a video should only take about 30 seconds of your allotted time.

One way to use a video within a speech would be to show short clips as examples. For example, in a speech about the innovative bass techniques of Victor Wooten showing video clips of each technique would connect the audience with the material. Just using words to describe the techniques would be too vague and not show the dynamic sounds of Wooten, but showing the audience the technique as well as describing it makes it much easier for the audience to grasp.

Another consideration is that you should not use a photograph just for the sake of using a photograph. Yes, it brings emotion with it, but at the same time it can be very distracting for the audience. This is why you can most likely identify "stock photography" or photos simply used for their ability to fill space. They appear posed and irrelevant. Consider this when selecting an image to further your presentation.

BAR/LINE GRAPHS. **Bar charts** and **line graphs** not only show the delineation of time, but also compare multiple items over that segment of time. There are a variety of these types of graphs that can show a wide range of information, but it is just as important to select one that best visually fits your presentation and conveys the information in the simplest and most easy-to-understand manner.

Bar chart: A chart consisting of horizontal or vertical bars that depict the values of several items in comparative terms.

Line graph: A visual display that shows the correlation between two quantities.

PIE CHARTS. Pie charts function to show parts to a whole. If you were explaining the annual budget of an organization, a pie chart is an easy visual to show the audience how much money is going to each part of the company. It is important to label a pie chart clearly with the percentage as well as the name of the part. It is also important to make sure that you select the right type of graph for the information you wish to show. Remember that you cannot show the delineation of time within a pie chart, so if you want to show the change in the number of employees over a set number of years within that same organization, a bar or line graph must be used. A pie chart cannot show that type of information.

Pictogram: A visual support that uses an artistic or pictorial variation of a bar, column, or pie chart.

Bar charts, line graphs, and pie charts can be useful for giving the audience information in an easy to understand way.

DIAGRAMS. A map or a drawing can show the audience the size, space, or shape of something. An architect's blueprint shows the layout and space of a building, so if you were trying to depict the type of office furniture to fill that space, an understanding of the space via a blueprint would assist your presentation.

PICTOGRAMS. **Pictograms** are more artistic versions of a bar or line graph. Common versions include the star rating given to movies where more stars equate to a better rating for the movie. If you were to show employee

© Andresr/Shutterstock.com

growth within an organization, this could be done via a pictogram where a drawing of a person could represent 100 people. More of the same drawing equals more employees in the organization.

BULLET POINTS. These are the easiest to create and most common visual aid, but there are rules you should follow when using them in a presentation. First, keep the points short, containing between five and eight words, making each line easy to read quickly. Along those lines, each slide should be limited to five lines total; otherwise, it can overwhelm the viewer. Using repetition or parallel structure in the wording also helps to keep the bullet point clear, concise, and easy for the audience to follow.

Determine How the Visuals Will Fit into the Delivery of Your Presentation

It is vital to the success of your presentation to not only select the proper visual aid, but also to make sure that you are able to display it to the audience in the most effective manner.

FLIP CHARTS AND POSTERS. Getting rid of the need for electronic means of display, **flip charts** and posters are easy to incorporate into your presentation. We must remember that each visual projector, sound system, and computer setup may be different, and sometimes the best solution is a low-tech one.

When using this type of visual delivery system, you must ensure that the audience will be able to see and to read the information presented. Flip charts and posters can be large and clumsy to use and can be damaged easily, but the largest drawback is the difficulty in making them appear professional. It is much easier to distract the audience with a bad poster than to engage them with a good one. You may deliver the best speech anyone has ever heard, but if your poster looks like you put it together at the last minute, then the audience will think that your speech is also last minute. Later in this chapter, techniques for designing quality looking visuals will be discussed.

Flip chart: A large pad of paper attached to an easel that is used to create and/or display visuals.

TRANSPARENCIES. **Transparencies** are probably the easiest means of producing a professional-looking visual aid all the while relying on much simpler technology than a computer. An overhead projector takes what is on the transparency and enlarges it for a group of people to see. Either purchasing transparency film that can be printed on through an ink jet printer or using a photocopy machine to transfer a printed image from

Transparency: A clear sheet used with an overhead projector to cast an image on a screen.

ordinary copy paper onto the transparency film easily produces these visuals. It is important to ensure that the audience will be able to read the information on the transparency by using no smaller than a 20-point font. Also, check the color quality of transparencies, as some overhead projectors dilute color. It is wise to use deep, saturated colors to ensure that they display properly on the overhead machine.

PRESENTATION SOFTWARE. The advent of the personal computer has brought the ability and potential for anyone to create professional-looking visual aids. Previously, businesspersons had to either craft them by hand or pay hefty fees to a professional designer. Now that nearly every business has access to a type of presentation software, it is easy and inexpensive to create a visually stunning presentation.

With any presentation at any time, you can create a visual that directly applies to your presentation for that day. Transitions between visuals become much easier, as you can incorporate video, pictures, and type into a set of slides. This eliminates the problem of having to switch back and forth between software programs during your speech. You can create graphs, tables, and charts easily and also prepare handouts of the visuals quickly.

With today's technology, it's much easier to create a professional-looking visual aid presentation.

Microsoft® PowerPoint is by far the leading software program in this genre. Being cross-platform compatible, PowerPoint is the choice for business presenters who have to use unknown equipment for presentations.

Prezi is fast becoming an alternative presentation tool. The platform has an optional cloud-based feature for retrieving the information and presentations. It also allows a traditional download feature with installation on Windows and Mac operating systems. When using the cloud-based function, users must have Internet access for the presentation. Therefore it is wise to consider a license and have a copy of the program on a USB drive in case Internet access is unavailable. There are also mobile options for the software.

When creating a Prezi, one should first think about the points that the audience needs to walk away with. Then a structure should be created to walk the audience to each and through each of those points. A great aspect of Prezi is that it allows the designer to help the audience see the overall focus of the presentation and main points at the beginning, or throughout the presentation. This is why the software is often referred to as storytelling software rather than a presentational aid. For shorter presentations, think about your presentation as a series of transitions (much like you would think of them as slides in PowerPoint). Consider making each step visible as one frame, and then zooming in and out of the main points of each frame. Simply keep your zooming to a minimum; remember it is a presentational aid, and the information within the Prezi should supplement, not distract from, your presentation. However, if you want to be more flexible with your presentation, consider also using a Prezi transition to supplement your verbal transition between points. Thus when you move from one point to another, have a frame that indicates what you just talked about and transition to a frame previewing your next point. Be cautious as this can take considerable amount of time away from the presentation. Again, it's also important not to overuse movement or zooming. Prezi provides more transitions than are possible in PowerPoint; however, more is not always better. If a transition itself becomes the attention the content of the presentation, your point can become lost. Just because you have the option to flip an image or zoom in, does not mean it needs to be used or enhances the presentation. Stated differently, avoid spinning and zooming too much.

It is important to not overuse any presentation software. There are templates and clip art files to select from, but keep in mind that everyone has access to these, uses them, and has seen them. How does a template set you apart from the competition? The old adage, "Keep it simple, stupid" applies here. Sometimes less is more. It takes an audience member time to process a complicated visual such as a graph in an orally delivered speech, but remember that you are also asking them listen to you at the same time. The simpler the visual, the more it will allow your audience to listen to your words, while at the same time being assisted through the presentation by the visual.

Because of the ease of use of presentational software programs, it is easy to become engrossed in the creation of your visuals. It is vital to your success as a business speaker that you devote the majority of your time to your speech itself and then allow the visual to support your speaking. Organization is key. No matter how sophisticated and flashy your visuals, if you don't have a strong organizational structure, your audience will not be able to follow the progression of your speech. It is a bad idea to construct your visuals prior to constructing your speech. The visual is there to assist you, not speak for you.

Strongly consider whether or not you absolutely need a visual for your particular presentation. Flash will not overcome lack of content. In speechwriting, function should come before form. Visual communication guru Edward Tufte has strong ideas about how visuals can help and hurt a presentation:

> If your numbers are boring then you've got the wrong numbers. If your words or images are not on point, making them dance in color won't make them relevant. Audience boredom is usually a content failure, not a decoration failure.[1]

DESIGN PRINCIPLES: SEEING WHAT HAS ALWAYS BEEN THERE

The four principles related to a visual's design are *contrast, repetition, alignment, and proximity.*

Contrast is about avoiding the similar. When two things contrast, they are different in some way. That old cliché of opposites attracting works here. If two things on your visual aid are too similar, then you need to make them appear to be *different* because when two things are too similar, they conflict visually on a page or screen to the viewer or audience. Often the most important visual attraction on a page is the one that is most contrasted. For example, when you think about the front page of a newspaper, how do you know what story is the most important story on the page? It is probably the one with the largest headline or the largest

Contrast: This is about avoiding the similar.

picture, right? You know this because of the contrast that was added to that headline or photo. You can create contrast in your visual aids by placing large type with small type; using a flowing, **oldstyle font** with a bold **san serif font**; placing a thin line next to a thick line; using a cool color with a warm color (this is why school colors are usually contrasting colors because they seem like they are "fighting" visually); and using a strong horizontal element with a strong vertical element. A widely spaced line contrasts with a closely packed line.

The design principle of contrast has two main purposes: to unify and to organize information. The following examples demonstrate the principles of contrast.

Contrast 1

Lisa Maxwell
123 Oak Lane
Santa Rosa, California 95405
707-555-1234

Related Skills
Excellent working knowledge of laboratory tests and their significance in oncology care through working in a clinical laboratory, reinforced while providing patient care. Assisted with bone marrow biopsy and aspiration, lumbar puncture paracentesis, thoracentesis, and intrathecal chemotherapy administration. Promoted self-care skills and adaptation of the client to their disease and particular treatment program.

Extensive experience with at-home care of AIDS and cancer patients, including IV line maintenance, pain management; understanding of medicare reimbursement and social service referrals.

Education
1990   Associate in Science Nursing, Los Angeles Junior College, Los Angeles, California.

Experience
1992–present   Registered Nurse for Los Angeles Hospital Oncology Unit, Los Angeles, California.

1985–1986   Nurse's Aide for Long Beach District Hospital, Long Beach, California.

1985–1986   Lab Assistant for Long Beach District Hospital, Long Beach, California.

Problems: Two alignments. Space between segments too similar.

Contrast 2

Lisa Maxwell
123 Oak Lane
Santa Rosa, California 95405
707-555-1234

Related Skills
- Excellent working knowledge of laboratory tests and their significance in oncology care through working in a clinical laboratory, reinforced while providing patient care.
- Assisted with bone marrow biopsy and aspiration, lumbar puncture, paracentesis, thoracentesis, and intrathecal chemotherapy administration.
- Promoted self-care skills and adaptation of the client to their disease and particular treatment program.
- Extensive experience with at-home care of AIDS and cancer patients, including IV line maintenance, pain management; understanding of Medicare reimbursement and social service referrals.

Education
1990   **Associate in Science Nursing,** Los Angeles Junior College, Los Angeles, California.

Experience
1992–present   **Registered Nurse** for Los Angeles Hospital Oncology Unit, Los Angeles, California.
1985–1986   **Nurse's Aide** for Long Beach District Hospital, Long Beach, California.
1985–1986   **Lab Assistant** for Long Beach District Hospital, Long Beach, California.

Solutions: strong alignments resulting in repetition, strong heads, and good separation.

Contrast 3

The Rules of Life
Your attitude is your life.
Maximize your options.
Never take anything too seriously.
Don't let the seeds stop you from enjoyin' the watermelon.
Be nice.

Contrast between rules (lines) is too similar.

The Rules of Life
Your attitude is your life.
Maximize your options.
Never take anything too seriously.
Don't let the seeds stop you from enjoyin' the watermelon.
Be nice.

Stronger contrast clearly shows the beginning and the end of the table.

Contrast 4

What is the focus? Eliminate all caps. Arrange similar information in close proximity. Center alignment is difficult to read. The border distracts from the message.

Contrast 5

Strong contrast in type, strong alignment, clean professional appearance, and information grouped.

Repetition: Repeating elements such as line, shape, color, or texture throughout a page in your presentation or throughout your entire presentation helps to keep the audience engaged.

Repetition is the next design principle. Just as it works in speech writing, repetition in visuals works to help make the audience remember things that you have deemed important. Repeating elements such as line, shape, color, or texture throughout a page in your presentation or throughout your entire presentation helps to keep the audience engaged. Repetition can be easily done by repeating bold fonts, rules or lines, a particular bullet type, colors, shapes, formats, or even spatial relationships such as your use of white space.

Repetition as a design principle has two major purposes: to unify a piece (useful in one page documents, critical in multipage documents) and to organize your information.

Repetition 1

The Three Bears

There were once three bears, who lived in the woods. Their porridge was thick, and their chairs and beds good. The biggest bear, Bruin, was surly and rough; His wife, Mrs. Bruin, was called Mammy Muff. Their son, Tiny-cub, was like Dame Goose's lad; He was not very good, nor yet very bad.

Now Bruin, the biggest—the surly old bear—Had a great granite bowl, and a cast-iron chair. Mammy Muff's bowl and chair you would no doubt prefer—They were both made of brick-bats, but both suited her. Young Tiny-cub's bowl, chair, and bed were the best,—This, big bears and baby bears freely confessed. Mr. B——, with his wife and his son, went one day

The stroll

To take a short stroll, and a visit to pay. He left the door open, "For," said he, "no doubt, if our friend should call in, he will find us all out." It was only two miles from dark Hazel-nut Wood, In which the great house of the three Bruins stood, That there lived a young miss, daring, funny, and fair, And from having bright curls.

▶ *She was called Goldenhair*

She had roamed through the wood to see what she could see, And she saw going walking the Bruins all three. Said she to herself, "To rob bears is no sin; The three bears have gone out, so I think I'll go in." She entered their parlor, and she saw a great bowl, And in it a spoon like a hair-cutter's pole.

The porridge

"That porridge," said she "may stay long enough there, It tastes like the food of the surly old bear," She tried Mammy Muff's, and she said, "Mrs. B——, I think your taste and my taste will never agree." Then she tried Tiny-Cub's bowl, and said, "This is nice; I will put in some salt, and of bread a thick slice."

Repetition 2

The Story of the Three Bears and Goldenhair

There were once three bears, who lived in a wood, their porridge was thick, and their chairs and beds good. The biggest bear, Bruin, was surly and rough; his wife, Mrs. Bruin, was called Mammy Muff. Their son, Tiny-cub, was like Dame Goose's lad; he was not very good, nor yet very bad.

Now Bruin, the biggest—the surly old bear—had a great granite bowl, and a cast-iron chair. Mammy Muff's bowl and chair you would no doubt prefer—they were both made of brick-bats, but both suited her.

The stroll

To take a short stroll, and a visit to pay. He left the door open, For," said he, "no doubt If our friend should call in, he will find us all out." It was only two miles from dark Hazel-nut Wood, In which the great house of the three Bruins stood, That there lived a young miss, daring, funny, and fair, And from having bright curls, she was called Goldenhair.

She had roamed through the wood to see what she could see, And she saw going walking the Bruins all three. Said she to herself, "To rob bears is no sin;

The three bears have gone out, so I think I'll go in." She entered their parlor, and she saw a great bowl, And in it a spoon like a hair-cutter's pole.

Goldenhair's choices

▶ the great granite bowl
▶ Mammy Muff's bowl and chair
▶ Tiny-cubs porridge bowl
▶ All the bears' chairs

All gone

She tried Mammy Muff's, and she said, "Mrs. B——, I think your taste and my taste will never agree."

Consistent: rules across top and bottom of page, typeface in headlines and subheads, spacing, page number and placing, bulleted points.

Repetition 3

Dots on page and in teapots and cups.

The third design principle is **alignment**. Alignment is more than just the four buttons at the top of the screen of Microsoft® Word. It is important to know that in your visual all elements should have a visual connection with the other elements on the visual. There should be a purpose for each of the places you put something on your visual. Place with care, as your audience will assume that you did.

There are two purposes associated with alignment as a design principle: to unify and to organize information.

Alignment: All elements should have a visual connection with the other elements on the visual.

Alignment 1

Ronald Birch
*Poems in Scots
and English*

The most
complete edition
available of
Scotland's greatest
lyric poet.

Mixed alignment: left and centered.

Ronald Birch
*Poems in Scots
and English*

The most
complete edition
available of
Scotland's greatest
lyric poet.

Still two alignments, left and right, but right aligns with H in Birch.

Alignment 2

*You are warmly
invited to attend!*

*You
are
warmly
invited
to
attend!*

If center aligning, be bold!

*You
are
warmly
invited
to
attend!*

**You
are
warmly
invited
to
attend!**

Alignment 3

Story of the Three Bears

The story of the three bears and Goldenhair.   by Anonymous

Describe the ten alignment errors as noted.

There were once three bears who lived in a wood. Their porridge was thick and their chairs and beds good. The biggest bear, Bruin, was surly and rough; his wife, Mrs. Bruin, was called Mammy Muff. Their son, Tiny-cub, was like Dame Goose's lad; he was not very good, nor yet very bad.

Now Bruin, the biggest—the surly old bear—had a great granite bowl, and a cast-iron chair. Mammy Muff's bowl and chair you would no doubt prefer. They were both made of brick-bats, but both suited her. Young Tiny-cub's bowl, chair, and bed were the best. This, big bear and baby bear freely confessed.

Mr. B——, with his wife and his son, went one day to take a short stroll and a visit to pay. He left the door open, "For," said he, "no doubt. If our friend should call in, he will find us all out."

It was only two miles from dark Hazel-nut Wood, in which the great house of the three Bruins stood, that there lived a young miss, daring, funny, and fair, and from having bright curls, she was called Goldenhair. She had roamed through the wood to see what she could see, and she saw going walking the Bruins all three.

Said she to herself, "To rob bears is no sin; the three bears have gone out, so I think I'll go in." She entered their parlor and she saw a great bowl, and in it a spoon like a hair-cutter's pole. "That porridge," said she "may stay long enough there. It tastes like the food of the surly old bear." She tried Mammy Muff's, and she said, "Mrs. B——, I think your taste and my taste will never agree." Then she tried Tiny-Cub's bowl, and said, "This is nice. I will put in some salt and of bread a thick slice." The porridge she eat soon made her so great, the chair that she sat on broke down with her weight. The bottom fell out and she cried in dismay, "This is Tiny-cub's chair, and oh, what will he say? His papa is, I know, the most savage of bears. His mamma is

a fury; but for her who cares? I'm sure I do not. As for her son, that young bear, Tiny-cub—from him shall I run? No, not I, indeed, but I will not sit here. I shall next break the floor through—that's what I most fear."

So up-stairs she ran, and there three beds she found. She looked under each one and she looked all around, but no one she saw, so she got into bed. It was surly old Bruin's and well stuffed with lead. Mammy Muff's next she tried; it was stuffed with round stones. So she got into Tiny-cub's and rested her bones.

Goldenhair was asleep when the three bears came in. Said Big Bruin, "I'm hungry—to eat, let's begin—"WHO HAS BEEN TO MY PORRIDGE?" he roared with such might. His voice was like wind down the chimney at night. "WHO HAS BEEN TO MY PORRIDGE?" growled out Mrs. B——. Her voice was like cats fighting up in a tree. "WHO HAS BEEN TO MY PORRIDGE AND EATEN IT ALL?" young Tiny-cub said, in a voice very small.

"WHO HAS BEEN SITTING IN MY GREAT ARM CHAIR?" In voice like a thunder-storm, roared the big bear. "WHO HAS BEEN SITTING IN MY GOOD ARM CHAIR?" growled out Mammy Muff, like a sow in despair. "WHO HAS SAT IN MY NICE CHAIR, AND BROKEN IT DOWN?" young Tiny-cub said, and so fierce was his frown, that his mother with pride to his father said, "There! See our pet Tiny-cub can look just like a bear," So roaring, and growling, and frowning, the bears, one after the other, came running up-stairs.

–Anonymous
Project Gutenberg EBook

ural: The three bears take a short stroll and a visit to pay.

Proximity: This is the idea that related items should be grouped together.

Proximity is the last design principle. This is the idea that related items should be grouped together. If you don't want your audience to associate a picture with certain words, then don't place them too closely together. Make sure that you have enough space to display all your work easily and well. If you need to purchase another posterboard, then do so—placing too many things on one area not only makes it look sloppy, but it will confuse the audience because of the too-close proximity.

Proximity has two purposes as a design principle: to unify and to organize information.

Proximity 1

Randy Parker   (717) 555-1234

Toad Hill

123 Willow Road   Albuquerque, NM

Toad Hill
Randy Parker

123 Willow Road
Albuquerque, NM
(717) 555-1234

Group like things together.

Proximity 2

CD ROMs
CD ROMs
Children's CDs
Educational CDs
Entertainment CDs
Laser discs
Educational
Early learning
Language arts
Science
Math
Teacher Tools
Books
Teacher tools
Videos
Hardware & Accessories
Cables
Input devices
Mass storage
Memory
Modems
Printers & supplies
Video and sound

CD ROMs

CD ROMs
Children's CDs
Educational CDs
Entertainment CDs
Laser discs

Educational

Early learning
Language arts
Science
Math

Teacher Tools

Books
Teacher tools
Videos

Hardware & Accessories

Cables
Input devices
Mass storage
Memory
Modems
Printers & supplies
Video and sound

Use contrast, repetition, and alignment with proximity.

Proximity 3

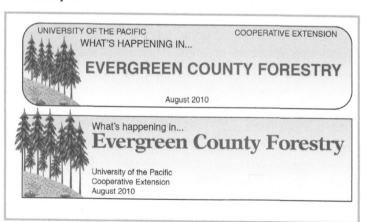

Group related items together. All caps are difficult to read. Squared lines relate to lines in trees.

Now you may have seen a theme here in the purposes of the design principles—yes, they are all about unification and organization of information. They work together to communicate to the audience what you want them to see. Be careful with what you present, and be intentional as well, as you don't want your audience to see something that you didn't intend. It is important to also avoid some fairly common design errors. Be careful not to put too many separate elements on a page. Avoid sticking elements in a corner or center of the page. Leave equal amounts of white space between elements. Be careful not to create a visual relationship between elements that don't belong together, and only use center alignment when a formal look is needed.

DESIGN EFFECTIVE VISUALS

As you design visual aids, make sure they enhance your presentation. The general rule for effective visuals is that they have the following characteristics:

1. **The information *must* be readable!** You don't want to find yourself saying in your speech, "I know you can't see this in the back, but . . ." A good rule of thumb for most slides, whether they are overhead transparencies or PowerPoint slides, is to test them in your speaking space first. A typical point size for fonts is somewhere between 16 and 24 points. Also, it is important to keep the typeface simple. Lots of scrolls and extras make the type hard to read, not interesting. Usually a sans serif such as Arial or a traditional serif such as Times works best.

2. ***You* are the most important visual**. Most novice speakers (and even some experienced ones) go overboard with PowerPoint. It is easy to become so caught up in the "gadgetry" of the software that you forget that you are the most important part of the presentation. You, your gestures, your eye contact, and body movements are much more interesting to the audience than the fact that you made the type fly in from the left side of the screen.

3. **You will not be able to cover up a lack of content with any visual aid—no matter the quantity of visuals.** Many top organizations are requiring their executives to "get back to the basics" and leave the PowerPoint at home. In fact shortly after 2001, former chairman of the Joint Chiefs of Staff, General Henry H. Shelton, had to remind his subordinates to stop using so many PowerPoint visuals

in their presentations. They were packing their presentations with so many pictures of rolling tanks and animated artillery pieces that they were forgetting to present the facts—something that should be the focus of any presentation.

PRESENTING WITH ANY TYPE OF VISUAL

It is very easy to start off your presentation with great energy and super eye contact, as you have practiced your introduction over and over, but many experienced speakers forget these basic speaking rules when they turn to their visuals. For some reason, their energy drains, and instead of looking outward at the audience, they turn their back to the audience and face their visual aid.

Three easy steps can be used when working with any visual aid. The following tips are described as if you are using an overhead transparency, as that is the most common type:

1. **Always stand next to the screen as you talk about the visual.** Make sure that you don't turn on the projector and speak from the projector, as this will give you a tendency to turn around to the screen while speaking. Also, standing next to the screen makes sure that you are not blocking the view of the screen for any of the audience, and by standing next to the screen the audience looks at you and the screen as one image. They will not have to look back and forth between you the speaker and the slide to which you are referring.

2. **Ensure that you introduce the visual aid.** Before diving into the details in the visual, give your audience an overview of the visual. As you would give them an introduction of your entire speech, give them an introduction of your entire visual. Presenting a visual as a complete entity without explanation will overwhelm your audience. Warm them up to your visuals with an introduction.

3. **Remember to talk *to* your audience and not to your visual itself.** Your visual is an inanimate object and won't react or learn from your speech. Look at the audience and teach them what the visual is about. It is appropriate to glance at the visual to make sure that the audience knows to what you are referring, but keep your focus on the audience. This is the hardest thing to deal with when speaking with visual aids, but having a conversation with your visual breaks the connection with the audience that you worked so hard to create in the introduction of your speech.

CONCLUSION

You have now learned that there are many different approaches to visuals when it comes to presentations and that there is no one way to present information visually. This chapter presented you with ideas on the role of visuals in public presentations, the best types of visuals for your own presentation, and the critical design elements of effective visuals. Above all, it is important to remember in today's technology-saturated world that your audience is very visually savvy. One minor slip up that you may not even be able to control will dramatically affect your credibility with your audience—just as Steve Jobs, former CEO of Apple, learned just by trying to connect to the Internet in front of the world.

ACTIVITIES

1. Select a visual based on each of the following speech claims. What visual(s) would make it easiest to present the following speech topics?

   a. Japan has the second-largest economy in the world.

   b. As the economy gets worse, enrollment at colleges rises.

   c. The population of California is decreasing.

   d. Small businesses are the key to finding the right job for you.

   e. The age of those getting married is increasing.

2. Recall the last presentation you attended on or off campus. What visual aids did the speaker use? Describe the effectiveness of the visuals. Did they follow appropriate design guidelines? Did they strengthen or detract from the speaker's message?

REFERENCE

[1] Tufte, E. R. (2003). *The cognitive style of PowerPoint*. Cheshire, CT: Graphics Press.

ADDITIONAL SOURCES

Azarmsa, R. (2004). *Powerful multimedia presentations*. Belmont, CA: Wadsworth.

Beardsley, M. (1982). *The aesthetic point of view*. Ithaca, NY: Cornell University Press.

Bernhardt, S. A. (1996). Visual rhetoric. In T. Enos (Ed.), *Encyclopedia of rhetoric and composition: Communication from ancient times to the information age* (pp. 746–748). New York: Garland.

Brown, J. C. (1983). Excellence and the problem of visual literacy. *Design for Art in Education, 85,* 11–13.

Fenner, D. E. W. (2003). Aesthetic experience and aesthetic analysis. *Journal of Aesthetic Education, 37,* 40–53.

Foss, S. R. (1994). A rhetorical schema for the evaluation of visual imagery. *Communication Studies, 45,* 213–224.

Fuller, P. (1984). Taste—You can't opt out. *Design, 423,* 38–43.

Ganzel, R. (2000, February). Destination: Presentation. *Presentations,* 48–66.

Ganzel, R. (2000, February). Power pointless. *Presentations,* 54–57.

Goggin, M. D. (2004). Visual rhetoric in pens of steel and inks of silk: Challenging the great visual/verbal debate. In C. A. Hill & M. Helmers (Eds.), *Defining visual rhetorics* (pp. 87–110). Mahwah, NJ: Erlbaum.

Hinkin, S. (1995, January). Not just another pretty face: 10 tips for the most effective use of type. *Presentations,* 34–36.

Jaffe, G. (2000, April 26). What's your point, Lieutenant? Just cut to the pie charts. *The Wall Street Journal,* A1.

Kosslyn, S. M., & Chabris, C. (1993, September/October). The mind is not a camera, the brain is not a VCR: Some psychological guidelines for designing charts and graphs. *Aldus Magazine,* 33–36.

Kostelnick, C., & Hassett, M. (2003). *Shaping information: The rhetoric of visual conventions,* Carbondale: Southern Illinois University Press.

Kress, G. (2000). Design and transformation: New theories of meaning. In B. Cope & M.

Kalantzis (Eds.), *Multiliteracies: Literacy learning and the design of social futures.* London: Routledge, 153–161.

Kress, G., & Van Leeuwen, T. (1996). *Reading images: The grammar of visual design.* New York: Routledge.

Lauer, D. A., & Pentak, Stephen. (2000). *Design Basics* (5th ed.). Fort Worth, TX: Harcourt Brace & Company.

Lawson, B. (1980). *How designers think.* Westfield, NJ: Eastview Editions.

Lucaiates, J. L., & Hariman, R. (2001). Visual rhetoric, photojournalism, and democratic public culture. *Rhetoric Review, 20,* 37–42.

Margolin, V. (Ed.). (1989). *Design discourse*. Chicago: University of Chicago Press.

Mayer, R. E. (2001). *Multimedia learning*. New York: Cambridge University Press.

Moore, P., & Fitz, C. (1993). Using gestalt theory to teach document design and graphics. *Technical Communication Quarterly*, *2.4*, 389–410.

Ogg, Erica. (2010, June 7). *Even Steve Jobs has demo hiccups*. Retrieved July 5, 2010 from: http://news.cnet.com/8301-31021_3-20007009-260.html

Parker, I. (2001, May 28). Absolute PowerPoint. *New Yorker*, 76–87.

Pearson, L. (1993, June). The medium speaks. *Presentation Products*, 55–56.

Simmons, T. (February 2000). MultiMedia or bust? *Presentation*, 40–50.

Simmons, T. (March 2004). Does PowerPoint make you stupid? *Presentations*, 25–31.

Scott, L. (1994). Images in advertising: The need for a theory of visual rhetoric. *Journal of Consumer Research*, *21*, 252–273.

Spagenberg, C. (1977, Summer). Basic values and the techniques of persuasion. *Litigation*, 64.

Stolnitz, J. (1960). *Aesthetics and philosophy of art criticism*. Boston: Houghton Mifflin.

Terberg, J. (2005, April). Font choices play a crucial role in presentation design. *Presentations*, 16–17.

Tuck, L. (1994, April). Using type intelligently. *Presentations*, 30–32.

Tuck, L. (1994, January). Improving your image with LCD panels. *Presentations*, 32.

Vesper, J., & Ruggiero, V. (1993). *Contemporary business communication: From thought to expression*. New York: Harper-Collins.

Vogel, D. R., Dickson, G. W., & Lehman, H. A. (1986, August). Driving the audience action response. *Computer Graphics World*, *5*, 25–28.

Vogel, D. R., Dickson, G. W., & Lehman, H. A. (1986). *Persuasion and the role of visual presentation support: The UM/3M study*. Austin, TX: 3M Corporation.

Zelazny, G. (2004). *Say it with charts: The executive's guide to visual communication*. New York: McGraw-Hill.

Zelanski, P., & Fisher, M. P. (1987). *Shaping space*. New York: Holt, Rinehart, and Winston.

Zelanski, P., & Fisher, M. P. (1990). *Color*. Englewood Cliffs, NJ: Prentice Hall.

Zelanski, P., & Fisher, M. P. (1996). *Design principles and problems*. New York: Harcourt Brace College Publishers.

Zielinski, D. (2001, July). The great web copyright crackdown. *Presentations*, 30–40.

section five

Presentation Competencies

chapter
fourteen

Informative and Special Occasion Business Presentations

After reading this chapter you will be able to:

- Form an organizational pattern for a business presentation
- Understand the difference in business speaking and public speaking
- Select a topic for your speech
- Understand the differences in types of informative speeches
- Understand the different types of special occasion speeches within the workplace
- Prepare and deliver multiple types of special occasion speeches based on various situational elements

CHAPTER OUTLINE

INTRODUCTION

Addison Garrett, a training coordinator for Syntec, an automotive supplier in Marysville, Ohio, has been working to coordinate a large-scale conference on lean manufacturing, a process for streamlining production and operations for maximum efficiency or "leanness." Participants from around the country will be in town for the conference. Some will be audience members, some will compete in quality circle competitions, and others will be there to network for potential business opportunities. From keynote speakers to informative conference presentations to awards ceremonies, Addison has multiple speakers to arrange. First, she'll need to set up several expert trainers to present on the basic and advanced elements of lean manufacturing. In addition to the main speakers, she plans to recruit some of her coworkers from Syntec to introduce speakers, present awards, and escort groups to dinner. She has also asked her boss to provide the opening welcome remarks. Although they have all agreed to participate, they bombard her with questions regarding the content and length of their presentations. Addison Garrett has much to consider given the number of speaking arrangements, and her team is looking to her to provide direction. To assist her group in preparing effective and smooth presentations, Addison plans to prepare a training workshop on developing and delivering **informative** and **special occasion presentations**.

INFORMATIVE PRESENTATIONS

The Goals and Strategies of Informative Presentations

The overarching goal of informative speaking is to build the audience's understanding and awareness by imparting knowledge to them on a particular subject. The speaker is attempting to provide listeners with new information on that subject.

A speaker must take a few steps to inform any audience effectively, whether in business or anywhere else. Developing an appropriate and effective presentation involves putting together the pieces laid out in previous chapters. First, the speaker must establish a mutual understanding and awareness with the audience. This means knowing who your audience is and what their needs are when it comes to the information you are presenting to them. Knowing your audience well will then allow you to take the other steps to preparing an effective informative presentation. Selecting an appropriate organizational pattern is key to presenting informative information clearly and directly to your audience. Providing effective preview statements and transitions will connect the subtopics within your speech together. Remember that we don't have visual cues

A skillful delivery combined with effective visual aids will create an engaging informative speech.

such as paragraph separations or bolding of important terms when delivering an oral presentation. Because of this, a preview statement, review statement, and connecting transitions allow the audience to follow the direction and organization of your speech more easily. Using language effectively for your specific audience is key to both engaging them in your topic as well as reaching the audience on their level. Be careful of jargon that may be specific to your area of business. Your audience may not know the meaning of those terms. This is why knowing your audience prior to constructing your presentation always has to be the first step. Finally, a skillful delivery of the speech combined with using effective presentation aids will create both an engaging and an effective speech for your audience.

A key step to knowing your audience is being able to gauge the audience's informational needs. What information do they know already? What information do they need to know to understand your speech? You also need to take into consideration the intended audience themselves. This includes factors such as background, age, gender, and religion. It is also important to consider the setting, the occasion, and the nature of the speech, which play an important role in shaping the information as it is presented to the audience.

There are several strategies for presenting information in an informative presentation. These include *defining, describing, explaining,* or *demonstrating* the material to the audience. Defining can take on five different forms. First, an operational definition shows what something does. For example, you could show your audience a product that your company makes and exactly the process for making that product work. Second, a definition by negation means to explain to the audience what something is not. This type of definition works well when talking about abstract ideas that your audience may not be familiar with. In this situation, comparing the unknown to something that they do know makes the abstract more concrete. Third, a definition by example provides the audience with solid examples of the subject under discussion. Telling the information in a variety of ways is a good idea to reach a wide, varying audience. Fourth, a definition by synonym works to compare something to another term or idea that has an equivalent or familiar meaning. Again, this can help to explain concepts that are abstract or unknown to the audience by defining them in terms that are familiar to the audience. Finally, a definition by etymology works to illustrate a word's history by explaining the root origins of the word or concept.

Other means of informing your audience include describing information by providing a picture of the subject at hand. Using effective language to paint a picture of the information for the audience can help to transport them into a new idea or concept. Explaining information involves providing reasons or causes between concepts as well as demonstrating relationships that exist within those concepts. Demonstrating information for the audience gives a step-by-step lesson on how to do something. This could be as simple as how to use a product or even how an audience member would or could react in particular situations.

Categories of Informative Presentations

There are many, many approaches to informative presentations, and the topics from which you can select are endless. Here we will try to categorize some of the approaches you may take in selecting a topic for your speech. First, speeches about objects are speeches that discuss anything that isn't human, including animate and inanimate objects. This could work well when discussing a new product that your organization has developed. Second, speeches about people are interesting topics that discuss historically significant individuals and groups. You should consider those who have made contributions to society (both positive and negative), or those who for one reason or another we simply find interesting. Perhaps the founder of an organization whom people may be unfamiliar with or a famous historical figure who has a business connection that we may be unaware of could be good topics. Third, speeches about events are interesting topics, as they can discuss noteworthy happenings, past, present, and future. Fourth are speeches about processes. These speeches discuss a series of steps that lead to a finished product or an end result by telling us how something is done, how it is made, or how it works. Some of the more interesting topics in this area are those that explain a product or item that we are very familiar with, but don't know where it comes from. For example, where does bubble gum come from? Your entire audience will know the product, but the history and business behind it is most likely something that they are unfamiliar with. Fifth, speeches about concepts are ways to discuss abstract or complex ideas and attempt to make them concrete and understandable for the audience. Finally, speeches about issues are ways to provide a report or an overview of problems or issues in dispute to increase understanding and awareness within the audience. These could be employee issues or other controversial issues within your organization's community.

> Informative speeches can be about objects, people, events, processes, concepts, or issues.

Guidelines for Great Informative Presentations

There are several steps that you should follow to construct an effective informative presentation. The following ideas should be taken into consideration for any type of informative speech in any setting.

1. **It is important not to say too much or too little about the subject being presented.** Remember that if you say too much and your audience is already familiar with this information, they will tune you out and not receive the message you intend for them. On the other hand, it is important not to say too little either. Keep in mind that some members of your audience may not be familiar with your jargon or even the broad subject on which you are speaking. Because of this, it is important to try to predict the knowledge level of your specific audience and adapt your presentation to those people.

2. **Emphasizing the topic's relevance to audience members is a good way to hold their interest.** One of the hardest things about any business presentation is keeping the audience engaged and interested. Most people only care about things that directly affect themselves. This appeal to self-interest may seem selfish at first, but this connection to the audience is key to your success. For example, why would college students want to hear a speech about retirement options? In this case, you should emphasize why preparing for retirement very early would make them dramatically more money and not focus on the differing retirement plans only.

3. **A speaker should always define terms that the audience may not understand.** Sometimes it can be difficult for us to realize that not everyone uses the same language set. Jargon refers to language specific to one particular group of people. You may notice this pattern if you have changed jobs within the same field. One company may refer to your computer operating system as one term or acronym, and your new employer may call their system something completely different. When presenting to a broad or diverse audience, you as the speaker should take the time to define the terms that you are using.

4. **Repeating the most significant idea in the speech reinforces the information presented.** Again, we don't have the visual cues in an oral presentation that we do in written communication; therefore, you must repeat key ideas that you wish your audience to remember the most. Repeating key words or phrases creates a distinct rhythm, and repeating the form of a sentence creates

parallel structure. Parallel structure may be difficult to identify at first, but you know it when you hear it. The majority of the greatest American speeches utilize parallel structure to reinforce ideas and keep the audience engaged. Speakers often use repetition to create a thematic focus within the speech. This means that you can use repeated words or phrases to generate an overarching theme for your speech. This was clearly demonstrated in the 2008 election when President Barack Obama used the phrase "Yes we can" to jump start the audience and keep them moving until the final election day. Repetition can be as simple as emphasizing a word several times or as sophisticated as continually relating main ideas back to the main theme of the speech.

5. **Try relating abstract concepts to things that the audience already knows or are at least familiar with.** This will both engage the audience and, again, make them realize how the information can be relevant to them. It is also important to try to relay compelling and fresh information during the course of the speech. If you believe that the audience already knows about your topic, you need to strive to present your information in a new and different manner to keep their attention.

6. **The entire message should be delivered with as much clarity as possible to ensure effective communication.** It is important to remember that keeping it simple is always a good idea. Use examples to define your ideas and keep them as clear as possible. You should use a preview statement in your introduction to make sure that the audience understands the overall goal of the speech right from the beginning. A review statement in the conclusion then reinforces that goal at the end of the speech. There is an old adage in speech writing that says, "Tell them what you're going to tell them. Tell them. And then tell them what you just told them." Preview your main points clearly and concisely in the introduction. Make sure that your main points are highlighted in the main body of the speech, and then repeat your main points one more time in the conclusion of the speech.

7. **Use visualization to increase understanding within your audience.** Visualization is the speaker's ability to paint a picture of the topic within the mind of the audience. Use vivid descriptions and concise and concrete language. If the audience understands your goal and you are able to get them to visualize your final idea as well, you will have an effective presentation.

8. **Presentation aids enrich the presentation by reinforcing the speaker's verbal message, not replacing it.** The chapter on visual presentations covers this extensively, but one key point is to remember that you are doing the talking, not your visual. Don't let your visual overstep the important parts of your speech.

Use examples to define your ideas and keep them as clear as possible.

SELECTING A TOPIC

The very first step in speech construction is what can seem to be a daunting task: choosing a topic. Always keep your audience and their needs in mind, but you should select a topic in which you have a personal interest and are enthusiastic about. This is advantageous because your research will be more enjoyable and your enthusiasm will actually show through in your oral presentation. Remember that you will have to spend a good amount of time with this topic, so it might as well be something that you are actually interested in. Good speech topics can be found easily within current events. These topics can be found in daily and weekly newspapers, magazines, as well as online publications. Controversial issues make relevant speech topics because they profoundly affect us as individuals and as members of society. Another direction that works well with an audience is grassroots topics, as they are issues that affect the audience directly. Consider issues that are specifically connected to your audience's school, community, or even state.

Brainstorming is just the process of generating ideas. There are many ways to go about brainstorming, but at this point the key is to remember to consider any and all possibilities. Creating lists of possible topics can help a speaker consider hobbies and topics and people with whom you identify. Word associations help to generate topics by thinking of words or phrases that fall in sequence to one another. Topic mapping may seem like something you did in grammar school, but it is a technique that works very well with speech writing. Topic mapping helps you by creating a picture of associated words or topic ideas from which to choose. This works well for speech writing because you can actually see how the speech will lay out and where your points will be grouped together.

Refining the topic and purpose to something that is manageable is the next step in putting together your presentation. Narrowing a topic involves focusing on specific aspects of the topic that interest you the most. You should also consider time and research constraints. If you don't have access to the information necessary for a particular topic, then choosing that topic may not be the best idea. The specific speech purpose expresses both the topic and the general purpose in action form and in terms of your overall objective for the presentation. The specific purpose focuses more closely and concisely than the general speech purpose on the main goal of the speech.

Moving from your topic and purpose to a solid thesis statement is the next step. A thesis statement in a speech, just as in a paper, is a single statement that expresses the theme or central idea of the speech and serves to connect all parts of the speech. Your thesis should make a *claim* about the speech. What do you specifically want the audience to take away from your presentation? Making the topic and the thesis statement relevant to audience members helps to maintain their interest and enthusiasm, and then motivates them to listen to the rest of the speech.

> Topic mapping creates a picture of associated words or topic ideas.

STRUCTURE OF A SPEECH

Any effective speech is made up of three basic main parts: an introduction, body, and conclusion. This applies to both informative and persuasive speeches. The parts of an introduction serve to: introduce of the topic, establish the purpose of the speech, and convey the relevance of the speech to the audience. The body of the speech presents the main points that support the purpose of the speech. Finally, the conclusion of the speech brings the purpose of the speech and the main points together. It also brings closure to the speech, restating the purpose and main points so that the audience can remember them.

The main points of the speech state the themes of the speech and support the thesis. These points should be stated as claims and be supported by facts. To create your main points, first identify the themes of your speech. Utilizing the specific purpose of the speech can help you to create the main points of your speech. Remember that the purpose statement expresses the goal of the speech, whereas the **thesis statement** expresses the theme of the speech. Three main points are ideal. Research shows that audiences are capable of processing two to seven main points. If you have more than seven main points, then group your ideas together. Have you ever gone to the grocery store and knew that you had to get nine items, but only ended up with half of them when you got home? Without written or visual backup, people are only able to remember about three main ideas; hence the reason we don't end up with everything we need from the store. By stating the main points at the beginning and end of the speech, the audience is more likely to remember them.

Main points should never introduce more than one topic or idea. The main points should be presented in a parallel structure or in a similar grammatical style to make them stand out from the rest of the speech. Main points need at least two subpoints, but no more than five. Each of these may also have supporting points. This tight format helps lend authority, formality, and power to the delivery of your presentation. Supporting points are used to justify the main points and lead the audience into accepting your ideas. Like main points, supporting points should be arranged in the order of importance or relevance from most important to least important. In creating an outline for you to follow when you deliver your speech, indentation among the points makes it easier to follow while speaking.

Well-organized, and hence effective, speeches have unity, coherence, and balance. Unity is developed by using only points relevant to the purpose, connecting the entirety of the speech together. If it doesn't seem like it belongs, then you don't need to include it. A coherent speech is logically organized and has clarity that is noticeable by the audience. The logical placement of the ideas that are relevant to each other and their ranking by their importance is critical for your audience to be able to

Thesis statement: A single sentence that summarizes the central idea of a presentation.

Topical pattern: An organizational arrangement in which ideas are grouped around logical themes or divisions of the subject.

Chronological pattern: An organizational arrangement that presents points according to their sequence in time.

Spatial pattern: An organizational arrangement that presents material according to its physical location.

Cause-effect pattern: An organizational arrangement which shows that events happened or will happen as a result of certain circumstances.

Problem-solution organizational pattern: An organizational arrangement in which the speaker first convinces the audience that a problem exists and then presents a plan to solve it.

follow the flow of your speech. Giving your speech balance means that you give each piece of the speech appropriate emphasis, relative to the purpose as well as the other main points.

Transitions are what make the difference between an okay speech and a great speech. Transitions are words, phrases, and sentences that tie a speech's ideas together. They allow the speaker to move from point to point smoothly, while giving the speech direction. There are several functions of transitions such as to: show comparison, illustrate cause and effect, show the sequence of events or time, contrast ideas, internally preview your points, generate an internal summary, and to summarize. Simple examples of transitions include the words or phrases: similarly, likewise, as a result, therefore, consequently, at present, until now, hence, following this, on the other hand, however, or in conclusion.

Five Major Types of Organizational Arrangements for Speeches

1. **Topically organized speeches**. In the topical pattern, each main point is of equal importance, and the order of the main points does not change the meaning of the speech. At the same time, you should still consider the organization of points depending on the audience, importance, and complexity of the topic.

2. **Chronological organization.** Use the chronological pattern when the main points of your speech happen in a specific order. The organization of the speech should then follow an order of natural sequence.

3. **Spatial or geographical pattern.** The spatial pattern is necessary when you are explaining either a physical arrangement of a place or object, or if logic suggests that the main points be arranged in accordance to their proximity or location.

4. **Cause-effect arrangement.** The cause-effect pattern should be used when the main points compare something that is known to be a cause with its effects following the cause. There can be multiple causes and a single effect or a single cause and multiple effects.

5. **Problem-solution patterns.** These types of arrangements are used to explain the significance of the problem as well as the nature of the problem and then provide justification for the solution. Most of the time, a speech using the problem-solution organizational pattern requires two main points.

Topic: Google, Inc.
General Purpose: To inform
Specific Purpose: To inform my audience about Google, Inc.
Thesis Statement: Google, Inc. is a global technology company with a rich history, innovative products and services, and a renowned organizational culture.
Organization Pattern: Topical

Topic: The Recession of 2007-2009
General Purpose: To inform
Specific Purpose: To inform my audience about the events contributing to the recession of 2007-2009.
Thesis Statement: The recession of 2007-2009 was marked by the deflated housing bubble, the bankruptcy of large banks, and an ensuing global economic contraction.
Organization Pattern: Chronological

Topic: University Traffic Plan
General Purpose: To inform
Specific Purpose: To inform my audience about the development of the traffic flow plan at Eastern University.
Thesis Statement: Eastern University develops transportation plans in a way that relieves congestion and enhances parking for North Campus, South Campus, and Central Campus.
Organization Pattern: Spatial/Geographical

Topic: Employee Wellness Plans
General Purpose: To inform
Specific Purpose: To inform my audience about the ways an employee wellness plan can offset health care expenses.
Thesis Statement: Health insurance costs at Grego, Inc. are decreasing due to smoking cessation programs, weight management clinics, and ergonomic troubleshooting workshops.
Organization Pattern: Cause-Effect

Topic: Motivation at Work
General Purpose: To inform
Specific Purpose: To inform my audience about how different organizational structures can positively influence motivation levels.
Thesis Statement: Traditional approaches to organizational motivation focus too heavily on extrinsic motivators, but creating more participative workplaces that stress autonomy can greatly increase motivation and productivity.
Organization Pattern: Problem-Solution

There are other alternate patterns than the five listed here that may be more appropriate for other classes or your future career. For example, if you are giving a scientific speech or technological presentation that may have more, complex main points, using a deductive or inductive arrangement of main points could be more effective. Remember that subpoints can also be arranged in any of these ways. Always consider audience diversity when choosing an organizational pattern, as with every other aspect of speech writing.

DIFFERENCES IN PUBLIC VERSUS BUSINESS SPEAKING

Although there are many similarities between public and business presentations, there are several differences. First, when selecting a topic, you generally have to adapt to the very specific topics and content that business speeches allow, whereas in public speeches, the topics are more broadly defined. Business presentations usually follow a traditional approach using specific, task-oriented, management, or client-directed topics. Second, the audience composition should be taken into consideration, as public speaking audiences are generally more diverse than audiences for a business presentation. Another difference is that audience participation is more frequent in business presentations and is found very rarely in public addresses. Finally, you should be aware that the audience members generally think that a public speaker has more knowledge than they do on a subject, whereas business speakers are thought to be more equal in terms of knowledge of their subject.

Audience participation happens frequently in business presentations as opposed to public speaking.

© wavebreakmedia/Shutterstock.com

Five Basic Types of Business and Professional Presentations

1. **Sales presentations**. In a sales presentation, you are attempting to lead a potential buyer to purchase a service or product that you describe in your presentation.

2. **Technical reports**. A technical report gives detailed information about a procedure or a device. Audiences for this type of presentation can vary from one person to a large group, and generally, someone in the audience is in charge of making decisions. Depending on the subject at hand, the report can be formal and long or relatively brief and loosely structured.

3. **Staff reports**. A staff report informs managers and other employees of new developments that directly affect them and their work. These reports can involve a new plan or a report on the completion of a project or a task. The audience is usually made up of a group, but could just be an individual. Staff reports usually include a statement of the problem or question under consideration, a description and a discussion of pertinent facts, and a statement of conclusions followed by recommendations.

4. **Progress reports**. A progress report updates clients or principals on developments within an ongoing project. The audience can vary greatly, and questions from them are usually common. There is no set pattern for a progress report, but they often begin with a brief overview of the progress up to the time of the last report.

5. **Investigative reports**. These are a study of a problem that includes recommendations, and they are usually conducted by a person or group outside the organization. The audience is usually made up of a group whose planning and decisions on a matter depend significantly on the results of the investigation, and it follows one of two forms. First, the indirect method presents conclusions and recommendations last, after background of the issue, a problem statement, the method of investigation, the findings, conclusions, and ending with recommendations for a plan of action. The direct method begins with conclusions and recommendations, then describes the problem, the method used to investigate, and the chief findings.

Sales presentation: A type of presentation aimed at persuading others to purchase a product or service.

Delivering the Business Presentation

Just as informative business presentations vary in type, they also require different delivery styles.

- An *informational style* is precise, disciplined, focused, clear, logical, and well organized. Use this approach when you know that the audience is concerned with getting the facts.
- An *instructional style* is stimulating, engaging, consequential, decisive, and action oriented. It involves audience interaction such as in a teaching or training situation.
- A *relational style* of delivery is open, candid, honest, believable, and trustworthy. These are usually extemporaneous presentations.
- A *transformational style* is emphatic, powerful, insightful, expansive, and visionary. These presentations are intended to motivate the audience and should also be extemporaneous. To see a transformative speaking style, check out this TED talk by Dan Pink, a career analyst who discusses motivation in the workplace.

www.ted.com/
talks/dan_pink_on_
motivation

Special Occasion Presentations

Special occasion presentations are an interesting mix between public and business speaking. Informative and persuasive business presentations are designed for clients, customers, employees, and shareholders, but other types of presentations are given for various reasons, including toasts, farewells, awards ceremonies, or even an introduction for a speaker. These types of presentations fall into the category of special occasion speeches or presentations. Chances are good that at some point in your career, you will be called on to deliver a brief presentation that falls into this category, or, like Addison Garrett, the training coordinator you read about at the beginning of the chapter, you might be in charge of arranging these types of presentations.

Special occasion presentation: Presentation that promotes goodwill or pays tribute in the form of welcomes, introductions, toasts, award presentations and acceptances, retirements, eulogies, and commemorations.

When planning a special occasion speech, many of the same rules for creating effective informative and persuasive presentations apply. You will want to keep in mind the elements of your situation, such as the place where you will present, the format of the presentation, the number of people attending the event, and the amount of time you are allotted. Special occasion speeches are typically shorter than most presentations, which means planning is even more important for communicating your sentiments.

The following sections review the most common forms of special occasion speeches in the business world, including welcomes, speeches of introduction, award acceptances and presentations, and toasts.

WELCOME SPEECHES

Formal events such as large meetings, conferences, and award ceremonies typically require a **welcome speech** to start the proceedings. Welcome speeches are positive, sincere, and brief. Your welcome speech should meet the same goals as a speech introduction, including an attention-getting

Welcome speech: Speech intended to welcome groups or audiences to an event or conference; designed to build anticipation, communicate enthusiasm, and preview the event.

© hxdbzxy/Shutterstock.com

Keep welcome speeches positive, sincere, and brief.

device, a specific purpose statement, and a preview of the main points. Additionally, since audience members may not know who you are, make sure you introduce yourself, your title, and your organizational affiliation; thank audience members for attending; focus on the importance of the meeting or ceremony; highlight the major events planned; and express enthusiasm. If your welcome speech lacks enthusiasm or an attention-getting device, you may be setting the audience up for a long day. Finally, the speaker should thank people or groups who made the event possible.

SPEECHES OF INTRODUCTION

Speech of introduction: Presentation designed to introduce a keynote speaker in a way that highlights his/her achievements, connects their topic to the audience, and builds anticipation.

Introducing speakers such as leaders, experts, or political figures is an important part of preparing the audience to listen and may serve to put the speaker at ease. Although speeches of introduction are relatively short presentations, they are critically important for setting the stage for a presentation and therefore require a certain amount of thought and planning. You may be asked to introduce someone you already know, but organizations often invite guest speakers from outside the organization, which may require you to do your homework and investigate the presenter. First, consider conducting an interview with the person and asking for basic details regarding their professional experience, awards, honors, qualifications, and the topic of their speech. Also, ask if they would share their résumé for you to glean specific points of interest.

Now that you have collected information, you should consider the structure of your introduction. Connecting to the concepts discussed in the chapter on persuasive presentations, you will want to describe the speaker's credentials and achievements (*ethos*), explain why the speaker's topic is relevant for the audience (*logos*), and set the tone by piquing the audience's interest in hearing this person present (*pathos*). You might also build anticipation by not stating the speaker's name up front (in the first sentence) and instead save it for the end.[8]

The following transcript provides a sample speech of introduction for Dr. Cooper Michaels, the keynote speaker at a conference on teaching public speaking. Notice how the speaker inspires the audience with a quote, highlights the keynote speaker's accomplishments, introduces the topic of the presentation, and finally, announces the main presenter's name.

Sample Speech of Introduction

Good afternoon. Please continue enjoying your lunch as we move on with the next segment of our program.

My name is Dr. Caleb Thomas and I am an assistant professor in the Department of Communication at West State University. I have the distinct pleasure of introducing our keynote speaker today who is both my mentor and my friend.

I'd like to begin by sharing with you one of my favorite Rumi quotes which embodies our speaker. "Let the beauty we love, be what we do. There are a hundred ways to kneel and kiss the ground."

I often reflect on the meaning of this quote, its relevance for my life and the lives of my students. The key message is that we should find beauty in our life's work, even when there doesn't seem like there is much to love. The quote inspires us to be open to the diversity of paths our lives and work lives might take and to be cognizant of the hundred ways to kiss the ground ... the hundred ways to be thankful for the things we have and the hundred ways to make a difference in the lives of others. Of course, living this motto is much easier said than done.

So, I'm always inspired when I meet people who embody this quote in terms of their purpose-driven life and their willingness to help others achieve. If you were to take a look at the 25+ page vita of our speaker today, you'd see the hundred ways he kisses the ground. From research, to teaching, to service, to administrating, he serves his students, he serves his colleagues, and he serves the public in untold ways.

Though he works on multimillion-dollar grants related to HIV, STDs, pregnancy, and drug prevention, he also researches and publishes in the area of instructional communication within engineering, mathematics, or communication classrooms. You'll find his name gracing the covers of *Communication Monographs, Communication Education, Media Psychology*, and countless others.

That said, you won't find him cloistered in his ivory tower beneath a pile of books and you won't find him lacking in interpersonal communication skills. When you're with him you're learning together. And, don't be surprised when you leave his office (or maybe his presentation today) with a new reference list, stack of books and articles, or even some new SPSS code he's written to analyze a new data set. He truly embodies continuous learning.

Our speaker today is a servant to those in the field. He's taken an incredible leadership role in the Regional Communication Association and in promoting communication education statewide. All of these are reasons we have invited him here today to share with us his insights on the state of the communication discipline in the region.

I know that in listening to him speak you'll understand Rumi's words and what it means to "Let the beauty we love be what we do." Please join me in welcoming Dr. Cooper Michaels, associate professor in the College of Communication at Central State University.

AWARD ACCEPTANCES

There may be times during your career where you will accept an award or honor for a personal achievement or on behalf of your organization. From watching award shows on television, we can all identify when this is done well or when the speech is so ill planned that music begins to play and a big hook practically pulls the speaker off the stage. To make sure this doesn't happen to you, consider planning your speech of acceptance in advance, even if you're uncertain of whether you'll be named the recipient of the award or honor.

The primary purpose of a speech of acceptance is to offer praise and thanks to the group giving the award, acknowledge the people who made your success possible, and give gratitude to the audience for being there to support your award acceptance.

To ensure that music does not begin playing to get you off the stage and to keep the attention of the audience, keep your comments brief. Also, be humble and only use humor if appropriate and if you can do it well. There might also be times where you need to explain the significance of the accomplishment, but avoid turning your acceptance speech into a political statement if it is not directly relevant to your award or accomplishment.

Award acceptance: Brief comments made by an award recipient providing credit and thanks to those who made the award possible and expressing sincerity.

Plan a speech of acceptance in advance, even if you don't know who will win the award.

© tmcphotos/Shutterstock.com

AWARD PRESENTATIONS

If you are presenting an award, keep in mind that, like the speech of introduction, your purpose is to present someone else to the audience, so your part should be brief. When presenting an award consider providing a brief anecdote about the person or organization and describe what makes them deserving of the award by explaining the significance of their accomplishment. If the audience is unaware of the purpose of the award, then also consider giving a history of the award itself. Finally, if the award is based on a public competition where other individuals or organizations have been publicly nominated, consider paying tribute to those who did not win first place. Review the following award presentation, analyzing each component.

Award presentation: Congratulatory comments made when presenting an award or honor to a deserving recipient, which explains the significance of the award, briefly summarizes the accomplishment, and introduces the recipient.

"Great things are not done by impulse, but by a series of small things brought together."

This quote from Vincent Van Gogh describes the achievements of our next award winner because she has truly focused her efforts in developing a successful undergraduate career in the Department of Communication at West State University. The Syntec, Inc. Scholarship Award for the Outstanding Organizational Communication Scholar is based on academic achievement, departmental citizenship, and scholarship in the area of intercultural business communication. It was a difficult decision for us this year, as we had to choose among top-quality competitors, so we would like to thank all of those who submitted outstanding applications for review.

   The recipient of this year's scholarship comes to us from Carbondale, Illinois, and has been quite a busy woman. Campbell Hunter has impressed the faculty members in her department and the scholarship committee with her ability to multitask. Not only is she graduating with a GPA of 3.96, but she is also taking a 21-hour course load, working part-time for the basketball team, actively participating in Kappa Delta Sorority, and planning a June wedding. Campbell Hunter's drive for achievement is exemplified by the completion of her degree in 3 years and we all know this in and of itself is a rare accomplishment. On top of all this, we would like to draw special attention to the training curriculum Ms. Hunter developed for use in preparing employees for business travel in Asia. The research support and the training materials she developed are quite impressive. The skills she has developed and the quality of her work will serve her well as she applies her communication skills in the workplace. Campbell, please come forward to accept the $10,000 scholarship award for the Syntec, Inc. Outstanding Organizational Communication Scholar.

TOASTS

Toast: Sentiments communicated at group meals, celebrations, or business meetings that convey goodwill and meet appropriate cultural etiquette.

Outside of the more traditional forms of toasting such as at wedding receptions or family celebrations, you may be asked to provide a **toast** as part of a business dinner or event. To avoid an embarrassing moment, always be prepared to give an impromptu toast. Because these moments may be unplanned, you can follow the same tips you might use for an impromptu speech. If you have time, make notes; otherwise, determine your main point, analyze how you might support it, and develop a strong introductory and concluding statement. Because toasts are typically short, avoid trying to cover too many points and stick to a few simple ideas.

   First, a toast (as opposed to a roast) is considered a mini speech of tribute, so enter into this by thinking of a noteworthy detail about the person, the event, or the accomplishment. Depending on the size of the group, explain your connection with the person you are toasting, be careful of using humor, and be sincere. Other situational considerations include whether to sit or stand. For large groups (10 or more) consider standing. Also, do your homework when traveling on business abroad because many cultures have standard rules of etiquette around toasting. For example, in many Asian cultures, toasts occur periodically throughout a multicourse meal with repetitive phrases about collaboration and friendship. Toasts are highly emphasized as an important, formal part of business meals, unlike the informal ways we toast in the United States.[9]

Here in the United States, you should verify with the host that is it okay for you to toast (unless your boss has assigned this task), look directly at the person or group you are toasting, clink glasses if you want or raise your glass, and make eye contact with those at the table instead of showing more enthusiasm for your beverage. Following these simple guidelines can help you make a good impression on your boss as well as your guests. And a final word: Avoid toasting if you have been drinking; sober toasting will ensure you are competent, brief, and appropriate.

Toasting Etiquette

For more tips on toasting etiquette, check out this video news segment from the CBS Saturday Early Show: http://www.cbsnews.com/sections/i_video/main500251.shtml?id=2015584n

CONCLUSION

This chapter reviews the basics of creating informative and special occasion business presentations, from selecting an appropriate topic to implementing a clear organizational pattern. Keep in mind that delivery is especially important for maintaining your credibility in business situations. By staying focused on the information needs of your audience, you are sure to compose a presentation that is perceived as appropriate and effective.

Additionally, several types of special occasions in the business world may require you to make a presentation. Unlike informative and persuasive presentations, special occasion speeches are brief, and the focus of attention is directed toward someone else. Using your words creatively can help the audience prepare for the main speaker, raise their interest, put them ease, and create goodwill, whether it's by welcoming groups, introducing speakers, accepting or presenting awards, or providing a toast. Competent communicators are able to pay tribute in small and large groups and in both impromptu and extemporaneous formats.

As in the case with Addison Garrett, training coordinator at Syntec, Inc., having the knowledge and resources to assist others in preparing informative and special occasion speeches can go a long way toward organizing a successful conference. If Addison properly coaches her coworkers, the conference planning will appear seamless and well coordinated. By helping others understand that they have the easy part of promoting goodwill and placing the focus on others, Addison will provide her colleagues with an experience to build their professional communication repertoire.

ACTIVITIES

1. Identify the following factors for the speech settings listed: your audience, the occasion, and yourself as a speaker.
   a. Fire an employee
   b. Recruit new students to your college
   c. Ask a professor for an extension on an assignment

2. Imagine that you are to give a presentation on your college or university. How would your presentation change based on the following audience groups?
   a. A group of grade school students
   b. A group of retired persons
   c. A civic group such as the Rotary Club
   d. A group of students looking to attend your school.

3. Think of a business leader you know and/or admire and develop an introduction speech as if they were visiting class for a discussion on communication in the workplace. How would you build in the persuasive elements of ethos, logos, and pathos?

4. When was the last time you heard a speech of introduction for a keynote speaker? Write down the specific elements of the introduction. What did the introducer do well? What advice could you provide him/her for improving? Describe the overall effect of the introduction on the audience and the keynote speaker.

5. Imagine you just received an award (scholarship, special honor in your field) or won a competition, and write an acceptance speech. Think of the qualities that make a strong acceptance speech based on examples viewed online (see box above), and create an outline of what you might include.

6. Based on the special occasion presentations discussed in this chapter, develop a speech of tribute for a retirement celebration. What specific elements should be included?

7. Conduct outside research on toasting customs and etiquette in different countries, such as Japan, Russia, China, Ireland, India, or Germany. Select one country, write an appropriate toast, and deliver it to your classmates.

REFERENCES

[1] Adler, R. B., & Elmhorst, J. M. (2008). *Communicating at work: Principles and practices for business and the professions*. New York: McGraw-Hill.

[2] Bovee, C. L., & Thill, J. T. (1989). *Business communication today*. New York: Random House.

[3] Brody, M. (1997). *Speaking your way to the top: Making powerful business presentations*. Boston: Allyn & Bacon.

[4] Foss, S. K., & Foss, K. A. (2003). *Inviting transformation: Presentational speaking for a changing world*. Prospect Heights, IL: Waveland Press.

[5] Inch, E. S., & Warnick, B. (2002). *Critical thinking and communication: The use of reason in argument* (4th ed.). Boston: Allyn & Bacon.

[6] Jaffe, C. (2007). *Public speaking: Concepts and skills for a diverse society* (5th ed.). Belmont, CA: Wadsworth.

[7] Lucas, S. E. (2001). *The art of public speaking* (7th ed.). New York: McGraw-Hill.

[8] Devet, B. (1995). Introducing a speaker: An assignment for students in business communication. *Business Communication Quarterly, 58*(4), 57–59.

[9] Beamer, L. (1993). Toasts: Rhetoric and ritual in business negotiation in Confucian cultures. *Business Forum, 18*(4).

ADDITIONAL SOURCES

Detz, J. (2006). *Can you say a few words? How to prepare and deliver a speech for any special occasion*. New York: St. Martins.

Kline, J.A. (2006). Introducing a speaker. *Armed Forces Comptroller, 51*(4), 42.

Kuryllowicz, K. (2002). How to introduce a speaker. *Profit, 21*(4), 11.

Starr, D. P. (2005). The speech of introduction. *Tactics, 12*(2), 24.

chapter fifteen

Persuasive Business Presentations

After reading this chapter you will be able to:

- Understand the concept of persuasion
- Differentiate the historical and modern approaches to persuasion
- Know how to pick a direct goal for your persuasive presentation
- Understand the role of audience in persuasion

CHAPTER OUTLINE

key words

Persuasion
Logos
Pathos
Ethos
Syllogism
Enthymeme

PERSUASIVE PRESENTATIONS

In order to understand how to construct a persuasive presentation, we must first understand what persuasion is. **Persuasion** is a process of influencing the attitudes, beliefs, values, and behavior of other people. According to Gass and Seiter, persuasion is "one or more persons who are engaged in the activity of creating, reinforcing, modifying, or extinguishing beliefs, attitudes, intentions, motivations, and/or behaviors, within the constraints of a given communication context." Persuasive speaking is a speech that is intended to do just that.

What methods do you use to try to persuade others?

© Konstantin Chagin/Shutterstock.com

405

As has been stated many times throughout this text, communication is key to professional success. The ability to persuade others well can provide a distinct and tangible success at work. Beyond just finding employment, your ability to use persuasion will help you achieve important career goals, and motivate others to say yes to your requests. Being a successful persuader means setting yourself up for success in business and your business relationships. The tools of persuasive speech will help you communicate arguments in a way that guarantees that they are heard by the people most important to your success.

CONTEXT

The role of context must be considered in any definition or model of persuasion. The context determines the nature of the persuasion process that is operating (e.g. linear, two-way, delayed, etc.). There are a number of context-based factors that affect the nature of the persuasion process. These include the number of communicators, whether communication is synchronous or asynchronous, the nature and type of media, the ratio of verbal to nonverbal cues that are present, the goals of the participants, and socio-cultural factors that shape participants' message construction and perceptions. Remember that not all human behavior is persuasive, although nearly all human behavior carries persuasive potential.

WHY STUDY PERSUASION?

Persuasion is an area of study that crosses the boundaries of both the arts and the sciences. The most important thing that you can remember is that persuasion is not a negative thing. It is essential to the process of human interaction. We study persuasion because it is pervasive, inevitable, and unavoidable in any human interaction. In any career that deals with people, persuasion is key to your success at that job. When you say that you have good people skills, what you are actually saying is that you are a persuasive person.

Persuasion is often found in not the most obvious places such as the natural sciences, the arts, interpersonal encounters, and many other communication situations. There are four basic functions of persuasion:

1. **Instrumental function**. Helps you to become a more competent persuader.

2. **Knowledge function.** Increases your understanding of how persuasion works. It is common that most people are unaware of their own patterns or skills of persuasion. .
3. **Defensive function**. Makes you a more discriminating consumer of persuasive messages. By knowing how persuasion works, you will be less susceptible to persuasive messages.
4. **Debunking function**. Alerts you to false or dated conceptions of how persuasion functions. There are many commonsense notions about persuasion that are often mistaken. There is much persuasion research that has yielded insightful, counter-intuitive findings to what you may initially think.

Common Criticisms of Studying Persuasion

First, many believe that studying persuasion is the same as studying manipulation. This is untrue as persuasion research focuses on the *means* of influence, which tend to be amoral rather than immoral or moral. Persuasion can be likened to a tool such as a hammer. The tool itself isn't good or bad, but the end purpose for which the tool is used may be good or bad. The motive behind the persuasion determines how ethical or unethical any given attempt to influence may be, not the means of persuasion. By studying persuasion, you can attempt to protect yourself from unethical influence. We must also remember that people who denounce the study of persuasion are themselves taking a persuasive position.

Second, some claim that persuasion findings are overly qualified or contradictory. On that same level, we must remember that human behavior is complex, so the complexity in persuasion should be expected. Remember that many meaningful, yet qualified generalizations have been established through meta-analysis and the results of empirical studies complement other ways of learning about how people influence one another. Regardless, in learning how to persuade, learning how to persuade ethically is vitally important.

WHAT EXACTLY IS PERSUASION?

The problem with that question is that there is no clear or concrete decision on what the term "persuasion" means. There are different definitions to emphasize different aspects of persuasion. Some definitions emphasize "pure" cases of persuasion, while others include "borderline" cases of persuasion as well. The various definitions of persuasion may be categorized by five limiting criteria:

1. **Intentionality.** These types of persuasion are emphasized by speaker-oriented definitions. To distinguish between persuasion and social influence, recognize that persuasion is intentional and social influence is not.

   Problems with the intentionality definition:
   - Influence may be accidental or unconscious or may operate at a very low level of awareness.
   - Persuaders aren't always aware of their intentions.
   - Unintended receivers may be influenced by persuasive messages.
   - It is difficult to determine a persuader's intent.
   - There may be intra-audience effects such as when receivers of the message persuade one another.
   - The intention definition requires a very linear approach to persuasion; meaning that one person persuades another in a direct fashion.

2. **Effects.** These types are emphasized by audience-oriented definitions.

   Problems with the effects definition:
   - This type of persuasion emphasizes persuasion as a product, or outcome, rather than a process.
   - It also entails a linear view of the persuasion process, from the source to the receiver. In reality, influence attempts are often mutual or reciprocal.
   - There are inherent difficulties in measuring or assessing persuasive effects. How do you know when the persuasion is effective?
   - The success of an influence attempt depends on the point of view of the perceiver or the audience. The one deciphering the persuasion is the one who determines its success or failure.

3. **Free choice or free will.** These definitions can be based on the free will of the audience.

   Problems with the free choice definition:
   - It is difficult to clearly differentiate persuasion from coercion.
   - Coercion can involve positive inducements and incentives, not just negative sanctions.

- Most influence attempts contain both persuasive and coercive features.
- The degree of coerciveness is largely in the eye of the beholder.

4. **Symbolic action.** As a limiting criterion, symbolic action takes into account all symbols involved in the persuasion.

   Problems with the symbolic action definition:
   - Nonverbal cues contain strong persuasive potential just as behaviors and physiological processes may hold persuasive implications.
   - Limiting persuasion to symbolic action excludes a host of non-symbolic features that affect persuasive outcomes.

5. **Interpersonal encounters.** This type of definition can be restricted to interpersonal, meaning between two or more people, rather than intrapersonal, meaning within the person.

   Problems with limiting persuasion to two or more persons:
   - Numerous examples of self-persuasion can be found and cognitive consistency theories, which are central to the study of persuasion, focus on intrapersonal processes.

PERSUASION, PROPAGANDA, AND INDOCTRINATION

Propaganda and *indoctrination* have derogatory meanings and are usually used to refer to persuasion done by those on the other side of an issue from where we stand. There are four basic characteristics of propaganda. First, propaganda has a strong ideological bent in that it does not have a purely informational function. Propaganda is working a specific agenda. Second, propaganda is institutional in nature in that organized groups practice it. Third, propaganda involves mass persuasion in that it is aimed at large numbers of people and relies on mass communication. Fourth, propaganda tends to rely on ethically suspect methods of influence. Propaganda is known to put results first and ethics second. This is what gives people their negative association with persuasion.

Indoctrination, on the other hand, is the act of indoctrinating, or teaching or inculcating a doctrine, principle, or ideology, especially one with a specific point of view.

Propagandists will use several different types of appeals to persuade an audience.

© VGstockstudio/Shutterstock.com

There are several questionable tactics, or types of appeals, used by propagandists:

- **Plain folks appeal**: "I'm one of you."
- **Testimonials**: "I saw the aliens, sure as I'm standing here."
- **Bandwagon effect**: "Everybody's doing it."
- **Card stacking**: presenting only one side of the story
- **Transfer**: positive or negative associations, such as guilt by association
- **Glittering generalities**: idealistic or loaded language, such as "freedom," "empowering," or "family values"
- **Name calling**: "racist," "tree hugger," "femi-nazi," "liberal"

GOALS OF PERSUASIVE SPEECHES

There are a few goals that are inherent in any persuasive speech. First, your goal really is to influence the audience's choices on your topic. Because persuasion is influence, so your goal in your speech is to influence your audience's decision about something. The best means of doing this is to present the audience with limited choices. As any topic has multiple viewpoints, limit the viewpoints within your speech to those that you believe are best for your audience. You should also seek some sort of active response from the audience. Encourage them to make a choice of some kind or to act on what they have heard. With these goals in mind, in order to be both ethical and successful at your persuasion, you must present the choice to your audience but then realize that that choice is ultimately up to the audience to make. This just means that you may lay the choices before your audience, but you may not force them to choose what you say is best.

There are four major occasions when using a persuasive speech works best. As persuasion is focused on changing attitudes, beliefs, and values, each of these situations focuses on altering a different aspect of these attributes within the audience. First is when you are trying to influence the audience's *attitudes* about your topic. You can do this by either making them more accepting or less accepting of your topic. Second, is when you are trying to get the audience to *accept* your own beliefs. Third, is when you are seeking to influence the audience's *behavior* by convincing the audience to take on a certain set of actions. This is commonly seen when an attorney seeks to persuade a jury to side with a particular verdict. The final occasion to use a persuasive speech is when you are seeking to *reinforce* the audience's existing attitudes about an issue. This is seen regularly when any religious minister preaches. They are persuading the audience by reinforcing their existing attitudes.

There are several factors that you can utilize to be more successful at persuasion. First, make sure that you are meeting the psychological needs of your audience. You need to ensure that your audience believes that changing will benefit them in some way. Second, seeking a minor change from the audience will be more likely to occur than seeking a major change. Think of it this way: no one likes change, therefore, getting them to make a small step toward change is bound to be more successful. Third, establish a common ground between you and your audience. This will show them that when they do change, they are not radically changing because in some way you are like them. Kenneth Burke called this *identification*. We like and trust people who are like us. Fourth, a way to ensure that your audience is going to be persuaded is to show them how not changing will keep them from being satisfied. They will be more receptive to change if they think that staying the way they are will not be good for them. Fifth, show that your position on the issue is only slightly different from that of your audience's. Finally, convince your audience that there will be an enduring reward for their changing. Show them how the change will benefit them in the long term, not just the short term.

ARISTOTLE ON PERSUASION

Logos: Concerns the nature of the message.

Pathos: The audience's feeling.

Ethos: The qualifications and the personality of the speaker.

Logos, pathos, and ethos are fundamental to forming a solid persuasive argument.

Over 3000 years ago, Aristotle developed the study of the liberal arts and he began with the study of rhetoric. Rhetoric is the first step to understanding democracy and is at the foundation of what we now know as any civilization. Aristotle believed that persuasive speakers should use three modes of persuasion or, what he called rhetorical proof. The first, logos, concerns the nature of the message; the second, pathos, the audience's feelings; and the third, ethos, the qualifications and the personality of the speaker.

Logos=Logic

Logos is any persuasive appeal directed at an audience's reasoning on a topic. We as humans like to believe that we are rational beings. Whether or not that is true is a completely different story, but regardless we would like to be rational about the decisions that we make. Logos helps to make use of arguments for or against an idea or issue through two main types of appeal to the rational side of humans.

© Africa Studio/Shutterstock.com

Syllogism. A syllogism is a three-part argument consisting of a major premise or general case, a minor premise or specific case, and a conclusion. Make sure that you attempt to avoid overgeneralizations in the major premise.

Example:

Major Premise: All communication courses rock!
Minor Premise: My class is a communications course.
Conclusion: My class rocks!

ENTHYMEME. The problem with syllogisms is that we don't speak in a three-part argument in everyday life. An **enthymeme** is a means of getting to an argument without sounding as if you are repeating yourself. An enthymeme is a syllogism stated as a probability rather than an absolute.

An enthymeme states either a major or a minor premise, with the unstated premise simply implied. This sort of works like an inside joke. Have you ever had a joke that you shared with a friend where either of you just had to say part of it and you both laughed? This works like an enthymeme. You only have to state part of the argument as you are relying on the audience to fill in the rest of the argument based upon their own knowledge. Enthymemes are useful because arguments are rarely based on absolutes; nothing is just black or white as there is a lot of grey in any argument.

Example: My communication course rocks!

Pathos=Emotion

Pathos consists of any persuasive appeal directed at the audience's emotions. There are two major ways of invoking pathos: through vivid description and through emotionally charged words. Keeping in mind that we like to believe that we are rational beings, what really persuades us and helps us make decisions are our emotions. At the same time, remember that pathos or emotion alone will fail if it is not combined with some sort of reasoning.

As an example, Howard Dean in the Iowa Caucus on January 19, 2004 let forth an excited scream that ended up ending his run for the presidency that year. The emotion was not misplaced, but the tenor of the emotion was off the mark. Emotion alone is not persuasive as it must be supported with rational argument.

Howard Dean speaking to supporters: https://www.youtube.com/watch?v=D5FzCeVOZFc

Ethos=Character

Ethos is the audience's perceptions and attitudes toward the speaker's perceived expertise, trustworthiness, similarity to audience members, and attractiveness. The key word there is *perceives*. Whether or not the speaker actually has credibility is a completely different story. The speaker can create a perception of credibility by highlighting the nature of the speaker's moral character and personality. These perceptions of a speaker's expertise and trustworthiness, or ethos, directly contribute to the speaker's persuasiveness. According to Aristotle, credibility consists of three elements:

- **Good sense** (competence): The speaker's knowledge and/or experience with the subject matter. We tend to give more credibility to a person who has either studied an issue extensively or to a person who has experience in the area. Experience is more important when talking about a specific incident or fact. Expertise is more important when talking about a general topic.
- **Good character**: The speaker's straightforward and honest presentation. We tend to believe people whom we trust. Trustworthiness is probably the most important speaker attribute as a loss in audience-perceived trustworthiness equates to a significant loss in credibility as credibility is in the eye of the beholder (or audience). For example: President Clinton after the Monica Lewinski affair.
- **Goodwill**: The speaker's interest in and concern for the welfare of the audience. Showing the audience how interested you are in them can create identification with the audience. We respond favorably to persuasive appeals when the speaker is like us. On the other hand, sometimes we attach more credibility to people who are actually dissimilar to us, as when an expert emphasizes facts and testimony. In addition, physical attractiveness does affect persuasive outcomes. In the U.S. culture, physically attractive people are perceived as competent, in control of themselves, well organized, and confident.

MODERN APPROACHES TO PERSUASION

Elaboration Likelihood Model (ELM) by Petty and Cacioppo. This approach to persuasion takes on the idea that audience members process messages in two different ways, centrally and peripherally. *Central processing* involves active mental effort or "issue-relevant thinking." If the audience finds the issue interesting or directly relevant to them, they will be more likely to focus and centrally process that information. For example, if you are in a class in your major one would assume that your focus would be on that material and you would centrally process the new material being presented. On the other hand, *peripheral processing* involves focusing on non-message-related or heuristic cues. If the audience finds the issue too complex or uninteresting, they will tend to peripherally process that information. For example, if you were in a class of difficult material for you, your peripheral processing might take over. Whether central or peripheral processing is used depends on the receiver's motivation and ability to engage in central processing. High involvement and motivation on part of the audience increases the likelihood that they will be motivated to engage in central processing. Also a high need for cognition increases the audience's likelihood of engaging in central processing. Persuasion via the central route is more persistent, or long lasting, than persuasion via the peripheral route, and is more resistant to counter-persuasion.

Heuristic-Systematic Model (HSM) by Chaiken and Eagly. This is a similar model to the ELM in that *systematic processing* is thoughtful and deliberate (similar to central processing), while *heuristic processing* relies on the application of mental shortcuts (analogous to peripheral processing). Heuristic cues, or simply "heuristics," such as the quantity of proof or credibility, help to simplify the thought process. Decision rules, such as brand loyalty, simplify the decision-making process. HSM posits that parallel processing is possible (e.g., both systematic and heuristic processing take place during any persuasion). The *sufficiency principle* posits that individuals balance their need for systematic and heuristic processing based on the importance of the issue.

STRUCTURING AND ORDERING PERSUASIVE MESSAGES

There are two types of approaches to persuasion, explicit or implicit. The *explicit conclusions approach* directly states the claim in the message. It works best when receivers are uninvolved or unable to draw their own conclusions as you are laying out the conclusion clearly for the audience. The *implicit conclusions approach* allows the audience to draw their own conclusions after hearing the message. This works best when receivers are involved and intelligent enough to draw their own conclusions and that conclusion is the one that the speaker wants them to draw.

Another issue to consider in persuasion is the quality versus the quantity of the arguments presented. Those who are not involved and are unlikely to scrutinize a message are the most persuaded by a large number of arguments. People who are involved and are likely to be critical of the message are most persuaded by a small number of good quality arguments.

There are competing theories of persuasion that say that repetition of the message may either help or hinder the persuasive quality of that message. On the one hand, the *mere exposure theory* says that people respond favorably to familiar stimuli and suggests that repeated exposure to a message should facilitate the persuasion. On the other hand, while repetition may increase comprehension of a persuasive message, too much repetition can lead to boredom and rejection of the message by the audience.

Three Types of Organizational Patterns for Persuasive Speeches

The importance of the quality of the arguments versus the quantity depends on the involvement of the audience.

- **Anticlimax order.** Place the strong arguments at the beginning of the speech.
- **Climax order.** Place the strong arguments at the end of the speech.
- **Pyramidal order.** Place the strong arguments in the middle of the speech.

© Andrey_Popov/Shutterstock.com

Anticlimax and climax are both more persuasive than the pyramidal order.

MONROE'S MOTIVATED SEQUENCE

As discussed in Chapter 11, Monroe's motivated sequence is an organizational pattern for planning and presenting persuasive speeches. It can be seen typically in many advertisements, especially the genre of ads known as "infomercials." This is because the form helps to ramp up the energy, or to motivate, within the audience. By the end of the infomercial, you feel compelled to buy a product, regardless of what that product may be.

There are five steps in the sequence:

1. **Attention**. Grabs the attention of the audience by appealing to core concerns and making the speech relevant to the audience. Why does your specific audience need to pay attention to your speech?

2. **Need**. The need step isolates and describes the issue to be addressed by showing audience members that they have a need the speaker can satisfy. If you buy into this idea, product, proposal, etc., your needs will be met.

3. **Satisfaction**. This step identifies the solution to the problem and offers audience members a proposal to reinforce or change their attitudes, beliefs, and values regarding the need at hand. This is where the persuasion starts to kick in. Show the audience how your idea, product, proposal, etc. is the way to go.

4. **Visualization**. The fourth step entails presenting the audience with a vision of anticipated outcomes associated with the solution by invoking needs of self-esteem and self-actualization. Paint a picture of the solution for them. Get the audience to see themselves enjoying your idea, product, proposal, etc.

5. **Action**. The final step involves making a direct request of the audience to do or not to do some specific thing. Get them to move on your idea, product, proposal, etc.

HOW TO MAKE AN AUDIENCE RESISTANT TO PERSUASION

The following are techniques to increase audience resistance to your message.

- **Inoculation effect (strategy).** This exposes people to a "weak dose" of the opposite side of your argument and then refutes it. This will make your audience more resistant to your opponent's persuasion attempts.
- **Supportive strategy**. This gives the audience reasons for why people should continue to believe what they already believe by supporting or reinforcing the ideas that the audience already holds.
- **Used together**. When two arguments are used together, they become more effective at making people resistant to an opponent's message than either one is when used alone.
- **Two-sided or refutational arguments**. These are messages that contain an argument while also refuting the opponent's argument. This type of argument is more persuasive than one-sided arguments or two-sided, non-refutational arguments.
- **Forewarning**. This is when the speaker tells the audience that they are about to be exposed to a persuasive message, hence, making them more resistant to persuasion.

CONCLUSION

This chapter reviewed the basics of what persuasion is, how persuasion functions with an audience, and skills that an effective persuader can utilize in the business setting. Additionally, this chapter covered historical and modern approaches to persuasion while also discussing organizing principles for potential persuasive presentations in the organization. Keep in mind that the only appropriate type of persuasion is an ethical one. Understanding the role of the persuader as one of presenting options to an audience that will exercise their free will in making the final decision, is important to being an ethical persuader in the business environment.

ACTIVITIES

1. Ask students to bring 50 cents to the next class period. At the beginning of the class, collect all the money in a jar or container. Each student will then give an impromptu speech on why he/she should get all of the money. Have the class vote on the winner. Then ask them to explain how they have used persuasion in their attempts to take home all of the money.

2. Divide students into groups and assign each a type of presentation:
   - Sales presentation
   - Technical report
   - Staff report
   - Progress report
   - Investigation report

   Then, as a class, come up with a type of company—real or hypothetical—and develop some demographics of the company: what the company does/makes/sells; the number of employees it has; its location; its current project. Once these items have been established, each group will work together to develop its report and its presentation.

3. Have the students pick a partner. Each team will be given two comparable objects, events, or issues. Each student picks a side and then argues as to why that side is better than the other. Each student has one minute to present their case.
   - Rap vs. rock and roll
   - Rural vs. city life
   - Giving a gift vs. receiving a gift
   - Hot weather vs. cold weather
   - Beer vs. wine
   - Telephone vs. e-mail
   - Women vs. men
   - Dieting vs. eating whatever you want
   - Basketball vs. football
   - Christmas/Chanukah vs. your birthday
   - Going to a movie vs. renting a video
   - Cake vs. pie
   - Living in the dorms vs. living off campus
   - Dogs vs. cats
   - Fact vs. fiction

ADDITIONAL SOURCES

Beardsley, M. (1982). *The aesthetic point of view.* Ithaca, NY: Cornell University Press.

Bitzer, L.F. (1968). The rhetorical situation. *Philosophy and Rhetoric, 1,* 1-20.

Bitzer, Lloyd F. (1959). Aristotle's enthymeme revisited. *Quarterly Journal of Speech, 45:*4, 399-408.

Black, E. (1965). *Rhetorical criticism.* Madison, WI: University of Wisconsin Press.

Black, E. (1980). A note on theory and practice in rhetorical criticism. *Western Journal of Speech Communication, 44,* 331-336.

Bostrom, R., & Donohew, L. (1992). The case for empiricism: Clarifying fundamental issues in communication theory. *Communication Monographs, 59,* 109-129.

Burke, K. (1966). Terministic screens. In *Language as Symbolic Action* (44-62). Berkeley: University of California Press.

Campbell, K.K. (1974). Criticism: ephemeral and enduring. *Speech Teacher, 22,* 9-14.

Carey, J. (1975). A cultural approach to communication. *Communication, 2,* 1-22.

Cohen, S. & Williams, R. (1999). *The non-designer's scan and print book: All you need to know about production and prepress to get great-looking pages.* Berkeley, CA: Peachpit Press.

Cosigny, S. (1974). Rhetoric and its situations. *Philosophy and Rhetoric, 7,* 175-186.

Dewey, J. (1916). *Democracy and education.* New York: The Free Press.

Dewey, J. (1934). *Art as experience.* New York: Perigee Books.

Enos, Theresa (Ed.). (1996). *Encyclopedia of rhetoric and composition: Communication from ancient times to the information age.* New York: Garland.

Forum. (1980). *Quarterly Journal of Speech, 66,* 85-93.

Forum. (1981). *Quarterly Journal of Speech, 67,* 93-101.

Foster, W. T. (1917). *Argumentation and debating.* Cambridge, MA: Harvard University Press.

Giddens, A. (1979). *Central problems in social theory: Action, structure, and contradiction in social analysis.* Berkeley, CA: University of California Press.

Gronbeck, B. (1975). Rhetorical history and rhetorical criticism. *Speech Teacher, 24,* 309-320.

Jaimeson, K. (1973). Generic constraints on the rhetorical situation. *Philosophy and Rhetoric, 6,* 163-170.

Kaufer, D.S., & Butler, B.S. (1996). *Rhetoric and the arts of design.* Mahwah, NJ: Lawrence Erlbaum Associates.

Keller, E., & Berry, J. (2003). Introduction. In *The influentials* (pp. 1-25). New York: The Free Press.

Kilbourne, J. (1999). Introduction: Buy this 24-year-old and get all his friends absolutely free. In *Deadly persuasion: Why women and girls must fight the addictive power of advertising* (pp. 33-56). New York: The Free Press.

Kostelnick, C., & Hassett, M. (2003). *Shaping information: The rhetoric of visual conventions.* Carbondale, IL: Southern Illinois UP.

Langer, S. K. (1937). *Introduction to symbolic logic.* Mineola, NY: Dover.

Langer, S. K. (1953). *Feeling and form: A theory of art developed from Philosophy in a New Key.* New York: Charles Scribner's Sons.

Langer, S. K. (1957). *Problems of art: Ten philosophical lectures.* New York: Charles Scribner's Sons.

Langer, S. K. (1979). *Philosophy in a new key: A study in the symbolism of reason, rite, and art.* 3rd ed. Cambridge, MA: Harvard UP.

Lucas, S. (1981). The schism in rhetorical scholarship. In Carl R. Burghardt (Ed.), *Reading in rhetorical criticism,* 2nd ed. State College, PA: Strata, pp. 88-106.

Luhmann, N. (1992). What is communication? *Communication Theory, 2,* 251-259.

Lyon, A. (1995). Susanne K. Langer and the rebirth of rhetoric. In Andrea A. Lunsford (Ed.), *Reclaiming rhetoric: Women in the rhetorical tradition.* Pittsburgh: University of Pittsburgh, pp. 266-284.

Rosenfield, L.W. (1968). The anatomy of critical discourse. *Speech Monographs, 35,* 50-69.

Rushkoff, D. (1999). Hand-to-hand. In *Coercion: Why we listen to what "they" say* (pp. 27-72). New York: Riverhead Books.

Rushkoff, D. (1999). Atmospherics. In *Coercion: Why we listen to what "they" say* (pp. 73-110). New York: Riverhead Books.

Rushkoff, D. (1999). Advertising. In *Coercion: Why we listen to what "they" say* (pp. 181-214). New York: Riverhead Books.

Simons, H.W. (1980). In praise of muddleheaded anecdotalism. *Western Journal of Speech Communication, 44,* 21-28.

Smith, C.R., & Lybarger, S. (1996). Bitzer's model reconstructed. *Communication Quarterly, 44,* 197-213.

Vatz, R.E. (1973). The myth of the rhetorical situation. *Philosophy and Rhetoric, 6,* 154-161

Ware, B. L., & Linkugel, W. A. (1973). They spoke in defense of themselves: On the generic criticism of apologia. *Quarterly Journal of Speech, 59,* 273-283.

Welch, K. (1996). Electrifying classical rhetoric: Ancient media, modern technology, and contemporary composition. In Amelie Oksenberg Rorty (Ed.) *Essays on Aristotle's rhetoric* (pp. 22-38). Berkeley: University of California Press.

glossary

A

Accommodating Smoothing over conflict by allowing the other person to get what they want.

Active listening Occurs when the listener is fully engaged in the moment, is aware of the message and sender, and is fully cognizant of the context of communication presently unfolding.

Adaptor Comforting gestures such as touching your hair, your face, or your body or adjusting your clothes or glasses.

Adjourning The final stage of group development. It is marked by a sense of pride at having accomplished the group's goal and a sense of loss at the disbandment of the group.

Alignment All elements should have a visual connection with the other elements on the visual.

Ambiguous word Leaves receivers uncertain as to its meaning.

Articulation Pronouncing the individual speech sounds.

Attention-getter A statement in your introduction that raises the interest of your audience.

Audience adaptation Adapting your speech to the needs of your audience before, during, and after the speech.

Audience analysis Knowing as much as you can about the audience to whom you will be speaking.

Audience oriented Keeping your audience in mind as you plan, write, and deliver your presentation.

Avoiding Withdrawing from conflict resulting in neither party gaining what they want.

Award acceptance Brief comments made by an award recipient providing credit and thanks to those who made the award possible and expresses sincerity.

Award presentation Congratulatory comments made when presenting an award or honor to a deserving recipient, which explains the significance of the award, briefly summarizes the accomplishment, and introduces the winner.

Awareness A state of consciousness when one is prepared to encounter, interpret, mentally record, and psychologically manage incoming stimuli of all types.

B

Bar chart A chart consisting of horizontal or vertical bars that depict the values of several items in comparative terms.

Behavioral interview An employment interview in which the candidate is asked to give concrete example of past behaviors that show how she or he behaved in certain situations.

Brainstorming An approach to idea generation that encourages free thinking and minimizes conformity.

C

Cause-effect pattern An organizational arrangement which shows that events happened or will happen as a result of certain circumstances.

Central idea or thesis statement Sums up your speech in a single statement.

Channel The means or mechanisms we use to send messages.

Chronemics Use of time.

Chronological pattern An organizational arrangement that presents points according to their sequence in time.

Claim A statement of fact or belief.

Co-cultures Subgroups of a larger culture who share a common set of values, beliefs, or attributes.

Collaborate When two parties work together to develop a joint solution that meets all the needs, goals, or demands of the situation.

Collectivism A cultural dimension describing the degree to which a culture focuses on the success of the group of which they are a member, including organizations and families.

Collegial peer Coworker with whom we discuss work-related topics as well as family and personal issues.

Communication context The situation or setting in which communication takes place.

Comparisons A type of support in which the speaker shows how one idea is similar to another; may be figurative or literal.

Compete When one person "wins" a conflict, and the other party loses.

Compromise A conflict strategy that allows both parties to gain a solution by each sacrificing a part of what they want.

Conclusion The closing, which lets the reader know the essay is ending and that the arguments have been adequately conveyed.

Concrete meaning Specific; leaves no uncertainty in its meaning.

Conflict The verbalized tension occurring between two or more people with differing goals or wants.

Conformity Adherence to the socially accepted behavior rules or the majority behavior rules.

Constructive feedback Communication intended to motivate others to change a process, procedure, or even a belief.

Context The environment of physical, social, chronological, and cultural variables that surrounds any process of communication.

Contrast This is about avoiding the similar.

Credibility The persuasive force that comes from the audience's belief in and respect for the speaker.

Culture A common set of beliefs, attitudes, customs, and ways of knowing agreed on and used by a group of people.

Curriculum vitae A very long resumelike document that details all the activities of a professional over the course of a lifetime.

D

Database Online information storage system including EBSCO, JSTOR, and LexisNexis.

Deafness When one cannot physically perceive vibrations as sounds.

Decode Translating messages and assigning meaning to messages.

Definition A form of support that explains the meaning of terms that are unfamiliar to an audience or are used in a specialized or uncommon way.

Delivery Bringing the words of your speech to life.

Demographic data The selected characteristics of a certain population.

Descriptive message Message that focuses on describing issues that have occurred, as opposed to stating an evaluation.

Designated chairperson The person that is there to make sure the group stays on task and that the group keeps going in an agreed-on direction.

Dewey Decimal System A library classification system which assigns a call number to materials based on subject areas. All library materials dedicated to certain subjects are placed together on the shelves.

Dialogue Meaning "through logic"; discussing all issues until they are dissected well and all perspectives are rendered identifiable.

Diversity maturity Having a clear understanding of diversity principles and the ability to practice this knowledge.

Downward communication Messages that travel "down" the organizational chart from members with power to those with lower levels.

E

Editing A close final review of your writing.

Egocentric Being primarily concerned about yourself.

Emblem Takes the place of a word or phrase, such as the peace sign or thumbs-up sign.

Empathetic message Communicating in a way that identifies with others on an emotional level.

Employment interview An interview designed to judge the qualifications and desirability of a candidate for a job.

Encoding The process of putting your thoughts and feelings into language.

Ethnocentrism The habit of observing situations and events from your own cultural perspective and making the judgment that your own culture is superior.

Example Form of supporting material that can add richness, relevancy, and a personal touch to your speech; brief illustrations that back up or explain a claim.

Expert testimony Information from someone who is a recognized expert or authority in their field.

Explicit norms Rules that have been clearly stated or written, and all members are expected to know them.

Expository A type of writing wherein you explain important concepts to your readers.

Extemporaneous Speech that is prepared and practiced ahead of time, but the exact wording of every sentence is determined at the time of delivery.

External noise Anything in the environment that disrupts or distorts a message.

F

Fallacy An error in the logic of an argument.

Feminine culture Feminine or nurturing cultures are more androgynous with less rigid sex roles and more openness to equality; these cultures focus on relational qualities of work environments and seek to resolve conflict using compromise and collaboration.

Feminine speech Uses communication as a primary way to establish and maintain relationships with others.

Finished writing "Draft" copy that begins to gel and solidify; begins where prewriting ends.

Flip chart A large pad of paper attached to an easel that is used to create and/or display visuals.

Form The writing structure.

Formal network Patterns of communication designed by management and inherent to a person's specific role within an organization.

Forming The initial stage of group development, marked by apprehension by its members and an overall tension throughout the group. The group must break this tension before it can proceed.

G

General purpose Your overall reason for speaking.

Gesture Nonverbal communication, such as talking with your hands, that can supplement or take the place of verbal communication.

Glass ceiling An invisible barrier preventing women and minorities from advancing in organizations, specifically into upper-management positions.

Globalization The term used to describe how the global economy is becoming interconnected through technology, more open trade agreements, and transportation.

Goodwill Shows your listeners what's in it for them; lets them know how they will benefit from listening.

Grammar The accepted structure of a language.

Graph A visual display that shows the correlation between two quantities.

Group building and maintenance roles A specific category of group roles that focuses on interpersonal relationships and group harmony.

Group roles Certain behavior is expected from all group members. Once a behavior is expected from an individual member, that member has officially been assigned the role.

Groupthink A major hindrance to group success when group members, for whatever reason, decide not to participate fully, allowing only one voice to be heard during meetings and that one voice to pour forth.

H

Hedges and qualifiers Words and phrases which make statements sound more tentative.

Hearing The ear's physical response to the auditory reception of sound waves.

High-context How a culture relies on different elements of a situation in communicating a message, which means noticing subtle cues in interaction and preserving harmony.

Horizontal communication Messages that flow between employees of similar status within or across the same departments.

Hostile work environment An uncomfortable workplace stemming from sexually charged messages.

I

Illustrator Hand gestures that help explain what we're talking about, such as pointing when giving directions.

Implied norms Rules that have not been written or clearly stated, and all members are expected to know them.

Impromptu A method of delivery done with very little or no preparation.

Individualism A cultural dimension describing the degree to which a culture places emphasis on the achievements of individuals.

Individual roles A specific category of group roles that focus on personal agendas to the possible detriment of the team.

Informal network Communication patterns based on friendships or relationships that are formed based on similarity in professional goals or personal interests.

Informational peer Coworker with whom we primarily share information about work.

In-group Being a member of a leader's inner circle, which signifies a higher level of liking and quality communication.

Inner ear The part of the ear where mechanical vibrations are translated into electric nerve transmissions that the brain can readily understand.

Intercultural communication competence The ability to communicate appropriately and effectively across various situations or settings.

Interdependence A characteristic of interpersonal relationships describing how people rely on each equally for both personal and professional support.

Internal noise The interference experienced within or internally to the communication event.

Internal preview Tells your audience what will be coming next.

Internal summary A review of the information you have already covered before you move on to the next part of your speech.

Interpersonal communication Communication of a relational nature between two or more people marked by interdependence, uniqueness, and quality.

Introduction The opening, which serves to entice and interest the reader in the writing.

Investigative A type of writing wherein you dissect an issue to its core elements.

J

Jargon Specialized terminology used by members of a particular group. The word is used in a derogatory sense when applied to language that is overly obscure.

Job interview A conversation between two people that both have a specific purpose in mind.

K

Kinesics The study of human body's motions and movements.

L

Leader-member exchange theory (LMX) A theory explaining how leaders have groups of employees who emerge as part of their in-group, middle-group, and out-group.

Library of Congress Classification System A library classification system which assigns all materials with a letter and call number based on subject areas. Using letters and numbers allows for more subject divisions.

Line graph A visual display that shows the correlation between two quantities.

Listening Occurs when we are receiving and appraising the stimuli that surround us.

Long résumé A two- to five-page document that denotes your professional potential more fully.

Long-term orientation A cultural dimension emphasizing the importance of methodically making decisions based on tradition.

Low-context How a culture focuses on the specific meaning of spoken words or messages and expects clarity, especially when giving an opinion.

M

Manuscript Writing down every word of your speech and then reading those words verbatim.

Masculine culture Culture that values assertiveness, competition, strength, and achievements; these cultures also have more rigid sex roles for men and women, with women holding fewer power positions within the organization.

Masculine speech Uses communication to exert control, preserve independence, entertain and enhance status.

Meaning A linguistic or symbolic mental value placed on the presence of some type of stimuli in the environment and is vested with the receiver.

Meeting A scheduled gathering of group members for a structured discussion guided by a designated chairperson.

Memorized Writing your speech out word for word and committing the entire speech to your memory.

Message of equality Message that recognizes the needs and rights of others.

Middle ear The portion of the ear between the ear canal and the cochlea.

Mixed-status relationship Relationship employee has with people above or below his/her own position in the organization.

Monochronic time orientation The view of time as something to be compartmentalized, segmented, or scheduled.

N

Negotiation A means to reach mutual agreement through communication.

Noise Anything that interferes with or interrupts the communication process.

Nonverbal communication Communication that consists of messages sent by nonlinguistic means, whether visually, physically, or vocally.

Norming The third stage of group development. It is marked by the group coming together and beginning to be productive. Rules for behavior will be firmly established during this point.

O

Opinion-based or argumentative A type of writing wherein you make a claim of some sort, backed with supportive evidence.

Organizational climate Describes the way the communication environment feels in an organization.

Organizational communication competence The impression of successful communication where the goals of the people in the interaction are met based on messages that are appropriate and effective within the organizational context.

Out-group Employees who are not in the supervisor's inner circle marked by lower-quality communication exchanges.

Outer ear A fleshy part of the human body, constituted by the pinna.

P

Paradigm Your frame of reference or worldview, which includes your thoughts, feelings, beliefs, experiences, values, and assumptions.

Paralanguage Vocal characteristics, including volume, rate, pitch, inflection, vocal fillers, resonance, and pauses.

Parallelism When you ensure that no one particular segment of your outline overpowers or outweighs any of the other segments.

Paraphrasing Listening to another and restating what has been said in your own words. Both feelings and factual content can be paraphrased.

Partially deaf Refers to one who can only moderately hear sounds.

Passive listening Occurs when the listener is not truly engaged in the moment or aware of the message coming from the sender or speaker.

Pattern of organization The order of your main points.

Peer-reviewed journal A journal which uses a more rigorous selection process involving review from professionals in a particular field.

Peer testimony Information that comes from people who have knowledge or an opinion on a subject, but they are not a recognized expert in the field.

Performing The fourth stage of group development. It is marked by extreme productivity and the slight breakdown of group roles.

Periodical Source which is periodically published such as magazines, journals, and some newspapers.

Persuasion The act of motivating an audience, through communication, to voluntarily change a particular belief.

Pictogram A visual support that uses an artistic or pictorial variation of a bar, column, or pie chart.

Pinna Part of the ear, it collects sound waves for the middle and inner ear.

Polite language Overly polite statements which include unneeded apologies or excessive expressions of thanks.

Polychronic time orientation The view of time as something that is free flowing and naturally occurring.

Power distance A cultural dimension describing the degree to which a society respects people, symbols, or structures of power.

Preview statement The last component of the introduction; you tell the audience exactly what you will cover in the body of your speech.

Prewriting "Rough draft" writing; the transfer of the sentence outline into a corpus of text.

Primary tension Ernest Bormann's term for the feelings of unease that group members feel when they initially meet. Members are unsure of social interaction rules and so are not sure how to act when first encountering a new group.

Problem-focused message Message that poses a request by focusing on how to solve problems together, as opposed to a message that communicates control over another person.

Problem-solution organizational pattern An organizational arrangement in which the speaker first convinces the audience that a problem exists and then presents a plan to solve it.

Pronunciation The way you put the sounds together to form a word.

Proofreading Carefully checking writing for errors.

Provisional message Message that acts as a provision or statement indicating that there are multiple meanings or that our assessment of situations may not always be correct.

Proxemics Use of personal space.

Proximity This is the idea that related items should be grouped together.

Psychological noise Internal stimuli that either enhance or detract from the processing of incoming stimuli.

Q

Quid pro quo A type of sexual harassment in which a person with power in the organization withholds resources from another employee unless offered sexual favors.

Quotation A form of support that uses the words of others who are authoritative or articulate to make a point more effectively than the speaker could on his or her own.

R

Rapport talk Shows support for others, fosters connections, support, closeness and understanding.

Reference material Resources which provide information on primary sources; material which refers you to something else.

Regulator Helps control the flow of conversation, such as glancing at your watch to show that you need to leave.

Repetition Repeating elements such as line, shape, color, or texture throughout a page in your presentation or throughout your entire presentation helps to keep the audience engaged.

Report An informative presentation that describes the state of an operation.

Report talk Exhibits knowledge, skill or ability, and is direct and assertive.

Rhetorical question A question with an obvious answer, which does not call for an overt response.

S

Sales presentation A type of presentation aimed at persuading others to purchase a product or service.

Same-status relationship Includes a wide variety of people in the organization, specifically at the same level of power and authority within or outside employees' department or work group.

Scheduled gathering A purposefully held meeting that was prearranged.

Search engine Software program designed to search Web sites for information based on search terms provided by the Web site owners. Search tools Tools such as catalogs, bibliographic databases, Internet search engines, and bibliographies designed to assist researchers in obtaining information.

Search tools Tools such as catalogs, bibliographic databases, internet search engines, and bibliographies designed to assist researchers in obtaining information.

Secondary tension Ernest Bormann's term for the struggle that group members go through while trying to find their identity within the group. As opposed to primary tensions, secondary tensions are likely to be more aggressive in nature and lead toward open hostility.

Sexual harassment Any unwanted physical or verbal action of a sexual nature, which creates a hostile work environment.

Short résumé Usually a one-page document that quickly canvasses your abilities and skills.

Short-term orientation A cultural dimension describing a culture's tendency to make quick decisions and expect quick results.

Signpost A key word or phrase that points to what the speaker is covering.

Situational analysis Includes knowing about the room size and arrangement, whether there is a stage, and whether it is an informal or formal, serious or humorous event.

Slang Informal language typically used or shared by a group.

Small group A collection of people, working together, interacting with the interdependent purpose of accomplishing some common goal.

Spatial pattern An organizational arrangement that presents material according to its physical location.

Special occasion presentation Presentation that promotes goodwill or pays tribute in the form of welcomes, introductions, toasts, award presentations and acceptances, retirements, eulogies, and commemorations.

Special peer Coworker who is considered the most intimate peer with whom we share personal information and from whom we receive emotional and social support.

Specific purpose What you want to accomplish with your presentation; your goal for the audience.

Speeches of introduction Presentations designed to introduce a keynote speaker in a way that highlights his/her achievements, connects their topic to the audience, and builds anticipation.

Spontaneous communication Communicating our thoughts and motivations in a way that indicates sincerity and objectivity and does not hide agendas.

Statistics Numbers used to represent an idea.

Stereotype A judgment made about individuals based on any observable or believed group membership.

Storming The second stage of group development. It is marked by actual work beginning, members trying to assert themselves, feelings perhaps getting hurt by other members pushing specific agendas.

Structured discussion Unlike idle chatter, structured discussion is a guided conversation with a specific purpose.

Subordination of ideas Deals with ensuring that all ideas contained within the subheading of an outline bear some logical, associated meaning to the principal heading.

Supporting material Material that backs up claims in a presentation.

Symbolic division Each heading under the outline tree must contain a minimum of at least two subheadings.

T

Tag question A statement that ends with a question which serves to seek agreement or confirmation from others.

Task roles A specific category of group roles that focus on the goal completion.

Testimony Using direct quotes or paraphrasing what someone says to support a main point.

Thesis statement A single sentence that summarizes the central idea of a presentation.

Toast Sentiments communicated at group meals, celebrations, or business meetings that convey goodwill and meet appropriate cultural etiquette.

Topical pattern An organizational arrangement in which ideas are grouped around logical themes or divisions of the subject.

Transition A statement used between parts of a presentation to help listeners understand the relationship of the parts to one another and to the thesis.

Transparency A clear sheet used with an overhead projector to cast an image on a screen.

U

Uncertainty avoidance A cultural dimension describing the degree to which a culture avoids things that are unknown or uncertain.

Uniqueness A characteristic of interpersonal communication signifying the special quality of the communication between individuals.

Upward communication Messages that travel "up" the organization chart from employees upward to managers.

Usage The conventions of both speech and writing that characterize particular groups of communicants.

U.S. Superintendent of Documents (SuDocs) A classification system which groups government documents by cabinet-level agency.

V

Verbal communication What you say or the message that you send.

Vocal filler Word or utterance used to fill the gaps in our language instead of using a silent pause.

Vocalics The voice.

Voice The personality conveyed in writing.

W

Welcome speech Speech intended to welcome groups or audiences to an event or conference designed to build anticipation, communicate enthusiasm, and preview the event.

Writing style The method by which a writer conveys and shapes text, thereby revealing their personality.

index _____

NOTE: Page references in *italics* refer to figures.

A

masculine and feminine cultures, 36–37, 52

power and language, 75

General Agreement on Tariffs and Trade (GATT), 31

general purpose, for speeches, 318–319

geographical (spatial) pattern of organization (speeches), 390–392

Gerstner, Louis, 353–354

gestures, 87–88

"Gettysburg Address" (Lincoln), 268–269

Gibb, J., 160–164

glass ceiling, 43–44

glittering generalities, 410

globalization, 28–64. *see also* cultural issues

    cultural dimensions of, 33–42, *41*

    defined, 30

    domestic diversity in workplace in, 42–52, *47, 48, 51*

    new economy and, 30–33

    overview, 28–30

    technology and, 24

    tips for communication with different cultures and co-cultures, 52–54, *55–57*

good sense/good character, 414

goodwill, 328, 414

government documents, 298–299, 304

grammar, for writing, 133–135

groups, 168–211. *see also* interpersonal communication

    group building and maintenance roles, 192

    group production, 176–177

    group roles, 192, *193–195*

    groupthink, 172–173, 181–182

    group work, advantages and disadvantages, 176–184

    meetings with, 197–208

    overview, 168–171

    small groups, defining and understanding, 171–176

    team building, 184–197, *193–195, 197*

Guffey, Mary Ellen, 42

H

Hall, Edward T., 38, 89

hearing, listening and, 97–103, *98, 100, 104*

hedges, 74

Heuristic-Systematic Model (HSM), 415

hierarchy of organizations, 19–21, *21*

high-context language, 38–39

Hispanic American population

    diversity in workplace and, 42–43

    terminology, 45–46

Hofstede, Geert, 34–38, 52

Holtz, Lou, 282

honors, included on résumés, 222

horizontal communication, 19

hostile work environment, 44

I

IBM, 353–354

"I" language, 156

illustrators, 88

implicit norms, 191

implied norms, 191

impression management

    interviewing and first impression, 242, 244–245

    with social media, 228–232

impromptu delivery, 280–281

individualism, 36

individual roles, 192

individuals, satisfaction of working in groups, 177

indoctrination, 409–410

inflection, 84

informational peers, 149

informational speeches, 318

information-seeking and traditional library skills, 294–313

    citation formats, 307–311

    classification systems, 296–300

    information organization, 296

    information sources, 300–305

    organizing research, 295–296

R

S

smell, as nonverbal communication, 85
Smitley, Bill, 256
social competencies. *see* interpersonal communication
social information processing theory, 227–228
social media
    impression management and, 228–233
    overview, 227–228
    professional networking sites, 233
Society for Human Resource Management, 48
solutions, myths about small groups and, 182–184
sources, for research. *see* information-seeking and traditional library skills
spatial pattern of organization (speeches), 331, 390–392
special occasion presentations, 394
special peers, 149
specific purpose, of speeches, 319–321
speeches. *see* delivery
speech of introduction, 396–397
spontaneous communication, 162
staff reports, 393
stage, for presentations, 267
"Stages of Small Group Development Revisited" (Tuckman), 188–197, *197*
standing, while speaking, 84
startling statements, by public speakers, 325
statistics, as supporting material for speeches, 341–342
stereotypes, 45
stimuli, listening and, 99–101, *100*
Stohl, Cynthia, 30
storming, 189–190, *197*
structure. *see also* pattern of organization (speeches)
    of meetings, 198–199
    structured discussion, 199
style, for writing, 133–135
subordination of ideas, 129
supporting material, for speeches, 341–344
supportive climates, developing, 160–164

supportive strategy, as audience resistance technique, 418
syllogism, 413
symbolic action, 409
symbolic division, 129
sympathetic listening, 113
synapses, 103
system-generated cues, 231–232

T

tag questions, 73–74
tall organizational hierarchy, 19–21, *21*
Tannen, Deborah, 75
task roles, 192
teams. *see also* groups
    overview, 184
    phases of small-group communication, 188–197, *193–195, 197*
    satisfaction of working in groups, 177
    types of, 184–188
technical reports, 393
technology. *see also* information-seeking and traditional library skills; social media; visual aids
    interviewing and, 256
    for meetings, 200–201
telepresence, 200–201
testimonials, as propaganda, 410
testimony, as supporting material for speeches, 342
text, working with. *see* writing
texting, slang and, 73
thank you notes, following interviews, 252–253
thesis statement
    for business presentations, 389
    for written works, *127,* 127–129
Thomas, R. Roosevelt, 53–54
time orientation
    chronemics, 89
    culture and, 40
    groups and, 180
Title VII, Civil Rights Act of 1964, 45, 90

toasts, 400–401
topical pattern of organization (speeches), 330–331, 332–333, 390–392
topic of speeches
    for business presentations, 387–388
    choosing, 316–318
    stating, 326–327
trade agreements, globalization and, 31–33
traditional résumé style, 216
transfer, for propaganda, 410
transitions, 340, 390
transparencies, 360–361
Tuckman, Bruce, 188–197, *197*
type (font), 364, 372

U

uncertainty avoidance, 35
uniqueness, 146
upward communication, 19
Urban Institute, 48
U.S. Census Bureau, 42, 45–46, 48
U.S. Department of Commerce, 32
U.S. Department of Labor, 214
U.S. Superintendent of Documents (SuDocs), 298–299
usage, for writing, 133–135
user-generated cues, 230

V

verbal communication, 66–93. *see also* nonverbal communication
    articulation and pronunciation, 75–77
    clarity, 70–71
    correct word usage, 77–78
    cultural issues of nonverbal communication, 40, *41*
    defined, 11, 69–70
    overview, 66–69
    powerful and powerless language use, 73–75

slang, jargon, buzz words, 71–73
    verbal communication, defined, 69–70
videos, 358
visual aids, 352–377
    audience's needs and, 355
    bar charts and line graphs, 358
    bullet points, 360
    choosing, 356–358
    design principles for, 363–372
    diagrams, 359
    effectiveness of, 372–373
    flip charts and posters, 360
    objects and models, 357–358
    overview, 352–354
    photographs and videos, 358
    pictograms, 359–360
    pie charts, 359
    presentation development and, 341–344
    presentation skills for, 373
    presentation software, 361–363
    speaking setting and, 355–356
    transparencies, 360–361
visualization, Monroe's motivated sequence on, 337, 417
vocabulary, skill assessment for workplace documents, 139–140
vocal delivery, 282–283, 288–289
vocal fillers, 74, 84
vocalics, 83–85
voice, for writing, 133–135
volume, 83

W

Walgreens, 50
Walther, Joe, 230
welcome speeches, 395–396
Wilen, Tracey, 37
word usage
    connectives in speeches, 340–341
    correct, 77–78
    for writing, 133–135
work experience, included on résumés, 218